Early Professional Development for Teachers

Early Professional Development for Teachers

This reader is part of a course: *Early Professional Development for Teachers* (E853), that is itself part of the Open University Masters Programme in Education.

The Open University MA in Education
The Open University MA in Education is now firmly established as the most popular postgraduate degree for education professionals in Europe, with over 3,000 students registering each year. The MA in Education is designed particularly for those with experience of teaching, the advisory service, educational administration or allied fields.

Structure of the Masters Programme in Education
The MA is a modular degree, and students are therefore to select from a range of options the programme which best fits with their interests and professional goals. Specialist lines in management, applied linguistics and lifelong learning are also available. Study in the Open University's Advanced Diploma can also be counted towards the MA, and successful study in the MA Programme entitles students to apply for entry into The Open University Doctorate in Education programme.

OU Supported Open Learning
The MA in Education programme provides great flexibility. Students study at their own pace, in their own time, anywhere in the European Union. They receive specially prepared study materials, supported by tutorials, thus offering the chance to work with other students.

The Doctorate in Education
The Doctorate in Education is a part-time doctoral degree, combining taught courses, research methods and a dissertation designed to meet the needs of professionals in education and related areas who are seeking to extend and deepen their knowledge and understanding of contemporary educational issues. The Doctorate in Education builds upon successful study within the Open University MA in Education programme.

How to apply
If you would like to register for this programme, or simply find out more information about available courses, please write for the *Professional Development in Education* prospectus to the Call Centre, PO Box 724, The Open University, Walton Hall, Milton Keynes MK7 6ZW, UK (Telephone +44 (0) 1908 653231). Details can also be viewed on our web page http://www.open.ac.uk

Early Professional Development for Teachers

Edited by Frank Banks and Ann Shelton Mayes

David Fulton Publishers
London

in association with

The Open University

David Fulton Publishers Ltd
414 Chiswick High Road, London W4 5TF

www.fultonpublishers.co.uk

Copyright © The Open University 2001
10 9 8 7 6 5 4 3 2

British Library Cataloguing in Publication Data
A catalogue record for this book is available from the British Library.

ISBN 1-85346-792-8

Typeset by Textype Typesetters, Cambridge
Printed in Great Britain by Thanet Press, Margate.

Contents

Acknowledgements

Any book is a joint enterprise, but this one in particular has been a team effort. Our intention has been to draw together a collection of articles covering different perspectives on an important range of topics for teachers in the early stages of their career. Even among the small group of people involved in making this selection, there were differences in the level of support for the positions adopted in the various articles. We consider this to be important in stimulating the debate around early professional development, and of course to provide an essential background to the key issues for students on the linked Open University course E853 *Early Professional Development for Teachers*. We would like to thank the representatives from the subject associations: ASE, MA, NAPE, NATE, who advised us on our selection of material and the structure of this Reader. Our colleagues at the Open

University, as usual, have been both supportive and constructively critical. We are particularly grateful in that respect to Hilary Burgess and Jane Devereux who are fellow members of the E853 course team. June Down and Julie Herbert gave the essential secretarial support. Most thanks, however, go to Di Harden who, as course manager, worked tirelessly on our behalf.

Grateful acknowledgement is made to the following sources for permission to reproduce material in this book:

Chapter 2: Sonia Blandford, 'Professional Development in Schools', from Blandford, S. (2000) *Managing Professional Development in Schools*, London, Routledge.

Chapter 3: David Berliner, 'Teacher Expertise', from Berliner, D. (1994) 'Teacher Expertise', in Moon, B. and Shelton Mayes, A. (eds) *Teaching and Learning in the Secondary School*, Chapter 14, pp. 107–13, London, Routledge.

Chapter 4: Brigitte A. Rollett, 'How do Expert Teachers View Themselves?', from Rollet, B. A. (1992) 'How do Expert Teachers View Themselves?', in Oser, F., Dick, A. and Patry, J. L. (eds) *Effective and Responsible Teaching*, San Francisco, Jossey-Bass Inc., a subsidiary of John Wiley & Sons, Inc.

Chapter 6: Geoff Whitty and Elizabeth Willmott, 'Competence-based teacher education: Approaches and Issues', from Whitty, G. and Wilmott, E. (1995) 'Competence-based teacher education: Approaches and Issues', in Kerry, T. and Shelton Mayes, A. (eds) *Issues in mentoring*, Chapter 18, pp. 208–18, London, Routledge.

Chapter 8: Michael G. Fullan, 'What makes change work for teachers', from, Fullan, M. G. and Stiegelbauer, S. (1991) *The New Meaning of Educational Change*, pp. 131–37, London, Cassell Educational Ltd. Published with the permission of Continuum International Publishing Group Ltd.

Chapter 12: Alistair Smith, 'What the most recent brain research tells us about learning', from Smith, A. (1998) *Accelerated Learning in Practice*, Section 1, Stafford, Network Educational Press.

Chapter 13: Howard Gardner, 'The theory of multiple intelligences', from Gardner, H. (1994), 'The theory of multiple intelligences', in Moon, B. and Shelton Mayes, A. (eds) *Teaching and Learning in the Secondary School*, Chapter 4, pp. 38–46, London, Routledge.

Chapter 15: Alistair Smith, 'The strategies to Accelerate Learning in the Classroom', from Smith, A. (1998) *Accelerated Learning in Practice*, Section 3, Stafford, Network Educational Press.

Chapter 16: Alma Harris, 'Effective Teaching: practical outcomes from research', from Harris, A. (1998) 'Effective Teaching: a review of the literature', *School Leadership and Management*, Vol. 18, No. 2, pp. 169–83, Carfax Publishing Ltd.
[Note: on 30 April 2001, Frank Banks contacted Alma Harris by phone about the title change and she confirmed that she is happy with it].

Chapter 17: Hay McBer, 'Research into Teacher Effectiveness', edited version of Hay McBer (2000) *Research into Teacher Effectiveness*, Norwich, HMSO, Crown Copyright. Published with the permission of the DfEE.

Chapter 18: John Munro, 'Learning More about Learning Improves Teacher Effectiveness', from Munro, J. (1999) 'Learning More about Learning Improves Teacher Effectiveness', *School Effectiveness and School Improvement* Vol. 10, No. 2, pp. 151–71, Swets & Zeitlinger.

Chapter 19: John Beresford, 'Matching Teaching to Learning', from Beresford, J. (1999) 'Matching Teaching to Learning', *The Curriculum Journal* Vol. 10, No. 3, pp. 332–44, British Curriculum Foundation.

Chapter 21: David McNamara, 'Vernacular Pedagogy', from McNamara, D. (1991) 'Vernacular Pedagogy', *British Journal of Educational Studies*, Vol. XXXIX, No. 3, August, pp. 297–310, Oxford, Blackwell Publishers Ltd.

Chapter 23: Richard Winter, 'Action Research as a Professional Ideal' from Winter, R. (1989) *Learning from Experience – principles and practice in action research*, Brighton, Falmer Press.

Chapter 24: Roger Hancock, 'Why Are Class Teachers Reluctant to Become Researchers?', from Hancock, R. (2001) 'Why Are Class Teachers Reluctant to Become Researchers?' *British Journal of Inservice Education*, 23:1, pp. 85–99.

Chapter 25: Dennis Thiessen, 'Classroom-based Teacher Development', from Thiessen, D. (1992) 'Classroom-based Teacher Development', in Hargreaves, A. and Fullan, M. G. (eds) *Understanding Teacher Development*, Chapter 6, pp. 85–109, London, Cassell. Published with the permission of Continuum International Publishing Group Ltd.

Chapter 28: Jennifer Moon, 'Learning Through Reflection', from Moon, J. A. (1999) *Reflection in learning and professional development: theory and practice*, pp. 68–9, and 187–201, London, Kogan Page.

Introduction

At the start of the twenty-first century Early Professional Development (EPD) for teachers is receiving long-overdue attention. In March 2001, the Department for Education and Employment (DfEE) published *Learning and Teaching: A strategy for professional development* which stated:

> We will pilot **Early Professional Development for teachers in their second and third years of teaching** in a sample of schools, building on the experience of the induction year. . . . This will encourage a firm base for career-long professional development.
> (DfEE, 2001, p.9) (their emphasis)

In Scotland the McCrone Report (SEED, 2000) suggested that 'every teacher should have a CPD plan agreed once a year with his or her immediate manager' (Vol. 1, p.9). Northern Ireland has for some time treated EPD as a part of the wider process of preparing teachers for the profession by having a common competence framework spanning initial education and training, through induction, to development in the early professional years (DoE, 1998).

As we see, the statutory frameworks which surround teachers' conditions of service and the political expectations that successive governments have of the teaching profession immediately come into focus. The context in which teachers work, particularly early in their career, needs to be carefully considered in order for sensible professional judgements to be made. How should teachers get to grips with the standards others use to judge their professional expertise? What models exist to describe a teacher's journey from 'novice' to 'expert'? How do expert teachers view themselves and how do they cope with and adapt to change? How can all teachers collaborate to make the structured observation of their work, such as that needed by appraisal requirements, a positive and enriching process? These issues are the subject of Section 1, 'Teacher Early Professional Development: the context'. Chapter 1 sets up the issues which are explored throughout the section, but it also suggests a way that professional development could be addressed within the pressured school environment by considering a framework of teacher professional knowledge.

The essential task for a teacher is to facilitate learning. As teachers we often need to consider the 'support' role as much as the 'academic' one, but our prime purpose is to enable the pupil to learn. The characteristics of an 'expert teacher' discussed in Section 1 are picked up in the following section by considering 'Teaching for learning'. The principal professional concerns of teachers develop throughout their career. Maynard and Furlong (1993) describe the initial teacher preparation period as one of a succession of stages: early idealism (before the first school placement!), survival, recognising difficulties, hitting the plateau, and moving on. But such concerns do not stagnate. In the early professional years, most teachers are ready to move on from an over-concern with their 'performance' or with routine discipline problems, to consider more fundamental teaching and learning issues. In a nutshell, how should we teach in order to provide richer learning experiences? Section 2 looks at what we currently know about how people learn and matches those understandings to how we might teach. The different theories of how people learn, often still speculative despite it being a concern of teachers for centuries, are considered in some detail. But the chapters never lose sight of the need to consider the pedagogy implied by such understandings. The outcome of studies on 'effective teaching' is the theme of the latter chapters of this section.

If one takes a decision to change one's classroom practice so that teaching and learning can be made more effective, a natural question follows: How will I know whether the change has had any impact, beneficial or otherwise? Teachers are frequently offered strong advice to follow certain approved teaching approaches. In England, the national numeracy and literacy strategies are two examples, but there are others set out in the 'Teacher Guides' to curriculum projects. The message is plain. Follow these techniques and all will be well. But if teaching is to develop as an evidence-based profession, teacher need to question such claims and make the classroom itself the site for their enquiry and their professional development. Section 3 of the Reader looks at 'The Classroom Teacher and School-based Research' and brings together different perspectives on the use of action research by classroom practitioners. The case is made that *small-scale* classroom investigations can be the vehicle to help a reflection on practice which acts as a focus of collaboration between colleagues and a topic for professional dialogue. The General Teaching Council for England agrees that this approach is suitable for the early professional years:

> The focus for these early years of professional development should be on engaging the individual teacher in reflection and action on pedagogy.
> (GTC, 2000)

Section 3 addresses both the ideal and the reality of implementing such a 'reflection and action on pedagogy' through a consideration of appropriate techniques and by offering a number of examples.

In describing their approach to professional development, the DfEE has coined the phrase 'Learning from each other . . . learning from what works' (DfEE, 2001, p.12). We agree with that wholeheartedly. However, 'learning from each other' needs to include the wider education community of researchers and scholars as well as our immediate colleagues, and 'what works' needs to be properly tested in the day-to-day reality of our own classrooms.

Frank Banks and Ann Shelton Mayes
The Open University
August 2001

References

Department for Education and Employment (DfEE) (2001) *Learning and Teaching: A Strategy for professional development.* Circular 71/2001. London: DfEE.

Department of Education (DoE) (1998) *The Teacher Education Partnership Handbook.* Belfast: DoE.

General Teaching Council (GTC) (2000) *Continuing Professional Development: Advice to Government.* London, GTC.

Maynard, T. and Furlong, J. (1993) 'Learning to teach and models of mentoring', in McIntyre, D., Haggar, H. and Wilkin, N. (eds) *Mentoring-Perspectives on School-based Teacher Education*, 69–85. London: Kogan Page.

Scottish Executive Education Department (SEED) (2000) *A Teaching Professional for the Twenty-first Century: the McCrone Report.* Edinburgh: SEED.

Section 1
Teaching Early Professional Development: the context

Chapter 1

Teacher early professional development: the context

Frank Banks, Ann Shelton Mayes, Malcolm Oakes and Dennis Sutton

Introduction

I was teaching about lenses, and I had taken my rather boisterous group of 14-year-old pupils outside on a sunny summer day to see whether they could scorch bits of scrap paper with a convex lens by focusing the sun's rays. They had a good time, marvelled at the bright spot formed, asked interesting and pertinent questions and, after a while, we went back inside. We talked about how their ideas about refraction, covered in the previous lesson, applied to this shaped glass block known as a lens. As I turned round from the diagram we were jointly constructing on the board to continue the discussion with the class grouped near me around the front, I spotted the Deputy Head Teacher who had just come in and was leaning silently against the back wall. I finished off the diagram, concluded the discussion and wound up the lesson. The pupils left. 'I came in earlier but it was like the Marie Celeste,' he said. 'We were outside,' I replied. 'Yes. That lot can be difficult, but if you can get them out, back and settled, there can't be much wrong. Well done.' 'Thanks,' I replied. He had watched me teach for about twenty minutes; it was the summer term and his only visit. That was it. I had just been assessed and passed my probationary year.

That story is true. It was how one of the authors passed an early and, in many ways, the most important 'rite of passage' as a new teacher in the mid-1970s. It was a successful personal outcome for the teacher in question but a totally unsatisfactory professional experience. Although the school was large and boasted its own 'professional tutor', the support and advice for new teachers was random, general and without any criteria for assessment other than 'seems to survive'. Moreover, as no one knew any teacher's individual needs, there was no continuity between receiving Qualified Teacher Status (QTS), the programme set up for the 'probationary year' and any strategy for further professional development. Except for certain exceptional schools and LEAs, the above tale of benevolent neglect was not an unusual experience at the time. Many of the current senior managers in schools will have been inducted into the teaching profession in a similar *ad hoc* way. Although the story, for that teacher, has a happy ending, life was not so sweet for a colleague who started at the same school at the same time. He failed his probation, and in the extension period struggled to restore credibility lost in the eyes of both staff and pupils. He eventually left the profession altogether. So much more could have been done to help *both* of these novice teachers, including the one considered 'successful', in the crucial early years of their careers.

How has the situation changed? In this chapter we will look at the current context for teacher Early Professional Development (EPD) at the start of the twenty-first century. We will consider the nature of the skills, knowledge and understanding needed by teachers and the practicalities of establishing activities to help them to develop professionally in the hectic environment of schools.

The context of EPD

In 1972 the James Report launched the idea of the triple-I. Education and training for teachers was described as falling into three cycles, initial, induction and INSET. The notion of a continuum of professional development has, until now, remained a professional ideal. The journey is worth re-visiting.

By the 1980s, many initial teacher education courses could be described as taking a 'knapsack approach' to course content. The view was that new teachers were unlikely to get access to further information and support once they started teaching full time. Consequently, they should be introduced to a whole range of issues, techniques and information to stuff into their knapsack for future use. It was almost as if Higher Education Institutions (HEI) were attempting to cram a lifetime of learning into one short period, with little thought as to whether this was an effective model for teacher professional development. Schools, for their part, saw new teachers (including student teachers) as the carriers of new ideas and techniques. In the early to mid-1990s this 'us and them' view of teacher development – HEIs do the training, schools allow them to practise on their pupils – gave way to a 'partnership' model. In this model, the time spent in schools considerably increased and supervising teachers took on an active training role as 'mentors' (DFE, 1992).

In most cases, in addition to coaching and support, this included assessment of practical teaching and sometimes of more knowledge-based aspects of the course (Bridges, 1993; Maynard and Furlong, 1993). In 1998, for England and Wales, the government set out the requirements for what should be covered in initial teacher education (DfEE, 1998). Although criticised for its 'technical skills' approach to teaching, the government circular did make clear what school/HEI partnerships should include in its teacher education curriculum. The school's full role in initial teacher training was confirmed as a foundation stone of the new regulations.

The consequence of these developments during the closing years of the last century has been far reaching. Setting aside the controversy that has surrounded the movement of many aspects of initial teacher education and training from higher education to schools, particularly in relation to funding, workload and consistency, the major impact has been the recognition of schools as *sites for professional learning*. Partnership with HEIs in initial teacher training has meant a generation of teachers has been trained in mentoring skills. These skills in classroom observation, assessment, debriefing and target setting against standards are directly transferable to supporting colleagues in general.

Other regulations have drawn explicitly on this newly developed school-based expertise. The restoration of formal induction in England and Wales (DfEE, 1999) (a probationary period or formal induction was retained in Northern Ireland and Scotland) requires that newly qualified teachers receive appropriate levels of support from teacher colleagues. Teachers now enter the profession with a 'career entry profile' to form the basis of early professional development in the induction year. At a stroke a proper connection, based on individual learning needs, has been made between initial teacher training and induction. Elsewhere in the UK, the development of a coherent framework for teacher professional development has gone one stage further. In Northern Ireland, the initial, induction and EPD years were brought together in a common competence framework (DoE, 1998) which took the view that stuffing all expectations into the initial teacher education 'knapsack' was also not a sensible strategy. And now in England, Wales and Scotland too, an expectation of teacher continuing professional development will be put in place (DfEE, 2001; SEED, McCrone Report, 2000).

As yet there is no coherent framework that seamlessly supports a teacher through career-long professional development, from novice to expert teacher, from classroom teacher to subject leader to school leader (see Chapter 7 for a fuller explanation). But the signs are that coherence, entitlement and support are back on the professional development agenda, along with schools and classrooms as the site for professional learning and learning from each other as part of teacher professionalism. It seems likely that we are about to see the realisation of the James Report's thirty-year-old professional ideal.

In this context, it is clear that early professional development, for many years the underdeveloped part of career-long teacher learning, needs to move centre stage. A focus on early professional development must be prioritised if teachers are to move swiftly towards expertise.

Teacher skills, knowledge and understanding

What do successful teachers do? What knowledge and understanding do they draw upon? In what ways is an 'expert' different from a 'novice'? Chapters 3, 16 and 17 explore these questions in detail.

Any group of experienced teachers can come up with a set of competences that describe what effective teachers should be able to do. They might be rather idiosyncratic and context specific, but for the group of teachers involved, they would be their view of 'what teachers do'. For example, one academic published in 1995 a checklist for evaluation of initial teaching skills, setting out 143 questions to be asked when assessing a student teacher (see Williams, 1995). It is unsurprising that national governments should seek to identify the set of knowledge, understanding and skills that describe effective teaching. And once established as a consensus view, use these descriptors as the basis for a rational approach to planned professional development from novice to expert. However, the different UK government officials drawing up such lists took a different view of the role of a teacher and consequently different parts of the UK have different types of standards. Also, as the standards were set out at different times, there are certain mismatches. Teachers are expected to improve throughout their career, but the clear framework for progression they might look for is absent. Ann Shelton Mayes looks at this issue in Chapter 7.

We may hope that the continual revision of standards will eventually lead to a rational framework for continued professional learning. But in the interim, there are thousands of teachers who complete induction each year and wish to focus on their own professional development. They need supportive frameworks for personal progress that help them aim towards excellence. Of course, in Northern Ireland such a framework already exists, at least in relation to the beginning years of early professional development. Elsewhere, in the UK, it has been the teacher associations who have focused on this neglected area for teacher professional development. The Association for Science Education (ASE), in particular, drew up a framework for Continuing Professional Development which classifies seven areas for development. The seven areas form a 'professional development matrix':

1. Subject knowledge and understanding

2. Pedagogical content knowledge
3. Development of teaching and assessment skills
4. Understanding teaching and learning
5. The wider curriculum and other changes affecting teaching
6. Management skills: managing people
7. Management skills: managing yourself and your professional development.
   (ASE, 2000)

Not only does this define what should be the focus of development for those in the first few years of their teaching career; it recognises the classroom itself as the site for learning and colleagues as key players in supporting professional growth. We look at this below.

Strategies for EPD

One of the first tasks of the newly established General Teaching Council for England was to set out recommendations for Continuing Professional Development for the profession.

> The Council believes that an entitlement to learning and development time for every teacher in their second and third years of teaching should be established as a priority. The benefits of new entrants learning from one another and from more experienced colleagues should become one of the norms of professionalism. Entitlement to extended professional development time in the early years of teaching will:
>
> - improve teaching and learning
> - support a culture of extended professionalism in schools
> - support retention.
>
> The focus for these early years of professional development should be on engaging the individual teacher in reflection and action on pedagogy, the quality of learning, setting targets and high expectations, equal opportunities, planning, assessment and monitoring, curriculum and subject knowledge, and classroom management.
> (GTC, 2000)

The ASE has developed a CPD model over a number of years which, in its focus on practical strategies for carrying out professional development activities, addresses the issue of 'engaging the individual teacher in reflection and action on pedagogy' in a meaningful way in the day-to-day turmoil of

5

busy schools and classrooms. The model adapts well for teachers of *any* subject and phase in an early stage of their career.

First, a further explanation of the seven aspects of the professional development matrix (adapted from ASE 2000). (See Figure 1.1 on pp. 10–11.)

1. Subject knowledge and understanding

Few would disagree that a sound grasp of subject knowledge is fundamental to good teaching. But, to be truly good, teaching should also demonstrate an enthusiasm for the subject. Pupils and some teachers talk about boring topics. We believe that the problem is often not the topic but the teaching. Enthusiasm cannot be maintained where a teacher is unsure of the material.

Common consequences of unsound subject knowledge are hesitancy in teaching, a lack of direction to the lesson and a lack of clarity in explanation. Over-reliance on books and worksheets as the primary sources of the information for the pupils is another outcome. Having a sound subject knowledge allows us to relax with pupils, ask pertinent and interesting questions which offer an appropriate challenge, respond to a wide range of questions from pupils, react positively to the unexpected and happily confess to not knowing a particular answer. It does not follow that we should all possess the same range of knowledge; although the introduction of the National Curriculum in schools and for ITT (Initial Teacher Training), in core subjects, does mean that we are moving to a position where a common minimum range is expected for primary teachers and secondary teachers of a National Curriculum subject.

In early professional development, we are looking for evidence that subject knowledge has been extended and/or deepened. It is something that all of us have to do and the means by which we can do it are varied. For a teacher in the early years of his or her career preparing to teach a new topic is the most common way of improving your subject understanding. We need to explore ways of maintaining and developing subject knowledge through personal study, learning from colleagues and the use of ICT.

2. Pedagogic content knowledge

Subject knowledge is a personal attribute, built up over many years and is being constantly reworked no matter how experienced we are as teachers. Once we feel secure in that understanding, we are then in a position to transform it so that it is appropriate for the level of understanding of a particular group of pupils. This is the key skill of the successful teacher. It is a complex procedure but essential to the teaching task. It involves a range of strategies to manipulate and transform personal understanding of a topic into a form that can be communicated to others, who are at a different stage in their development of understanding, to enable them to learn.

3. Development of teaching and assessment skills

The range of skills employed by any teacher is very wide. Managing a class of 30 pupils engaged on a variety of practical tasks, discovering a group's prior ideas about a topic and presenting information in different ways are techniques used daily. Research on the ways in which we learn has shown that even a narrowly setted class of pupils contains individuals with many different interests, motivations and preferred ways of learning. It follows therefore that a teacher who practises a range of different methods in presenting and explaining work is more likely to engage a greater portion of the minds of the pupils for more of the time than one who does not. Teachers undertaking early professional development should develop an awareness of a range of different strategies, and experiment and evaluate new techniques.

4. Understanding teaching and learning

The past 25 years has seen a great increase in research findings about how children learn. An awareness of such findings and their significance is an appropriate background for anyone who is reflecting upon the best ways to teach children.

5. The wider curriculum and other changes affecting teaching

Since the introduction of GCSE in 1986 and the National Curriculum in 1988, teachers have been facing a world of constant change. The accountability to students, parents and colleagues has become more marked. These changes continue to transform the lives of all teachers. The reasons for the changes are many and varied and you should be aware of the issues and the measures that are introduced to resolve them.

6. Management skills: managing people

Taking on extra responsibilities goes hand in hand with professional development. The reasons for taking them on are many, but from their early years in teaching teachers are encouraged to make contributions to team, department and school life. Teachers in the early stage of their career are encouraged to take on some extra responsibilities. For instance you might take on responsibility for reviewing a section of a scheme of work or leading a workshop on the use of ICT. In doing so you will be developing the skills necessary at a later stage to lead a team.

7. Management skills: managing yourself and your professional development

This final part of the matrix is about the ways in which you manage your workload and the ways in which you manage any responsibilities you undertake. This might include: managing your time; organising work to min-imise stress; the organising regimes you use to manage such activities as administering a topic or looking after team resources.

This model of supporting early professional development works because it takes the teacher through a structured process:

1. The professional development matrix is used as a planning tool for identifying personal needs and setting priorities for professional development.
2. Working with an experienced colleague, the teacher identifies and plans to carry out a number of small-scale classroom-based activities. Each activity is specially planned to address different elements of the matrix.
3. The teacher, supported by an experienced colleague, considers the evidence from carrying out the activities and analyses the teaching and learning taking place in her own classroom. She also reflects on what she, as a teacher, has learned in the process.

Such a model of early professional development incorporates all the key elements needed to support teachers at this stage in their learning:

- a focus on personal needs;
- teacher ownership of professional development;
- developing skills to carry out classroom-based enquiry; directly focused on practical strategies to improve teaching and learning in the classroom; working with other experienced teachers; an incremental approach to learning.

This focus on teaching and learning is explored in great detail in Section 2 and the ways teachers can themselves explore their own practice is the theme of Section 3.

At the beginning of this chapter we reminisced about the 'bad old days' when teacher professional development was a lottery. Some won, some lost. The real winners and losers of a professional development lottery, of course, are children. Every child deserves to be taught by an outstanding teacher who is able to inspire a real love of learning. The authors feel optimistic about the current climate where early professional development is finally being prioritised. If more teachers are to become outstanding teachers then we need to ensure that every teacher can take advantage of structured professional development from the earliest stage in their career.

References

Association for Science Education (ASE) (2000) *The Certificate of Continuing Professional Development Handbook*. Hatfield: ASE.

Bridges, D. (1993) 'School-based teacher education', in Bridges, D. and Kerry, T. (eds) *Developing Teachers Professionally*, 51–66. London: Routledge.

Cynulliad Cenedlaethol Cymru (CCC) National Assembly for Wales (2001) *Supporting New Teachers: Early Professional development including Induction*. Cardiff: CCC.

Department For Education (DFE) (1992) *Initial Teacher Training (Secondary Phase)*. London: HMSO.

Department for Education and Employment (DfEE) (1998) *Teaching: High Status, High Standards. Requirements for Courses of Initial Teacher Training*. Circular 4/98. London: DfEE.

Department for Education and Employment (DfEE) (1999) *Induction Arrangements for School Teachers (England) Regulations 1999 and amendments*. Circular 5/99. London: DfEE.

Department for Education and Employment (DfEE) (2001) *Learning and Teaching: A Strategy for professional development*. Circular 71/2001. London: DfEE.

Department of Education (DoE) (1998) *The Teacher Education Partnership Handbook*. Belfast: DoE.

General Teaching Council (GTC) (2000) *Continuing Professional Development: Advice to Government*. London: GTC.

Maynard, T. and Furlong, J. (1993) 'Learning to teach and models of mentoring', in McIntyre, D., Haggar, H. and Wilkin, N. (eds) *Mentoring-Perspectives on School-based Teacher Education*, 69–85. London: Kogan Page.

Scottish Executive Education Department (SEED) (2000) *A Teaching Professional for the Twenty-first Century: the McCrone Report*. Edinburgh: SEED.

Teacher Training Agency (TTA) (1998) *National Standards for Subject Leaders*. London: TTA.

Williams, A. (ed.) (1995) *Partnership in Secondary Initial Teacher Education*. London: David Fulton Publishers.

Professional development area	Description of understanding to be developed in each area	Possible elements of an activity	Examples of appropriate evidence
1. Subject knowledge and understanding	*Having a sound knowledge of the subject area that you have to teach* • development of understanding of recent advancements and changes in your taught subject • security of subject knowledge in areas to be taught	• course/meetings attendance; • library research; • self-study packs; • industrial placements or links	• written report on impact of 'new' subject knowledge; • presentation at team or department meeting
2. Pedagogical content knowledge	*Translating one's own understanding of the subject into forms that will be understood by pupils of varying abilities and ages* • examination of the teaching of particular parts of the curriculum including translation of one's own subject knowledge into suitable classroom activities	• classroom-based curriculum development or research; • comparison of own approaches with other teachers or researchers; • course attendance	• documentary evidence of classroom innovation or evaluation e.g. • teaching materials; • evaluations; • pupil reactions; • learning outcomes, etc.
3. Development of teaching and assessment skills	• development of teaching skills which are felt to be underdeveloped or under-used e.g. use of ICT in assisting learning; use of particular teaching techniques; promotion of classroom discussion; individualised learning; strategies for differentiation and equal opportunities, etc.	• course attendance and classroom implementation; • departmental implementation; • team teaching; • evaluation of teaching and learning strategies	• documentary evidence of teaching strategies – e.g. evaluations; • pupils' responses and learning outcomes; • observation report by fellow teacher; • demonstration to colleagues, etc.

4. Understanding teaching and learning	*Being aware of the significance of the findings of recent years on the ways in which pupils learn best* ● reflection on the basis for the classroom practice of oneself and of others – why do you teach this way? e.g. an examination and comparison of learning theories; learning styles; theories of classroom management, etc.	● observation of teaching and learning – examination of theoretical underpinning; ● library research; ● course attendance; ● departmental review	● self-review report; ● written report explaining the practice seen; ● written comparison of some current theories with own practice
5. The wider curriculum and other changes affecting teaching	*Being able to place one's teaching in the context of national developments* ● development of knowledge relating your context to wider teaching issues e.g. awareness of curriculum policy developments at national level; links with industries; regional and national initiatives	● active membership of ASE and other professional bodies; ● industrial placement; ● activities within school cluster; ● liaison with feeder schools; ● liaison with FE/HE	● documentary record of activities which have been undertaken as developments in this area with a comment on the outcomes for the individual and for the department
6. Management skills: managing people	*Being able to manage others effectively* ● development of any changing responsibilities ● taking on a management role	● reflection on current role and responsibilities; ● participation in pupil extracurricular activities; ● taking the lead in departmental activities, etc.	● documentary record of responsibilities and activities, with comments on the outcomes
7. Management skills: managing yourself and your professional development	*Being able to manage oneself effectively* ● development of skills such as time management; stress management; course administration; resource management; team management	● course attendance – implementation and reflection on outcomes; ● participation in activities requiring additional skills, etc.	● self-review report; ● documentary evidence of skills demonstrated

Figure 1.1 The ASE professional development matrix

Chapter 2

Professional development in schools

Sonia Blandford

Editors' Note: This chapter explores what is meant by professional development from the perspective of an individual teacher. It places professional development firmly within the context of schools as learning organisations and the national framework of standards that provide a staging for teachers' careers.

The purpose of professional development

The purpose of professional development can be summarised as the acquisition or extension of the knowledge, understanding, skills and abilities that will enable individual teachers and the schools–learning organisations in which they work to

- develop and adapt their range of practice;
- reflect on their experience, research and practice in order to meet pupil needs, collectively and individually;
- contribute to the professional life of the school, and as a practitioner interact with the school community and external agencies;
- keep in touch with current educational thinking in order to maintain and develop good practice;
- give critical consideration to educational policy, in particular how to raise standards;
- widen their understanding of society, in particular of information and communication technology (ICT).

An educational institution's approach to professional development will depend on whether it views employees as a resource or a cost–commodity, its view of adults as lifelong learners, its educational goals and preferred methods for achieving them. Ultimately, in each school, the aim of professional development is to improve practice in the classroom.

Management teams

In their early professional years individual teachers, assisted and guided by the management teams responsible for their employment and the support of their development, should seek to develop abilities in respect of

- recognising the diverse talents and capabilities of their individual pupils;
- identifying and providing for the special learning needs, strengths and weaknesses of all pupils;
- evaluating, assessing and reporting on their pupils' learning and adjusting their expectations as teachers accordingly;
- providing for the social, moral, spiritual and cultural development of their pupils;
- their own professional knowledge, skills, strategies, techniques, beliefs and values, and personal characteristics such as awareness, imagination and enterprise;
- their working relationships with their teaching and support colleagues, the parents of their pupils, the governors of the school, and members of external agencies;
- their administrative, pastoral and legal responsibilities.

Types of professional development

Teachers and support staff will normally associate professional development with In-service Education and Training (INSET), defined as 'planned activities practised both within and outside schools primarily to develop the professional knowledge, skills, attitudes and performance of professional staff in schools' (Hall and Oldroyd, 1990). INSET has been a 'catch-all' term encompassing diverse continuing professional development and training opportunities. In practice, the only experience of INSET for the majority of teachers is of the compulsory training days managed by either LEA advisory teams or senior managers in schools. This should change, as the government requires all schools to have a professional development policy that affords a range of opportunities and modes of participation.

The management of professional development will involve consideration of different types of professional development activity (Bolam, 1993), including:

Practitioner development – School-based development, self-development, induction, mentoring, observation, job-shadowing and team teaching.
Professional education – Award-bearing courses managed and taught at higher education institutions (HEIs), focusing on the relationship between

educational theory and practice, and leading to higher education accreditation and professional qualifications.

Professional training – Conferences, courses and workshops that emphasise practical information and skills, managed and delivered by LEAs, schools' external consultants or trainers from HEIs. Such courses may lead to academic awards or accreditation towards national standards.

Professional support – Provided by colleagues and managers in fulfilment of contractual conditions of service; e.g. recruitment and selection procedures (including job descriptions), promotion, career development, appraisal, mentoring, team building, redeployment and equality of opportunity.

How each of the above is implemented will depend on the knowledge, skills and abilities of individuals, teams, managers and advisers. The quality of school-based professional development activities will depend, in turn, on the extent to which a school approximates a learning community with a positive developmental culture.

Policy

The effective school will have a professional development policy which is generated by a team representing the views of staff at all levels. To begin with, the analysis of institutional strategies for development and individual appraisal targets provides the information that will determine the content and direction of the policy. That there is tension between the individual and institutional requirements of staff development is well known, therefore when planning a professional development programme it is important to try to find a balance between the needs of the institution and the aspirations of all who work within it. These two elements generally overlap, though initially differences in priorities will have to be accommodated. It is through the management of a detailed planning process that the professional development policy will be able to relate individual needs to school targets.

A professional development programme should encompass provision by LEAs, external agencies, in-school initiatives and, where appropriate, HEIs. Relevant data, such as that on inspection outcomes, will inform senior managers and the professional development coordinator of the needs of the school and its teachers in the context of external demands and opportunities. Having decided on the content and direction of the policy document, the next stage is to plan the provision of resources to enable targets to be met. The final part of the policy process is monitoring, evaluating and reviewing activities to ensure that each target has been properly addressed. Any evaluation of practice should provide managers with the information relevant to the development of their organisation.

The learning organisation

Learning organisations are created and sustained by learning communities. A learning community is comprised of individuals each of whom, in addition to performing his or her duties, has opportunities for learning. A learning community will formally recognise and value the learning that takes place within and beyond itself. In such a community learning is managed by individuals, their teachers and helpers, team leaders and managers. It is through the recognition of itself as a learning community that a school becomes a learning organisation, and this requires the formal acknowledgement of the right to learn of each member of the organisation. Schools that are learning organisations are centred upon the teaching, support and administrative staff who lead, direct and contribute to its evolution and development. A learning organisation is one that is able to set, plan and meet targets. It is also a reflective organisation, able to identify strengths, weaknesses, opportunities and threats, and professional in the way it manages and develops staff. Crucially, a learning organisation is continually in search of ways in which to improve itself.

In a learning organisation opportunities are provided to learn how to learn. This enables staff to assimilate and respond to new areas of knowledge and to develop the skills required to address issues as they emerge. It is now recognised that central to lifelong learning is the ability of individuals to absorb new information and to encounter new situations (Fryer, 1998). This is particularly pertinent to practitioners in the current climate, where professional and career initiatives for teachers and managers require individuals to manage their own learning accounts and to develop their own quality goals.

Within a learning organisation the close relationship between professional and organisational development is reflected in the community's culture. If a school is to become a learning organisation, a culture of learning that encompasses and celebrates the professional and personal development of its staff is required. Such development should be funded and supported through government policies and training initiatives (DfEE, 1999). Further and higher education institutions are also able to support schools: with their combined knowledge and skills they can provide the stimulus required for individual and institutional growth. It is within a learning organisation that professional development will become fully effective.

Culture

A good professional development culture is crucial to the creation of a learning organisation, as also is effective implementation of the staff development policy. The management of a professional development culture involves

- the acceptance that professional development continues throughout working life, i.e. lifelong learning;
- establishing, through induction and appraisal, an awareness of the importance of continuous learning;
- providing staff with access to a variety of learning experiences;
- providing expert support and guidance on professional development issues for all staff;
- encouraging reflection and development;
- motivating, valuing and rewarding all staff in the learning community.

Career management

Those who manage professional development will recognise that teachers' career development is most effectively managed by the individuals themselves, with guidance and support from management teams. Managers should recognise also that the importance of continuous support in the development of a teacher's career stems from modifications to the role of educational practitioners (see Table 2.1); moreover, the rapid changes to the curriculum and the devolution of management responsibilities from LEAs to schools have led to a shift in management styles affecting schools as organisations.

Table 2.1 indicates changes in the roles of managers and practitioners. All teachers now are involved in a range of day-to-day management tasks: teaching, planning and primary learning, and resources; collaboration on clearly defined tasks; monitoring and evaluation. They participate by representation in working groups set up by the senior management team to discuss specific tasks or directives issuing from governing agencies or school policy groups. Such changes will, inevitably, impact on each teacher's career.

Table 2.1 Changes to teachers' practice

From	To
Fixed roles	Flexible roles
Individual responsibility	Shared responsibility
Autocratic	Collaborative
Control	Release
Power	Empowerment
Managed	Managing

As professionals, teachers are enabled to make their own decisions concerning their careers, though, as members of a learning organisation, they will be assisted and guided in their career development. This investment in a teacher's development will be reflected in his or her commitment to teaching.

How this is achieved in practice requires further elaboration. Table 2.2 on p. 18 illustrates the learning organisation's commitment to a teacher's career, beginning with his or her recruitment and selection for a particular post. This leads to appointment, positioning and induction, followed by the process of appraisal and its outcome – targeted training and development. The final component in a career framework is the diversity of options that present themselves at the end of a contract in a school (or indeed the end of a career).

Table 2.2 illuminates the importance of a collegial approach to the management of professional development, indicating that effective professional development opportunities are the result of collaboration, participation and negotiation. A teacher's career should be viewed as a continuum in which is embedded the right of access to support at any point. Such an approach, wider than simply succession planning for promotion to senior management, requires a detailed analysis of the needs and aspirations of the profession in order to meet them as fully as possible.

The Teacher Training Agency's national standards' framework is a significant government initiative for professional development. Figure 2.1 on p. 19 illustrates the stages of a teacher's career in relation to the Teacher Training Agency's *National Standards for Teachers* (1998).

The introduction of the *National Standards for Teachers* is the latest in a series of governmental drives to raise standards in schools.

References

Bolam, R. (1993) *Recent Developments and Emerging Issues in the Continuing Professional Development of Teachers*. London: General Teaching Council for England and Wales.

Department for Education and Employment (DfEE) (1999) *Teachers Meeting the Challenge of Change*, Technical Paper. London: HMSO.

Fryer, R. (1997) 'We've got to get a handle on change', *Times Educational Supplement*, 28 November.

Hall, V. and Oldroyd, D. (1990) *Management of Self-development for Staff in Secondary Schools, Unit 3: Team Development for Effective Schools*. Bristol: NDCEMP.

Teacher Training Agency (TTA) (1998) *National Standards for Teachers*. London: TTA.

Table 2.2 Aspects of career management and related human resource planning

Career management	Human resource planning
Recruitment	Knowing/influencing the supply of available talent
• Attracting applicants	Use of agencies or search firms
• Defining requirements	Defining staffing needs
• Selection	Defining bona fide job requirements
• Induction and orientation	Providing information to recruits
	Validation of selection process
	Shortening the learning curve
	Minimising early turnover
Placement	Defining professional and managerial job requirements and job families/career paths
• Identifying job requirements and career paths	Designing job descriptions
• Inventories and placement systems	Defining the level of employee involvement
• Job posting and bidding	Validation of internal selection procedures
• Fast-track programmes	Managing accelerated career progress for high-potential employees
• Management succession programme	Controlling relocations and minimising their disruptive effects
• Relocations	
Training and development	Enabling employees to do their own career planning effectively
• Individual career planning	Managing raised expectations
• Training needs' analysis	Defining developmental needs
• Programme design and development	Weighing alternative means of meeting needs
• Research and evaluation	Evaluating the costs, benefits and quality of programmes
De-recruitment and alternatives	Policy and philosophy regarding reverse or lateral career steps
• Termination	Policy governing termination and consideration of legality
• Retirement	Devising flexible retirement policies and practices
• Demotion and transfer	

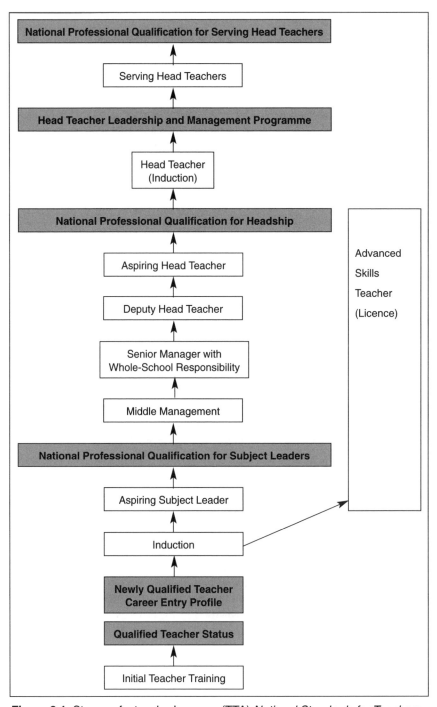

Figure 2.1 Stages of a teacher's career (TTA) *National Standards for Teachers*

Chapter 3

Teacher expertise

David Berliner

Editors' Note: David Berliner identifies the characteristics of expert teachers and compares them with experts in professional and other domains. He suggests a five-stage professional development journey from novice to expert teacher, each with defining features linked to classroom interpretation, teaching performance and development of responsibility.

Experts in areas as divergent as chess, bridge, radiology, nursing, air traffic control, physics, racehorse handicapping, and pedagogy show certain kinds of similarities. Despite their apparent diversity, experts in these fields seem to possess similar sets of skills and attitudes and to use common modes of perceiving and processing information (Chi *et al.*, 1986; Berliner, 1986). These abilities are not found among novices. Experience allows experts to apply their extensive knowledge to the solution of problems in the domain in which they work. To the novice, the expert appears to have uncanny abilities to notice things, an 'instinct' for making the right moves, an ineffable ability to get things done and to perform in an almost effortless manner.

Although we have gained some insight into the differences between experts and novices in various fields, we have only the scantiest knowledge about the ways that one progresses from novice to expert within a field. In part, this is because scientific knowledge about expertise is relatively new. But such research also requires longitudinal studies, and these studies are among the most difficult for which to get support.

Despite the shortage of scientific research in this area, some thoughtful speculation about the ways in which one becomes expert in a particular field is needed, because the planning of instruction for novices and the evaluation of others in a field are inherently related to theories of the development of expertise within the field. If we focus on the field of teaching, then answers to questions about what to teach novices, when to teach it, and how to teach it depend in part on implicit theories about the role of experience in the ability to learn the pedagogical skills, attitudes, and ways of thinking that teacher educators believe to be desirable. The evaluation of teachers also depends on such implicit theories of development. What one chooses to observe or test for, when one expects to see it, how it should be measured, and the criteria by which successful performance is judged all depend on some notions, perhaps fragmentary, about the development of ability in pedagogy. To make these often implicit and incomplete theories more explicit and complete, I report here on a general theory about the development of expertise.

A theory of skill learning

There are five stages to consider in the journey one takes from novice to expert teacher. We begin with the greenhorn, the raw recruit, the *novice*. Student teachers and many first-year teachers may be considered novices. As experience is gained, the novice becomes an *advanced beginner*. Many second- and third-year teachers are likely to be in this developmental stage. With further experience and some motivation to succeed, the advanced beginner becomes a *competent* performer. It is likely that many third- and fourth-year teachers, as well as some more experienced teachers, are at this level. At above the fifth year, a modest number of teachers may move into the *proficient* stage. Finally, a small number of these will move on to the last stage of development – that of *expert* teacher. Each of these stages of development is characterised by some distinctive features.

Stage 1: Novice

This is the stage at which the commonplace must be discerned, the elements of the tasks to be performed must be labelled and learned and a set of context-free rules must be acquired. In learning to teach, the novice is taught the meaning of terms such as 'higher-order questions', 'reinforcement', and 'learning disabled'. Novices are taught context-free rules such as 'Give praise for right answers', 'Wait at least three seconds after asking a higher-order question', 'Never criticise a student', and that old standby, 'Never smile until Christmas'. The novice must be able to identify the context-free elements and rules in order to begin to teach. The behaviour of the novice, whether that person is an automobile driver, chess player, or teacher, is very rational, relatively inflexible, and tends to conform to whatever rules and procedures the person was told to follow. Only minimal skill should really be expected. This is a stage for learning the objective facts and features of situations and for gaining experience. And it is the stage at which real-world experience appears to be far more important than verbal information, as generations of drivers, chess players, and student teachers have demonstrated.

Stage 2: Advanced beginner

This is when experience can meld with verbal knowledge. Similarities across contexts are recognised, and episodic knowledge is built up. Strategic knowledge – when to ignore or break rules and when to follow them – is developed. Context begins to guide behaviour. For example, advanced beginners may learn that praise does not always have the desired effect, such as when a low-ability child interprets it as communicating low expectations. The teacher may also learn that criticism after a bad performance can be quite motivating to a usually good student. Experience is affecting behaviour, but the advanced beginner may still have no sense of what is important. Benner (1984, pp. 23–4) makes this point in describing the difference between novice and advanced beginner nurses on the one hand and competent nurses on the other:

> I give instructions to the new graduate, very detailed and explicit instructions: When you come in and first see the baby's vital signs and make the physical examination, and you check the I.V. sites and the ventilator and make sure that it works, and you check the monitors and alarms. When I would say this to them, they would do exactly what I told them to do, no matter what else was going on. . . . They couldn't choose one to leave out. They couldn't choose which was the most important. . . . They couldn't do for one baby the things that were most important and then go on to the other baby and do the things that were most important, and leave the things that weren't as important until later on . . . . If I said, you have to do these eight things . . . they did those things, and they didn't care if their other kid was screaming its head off. When they did realize, they would be like a mule between two piles of hay.

The novice *and* the advanced beginner, though intensely involved in the learning process, may also lack a certain responsibility for their actions. This occurs because they are labelling and describing events, following rules, and recognising and classifying contexts, but not actively determining through personal action what is happening. The acceptance of personal responsibility for classroom instruction occurs when personal decision making, wilfully choosing what to do, takes place. This occurs in the next stage of development.

Stage 3: Competent

There are two distinguishing characteristics of competent performers. First, they make conscious choices about what they are going to do. They set priorities and decide on plans. They have rational goals and choose sensible means for reaching the ends they have in mind. In addition, they can determine what is and what is not important – from their experience they know what to attend to and what to ignore. At this stage, teachers learn not to make timing and targeting errors. They also learn to make curriculum and instruction decisions, such as when to stay with a topic and when to move on, on the basis of a particular teaching context and a particular group of students.

Because they are more personally in control of the events around them, following their own plans, and responding only to the information that they choose to, teachers at this stage tend to feel more responsibility for what happens. They are not detached. Thus they often feel emotional about success and failure in a way that is different and more intense than that of novices or advanced beginners. And they have more vivid memories of their successes and failures as well. But the competent performer is not yet very fast, fluid, or flexible in his or her behaviour. These are characteristics of the last two stages in the development of expertise.

Stage 4: Proficient

This is the stage at which intuition and know-how become prominent. Nothing mysterious is meant by these terms. Consider the micro-adjustments made in learning to ride a bicycle – at some point, individuals no longer think about these things. They develop an 'intuitive' sense of the situation. Furthermore, out of the wealth of experience that the proficient individual has accumulated comes a holistic recognition of similarities. At this stage, a teacher may notice without conscious effort that today's mathematics lesson is bogging down for the same reason that last week's spelling lesson bombed. At some higher level of categorisation, the similarities between disparate events are understood. This holistic recognition of similarities allows the proficient individual to predict events more precisely, since he or she sees more things as alike and therefore as having been experienced before. Chess masters, bridge masters, expert air traffic controllers, and expert radiologists rely on this ability. The proficient performer, however, while intuitive in pattern recognition and in ways of knowing, is still analytic and deliberative in deciding what to do. The proficient stage is the stage of most tournament chess and bridge players. But the grand masters are those few who move to a higher stage, to the expert level.

Stage 5: Expert

If the novice, advanced beginner, and competent performer are rational and the proficient performer is intuitive, we might categorise the experts as often arational. They have both an intuitive grasp of the situation and a non-analytic

23

and non-deliberative sense of the appropriate response to be made. They show fluid performance, as we all do when we no longer have to choose our words when speaking or think about where to place our feet when walking. We simply talk and walk in an apparently effortless manner. The expert striker in football, the expert martial artist in combat, the expert chess master, and the expert teacher in classroom recitations all seem to know where to be or what to do at the right time. They engage in their performance in a qualitatively different way than does the novice or the competent performer, like the racing-car driver who talks of becoming one with her machine or the science teacher who reports that the lesson just moved along so beautifully today that he never really had to teach. The experts are not consciously choosing what to attend to and what to do. They are acting effortlessly, fluidly, and in a sense this is arational, because it is not easily described as deductive or analytic behaviour. Though beyond the usual meaning of rational, since neither calculation nor deliberative thought is involved, the behaviour of the expert is certainly not irrational. The writings of Schon (1983) about knowledge in action characterise the behaviour of the expert practitioner.

Experts do things that usually work, and thus, when things are proceeding without a hitch, experts are not solving problems or making decisions in the usual sense of those terms. They 'go with the flow,' as it is sometimes described. When anomalies occur, things do not work out as planned, or something atypical happens, they bring deliberate analytic processes to bear on the situation. But when things are going smoothly, experts rarely appear to be reflective about their performance.

Findings and implications

1. *There are differences in the ways that teachers at various levels of experience and expertise interpret classroom phenomena.* Because of a lack of experience, those near the novice end of the developmental continuum can be expected to have trouble interpreting events. Until episodic knowledge is built up and similarities can be recognised across contexts, confusion may characterise the interpretations of classroom phenomena made by novices and advanced beginners. Experts are more likely than those with less ability to discern what is important from what is not when interpreting classroom phenomena. And we should also expect that experts will show more effortless performance and rely more on experience for interpreting information. We obtained data supportive of these ideas in some of our studies.

2. *There are differences in the use of classroom routines by teachers at various levels of expertise and experience.* The effortless and fluid performance that often characterises the experts' performance may be due, in part, to their

use of routines. Adherence to routines by teachers and students makes classrooms appear to function smoothly. In studying elementary school mathematics lessons, Leinhardt and Greeno (1986) compared an expert's opening homework review with that of a novice. The expert teacher was found to be quite brief, taking about one-third less time than the novice did. This expert was able to pick up information about attendance, about who did or did not do the homework, and was also able to identify who was going to need help later in the lesson. She elicited correct answers most of the time throughout the activity and also managed to get all the homework corrected. Moreover, she did so at a brisk pace and never lost control of the lesson. She also had developed routines to record attendance and to handle choral responding during the homework checks and hand raising to get attention. This expert also used clear signals to start and finish the lesson segments. In contrast, when the novice was enacting an opening homework review as part of a mathematics lesson, she was not able to get a fix on who did and did not do the homework, she had problems taking attendance, and she asked ambiguous questions that led her to misunderstand the difficulty of the homework. At one time the novice lost control of the pace. She never did learn which students were going to have more difficulty later in the lesson. It is important to note that the novice showed lack of familiarity with well-practised routines. She seemed not to act in habitual ways.

3. *There are differences in the emotionality displayed by teachers at various levels of expertise and experience.* When the developmental stage of competence is reached, it is said to be accompanied by a qualitatively different kind of emotionality and sense of responsibility for the work of the performer. We have some evidence for that, obtained in a curious way, in the study in which experts, advanced beginners, and novices planned and then taught a lesson [in a University-based laboratory context] (Berliner, 1988). The novices in that study were quite happy about their performance, although we did not rate it highly. Advanced beginners were generally affectless in describing their experience. They had a task to do and they did it. The experts, however, were quite angry about their participation in the task and disappointed about their performance.

In retrospect, and on the basis of our interviews, it appears that we had inadvertently taken away some of the experts' edge. First, we had created an artificial teaching situation. Second, according to their standards, they did not have enough time to prepare the lesson. Third, the students were not trained in the routines that make the experts' classrooms hum. One expert expressed his anger by walking out of the study. Another stopped in the middle of the lesson and had to be coaxed to continue. One started crying during the playback of her videotape. All were upset. Two weeks after the study, one expert, when asked what she remembered of her experience, said:

'I just remember it as the worst experience in my entire life, and I was depressed. . . . The things that stick out in my mind are the negative things. I remember just being frustrated the whole time I taught the lesson . . . . I don't like what happened. I've been real depressed and down [since then].'

Other comments by experts were about their feelings of uncomfortableness, stress, terror, and so forth. In this situation, advanced beginners and novices were virtually untouched at any deep emotional level, but our experts were affected deeply. In addition, they felt that in some way they had let us down – their sense of responsibility played a part in their feelings. Expert teachers, apparently like other experts, show more emotionality about the successes and failures of their work.

Summary

A growing body of literature is documenting the ways in which individuals at different levels of experience in classroom teaching and other fields differ in their interpretive abilities, their use of routines, and the emotional investment that they make in their work. From this one can extract a general principle, namely, that very important qualitative differences exist in the thinking and the performance of novices, experts, and all those who fall between these two points on the continuum. The developmental sequence involved in the acquisition of expertise, however, is not yet as clearly described. The five-stage theory of the development of expertise presented above is intended to help us think more about that issue and is well supported by data that were collected for other purposes.

References

Benner, P. (1984) *From Novice to Expert*. Reading, Mass.: Addison-Wesley.

Berliner, D. C. (1986) 'In pursuit of the expert pedagogue', *Educational Researcher* **15**, pp. 5–13.

Berliner, D. C. (1988) 'Memory for teaching as a function of expertise'. Paper presented at meetings of the American Educational Research Association, New Orleans, April.

Chi, M. T. H., Glaser, R. and Farr, M. (eds) (1986) *The Nature of Expertise*. Hillsdale, NJ: Erlbaum.

Leinhardt, G. and Greeno, J. (1986) 'The cognitive skill of teaching', *Journal of Educational Psychology* **78**, pp. 75–95.

Schon, D. (1983) *The Respective Practitioner*. New York: Basic Books.

Chapter 4

How do expert teachers view themselves?

Brigitte A. Rollett

Editors' Note: This exploration of expert teachers' interpretations of critical incidents in their classrooms is based on research projects carried out in three western industrialised cities, London, New York and Vienna, focusing on multi-ethnic classrooms. It reveals broad similarities in teacher attitudes towards children and their views on what contributes to their success.

What does it mean to be an expert in teaching? We know already that there are different kinds of knowledge (Shulman, 1986), and we also know that experts possess most or all of these. More specifically, experts rely on a large repertoire of strategies and skills that they can call on automatically, leaving them free to deal with unique or unexpected events. They have been shown to possess a distinct and original way of approaching the task of teaching, getting right to the core of problems rather than paying attention to peripheral features. They analyse situations for a longer time and in greater depth than novices before deciding on a plan of action. The wealth of knowledge and routines that they employ, in fact, is so automatic that they often do not realise why they preferred a certain plan of action over another. However, when questioned, they are able to reconstruct the reasons for their decisions and behaviour. And it seems that we in teaching research have finally begun to appreciate the fact that expert teachers also have a caring attitude towards their students. In fact, it is this caring attitude that enables them to be not just efficient but also responsible in carrying out their activities.

That is how researchers see teachers. But how do teachers see themselves? What is their self-image, and does this also have an effect on their teaching? In an international study described in this chapter, my colleagues and I tried to find answers to those questions on the basis of a belief that good teachers have positive self-images and that this optimistic, positive way of seeing themselves and their teaching plays an important role in their high capability. A positive self-image allows teachers to think positively about their work and, thus, about their students. This positive view of their students is reflected in their caring attitude towards them and also forms the basis for it.

Now, of course, one might ask, 'Yes, but can't a teacher have a positive self-image and still be an uncaring teacher, more interested in his or her own professional ego than in the students?' A positive self-image, it is true, is not something easily come by or easily assessed. In fact, it is much easier to assess teachers' didactic skill or the results achieved at the end of a lesson than to assess their self-image. However, by using the 'critical incident' methodology of Flanagan (1954), it is possible to approach a realistic impression of teachers' self-image.

In much of the research on expert teachers, the teachers had been prepared in one way or another before the investigation was begun. We felt that if we asked teachers in an impromptu way to explain or write about two critical incidents, a negative one and a positive one, it would be possible to carefully analyse the events for the values that entered in and to evaluate these and to thereby arrive at a more spontaneous view of teachers' thinking. We were also interested in the possibility of cross-cultural variation in how teachers valued themselves. To investigate this, a three-country research project that included researchers in New York, London, and Vienna was organised. While these countries all participate in the Western cultural tradition, there is enough of a difference that anyone moving from one culture to the other for the first time would sense a clear need to shift his or her cultural expectations in order to function smoothly and without incident in the new culture. Furthermore, when setting out to examine thought processes across very disparate cultures, one runs a risk of either comparing the wrong phenomena or asking questions inappropriate for discovering what one wants to discover (see Cole *et al.*'s 1971 classic work on this subject).

Simply put, then, our question was, if expert teachers have a positive self-image reflected in their caring attitude, is this self-image the same across three Western cultures? The answer turned out to be yes and no. Although how the teachers in the three cultures defined themselves as good teachers differed, our detailed analysis showed that the items that they viewed as contributing to their success were largely the same. This finding encouraged us to expand our hypotheses to include the consideration that it might be possible to create a sort of knowledge base for beginning teachers that is based on teachers' own perceptions of what is important and that might have international usefulness.

Intercultural research project

The crucial question for our study (Beckum *et al.*, 1989; Garcia and Otheguy, 1988; Perry and Lord, 1988; Rollett, 1988, 1989) was what expert teachers see as the source of their success (knowledge base, teaching skills, belief system) and how this reflects how they view themselves as teachers. We also wanted to determine whether expert teachers interpret and handle problem situations similarly in different cultural environments. The last question becomes especially significant when we think about the growing internationalisation of society caused by increasing worldwide mobility. In what follows, I outline the main thrust of our international research effort undertaken to shed light on this aspect of expert teachers.

A set of three parallel studies was organised and conducted by research groups in three different countries: Austria, the United Kingdom, and the United States. The research centres that took part in this study were the City College of the City University of New York, led by Leonard C. Beckum (who headed the research team), Ofelia Garcia, and Ricardo Otheguy; the South Bank Polytechnic in London, headed by Pauline Perry and Eric Lord; and the University of Vienna, Austria, headed by myself and my colleague Barbara Reisel. Each of these institutions is involved in training programmes for teachers in urban, multiethnic, multilingual, multicultural classrooms.

Each research centre selected teachers from elementary schools in its area and then asked school authorities to make the final selection of teachers. They were asked to choose teachers who met the following prerequisites: a minimum of three years' teaching experience, proven professional excellence, and continued participation in various higher-level teacher training seminars. Furthermore, we asked that the teachers have classes with a multiethnic character. The final project included 102 elementary teachers: 50 teachers in 20 schools from four community school districts in New York City; 21 teachers in four schools from two districts in London; and 31 teachers in 15 schools from nine districts in Vienna.

The expert teachers were asked to 'think back on two different kinds of situations. One should be an event or practice that you think you handled in a competent manner and that worked out well. The second situation should be an event or practice that you feel did not work out so well'. Their answers could be in either written or oral form (essay or taped interview). The teachers were encouraged to analyse and describe the incidents as fully as they could, reflecting on the skills and knowledge that they thought had enabled them to cope with the positive situation successfully and had caused failure in the negative instance.

The teachers' descriptions of their successes and failures were analysed for content through a category system developed by the New York research group (Garcia and Otheguy, 1988). On the basis of an initial reading of the essays and interview transcripts, a coding manual was developed in order to guarantee an exact application of the categories. Through this process, 105 topics were identified and coded according to the positive and negative affect expressed by the teachers. The topics were then organised into four domains that we felt were basic and essential spheres of operation for teachers: community characteristics, institutional characteristics, student characteristics, and teacher characteristics.

Community characteristics took into consideration items of social or cultural significance, mostly pertaining to the students mentioned in the description of critical incidents, such as cultural and linguistic background, household structure, school orientation of families, and so on. Institutional characteristics included more official elements of the classroom and school context that the teacher had to respond to, such as administrative support, type of curriculum, and class size and groupings. Student characteristics pertained to psychological characteristics of the students as they interacted in the classroom and included such areas as ability of students to concentrate, particular behaviour problems, poor language skills, and emotional needs (the latter two could also be correlated with an item in the community characteristics group, for instance). The teacher characteristics ranged the furthest, running the full spectrum from teachers' concern for and under-standing of individual children, class management, and handling of the intricate social relationships in the school community to considerations and initiatives regarding the curricula, didactic skill, and providing for their own professional development.

Obviously, there is overlap among these items, especially between those in the community and the student domains. However, if we go back to the original question, 'What image do expert teachers have of themselves?', any overlap or lack of clarity becomes more a formal question than a true methodological one. Qualitative research aims at getting to the *quality* of something, not at quantification of the exact composition of elements that would be imposed by the research question. Another goal of our categories and domains was to see whether it would be possible to determine what it is that teachers themselves feel is most important to their success and whether that could be formulated into a knowledge base for beginning teachers.

The results of the analyses from all three parallel research groups were surprisingly similar. We had expected to find greater, more substantive differ-ences in how teachers in the three different cultures viewed their teaching and to what they attributed their success. When we analysed the data for cultural differences in their thought processes, we could identify only a few characteristics.

For example, a comparison between the New York and the Viennese data showed some interesting differences in the ranking of the categories that the teachers used to describe teacher characteristics and aims that they thought significant. New York teachers especially stressed the importance of self-esteem as a person and a teacher, of upholding high expectations, and of developing self-esteem and pride in their students, while Viennese teachers' first priority was the ability to create a general atmosphere of understanding and love in their classrooms. The London and Vienna teachers did not emphasise helping their students develop self-esteem and pride, because the

European tradition holds that pride is too 'self-congratulatory' (a term used by the London group) and not something to strive for. However, it is clear that having a positive self-image (self-esteem) is the foundation for having respect of others, which is again the basis for creating an atmosphere of understanding and love. Thus, while the definitions among the cultures vary, the basis seems the same.

Another area where there was apparent cultural variance was the protocols dealing with unresolved situations. Teachers across all three cultures generally showed a tendency to blame failures on extrinsic factors (community, administrative, and student domains). In Vienna, the teachers agreed that a non-school orientation of parents was one of the main reasons for their inability to resolve a problem situation satisfactorily. In New York, on the other hand, teachers cited the disintegration of families caused by the absence of one or both parents as the predominant cause of failures. While it is statistically obvious that there are more divorces in the United States than in Austria, the two explanations come down to the same thing: parents are occupied with matters other than school and are, for economic or emotional reasons, not able to give their children or the teacher the support that the teacher feels is necessary to solve certain problems.

In the two examples just cited, where we thought we would find cultural variance, closer analysis showed that teachers, especially expert teachers, in our Western cultural tradition seem to resemble each other regardless of their specific cultural or ethnic backgrounds. Who is this culturally non-specific expert teacher as seen through the teachers' own eyes? Our research shows that above all, it is someone who favours the positive.

A first general analysis of the teachers' narratives of critical incidents in the classroom disclosed one characteristic that all teachers had in common: they found it much easier to recall positive events than negative ones. In some cases, it was necessary to ask the teachers to go back more than two weeks in order for them to remember an event that had not worked out favourably. In addition, the teachers found it much harder to describe the negative episodes and seemed reluctant to do so. When explaining their successes, expert teachers used much more detailed information and gave more reasons for their behaviour than they did in relating their failures. . . . Both descriptions and explanations of positive episodes were more numerous and detailed than those of the negative ones.

That teachers across three cultures preferred to remember positive events over negative ones is a noteworthy result, since the typical outcome in studies of recall of past events is that unfavourable memories are described in greater detail. To check this, I organised a preliminary adjunct study at the University of Vienna. Sixty-eight students who were participating in an educational psychology course were asked to describe the most pleasant incident and the most unpleasant incident that they could remember happening to them during their own schooling. When we compared the lengths of the descriptions, we found that they went into much greater detail about the unpleasant events than the positive ones.

Our teachers, however, showed a strong inclination to concentrate on the brighter side of their professional experiences. In all three samples, the experts showed themselves to be a strikingly optimistic group of people: they thought of themselves positively, as teachers who enjoy teaching and who have great trust in their abilities to ensure their success. As one Viennese teacher expressed it, 'Every morning I look forward to going to school, and I tremendously enjoy teaching'.

Another interesting strong tendency of the teachers, along with their positive self-image and attitude towards their work, was the importance that they attributed to emotions in their descriptions of critical incidents. In all three cities, teachers most often chose categories dealing with emotions and attitudes in explaining success or failure. For instance, in explaining success in dealing with a critical incident, teachers attributed affective qualities such as patience, tolerance, empathy, and love for and acceptance of children. When describing a negative experience or an incident with a negative outcome, they again chose affective qualities, such as disappointment, anger, and frustration.

This shows that emotions play a critical role when teachers think about important incidents in the classroom. As Zajonc (1980) proposed, processing meaningful information in general seems to be mediated by 'hot cognitions'. He found that emotions are not post-cognitive but precognitive and that conclusions based on emotions are made with much more confidence than purely rational judgements. In this way, cognitions produce the intimate meaning that a person attributes to his or her experiences. By preferring positive occurrences, expert teachers set the emotional stage for interpreting classroom situations in a favourable way, thereby producing a positive feedback loop for themselves.

Critical incidents

The teachers in our study were chosen to participate by their school principals because they were considered good teachers who were well liked by both students and fellow staff. As noted above, an analysis of their reports of critical incidents in their classroom showed that they tended to prefer reporting on positive incidents rather than negative ones and, in fact, had difficulty remembering the negative ones and that they tended to think of these experiences in emotional terms, indicating that they made decisions and acted on these decisions in a more affective than cognitive way. What were the types of incidents that they tended to report as critical? In analysing the issues that teachers concentrated on in the incidents that they reported, our research showed that, across all three countries, the highest percentage of episodes centred around problems generated by the teachers' interest in their students rather than curricular or managerial matters.

In all three studies, two-thirds of the incidents reported had to do with problem situations involving *individual* children, while only about one-third of the episodes dealt with situations caused by other factors. When researchers discussed these results with teachers, they mentioned that they felt at ease when handling instructional or managerial tasks but that the 'emotional highlights and frustrations' of their work at school were created by their successes and failures with children who had behavioural or academic difficulties.

The content analysis also pointed out that the major concerns of beginning teachers – perfecting their knowledge of subject matter, sharpening their pedagogical skills, familiarising themselves with the curriculum, and developing their organisational and classroom management techniques – had long ceased to be problems for these experts. What they were interested in was not the routines of the teaching profession but the extra challenges.

This finding supports what Berliner in Chapter 3 of this volume calls a characteristic attitude of experts: that they attend more to the atypical or unique events than the typical or ordinary events in the domain in which they have expertise. From this, I think we can also conclude that it is exactly this ability to deal efficiently with the curriculum or subject matter that allows expert teachers to go on to deal with their students in a caring, responsible way. It is hard to imagine that a novice teacher struggling to master presentation of the content could also find energy to negotiate particular issues on a more moral level with students in a responsible way. Our study also shows that it is exactly this level beyond the curriculum that expert teachers find the most challenging and interesting in their jobs.

At least half of the positive incidents recalled by the teachers dealt with their ability to integrate into the learning group a child who had been, for various reasons, an outsider. The next highest category of positive incidents was teachers' ability to successfully teach an individual child something that the child had previously found difficult to grasp. An example of this child-centred aspect of the teachers in our study is a teacher in the London project. One of the critical incidents that this teacher with 15 years' experience found very important involved an 11-year-old pupil who went 'berserk' on the playground during a physical education period. The teacher was able to calm the child down by removing him from the situation and discussing the incident with him. She interpreted his loss of control as the result of his worries about his grandmother's health and his upcoming move to a secondary school. She attributed her success to her knowledge of his home situation, her ability to sympathise with his grief and anxiety, and her willingness to understand his emotions instead of punishing his behaviour. Thus, her image of herself as an understanding, empathetic, caring teacher allowed her to act in a very responsible way, and her success in dealing with the situation reinforced her positive feelings not only about herself but about her student.

In all three cities, what teachers complained about (and saw as the extrinsic factors having a negative impact on their teaching success) was institutional and time pressures imposed on them by authorities. They saw these pressures as preventing them from being as flexible in their teaching as they thought was necessary to get the best out of every child in their class. They were especially interested in developing ways to find a compromise between these institutional limits and the needs of individual students.

This personal, child-centred way of interacting with their students seems to be one of the major reasons for these teachers' feelings of success and satisfaction. In all three samples, the detailed analysis of the teachers' descriptions revealed their conviction of the importance of being able to reach individual children and to deal with their problems in a responsible and competent way. If the teachers had generally found their successes in academic or curricular incidents, such as high overall test scores for a partic-ular subject, we would have to have said that school efficiency was more important for them and that they saw themselves primarily as transmitters of content knowledge. Given our findings, it is clear that the large majority of them see themselves as *caring* individuals.

This is not to say, of course, that knowledge of subject matter and its competent presentation, supported by efficient classroom management techniques, is not important to them. In fact, it is these things that form the basis of successful teaching. The results of our studies indicate, however, that in teachers' views of themselves, another component plays a more important role in their conceptions of what it means to do a good job of teaching: the teachers felt that for them to be successful, it was vital to have an intimate knowledge of each student's personality and to understand how classroom, home, and community experiences affected each child. They also thought that it was important that the teacher could work with children on an individual basis as well as on a group basis in a quasi-therapeutic way so that children could make the most of their abilities and their personality growth could be enhanced. This is clearly an attitude of taking moral responsibility for their students.

One teacher felt extremely uplifted when, after four frustrating years of trying to teach a boy to read, he surprised her one day by suddenly reading aloud a whole paragraph in the book that they were discussing. She was especially pleased about the fact that the whole class started clapping and congratulated the child for his achievement, shouting excitedly, 'Our Tommi can read!'

We found further support for the child-centred orientation of the teachers in our detailed analysis of the items in the category of student characteristics. In their narratives recalling problems within a critical incident, about half the teachers mentioned students' poor study habits and/or their disruptive behaviour. Their perceived success or failure in dealing with the incident was based on the degree of cooperation that they felt they were able to establish with individual students in social or academic settings. This finding is closely related to one mentioned earlier in the discussion, that teachers in all three cultural settings tended to blame the child's family or home situation for failures. Now we can better see why: if the teachers view themselves as being able to establish positive rapport with their students, on both an individual and a group basis, and this effort fails with certain children, they generally choose to maintain their own positive self-image and that of their students and blame extrinsic factors such as the family instead. Of course, we could also ask why they do not blame the student directly. We can hypothesise that doing so would require them to view at least part of the teaching relationship in a directly negative light. For example, since one of the main concerns of the Viennese teachers was forming good and loving relationships with their students and a pleasant work atmosphere in their classrooms, they probably preferred to view all their students as being capable of joining this effort.

Since we specifically chose classrooms with a high ratio of students from ethnic backgrounds other than the target culture, we also found that the teachers in our study were highly sensitive to minority children's particular cultures in their dealings with them. Their interest in learning more about those cultures in order to understand their students better again reflects this important student-centred attitude. A striking feature of the reports was that ethnicity was never mentioned in a derogatory way but was seen as a challenge (which we know is not always the case, especially as racism becomes an increasingly more important topic in many Western industrialised nations). Quite a few of the teachers in fact blamed teacher training authorities for not providing enough information about the customs and traditions of specific nationalities, so that the teachers had to acquire the necessary knowledge by trial and error. In a critical incident reported by an Austrian teacher, a Turkish boy ordered a female classmate to pick up something that he had dropped. When the classmate refused, he then ordered the teacher herself to pick it up. The teacher, needless to say, was annoyed and baffled by this incident. Only after she had been able to reflect on it did she realise that he had acted in accordance with the customs of his culture, where males are superior to females and never bend down in the presence of females.

This insight made such an impression on her that she decided to develop a cross-cultural awareness programme in her classroom.

This example also shows how expert teachers are able to build the positive feedback loop mentioned earlier. This teacher felt very good about her success at understanding what was behind her Turkish student's 'inappropriate' (as seen from her own culture) behaviour and was further motivated to increase mutual understanding in her classroom by initiating a cultural awareness programme. The success of this programme, fuelled by her desire to care for each one of her students, further contributed to her positive self-image and her ability to feel responsible in her teaching.

It is interesting to note at this point a study conducted at the University of Vienna by Fiedler (1987). Fiedler was interested in finding out which of the competencies acquired during teacher training at the university made young teachers more appreciated by their classes. She collected the grades received by 27 prospective secondary school teachers in their final exams and compared them to their rankings on the Dortmund Scale of Teacher Behaviour (Masendorf *et al.* 1976), a test designed to determine whether teachers use a positive (supporting), a negative (authoritarian), or an intermediate teaching style. The test was administered to 635 students in classes taught by these 27 teachers. An analysis of the data showed that the only predictor for a supportive teaching style as perceived by the students was the grade that the teacher had received on his or her psychology exam at the university.

We can suspect that the teachers who feel positive and responsible towards themselves and their students are likely to possess a certain amount of psychological tact and to be similarly perceived by their students. Thus, we can expand our hypothesis to include the assumption that an interest in and knowledge of psychology and the ability to apply it to the problems in the classroom are crucial to developing a teacher's sense of success in the classroom and thus also to developing a sort of positive feedback loop as mentioned earlier. The benefit for the students is that teachers are able to create a climate of mutual trust and support in which they can efficiently and responsibly carry out their work. In terms of teacher training, it seems to me that this insight supports the recommendation that teacher training programmes try to include psychology courses, preferably with a practical focus.

At this point, it is useful to return to our discussion of teachers' self-image. We hypothesised that expert teachers have a positive self-image that allows them to view their classrooms and their students in a positive, optimistic way. In addition to expert teachers' interest in the psychological well-being of their students, analysis of our data revealed that teaching was a very personal issue for them. This can best be illustrated by a Viennese teacher in our sample who declared, 'I realised in the course of my teaching experience how much the problems of my students have to do with myself'.

This attitude of taking personal responsibility for what goes on in the classroom may seem to contradict what was said earlier about teachers tending to blame extrinsic factors for their failures – why do they not also take direct responsibility for negative outcomes? – but, in fact, it does not: the teachers represented in all three research projects showed that they earnestly strove to improve themselves as persons and as professionals. They were interested in attending teacher training courses and eager to consult with other teachers at their school to share knowledge and skills, to exchange materials, and to discuss problems (items mentioned in the domain of teacher characteristics). A New York teacher expressed this connection between success and interest in personal improvement by saying, 'I am successful because I am good at looking for resources'. The responsibility that the teachers felt for maintaining a good relationship with their students extended to themselves: by improving themselves, they could feel more positive about themselves. This characteristic of experts is also discussed by Greeno (1990), who found that experts are especially able to draw on the resources in their environment to solve problems in their field of expertise.

Conclusion

As Clark and Peterson (1986) concluded from their review, teachers' thought processes play a crucial role in teaching. Teachers are revealed as responsible 'reflective professionals', whose theories and belief systems influence, to a large degree, their perceptions of classroom occurrences and who thus monitor their thoughts and actions involved in the teaching process (see also Bromme and Brophy, 1986; Clark and Lampert, 1986; Corno and Edelstein, 1987; Floden and Klinzing, 1990; Lampert, 1984; Leinhardt and Greeno, 1986; Peterson and Comeaux, 1987; Peterson, 1988; Shavelson and Stern, 1981; Shavelson, 1983; Shulman, 1986). A strong positive self-image is part of the belief system that influences teachers' perception of classroom occurrences and their feeling of power to have a positive effect on such occurrences.

When the results of our three studies are summarised, the parallels outweigh the differences. In their accounts of critical incidents in the classroom, the expert teachers revealed themselves as optimistic, outreaching, loving personalities, interested in children and concerned about their needs, able and happy in relating with them and willing to put in any amount of time and effort necessary to make a success of this. Furthermore, the expert teachers had a firm picture of what they wanted the individual learners to achieve academically and in social and personality growth, and they were convinced that it was important to give the children the time needed to achieve these things, even when this meant departing from the prescribed curriculum.

As competent professionals, the teachers were able and eager to produce what De Corte (1990) calls a 'powerful learning environment', fashioning the standardised curriculum to the requirements of their pupils. The reports of the resolved situations reflect the wealth of pedagogical and psychological knowledge that these expert teachers possess. The unresolved incidents mirror this in a way: they were experienced as doubly frustrating because the teachers were used to handling problems smoothly and successfully. As the London researchers expressed it, 'It was as though in these situations what stayed in the teachers' mind was simply their bafflement. They had run through their repertoire of skills and were at a loss to know what other strategies they could try' (Perry and Lord, 1988, p.22). The fact that they tended to avoid pondering on the negative incidents, thus possibly depriving themselves of the chance to hit on a solution, reflected their optimism and their positive self-image rather than a denial of the problem or an unwillingness to improve their skills and knowledge. Many of the positive incidents were the unresolved problem situations of the past. We can thus infer that the teachers seemed to prefer to shelve a problem for the time being when they did not have a solution rather than take a trial-and-error course of action. This kind of strategic thinking allows the teachers to further reinforce the positive feedback loop that seems to be basic to their success.

Thus, expert teachers seem to attribute an integral part of their success to their ability to understand children and their willingness to observe and listen to them, making responsible interaction the keynote of their everyday work with their students. If the driving force in the professional life of expert teachers seems to be the overwhelming conviction that, regardless of adverse factors, all children are able to learn, then it is the teachers' responsibility to enhance this growth. Their effectiveness is constantly being shaped by this force. Our study reflects the interpretative synthesis model of effectiveness and responsibility, in which morality is implicitly present wherever certain humane forms of effectiveness are employed.

References

Beckum, L. C. *et al.* (1989) *Moving Towards Developing a Knowledge Base for Beginning Teachers of Multicultural, Multilingual Populations: An International Study Focussing on Effective Teacher Behaviors.* New York: City College of New York.

Bromme, R. and Brophy, J. (1986) 'Teachers' cognitive activities', in Christiansen, B., Howsen, G. and Otte, M. (eds) *Perspectives on Mathematics Education.* Dordrecht: Reidel.

Clark, C. M. and Lampert, M. (1986) 'The study of teacher thinking: implications for teacher education', *Journal of Teacher Education* **37**(5), 27–31.

Clark, C. and Peterson, P. (1986) 'Teachers' thought processes', in Wittrock, M. C. (ed.) *Handbook of Research on Teaching*. New York: Macmillan.

Cole, M. *et al.* (1971) *The Cultural Context of Learning and Thinking*. London: Methuen.

Corno, L. and Edelstein, M. (1987) 'Information processing models', in Dunkin, M. J. (ed.) *The International Encyclopedia of Teaching and Teacher Education*. New York: Pergamon Press.

De Corte, E. (1990) 'Towards powerful learning environments for the acquisition of problem-solving skills', *European Journal of Psychology of Education* **5**(1), 5–19.

Fiedler, R. (1987) 'Einige Aspekte der Praxisrelevanz der Universitätsausbildung von Lehrern fur Allgemeinbildende Höhere Schulen' [Some practice-relevant aspects of the university's teacher training programme for prospective teachers at the college-preparatory level]. Unpublished doctoral dissertation, University of Vienna.

Flanagan, J. C. (1954) 'The critical incident technique', *Psychological Bulletin* **51**(4), 327–58.

Floden, R. E. and Klinzing, H. G. (1990) 'What can research on teacher thinking contribute to teachers' preparation? A second opinion', *Educational Researcher* **19**(5), 15–20.

Garcia, O. and Otheguy, R. (1988) 'The knowledge base of experienced teachers of minority children in New York City Public Schools'. Report submitted to the Exxon Foundation Project on the Knowledge Base of Beginning Teachers.

Greeno, J. G. (1990) *Number Sense as Situated Knowledge in a Conceptual Domain*. Report NOIRL 90-0014. Palo Alto, Calif.: Institute for Research on Learning.

Lampert, M. (1984) 'Teaching about thinking and thinking about teaching', *Journal of Curriculum Studies* **16**, 1–18.

Leinhardt, G. and Greeno, J. (1986) 'The cognitive skill of teaching', *Journal of Educational Psychology* **78**, 75–95.

Masendorf, F. *et al.* (1976) *Dortmunder Skala zum Lehrerverhalten* [Dortmund Scale of Teacher Behaviour]. Braunschweig, Germany: Westermann.

Perry, P. and Lord, E. (1988) *Knowledge-Base for Beginning Teachers in Multicultural, Multilingual, Deprived Urban Schools*. Report of the London Project.

Peterson, P. L. (1988) 'Teachers' and students' cognitional knowledge for classroom teaching and learning', *Educational Researcher* **17**(5), 5–14.

Peterson, P. L. and Comeaux, M. A. (1987) 'Teachers' schemata for classroom events: the mental scaffolding of teachers' thinking during classroom instruction', *Teaching and Teacher Education* **3**, 319–31.

Rollett, B. (1988) *Expert Teachers' Interpreting and Handling of Difficult Classroom Situations: Preliminary Report of a Study of 31 Primary Grade Teachers Using Flanagan's Critical Incidents Technique.* Vienna: University of Vienna.

Rollett, B. (1989) *An Examination of Knowledge Bases for Beginning Teachers in a Multicultural Environment.* Report to the Vienna Project, University of Vienna.

Shavelson, R. J. (1983) 'Review of research on teachers' pedagogical judgments, plans, and decisions', *Elementary School Journal* **83**(4), 392–413.

Shavelson, R. J. and Stern, P. (1981) 'Research on teachers' pedagogical thoughts, judgments, decisions, and behavior', *Review of Educational Research* **51**(4), 455–98.

Shulman, L. S. (1986) 'Paradigms and research programs in the study of teaching: a contemporary perspective', in Wittrock, M. C. (ed.) *Handbook of Research on Teaching*, 3rd edn. New York: Macmillan.

Zajonc, R. B. (1980) 'Feeling and thinking: preferences need no inferences', *American Psychologist* **35**, 151–75.

Chapter 5

The meaning of teacher professionalism in a quality control era

Anne Storey and Steven Hutchinson

Editors' Note: Storey and Hutchinson present an overview of the recent government-imposed changes for the teaching profession. They argue that, far from this being a deskilling agenda, there exists a new opportunity for reprofessionalisation for teachers, in the light of the Hay McBer Report.

Section 1

Professions in change

As Wilensky (1964, p.137) pointed out: 'Many occupations engage in heroic struggles for professional identification; few make the grade'. Teachers in the early years of their career will have sensed from their reading and contact with more experienced colleagues in schools that this is a source of some unease; teachers, far from progressing in their route to professional recognition, have been in retreat in the face of adverse conditions. The idea of 'the teaching profession' has served as shorthand for a number of interlocking values. Many of these values echo the classic attributes that mark out a liberal profession. These include access to and application of a systematic and codified body of specialist knowledge; an exclusive jurisdiction; regulation and certification by a professional body; and adherence to a set of professional norms which transcend pecuniary gain and which stem from a code of ethics supported by public trust.

These markers of the classic liberal professions bestow status and permit measures of autonomy. Intrinsic satisfaction is deemed to be gained by the idea of socially useful work and service. The concept implies the exercise of degrees of self-regulation both in terms of individual autonomy and judgement and also in terms of professional issues. In times past, governments have indeed appeared to endorse a large measure of teacher professional autonomy. In 1960, for example, the then Minister of Education was stating that 'Of course Parliament would never attempt to dictate the curriculum, but from time to time, we could, with advantage, express views on what is taught in schools and in training colleges' (Whitty, 1989).

The kind of work done by professionals has traditionally been regarded as complex, esoteric even, and not easily able to be evaluated by others who are not members of the professional group. The work done by them is regarded as socially useful and possessing a moral dimension. In the ideal-type descriptions available, society benefits from this package of elements. 'Being professional', an adjunct to these, is seen to involve a demonstrated sense of quality, discretion, high standards and an attention to improvement of self and service offered. A counterbalance to this range of requirements and responsibilities has been a public acceptance of such a group's right to a high level of self-regulating autonomy.

In the first part of the twentieth century, Emile Durkheim (1933) viewed such a group as a bulwark against narrow industrial and economic individualism and in the same era the historian, R. H. Tawney (1921/1961), made a clear and moral distinction between 'industry' and 'profession':

> The former is organised for the protection of rights, mainly rights to pecuniary gain. The latter is organised, imperfectly indeed, but nonetheless genuinely, for the performance of duties. The essence of one is that its only criterion is the financial return which it offers to its shareholders. The essence of the other is that, though men enter it for the sake of livelihood, the measure of their success is the service which they perform, not the gains which they amass.

This is a stark but useful early definition. The passage of time, social changes and the bureaucratisation of work as described by the sociologist Max Weber (1964, 1972), for example, have made such definitions contingent and partial. The results have undercut a number of occupational groups who aspire to become and to be regarded as 'professionals' – teachers are among them.

While the professional practitioner draws upon a body of accumulated knowledge, she or he is expected to use situation-specific expertise in everyday practice. In return for this socially useful and expert contribution, members of such professions in the twenty-first century expect a commensurate level of reward, in a wide sense. In contemporary terms, a 'psychological contract' is struck between the professional practitioner and the 'client', or as here, the state agency paying for that service. As in other work contexts, however, in teaching this psychological contract has been severely strained. A number of things have occurred to produce this situation.

Complex social and economic changes are in part to blame. It could be argued that the two great expansions of the education system itself, in the UK, in the 1870s and the 1960s onwards, contributed to the dissipation of the social and 'professional' standing of teachers who no longer were perceived to have a number of its distinguishing features. The 'learned' respected teacher, set apart from the local uneducated populace, was a stereotype in literature but it was less tenable or credible as levels of education improved generally. As national standards of education rose, along with official school-leaving ages and the emergence of self-education groups, the complex and not-easily gained special knowledge owned by teachers was not so apparent as it had been. Indeed, in the new millennium, trainee teachers are required to take tests in the *application* of 'basic' skills to their teaching posts: the maths graduate taking a numeracy test, for example, has to renegotiate the traditional 'meanings' of what it is to be a professional, outlined above.

It is both revealing and needful for teachers in the first phase of their career to note the ebb and flow of relationships that have occurred between professional groups and the state in the UK in order to make sense of the newly-shaped set of expectations required of teaching professionals. These relationships have varied in nature from being mutually supportive to antagonistic. The construction of state bureaucracies as ways of enacting the post-war 'welfare state' gave a huge impetus to the rise of a number of occupational groups which laid some claim to professional status. These included nurses, social workers and teachers. The subsequent working arrangement between professionals and the state was mutually beneficial. 'The professions provided the means for the implementation of government policy in the field of welfare and a source of expertise on which the state could draw to legitimate its power. The state supported the development of professional monopolies as a way of ensuring quality of service and provided professionals with a ready supply of clients, financial security and a voice in the development of government policy' (Quicke, 1998, p.328). Allied with this post-war settlement was the strengthening of the professional associations and the trade unions and for a time the state was content to negotiate on a collective basis with these representative bodies. It was through the mechanisms of collective bargaining and consultation that a valuable negotiated order was accomplished.

But this state of affairs was not to persist. The system came under challenge most notably and strongly in the Thatcher era with the application of the economic market to ever-increasing segments of former state bureaucracies. But there had been signs of strain even before this when Labour was in power: as early as 1976, James Callaghan's Ruskin College speech had questioned standards and productivity in the education service.

Value for money and accountability became new watchwords in public debates. The introduction of the National Curriculum, of school inspections by OFSTED, Key Stage testing, the publication of results and league tables as indications of a school's performance, and appraisal systems were, we would argue, some of the control systems placed upon teachers and schools to check power and to produce improved levels of consistency in educational achievement. Nor, as became abundantly evident, was this new agenda simply a temporary phase to be thrown into reverse by a change of government. In 1997, New Labour pressed ahead with many of the same ideas and mechanisms. 'Old' versions of professionalism in teaching, based on notions of autonomy and individual creativity, and resistance to state interference in matters of curriculum or methods, were in tension with a series of governments intent on driving through far-reaching changes relating to consistency, higher standards and accountability in an education *system*.

Section 2

The modernisation drive and new agendas

Teachers located in the first phase of their careers will be well aware of a much-aired 'modernisation agenda'; one which actually has its roots in the final quarter of the last century, though the term is formally claimed by New Labour (1998). This political party made no secret of its aim to 'modernise' Britain, one of its central missions being the improvement of education within this declared endeavour. Issues of quality enhancement and quality control were promoted publicly in the 1997 *Excellence in Schools* initiative but they were hardly new to experienced teachers in post, simply because of the structural processes and checks referred to earlier. The Green Paper, *Teachers: meeting the challenge of change* (DfEE, 1998), and the subsequent technical amplification documents, set out the vision for modernisation, which was to be directed towards the 'raising of standards in schools'. In these documents, teachers were asked to 'rise to the challenge of modernisation' and they were invited 'to grasp the historic opportunity that now presents itself' (1.35). The mechanisms put in place for achieving these objectives were: externally-imposed targets; assessment of performance (of pupils, schools and teachers); increased attention to the training of teachers; and performance-related reward and penalty. In February 2000, a *Professional Development Framework*, to support the vision, was published. The National College for School Leadership and the General Teaching Council were other structures created and designed to complete the plan for modernisation. Ensuing publications, *Learning and Teaching: A Strategy for professional development* (DfEE, 2001a); *Good Value CPD: A Code of Practice for Providers of Professional Development for Teachers* (2001b), and the Green Paper *Schools: Building on Success* (2001c) have confirmed the 1997/8 agenda and vision and provided details for the further implementation of it. Success and achievements have notably been celebrated within the pages of the 2001 publications cited.

The vision itself was focused on securing a 'world class' system, producing able, enquiring teachers, in training, in induction and as developing professionals. It was seen too as a way in which the system could produce a workforce able to compete internationally and able to contribute to national growth. This was designed to be a system that raised standards for every pupil and at all school ages. The projected changes, building on the gains of the national numeracy and literacy strategies, were consciously formulated to push systems and people within them to deal with continued change and innovation, in a fast-moving world. The changes, designed to aid recruitment and retention, offered a new, 'robust system' for appraising staff 'against clear objectives and outcomes'.

This is a system consciously designed to appeal to teachers relatively new to the profession and to those who are considering a career move into teaching; in fact all those who are assessing the relative merits of different career options in a market economy and in conversation with peers who are knowledgeable about the pay, prospects and perceived status of other careers on offer. It is a system notable too for an attempt to reward and retain capable, experienced classroom teachers, offered in return for the 'new professionalism'. Accompanying this has been the view that professional development is taken to be a career-long expectation of teachers in order to fulfil new training and teaching requirements. Within the system, annual appraisal was linked to classroom observations, together focusing on three key areas: improved teacher performance, target setting for improved pupil performance, and professional development. A core component of the scheme was the introduction of a 'threshold', an opening (or barring) of the way to a higher pay spine, so establishing a pay–performance link. In addition, the body of Advanced Skills Teachers, already established, was expanded, as were the leadership spines in schools. Rapid advancement for high performers on the pre-threshold spine was also integrated into the scheme. A key element of the re-setting of pay and rewards in the scheme was the premise that quality of input as well as years of service were to be rewarded. Systems of reward for quality-in-evidence as well as quality control systems were core drivers of the reforms introduced.

While these classic elements of a human resource management approach were to the fore there was also a clear statement which challenged and indeed rejected the claim to teacher autonomy: 'the time has long gone when isolated, unaccountable professionals made curriculum and pedagogical deci-sions alone, without reference to the outside world' (DfEE, 1998, 1.13). The old order was transparently being challenged and refuted. The traditional contract with all teachers, it appeared, was to be replaced with a new one based not on individual teacher autonomy but on a mix of state regulation and managerialism: these were opportunities for a 'new professionalism'.

Section 3

Deprofessionalism or reprofessionalism?

An argument to be considered is that teachers currently in the first, pre-threshold phase of their careers may find the details of what is essentially a performance management scheme, containing its language and grammar, less threatening and more familiar than their more experienced colleagues in schools. More recent entrants to teaching may well be related to members of other professional, clerical or manual groups, and well-versed in what are now commonplace systems in other careers. Specific details and the particular strictures governing teaching (such as resources and the fixed arrangements of school life and routines, for example) may account for differences to be accommodated. But these may be small in scope. More mature, recent entrants to teaching will undoubtedly have encountered performance management systems of some variety in other occupations.

What such systems have at their core are the notions of defined standards and requirements about consistency. Familiarity with the terms and the practice of such systems may well, for the teacher groups referred to above, simply express the *expected norms* for a post rather than pose *quality control* issues to be negotiated and internalised as part of a new and potentially difficult agenda. These teachers may indeed, in practice, recognise more opportunities than threats in the performance–reward system in place. We will return to the issue of opportunities for teachers in the final section of this chapter.

Discussions about the nature of education, the role of teachers, learners, expected outcomes, consistency and effectiveness issues are, however, as unfinished as they have always been. There are different agendas in contest in these matters and they go to the heart of the debates about professionalism.

It is the proposed nature and scope of *what kind of performance* is to be managed and how this relates to perceptions about the nature of professionalism in teaching that have elicited enormous debate by experienced teachers and others, not least those unpersuaded by the relatively new structures, systems and the values which appear to be promulgated by them. Hodkinson (1997) argues that the division of labour, notably in the (Ford) motor industry in the early part of the twentieth century has been revived in new contexts. Teachers, it is reasoned, have become neo-Fordists: directives organise their work, inspectors assess its degree of accuracy in meeting the stipulated norms. This is retrograde strategic

46

planning in his view, given the demands of the future: 'We need to commence the education and re-education of teachers today, in order to meet the challenges of the day after tomorrow. A reductionist, technical de-professionalising control agenda will do nothing to achieve this' (Hodkinson, 1997, p.80).

A clear thread in the academic literature relating to the issue, is that teaching, far from improving or even maintaining its professional standing, has become 'de-skilled'. For example, even before a New Labour phase of the modernisation programme was launched, Hyland (1993, p.130) was arguing that: 'programmes based on the functional analysis of work roles are likely to produce teachers who are judged competent yet are ill-equipped for further professional development, uncritical of educational change and largely ignorant of the wider cultural, social and political context in which the role of teachers needs to be located'. Golby (1998) maintained that the nature of teachers' professionalism is in deep contention; indeed that the concept itself is patently problematic. The whole business orientation of education (Weir 1997) has been a key focus for criticism in subsequent literature. Harris (1997) went further and interpreted the process of change as one of 'proletarianisation'. What is a key assumption, consciously explicated or not, in much of the critical analysis of these trends, is a correlation of professional autonomy with the freedom of teachers to make creative inputs to the content and methodology of courses in schools. The application of 'rigour' and of 'robust' standards and procedures by successive governments, has widely been viewed as an undermining of autonomy and creative potential in the classroom, with teachers as ciphers, simply technicians of the process, with a resulting perceived reduction of a values dimension (Apple, 1986; Young, 1998).

Other arguments have been pressed against the culture changes affecting teachers. One major counter-thrust relates to all the things that teachers *do* and are expected *to be* that must reside outside the easily visible and measurable behaviours of a performance reward system (Young 1998). Arising out of their study, Helsby and Saunders (1993) suggest rather more optimistically that *teacher-generated* indicators point a way forward and that performance indicators *can* be made professionally relevant and useful.

Quicke (1998, 2000), however, taking up similar issues, maintains that professionals can only function as moral leaders, an enduring professional requirement of British teachers, if they are given autonomy and allowed to develop strategies and approaches in ways which in their view will benefit society. Market strategies reinforce inequalities and divisions, repulsing collaborative efforts and are an expression of the absence of trust, he argues. This absence was described in a different way by Nick Tate, Chief Executive of the QCA. He attributed it to the situation which accompanies top-down reform, not owned by the mediators of it, so that, 'requirements are always likely to feel oppressive in the absence of an explicit and shared rationale'

(1999, p.12). The response to this view, from many teachers and other observers at that time, was that the rationale for modernisation was perfectly explicit. The correlation made of improved pay–performance opportunities, clearer and transparent appraisal processes for teachers, fast tracking of very able classroom teachers and better training and support for career-long professional development with enhanced achievement nationally and consistently by pupils was absolutely clear: it simply was not shared (Storey, 2000).

Nevertheless, though teaching may have presented an 'easy' target for the systems and perspectives described, it is worth accenting the point that it has not been the only service in recent years to be touched by them. The Health Service particularly, has been subject to similar modes of control with management tiers, cost effectiveness drives, and appraisal and performance management systems firmly in place, but still with only a limited brake on consultants' autonomy and recourse to private clients. In *both* these service areas, however, standards, targets, competitiveness and results analysis and publication, represent the warp and weft of a market-driven economy approach which in the 1980s and 1990s was pressed as a global one.

But what emerges through the debates about such terms is how complex they actually are. Multifaceted strands interact, individual ones more dominant and important in some occupational groups than others. Status, too, an important facet of 'professionalism', can be a complex and shifting element. It is an argument here, however, that an irreversible reshaping of what it means to be a professional in teaching has taken place. Further, it is contentious whether teachers as a body in the past thirty years have owned or been perceived to possess, the exclusive knowledge or socially scarce skills which have traditionally described a professional group. However, the opportunity now may be available for all teachers, in any phase of career development, to take the content, processes and structures of the modernisation scenario and seek to shape them in specific educational contexts in order to *reprofessionalise* and to write their own version of an educational vision through dialogue and action. Wresting a greater share of the contested terrain of education through participation may, ironically, be one tangible and possible outcome beyond the current era's accent on quality control.

Section 4

Challenges and opportunities for teachers

Whatever the relative merits of these particular interpretations, it can be reasonably concluded that a cultural change of some sort has taken place in the UK and that perceptions and debates about educational quality will continue to be set in the context and language of international competition, and of standards, rigour and effectiveness. Moreover, it appears unlikely that the broad thrust of the changes will be withdrawn whichever of the political parties assumes control in subsequent General Elections.

An important part of the challenge for teachers can be found, we maintain, in the government-funded Hay McBer Report (2000) which pointed the way for standards of classroom teaching and learning from the Induction period, through to Advanced Skills Teacher status. The significant recognition here – that real life in classrooms has to be part of any creditable assessment of what teachers need to do and how they do it – may be seen as a route to re-professionalisation. In tune with this, the model emerges from a study of what effective teachers *actually do* in the classroom (see Chapter 17). 'Effective' here is tellingly given a much wider definition than in earlier documents referred to in this chapter.

The wider definition nets in three core aspects: *teaching skills*, *professional characteristics* and *classroom climate*. Teaching skills refer to those 'micro behaviours' constantly exhibited by effective teachers and clustered under the seven OFSTED classroom observation areas. Professional characteristics 'are deeper-seated patterns of behaviour' – demonstrated more often and to a greater degree of intensity than less effective colleagues. There are 16 of these, arranged in clusters such as 'professionalism', thinking, planning and setting expectations, leading and relating to others. 'Professionalism' here is seen to relate to 'a core of strongly held and enacted values' (Hay McBer 2.3.7). Not all of these 16 characteristics were cited as being needed to demonstrate 'effectiveness'; strength in five of these would meet the official definition. An effective classroom climate includes lack of disruption, opportunities to engage, high expectations and a sense of security and order. The point was made here that 'In both primary and secondary samples, pupil progress correlated strongly with classroom climate' ('Executive Summary': 3).

But it may also be argued that what is here is a more realistic recognition about the need to look at the wider picture in terms of what a teacher actually does and ought to do that takes future practice beyond the narrow confines of what practitioners and writers have characterised as trends to deskilling. This Phase II Report recognised that teaching is 'a cultural activity' (5.1.6), that because of this 'changes in teaching practice can only take place over a long period of time' (6.2.3), and that the 16 professional characteristics do 'not provide a one-size fits-all picture' (2.3.2) since 'teachers are not clones' (2.1.4). It refers also to respected practitioner-researcher findings. Peter Mortimore and associates' *School Matters* (1988) for example, is cited as a supportive platform for the findings of their own study: that structured sessions, intellectually challenging lessons, a work-oriented environment, communication between teacher and pupils and a well-defined focus to individual lessons resulted in more effective lessons – for *everyone.* Moreover, a (re)emerging sense, perhaps, of the real need for teachers to apply judgement and professional skill in *meeting different needs in varying contexts* and implementing well-judged and creative responses to them, supports the view that skilled and inspiring teachers are *not* simply facilitators or technicians (Hay McBer, 2.1.4). Teachers in the early phase of their careers in a performance management era can take heart that a collaborative effort with colleagues *is* part of a standards agenda that has the goal of improving pupils' learning in the 'average' classroom. The 'star teachers of the twenty-first century . . . will be teachers who collaborate to build a system . . . who work every day to improve teaching – not only their own but also that of the whole profession' (6.1.2). 'Working every day to improve teaching' links here to the 'teacher-as-researcher' aspect of professional development and the potential for enhanced professional status as a result.

The elements of rigour and autonomy which suggest themselves were well aired in the Hay McBer Report. There, 'a system of continuous improvement' was pressed and a Japanese variant (6.2.2) outlined as a potentially fruitful one to consider. One component of this, a 'lesson study', involved professional development groups of teachers working to pursue school goals, designing, implementing and evaluating new teaching and learning strategies. 'Lesson fairs' at year end provide platforms for sharing innovations and the rationales for them between schools. Such developments could potentially offer an enhanced professional base for teachers through a syncopation of study and action, with the proviso that such a process would not profit from any simplification towards systematised tricks-of-the-trade.

The pre-threshold teacher can also look to other supportive strains in the debate about rigour and its perceived tension with creativity – an element associated with professional autonomy. Bodies such as the National Advisory Committee on Creative and Cultural Education (NACCCE) in its publication *All Our Futures: Creativity, Culture and Education,* presents a not unexpected case for:

> a broad, flexible, and motivating education that recognises the different talents of all children and delivers excellence for everyone . . . to engage with the growing complexity and diversity of social values and ways of life.
> (NACCCE,1999, p.6)

The point is stressed:

> We live in a fast-moving world . . . employers continue to demand people who can adapt, see connections, innovate, communicate and work with

others . . . many businesses are paying for courses to promote creative abilities, to teach the skills and attitudes that are now essential for economic success but which our education system is not designed to promote.
(NACCCE, p.12)

Pressing, prestigious and public voices of this kind in the debates about autonomy, and the complexities of the teaching–learning dynamic, have undoubtedly led to more subtle reworkings of the original, simpler performance management scheme devised as part of the modernisation agenda of 1998.

Conclusion

The road ahead for all teachers, irrespective of career phase, may well be a smoother one than was thought possible in recent years. A growing recognition that willing, able teacher-partners in sufficient numbers will be needed for the new challenges of teaching in the twenty-first century has been making itself felt. This chapter has presented the argument that positive signs relating to pragmatic adjustments by the major parties have been born of necessity. What has been declared: much greater autonomy for schools and teachers who have performed competently; more subtle and wide-ranging descriptions of what being an 'effective teacher' means, to include, for example, values, thinking skills, a passion for learning and the ability to relate to and influence others, can be seen as far less prescriptive and restricting for all teachers and for the future, than first indications suggested.

The outlook for professionalism looks brighter, too. It is worth considering the argument that many teachers are able to go well beyond the 'new professionalism' of the 1998 Green Paper, where the term was used notably to contrast with the poor motivation and lacklustre underperformance identified and which was to be replaced with an 'unprecedented opportunity' for culture and classroom change; and beyond too, subsequent pragmatic re-versionings of the term. In practice, and given the wider framework emerging of what 'teacher effectiveness' is deemed to be, drawn from observations of classrooms and used as a flexible tool to encourage consistency, there may well be an opportunity to reskill rather than deskill. The wider range of pedagogic and personal skills and attributes expected and the training opportunities that must accompany them as part of the career-long professional development requirement of teachers, linked to appraisal, may well contribute to the special skills and attributes that the teaching 'profession' has arguably lacked. Since this will apply to the whole cohort of teachers, the general standard of what is offered and how it is offered to pupils could be rather higher, and consistently so.

Moreover, the General Teaching Council and the National College for School Leadership may come to be commonly viewed as providing the kinds of support and regulation strategies, and in an appropriate balance, that are valued by teachers as well as government agencies. These newer organisations might make a real contribution to the discrete body of professional knowledge and skills owned by teachers. In another context, Marsden (2000) has argued that it is the perceptions of teachers that really count. This applies, too, in relation to the actual and imagined levels of autonomy teachers feel themselves to have in the management of their performance and in their sense of selves as 'professionals'.

The meaning of the term is, of course, contingent of time and context. Whatever strengths emerge from what has been a volatile period of change, a reskilling or 'reprofessionalisation' will not relate to traditional versions of the term – and other service sectors will experience this too. If, however, a sufficient degree of autonomy can be blended with the controls realistically required from any nationally-provided service, then there may well indeed be a net benefit for all teachers in terms of status and special skills as well as in other career prospects. If the 'standards' required of teachers are seen, ultimately, as wide-ranging and multifaceted and teachers can look beyond checklists to personal 'repertoires' of approach, then the familiar creativity–rigour debates, at the heart of many discussions that define professionalism and its links with teaching, might well be resolved to great advantage. Such an outcome might impact particularly on that body of teachers now joining the profession who have hopes of becoming the star teachers of the twenty-first century and who have aspirations too, to gain a greater control of both the definitions and the practice of 'quality' in education.

References

Apple, M. W. (1986) *Education and Power*, 2nd edn. London: Ark.

Department for Education and Employment (DfEE) (1998) *Teachers: meeting the challenge of change* (Green Paper). London: The Stationery Office.

Department for Education and Employment (DfEE) (2001a) *Learning and Teaching: A Strategy for professional development*. London: DfEE Publications.

Department for Education and Employment (DfEE) (2001n) *Good Value CPD: A Code of Practice for Providers of Professional Development for Teachers*. London:DfEE Publications.

Department for Education and Employment (DfEE) (2001c) *Schools: Building on Success* (Green Paper). London: The Stationery Office.

Durkheim, E. (1933) *The Division of Labour in Society* (1893). Glencoe, Il.: Free Press.

Golby, M. (1998) 'Editorial' *Teacher Development* **2**(3).

Harris, A. (1997) 'The deprofessionalization and deskilling of teachers', in Watson, K., Modgil, C. and Modgil, S. (eds) *Teachers, Teacher Education and Training*, 57–65. London: Cassell.

Hay McBer (2000) *Research into Teacher Effectiveness: Phase II Report A Model of Teacher Effectiveness*. London: Hay McBer.

Helsby, G. and Saunders, M. (1993) 'Taylorism, Tylerism and performance indicators: defending the indefensible?', *Educational Studies* **19**(1), 55–77.

Hodkinson, P. (1997) 'Neo Fordism and teacher professionalism', *Teacher Development* (1), 69–82.

Hyland, T. (1993) 'Professional development and competence-based education', *Educational Studies* **19**(1), 123–32.

Marsden, D. (2000) 'Teachers before the "threshold"', Discussion Paper 454. London: Centre for Economic Performance, London School of Economics.

Mortimore, P. *et al.* (1988) *School Matters*. Shepton Mallett: Open Books.

National Advisory Committee on Creative and Cultural Education (NACCCE) (1999) *All Our Futures: Creativity, Culture and Education*. London: DfEE Publications.

Quicke, J. (1998) 'Towards a new professionalism for new times: some problems and possibilities', *Teacher Development* **2**, (3), 323–38.

Quicke, J. (2000) 'A new professionalism for a collaborative culture of organizational learning in contemporary society', *Educational Management and Administration* **28**(3), 299–315.

Storey, A. (2000) 'A leap of faith? Performance pay for teachers', *Journal of Educational Policy* **15**(5), 509–23.

Tate, N. (1999) 'What is education for?', *English in Education* **33**(2), 5–18.

Tawney, R. H. (1921/1961) *The Acquisitive Society*. London: Fontana.

Weber, M. (1964) *The Theory of Social and Economic Organisations*, Parsons, T. (ed.). London: Macmillan.

Weber, M. (1972) *The Interpretation of Social Reality*, Eldridge, J.E.T. (ed.). London: Nelson.

Weir, A. D. (1997) 'Professions under change', in Watson, K., Modgil, C. and Modgil, S. (eds) *Teachers, Teacher Education and Training*, 18–26. London: Cassell.

Whitty, G. (1989) 'The New Right and the National Curriculum: state control or market forces?', *Journal of Educational Policy* **4**(4).

Wilensky, H. L. (1964) 'The professionalization of everyone?', *The American Journal of Sociology*, September, 137–58.

Young, M. (1998) 'Rethinking teacher education for a global future: lessons from the English, *Journal of Education for Teaching* **24**(1), 51–62.

Chapter 6

Competence-based teacher education: approaches and issues

Geoff Whitty and Elizabeth Willmott

Editors' Note: This contribution first appeared in the early 1990s prior to the government's introduction of the first competences for teacher assessment in initial teacher training. It set the scene for a decade of debate on competence-based approaches to teacher education.

[. . .]

Definitions

In any debate about a value-laden activity such as teacher education, difficulties are bound to be encountered in relation to the key concepts employed. Many teacher educators reject the idea of competence-based teacher education on the grounds that it encourages an over-emphasis on skills and techniques; that it ignores vital components of teacher education; that what informs performance is as important as performance itself; and that the whole is more than the sum of the parts. This rejection partly derives from a reading of early American checklists of teacher behaviour, which are ticked by an observer. Yet there are others who argue that a 'reflective practitioner' approach, which often claims to be the very antithesis of a technicist and behaviourist view of teacher education, can itself be expressed in competence terms. Hextall *et al.* (1991, p.15), for example, argue that 'teaching is not reducible to a set of technical operations'. However, they go on to say that 'they are not running away from the issue of the systematic appraisal of teaching competence' and that even the quality of reflectivity can be formulated as a series of competences that can be monitored. Clearly 'competence' is a term capable of a number of different interpretations.

The courses we have looked at that use the term 'competence' are less than explicit about what it is meant to convey. However, two major approaches to the definition of a competence can be discerned:

- competence characterised as an ability to perform a task satisfactorily, the task being clearly defined and the criteria of success being set out alongside this;
- competence characterised as wider than this, encompassing intellectual, cognitive and attitudinal dimensions, as well as performance; in this model, neither competences nor the criteria of achievement are so readily susceptible to sharp and discrete identification.

Additionally, there is often a lack of clarity about the relationship between different types of competence. Some competences appear to be person related and others task related. While some courses restrict themselves to defining a short list of generic professional competences and others embrace literally scores of discrete behaviours, many fail to distinguish between these different types of competence or specify the ways in which they are presumed to relate. Nor are the course documents we have read usually explicit about how performance in terms of the identified competences relates to overall 'competence'. This is reminiscent of some of the early US examples, where it seemed possible to get a tick on a whole list of individual competences and still appear incompetent! Some people therefore argue that competence is more than the sum of a variety of individual competences and that it is more like communicative competence, derived from an underlying grammar that generates individual competences in different unpredictable situations.

In the light of these variations, it would be difficult and probably undesirable to prescribe a particular definition of competence-based teacher education, or to specify particular competences that need to be included in any scheme. Nevertheless, teacher educators attracted by the idea of competence-based approaches will need to clarify their own approach to these issues. As we shall see later, different definitions will have different implications for teaching, learning and assessment.

The attraction of competence-based approaches

To some extent, even the reasons for choosing competence-based approaches will differ according to the definition of competence employed. Nevertheless, a number of general points can usefully be made. One advantage, which might commend itself to critics of more traditional approaches to teacher education, was put forward by an early advocate of the approach who argued that it would help to 'remove some of the mystique and institutional restrictions that surround teacher education' (Tuxworth, 1982). However, that is essentially a plea for clarifying and making public the aims and objectives of a course and the ways in which they are evidenced in assessment, something which arguably should apply to all courses, whether competence-based or not. Beyond that, competence-based approaches can be justified as giving students clear targets of achievement and explicit evidence of their progress, enabling schools to share an understanding of the function of placements, and giving employers a clear idea of what to expect. A subsidiary reason for introducing competence-based approaches, which has been particularly influential in the FE sector, is that it allows teachers to experience the same approach as the students they teach.

Justifications for the particular competences selected also seem to vary. This may relate to the aims of the course in question: whereas an initial B.Ed. is expected to provide a general programme of higher education as well as a professional preparation for teaching, a PGCE is geared to entrants who already have a general education and focuses on their professional preparation. Much of the . . . debate about the competences that might inform a competence-based approach to teacher education sees them as derived from an analysis of the required competences of the beginning (or continuing) teacher, usually related to performance in the workplace. This is consistent with other forms of training which utilise the approach, as exemplified in the following statement from NCVQ (1989, p.4):

- the area of competence to be covered must have meaning and relevance in the context of the occupational structure in the sector of employment concerned;
- the statement of competence must be based on an analysis of occupational roles within the area of competence to which it relates;
- the statement of competence must encompass the underpinning knowledge and understanding required for effective performance in employment.

While this last statement extends the notion of competence beyond observable workplace skills, it does not necessarily encompass all the elements of personal education which may be the concern of courses of teacher education. It may well be that an even broader approach to the definition of competences will be necessary in teacher education, especially in B.Ed. courses. All CNAA courses, for example, are required to address the following general educational aims:

> the development of students' intellectual and imaginative powers; their understanding and judgment; their problem solving skills; their ability to communicate; their ability to see relationships within what they have learned and to perceive their field of study in a broader perspective. Each student's programme of study must stimulate an enquiring, analytical and creative approach, encouraging independent judgment and critical self-awareness.
> (CNAA, 1990, Section 4.3.3)

However, such elements of education are notoriously elusive in practice and some argue that, in a competence-based approach to education, they can be addressed more explicitly (Jessup, 1991). The notion of transferable skills is now seen as significant in relation to a wide range of degrees that are not, on the face of it, vocational (see UDACE, 1991) and it is particularly significant in the context of credit accumulation and transfer and the assessment of prior learning. These concerns are part of a wider concern to relate life and work-based learning to award-bearing higher education courses, and vice versa.

Those considering adopting a competence-based approach will therefore need to address the extent to which it is possible to adapt B.Ed., PGCE, Cert.Ed. (FE) and INSET courses to a method which appears to judge the value of a learning experience largely in terms of the ability to demonstrate competence. Whether broader aims can be accommodated within a competence-based approach may well depend on how broad a definition of competence is employed. A narrow definition based on observable workplace skills is certainly in some tension with the rationale of a liberal education and even with the notion of the reflective professional. On the other hand, a broader definition can make it difficult to define criteria of competence in any meaningful way. The possible limitations of a competence-based approach need not, however, lead to its out of hand dismissal or to the assumption that there is no place for competences in a broader view of teacher education. A parallel from which some lessons might usefully be learnt is the development of the Certificate in Management Education award which incorporates the competences identified as a result of the Management Charter Initiative (CNAA and BTEC, 1990).

The use of competences in course design

A few teams have designed courses on criteria other than competences but then tried to define exit competences for use in student profiles. A distinctively competence-based approach to teacher education implies that competences play a more significant role in the planning and implementation of courses. All course design should be informed by the characteristics of the learners who are to benefit from the course. In a competence-based course, it might be expected that those learner characteristics which provide a basis for entry to the course will be identified in greater detail, thus facilitating a common understanding of the skills, knowledge and attitudes which potential students should bring to the course, and affording a foundation upon which the programme of study will build.

The philosophy underlying extreme competence-based approaches implies that if a student can demonstrate a competence he or she can gain credit for it without necessarily having followed a course at all. Such a strategy places the entire burden of assuring the attainment of the required standards on the assessment process. It has also been suggested that students might be permitted to leave a course of initial teacher education and enter teaching once they have reached a certain threshold of competence (Hargreaves, 1989) [*Editors' Note:* This approach underpins the flexible PGCE Initial Teacher Training routes introduced in 1999]. There are, however, legitimate concerns about the extent to which this approach can undermine the experience of a coherent programme of study, often seen as a necessary part of teacher education. Whether or not the extreme approach is adopted, there is considerable scope for using competences as a basis for the accreditation of prior learning – including experiential learning – and thus giving access to courses with advanced standing. Judgement about prior learning, even expressed in competence terms, may though prove difficult to agree upon. Competences have, however, been seen as providing a particularly useful basis for designing bridging courses into the Cert.Ed. (FE) and shortened B.Ed. courses.

The extent to which a competence-based approach will inform mainstream course design will vary. Some course teams have used the approach only for part of their courses and it is perhaps not surprising that the most extensive use of competences has been in relation to school experience and to the work-based elements in FE courses. Indeed, some tutors believe that, in principle, the approach should be limited to this area, particularly where a narrow definition of competences is being used. Other course teams, usually working with a broader definition, have tried to adopt a competence-based approach to a whole course.

The specific competences used in course design can be derived from a variety of sources. The various task analyses of teaching or attempts to specify the attributes of the teacher as professional might be one starting point. Some competences may be specified by external agencies. In other cases, they might be determined by the staff designing the courses, probably in consultation with teachers and LEA advisers. There is also considerable scope for students to negotiate the competences which they wish the course to help them develop and this is likely to be a central feature of INSET provision which adopts this approach.

Teaching, learning and assessment

It may be argued that a competence-based approach has no epistemological basis: it is concerned with what can be done (and perhaps what has been understood), rather than with *how* skills are developed and knowledge acquired. This creates tensions for higher education courses which are concerned with fostering learning through course curricula and learning processes as well as with the assessment of achievement. Nevertheless, Jessup (1991, p.138) argues that the whole point of specifying outcomes is to promote learning. If competence-based approaches encourage teacher educators to be more explicit about the characteristics of skilled professionalism that they seek to encourage, this is likely to have implications for teaching and learning. In some cases, it will lead to whole-course policies on teaching and learning. In theory, courses designed with an emphasis on exit competences might be expected to be non-prescriptive about the methods used to encourage their attainment. Indeed, they should provide considerable scope for the negotiation of teaching and learning methods. In practice, teaching methods are likely to be influenced by the particular definition of competences adopted and by the actual competences being encouraged. The competences required of the reflective teacher are likely to require rather different methods of teaching and learning from those of the instructor.

The early association of competence-based approaches with vocational training, especially in some of the narrowly behavioural approaches adopted in the USA, has nevertheless led to a view among teacher educators that competence-based education implies an instructional form of pedagogy. A narrowly skills-based definition of competence has, as in earlier courses based upon behavioural objectives, sometimes led to teaching that stresses performance at the expense of understanding. Narrow competence-based approaches to education and training have also relied particularly heavily on the assessment of observable workplace skills. Again they are associated in the minds of many teacher educators with the behaviourist and technicist approaches of their American pioneers, such as one scheme in which 121 separate teacher behaviours had to be checked off by an independent observer and fed into a computer to produce a competence level (see Gitlin and Smyth, 1989).

The early work of NCVQ was sometimes criticised for similar excesses, but it is now widely accepted that such an approach is inappropriate in the assessment of higher level professional skills. NCVQ now acknowledges that for levels four and above, it may be necessary to assess underpinning knowledge and understanding separately from performance. One of the last acts of the Training Agency was to mount a research project to look at the assessment of underpinning knowledge and understanding, because it was recognised that, while knowledge was essential to performance, it could not always be inferred from direct observation in the workplace. It is therefore likely that, in a field such as teacher education, a range of assessment methods will be employed, even in a course based entirely around the achievement of workplace competences. In this context, some useful lessons might be learned from the field of management education, where some guidelines for the assessment of management competences have been identified (CNAA and

BTEC, 1990). Those guidelines suggest that the following principles should govern assessment. It should:

- meet national standards, be based upon criterion-referenced processes and explicit criteria;
- employ a wide and appropriate array of methods;
- include work-based assessment of candidates' performance;
- involve collaboration between candidates, course providers, employers and assessors: there should be a clear delineation of the various participants' roles and of the weighting of their contribution to the assessment;
- be independent of the pathway to assessment, although assessment may contribute to learning;
- be available to individual candidates as well as to a cohort of students.

Knowledge and understanding should be explicitly related to past and current work-based performance and indicative of future performance. If it were possible to arrive at some form of consensus about the levels of competence for beginning teachers, it might be possible to ensure similar standards of entry to teaching despite the diversity of routes into the profession.

Definitions of competence that go beyond skills to include knowledge, values and attitudes raise particular problems for assessment. Some lists of professional competence include personal attributes which demand considerable sensitivity in assessment. On the other hand, many competence-based approaches make extensive use of self-assessment. Indeed, the competences of the reflective practitioner can be expected to include the capacity for self-assessment and the exclusive use of observer checklists on a course designed to develop this mode of professionalism would seem to be a contradiction in terms.

The assessment of competences obviously raises issues of validity and reliability, though arguably these only seem greater than in other types of courses because they sometimes take different forms. Nevertheless, Jessup's view that reliability diminishes in importance in competence-based approaches (Jessup, 1991, pp.191–3) is surely contentious, while ensuring validity is itself by no means straightforward in the assessment of sophisticated professional competences. Whatever approaches are adopted, we need to acknowledge that assessment of the attainment of competences requires inferences to be made on the basis of a range of evidence: the less specific the criteria enunciated, the higher the level of inference will be, and the more informed judgement will be called for. One strategy for attempting to ensure that the competences being assessed are not based on too narrow an experiential context is to specify range indicators which describe the context within which a performance should take place; for example, a student-teacher may be required to demonstrate practical ability in more than one type of school.

The competences specified in some courses are the minimum or threshold competences necessary to perform particular teaching activities and, in others, those characteristic of the 'good teacher'. More generally, there are differing views about whether a competence is something that is either a specific achievement or, alternatively, a dimension of performance in terms of which one can perform at different levels. In the former case, one might expect distinct lists of competences for ITT and INSET courses, while the latter approach implies a similar (or overlapping) list of competences with different levels of attainment. Specialist courses may, of course, use a restricted range of competences or introduce additional ones. Courses in education management, for example, draw upon generic management competences. In any case, the criteria and/or indicators to be used in determining whether a particular achievement or level of achievement has been attained need to be specified as clearly as possible. Furthermore, it is necessary to decide how the assessment of individual competences relates to the criteria used in making the overall award. In hybrid courses the relationship of the assessment of competences to any other forms of assessment employed on a course also needs to be clarified.

Competence-based approaches lend themselves to clear reporting of assessments for both students and potential employers. They are therefore highly compatible with current trends towards the use of profiles in teacher education courses. Like other approaches to profiling, their use can be formative and/or summative and they raise similar issues about ownership to the profile of achievement. This could become particularly significant in the context of teacher appraisal.

Implications for institutions

In so far as the adoption of a competence-based approach to teacher education brings about significant changes to the nature of courses, it will make new demands on staff and on the quality assurance processes of institutions. Institutions that choose to employ a competence-based approach will need to examine the implications of that approach for course design, assessment, course structures, admissions and innovation and the management of change. A further consideration will be the resource and staff demands; these become increasingly acute if a competence-based approach is associated with a student-centred learning approach, negotiated programmes and learning contracts. If the assessment is to involve a large number of competences, that will have implications for academic and support staff resources. Assessment of prior learning is particularly demanding in terms of staff time.

Conclusions

Competence-based approaches to education are often considered problematic because of the central focus of competence upon outcomes rather than upon course content and the learning process. However, such approaches may have a number of benefits:

- demystification of teacher education;
- a clearer role for schools/colleges in the training process;
- greater confidence of employers in what beginning teachers can do;
- clearer goals for students.

The difficulties of the approach have also been rehearsed:

- it may lead to reductionism;
- it may shift the emphasis towards outcomes at the expense of learning processes;
- it may be difficult to reach agreement on a definition of competence;
- it may be difficult to specify which competences should be included;
- it may be difficult to arrive at valid and reliable criteria for assessment.

Given the growing official interest in competence-based approaches, teacher educators can expect to come under increasing pressure to explore the extent to which the use of competences can enhance the quality of teacher education. Nevertheless the advantages of using a competence-based approach remain to be proven, and it seems unlikely to be the panacea that its staunchest advocates often imply.

[. . .]

References

Council for National Academic Awards (CNAA) and Business and Technician Education Council (BTEC) (1990) *The Assessment of Management Competence: Guidelines*. London: CNAA/BTEC.

Eraut, M. (1989) 'Initial teacher training and the NVQ model', in Burke, J. W. (ed.) *Competency-based Education and Training*. Lewes: Falmer Press.

Gitlin, A. and Smyth, J. (1989) *Teacher Evaluation: educative alternatives*. Lewes: Falmer Press.

Hargreaves, D. (1989) 'PGCE assessment fails the test', *Times Educational Supplement*, 3 November.

Hextall, I. *et al.* (1991) *Imaginative Projects: arguments for the new teacher education*. London: Goldsmith's College.

Jessup, G. (1991) *Outcomes: NVQs and the emerging model of education and training*. Lewes: Falmer Press.

National Curriculum Council (NCC) (1991) *The National Curriculum and the Initial Training of Student, Articled and Licensed Teachers*. York: NCC.

National Council for Vocational Qualifications (NCVQ) (1989) *National Vocational Qualifications: criteria and procedures*. London: NCVQ.

Spady, W. G. (1977) 'Competency-based education: a bandwagon in search of a definition', *Educational Researcher* **6**, 9–14.

Tuxworth, E. N. (1982) *Competency in Teaching: a review of competency and performance-based staff development*. London: FEU Research Development Units.

Unit for the Development of Adult Continuing Education (UDACE) (1991) *What Can Graduates Do? A Consultative Paper*. Leicester: National Institute of Adult Continuing Education.

Chapter 7

National standards for teachers: twenty-first century possibilities for professional development

Ann Shelton Mayes

Editors' Note: After a decade of national standards for teachers and, following government pronouncements on the importance of professional development, Ann Shelton Mayes explores whether existing national standards provide a supportive framework for a continuum of professional development, from initial, through induction to threshold levels.

A revolution in the way teachers are assessed has taken place in England in the last decade. Ten years ago, there were no public, externally set, standards to define, measure and monitor teacher performance. Now, national standards, set by government, have proliferated to cover key stages and roles within the teaching profession. In this chapter, I will explore the link between national standards, teacher performance and teacher professional development and consider whether, after a decade of national standards, there is the potential for a supportive framework to encompass career-long teacher development. The chapter focuses on the position in England but, given the widespread development of standards throughout the UK and in other countries, most of the general argument developed in this chapter will apply to other contexts.

The first explicit statements of teacher performance, called teacher competences, were introduced in England, in 1992, as assessment require-ments for entry to teaching (DFE, 1992). In less than a decade, national standards were in place for newly qualified teachers, subject leaders, special educational needs coordinators and head teachers (TTA 1998a, b, c, d). Though identified as a significant government initiative for professional development (Blandford, 2000), these standards have essentially served a 'gatekeeping' function at key points in a teacher's career, primarily to quality control teacher progression, at entry to teaching, end-of-induction and to cross the threshold to higher pay scales. Moreover, in the same period, the extent and detail of national standards has rocketed. The first set of teaching standards (DFE, 1992) identified 27 competence statements, defining the expected standards of teaching performance for newly qualified teachers (NQTs). By 1998, the number of standards regulating entry to teaching for primary teachers had grown to 851 (DfEE, 1998a).

The proliferation of standards, within such a short space of time, raises a number of important questions. Why were national teaching standards introduced? What purpose do they serve? What is the link between national standards and teacher professional development?

The introduction of national teaching standards is directly linked to government concern about the quality of schools and, hence, the quality of teaching and teachers. The assessment of performance of pupils, schools and teachers has been viewed by government as a key tool in raising standards in education (DfEE, 1998b). Indeed, establishing standards in order to 'set targets for improvement, measure progress towards those targets and monitor and compare performance between individuals, groups and schools' is one of the key principles of the National Curriculum (QCA, 1999 p.12). The introduction of national standards for teachers, therefore, mirrors the setting of outcome standards for pupil achievement in the National Curriculum, and standards for schools monitored through OFSTED inspection.

Against this background, national standards for teachers can be viewed as the logical outcome of succeeding governments' agenda to raise the quality of the education system. A national system of teaching standards is an important tool in achieving this aim as it provides the means by which teacher quality can be monitored and controlled. Basically, the standards are constructed to permit summative assessment by setting explicit standards of performance that are required at specific points in a teaching career. Only teachers who demonstrate the standards can progress. Such a system matches well with the principles of accountability identified by government as one of the key features of a twenty-first century teaching profession (DfEE, 2001a). It also provides important information to parents and employers about expectations of the quality of teaching, the latter being identified as an important benefit of using standards-based assessment for teachers (see Chapter 6).

Government is not only interested in issues of accountability and monitoring. It also has a stated aim in developing a teaching profession committed to professional development and providing teachers with greatly increased opportunities for relevant, focused and effective professional development (DfEE, 2001a). An important question to pose, therefore, is what kind of national standards provide a supportive framework for professional development? And do the national standards operating in England at the start of the twenty-first century provide such a framework?

It is worth, at this point, reviewing some of the background to the national standards. Prior to the introduction of the first teacher standards in England, a great deal of debate had focused on the pros and cons of using competence-based teacher assessment systems. Teacher competences for assessment of performance had been pioneered in the USA in the 1970s, and critics pointed to the dangers of similarly constructed competences promoting a narrow technicist model of teacher as instructor (Hyland, 1995). Whitty and Willmott's (see Chapter 6) analysis identified a number of benefits and difficulties that such competence-based systems might have for course design, pedagogy and assessment, which are particularly pertinent to the issue of continuing professional development. Others identified the potential for including professional values (Moon and Shelton Mayes, 1995) and reflection-on-practice (Hextall *et al.*, 1991) as elements of competence-based teacher assessment models. Though the term competences, in England at least, has been replaced by standards, the analysis remains the same. Ultimately the balance between the potential benefits and disadvantages of using standards-based approaches for teacher education and assessment appears to come down to a single critical issue: *what model of teaching do the standards represent?* If the design of teacher education courses and systematic training is directly linked to the standards (see Chapter 6) then it is important that the standards relate to a full and rounded picture of the twenty-first century teacher. For example, scant attention is likely to be paid to training teachers in effective techniques for enquiry into their own practice if this aspect of the teacher's role is not explicitly captured in the language of the standards.

If the national standards are to provide the basis for effective teacher professional development programmes, we need to ask these questions:

- Are the standards constructed broadly in order to capture the complexity of teaching, incorporating knowledge, understanding and professional values as well as teaching skills?
- Do the different sets of national standards, operating at different points in a teacher's career, relate to each other, providing a coherent model of teaching and a framework for professional progression?
- Can the standards be used for formative assessment, as well as summative assessment, to identify an individual's current strengths and support the teacher in planning targets for development to meet the next level of standards?

The issue of broad versus narrow constructions has been well rehearsed elsewhere (see Chapter 6; Furlong, 1995). Fortunately, none of the sets of national standards operating in England has focused exclusively on the technical skills of teaching and all incorporate extensive elements of knowledge and understanding. The extremes of a behaviourist, mechanistic model of teaching have, therefore, been avoided. However, a review of the three key sets of national standards – those linked to initial teacher training, through induction and onto the threshold level of performance – reveals a significant weakness in their usefulness for supporting progression through a teacher's career. The difficulty is that different models of teaching appear to underpin the standards and so no coherent, progressive framework of professional development can easily be built from one set of standards to the next.

An analysis of the generic standards linked to initial teacher training (secondary) (DfEE, 1998a) show only seven per cent (five out of 69) relate to professional values. In contrast 37.5 per cent (three out of eight) threshold standards (DfEE, 2000a) have a professional values dimension. Moreover, the way the ITT and threshold standards have been developed is based on quite different processes. The standards for NQTs were not developed from a systematic analysis of teaching as an occupation, but derive from previous DfEE and HMI reports, advice and directives on initial teacher education (Furlong, 1995). In contrast, the threshold standards are linked directly to research carried out by Hay McBer on effective teachers (DfEE, 2000b, 2000c) which identifies 16 professional characteristics underpinning effective teaching. Put simply, the model of teaching promoted by the NQT and induction standards is quite different from that of the threshold standards. The former emphasises technical capability with minimum regard for the development of critical analysis or professional values, and is caricatured by Ted Wragg as 'preparing people brilliantly for a life of tick-boxing' (Wragg, 2001). The latter emphasises how professional characteristics, such as professionalism, thinking, and relating to others, make the key difference in teacher performance, moving it beyond adequate to effective and outstanding teaching. It is, of course, important to prioritise different dimensions of teaching for training and development at different points in a teacher's career, and therefore, a focus on teaching skills is perfectly appropriate for the novice stage (see Chapter 3). However, the mismatch between the conceptions of teaching underpinning the two sets of standards reduces the potential for developing a coherent system of professional development spanning initial, induction and continuing professional development. This is a lost opportunity to ensure that teacher training from the outset includes the key professional dimensions that underpin effective teaching and ensures all NQTs have an awareness of longer-term professional development goals. Standards for initial teacher training that incorporated a stronger 'professional characteristics' dimension would drive initial training in that direction, and, critically, introduce teachers to professional development methods that they can use subsequently, in induction and early professional development, to work towards the threshold standards.

It is interesting to note that elsewhere in the UK such a system of national standards designed to support progression from initial teacher training, through induction into early professional development already operates. In Northern Ireland, the approach has, from the outset, been characterised by the need to include professional characteristics as well as professional competences, and moreover, to prioritise phased development of competences at different stages in a teacher's career (DENI, 1993).

Although this is not yet the system in England, there is much to be optimistic about. First, it is important to remember that national standards only set out the minimum requirements. Many HEI providers of initial teacher training have developed curriculum and assessment models that go beyond the standards required for QTS. The 'reflective practitioner' model of teaching underpins most ITT courses and many have an explicit focus on professionalism. The Open University's PGCE, for example, emphasised the importance of professional values by incorporating additional standards into the assessment model (Moon and Shelton Mayes, 1995), and the use of developmental portfolios as preparation for career-long continuing professional development. Teachers trained in this way have a head start in beginning the process of improving their practice to meet the threshold standards. Individual teachers, too, have sought to go beyond minimum external standards. The popularity of the Masters in Education degree for serving teachers is evidence of this.

Second, the government has made clear its commitment to the development of 'reflective practitioners'. It has directed the Teacher Training Agency to slim down the standards relating to initial teacher training and strengthen those aspects relating to 'trainees' understanding of responsibility for professional development and the importance of CPD' (DfEE, 2001a). Its CPD website, launched in March 2001, gives information on a new standards framework which 'will set out the standards of practice that teachers should expect to demonstrate at particular points of their career. It will suggest ways of supporting professional development activity. The framework will also support career planning and performance management, and will help to target Continuing Professional Development to the individual teacher's needs and aspirations' (DfEE, 2001b). There is much here to suggest that we are moving slowly towards a more coherent framework of national standards that can support planned professional development and progression.

Third, and most important, is the government's acceptance of the Hay McBer model of effective teaching, which has been incorporated into the threshold standards. This model has reinforced the importance of developing professional characteristics in teacher training and education programmes, providing a clear rationale for their inclusion.

The model also makes clear the importance of using standards for formative as well as summative assessment. The Hay McBer Report states that:

> the detailed framework is intended to support teachers by painting a picture of what all the characteristics look like in action, at progressively higher

levels of display. It can inform teachers' continuous professional development and performance management. Teachers would be able to confirm their strengths as a professional, and to pinpoint areas for further development, to improve their performance and to equip them to progress up through the profession.

(DfEE, 2000b, p.2)

The report models the unpacking of professional characteristics to provide a range of levels which teachers can use as a guide to identify their strengths and weaknesses and plan their personal professional development towards new targets. This model of unpacking standards for formative assessment will be particularly useful for planning the early professional development for individual teachers.

Using the threshold standards to provide scaffolding for teacher learning will have a bold impact on the professional development of individual teachers in the early years of their career, who are aiming to 'cross the threshold'. Making the leap to integrate the standards for initial teacher training, induction and threshold into a genuinely, coherent continuum would ensure that teachers coming into the profession have the necessary skills, understanding and commitment to take their professional development forward fast. Such a framework could transform professional development in the twenty-first century.

References

Blandford, S. (2000) *Managing Professional Development in Schools.* London: Routledge.

Department of Educational for Northern Ireland (DENI) (1993) *Review of Initial Teacher Training (ITT) in Northern Ireland: Report of the Working Group on Competences (Working Group I).* Bangor: DENI.

Department For Education (DFE) (1992) *Initial Teacher Training (Secondary Phase).* Circulars 9/92, 35/92. London: DFE.

Department for Education and Employment (DfEE) (1998a) *Teaching: High Status, High Standards. Requirements for Courses of Initial Teacher Training.* Circular 4/98. London: DfEE.

Department for Education and Employment (DfEE) (1998b) *Teachers: Meeting the Challenge of Change.* London: The Stationery Office.

Department for Education and Employment (DfEE) (2000a) Threshold Standards http://www.dfee.gov.uk/teachingreforms accessed 30 April 2001.

Department for Education and Employment (DfEE) (2000b) *Raising Achievement in Our Schools: Model of Effective Teaching.* An interim report from Hay McBer on the research findings. Version 9.1. HayGroup.

Department for Education and Employment (DfEE) (2000c) *A Model of Teacher Effectiveness*. Report by Hay McBer to the DfEE, June 2000.

Department for Education and Employment (DfEE) (2001a) *Learning and Teaching: A Strategy for professional development*. Circular 71/2001. London: DfEE.

Department for Education and Employment (DfEE) (2001b) *Standards framework* DfEE CPD website. http://www.dfee.gov.uk/teachers/cpd/ accessed 30 April 2001.

Furlong, J. (1995) 'The limits of competence: a cautionary note on Circular 9/92', in Kerry, T. and Shelton Mayes, A. (eds) *Issues in Mentoring*, Chapter 20. London: Routledge.

Hextall, I., Lawn, M., Menter, I., Sigwick, S. and Walker, S. (1991) *Imaginative projects: Arguments for a New Teacher Education*. London: Goldsmith's College.

Hyland, T. (1995) 'Expertise and competence in further and adult education', in Kerry, T. and Shelton Mayes, A. (eds) *Issues in Mentoring*. London: Routledge.

Moon, B. and Shelton Mayes, A. (1995) 'Integrating values into the assessment of teachers in initial education and training', in Kerry, T. and Shelton Mayes, A. (eds) *Issues in Mentoring*. London: Routledge.

Qualifications and Curriculum Authority (QCA) (1999) *The National Curriculum: Handbook for secondary teachers in England*. London: QCA.

Teacher Training Agency (TTA) (1998a) *National Standards for Qualified Teacher Status*. London: TTA.

Teacher Training Agency (TTA) (1998b) *National Standards for Subject Leaders*. London: TTA.

Teacher Training Agency (TTA) (1998c) *National Standards for Special Educational Needs Co-ordinators*. London: TTA.

Teacher Training Agency (TTA) (1998d) *National Standards for Headteachers*. London: TTA.

Wragg, T. (2001) 'Welcome to the Dalek Factory', *Times Educational Supplement*, 23 February.

Chapter 8

What makes change work for teachers

Michael G. Fullan

Editors' Note: In this seminal work, Michael Fullan explores many facets of educational change. He argues that opportunities for teacher interaction and collaboration, both within and outside schools, can support the type of educational change that brings benefits for both pupils and teachers.

Change is necessary because high proportions of students are alienated, performing poorly or below par or dropping out. Change is needed because many teachers are frustrated, bored, and burnt out. Good change processes that foster sustained professional development over one's career and lead to student benefits may be one of the few sources of revitalisation and satisfaction left for teachers. And as Sarason (1971, pp.166–7) observes, 'if teaching becomes neither terribly interesting nor exciting to many teachers can one expect them to make learning interesting and exciting to students?'

What can be done to increase the teacher's and the school's capacity for managing change and bringing about improvements on a continuous basis?

[. . .]

Teacher isolation and its opposite – collegiality – provide the best starting point for considering what works for the teacher. I shall first examine the positive side of teacher collaboration for that is where the power for change lies. As with most solutions, we must also identify the 'dark side' and potential misuses of this powerful research finding.

This book suggests that at the teacher level, the degree of change is strongly related to the extent to which teachers *interact* with each other and others providing technical help. Within the school, collegiality among teachers, as measured by the frequency of communication, mutual support, help, etc., is a strong indicator of implementation success. Virtually every research study on the topic has found this to be the case. Significant educational change consists of changes in beliefs, teaching style, and materials, which can come about *only* through a process of personal development in a social context. As Werner (1980) observes in explaining the failure of social studies curriculum in Alberta,

> Ideally, implementation as a minimum includes shared understanding among participants concerning the implied presuppositions, values and assumptions which underlie a program, for if participants understand these, then they have a basis for rejecting, accepting or modifying a program in terms of their own school, community and class situations. To state the aim another way, implementation is an ongoing construction of a shared reality among group members through their interaction with one another within the program.
> (pp.62–3)

There is no getting around the *primacy of personal contact*. Teachers need to participate in skill-training workshops, but they also need to have one-to-one and group opportunities to receive and give help and more simply to *converse* about the meaning of change. Under these conditions teachers learn how to use an innovation as well as to judge its desirability on more information-based grounds; they are in a better position to know whether they should accept, modify, or reject the change. Sometimes teachers cannot answer this question until they have had a chance to try out the new programme and to discuss it.

It is essential to recognise that I am not referring only to innovations developed externally to the school. Innovations decided on or developed by teachers within a school also require teacher–teacher interaction, if they are to go anywhere. Whether innovations are external or internal, the more teachers can interact concerning their own practices, the more they will be able to bring about improvements that they themselves identify as necessary. Even wanted changes have costs and create ambivalence. Social support is necessary for reducing costs and resolving the ambivalence in terms of how much change is needed and what can feasibly be accomplished. Thus, whether the source of change is external or internal to the school (and either may be good or bad, feasible or infeasible), it is teachers as interacting professionals who should be in a position to decide *finally* whether the change is for them.

[. . .]

Up to this point, we have been discussing the relationship between single innovations and teachers. When we shift our perspective to managing multiple innovations, we immediately confront the culture of the school. The school is the centre of change because the norms, values, and structure of the school as an organisation make a huge cumulative difference for individual teachers. Rosenholtz (1989) provides a thorough description of the collaborative work culture of the 13 'moving' or 'learning-enriched' work environments in her study. Figure 8.1 contains an adapted summary of the main school-based elements associated with the successful schools in Rosenholtz' research. There are other factors influencing the six themes depicted in Figure 8.1 and the interactions among the themes are multifaceted, but the composite picture of how successful collaborative schools work is clear and convincing.

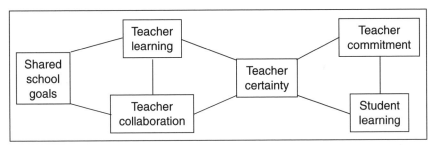

Figure 8.1 Learning enriched schools

As Rosenholtz observes, teacher uncertainty (or low sense of efficacy) and threats to self-esteem are recurring themes in teaching (Ashton and Webb, 1986). In learning-enriched compared with learning-impoverished schools, Rosenholtz found that teachers and principals collaborated in goal-setting activities (or vision-building) that 'accentuated those instructional objectives toward which teachers should aim their improvement efforts' (p.6), and that shared goals served to focus efforts and mobilise resources in agreed upon directions. Principals and teacher-leaders actively fostered collegial involvement: 'Collective commitment to student learning in collaborative settings directs the definition of leadership toward those colleagues who instruct as well as inspire, awakening all sorts of teaching possibilities in others' (p.68). In effective schools, collaboration is linked with norms and opportunities for continuous improvement and career-long learning: 'It is assumed that improvement in teaching is a collective rather than individual enterprise, and that analysis, evaluation, and experimentation in concert with colleagues are conditions under which teachers improve' (p.73). As a result teachers are more likely to trust, value, and legitimise sharing expertise, seeking advice, and giving help both inside and outside the school. They are more likely to become better and better teachers on the job: 'All of this means that it is far easier to learn to teach, and to learn to teach better, in some schools than in others' (p.104).

Becoming better teachers means greater confidence and certainty in deciding on instructional issues and in handling problems. Rosenholtz found that

Where teachers request from and offer technical assistance to each other, and where school staff enforces consistent standards for student behavior, teachers tend to complain less about students and parents. Further, where teachers collaborate, where they keep parents involved and informed about their children's progress, where teachers and principal work together to consistently enforce standards for student behavior, and where teachers celebrate their achievements through positive feedback from students, parents, principal, colleagues, and their own sense, they collectively tend to believe in a technical culture and their instructional practice.

(p.137)

Teacher certainty and teacher commitment feed on each other, as Rosenholtz found, increasing teachers' motivation to do even better. All of these factors served to channel energy towards student achievement. . . .

I must caution the reader that the story up to this point is a little too smooth. Other factors feed into the equation. . . . Moreover, the relationships among Rosenholtz' themes are not linear and hide an array of subvariables at work, which must be understood to avoid drawing superficial lessons from Rosenholtz' research. And the relationship between collaboration and autonomy is not unproblematic. Nonetheless, the gist of Rosenholtz' main findings is backed up by a lot of other research. Most of Mortimore and associates' (1988) 12 key factors are related to Rosenholtz' themes – including the involvement of teachers, consistency among teachers, intellectually challenging teaching, work-centred environment, purposeful leadership, positive climate, and so on. Teacher and student commitment is heavily influenced by these school characteristics. Similar themes are found in studies of secondary school improvement (Firestone and Rosenblum, 1988; Louis and Miles, 1990; Wilson and Corcoran, 1988) as well as in all other major studies of collaboration at the school level (Goodlad, 1984; Little, 1982). As Nias (1989) concludes from her study of school cultures in England,

[Teachers] are happiest in a social environment characterised by mutual dependence in which 'sharing' is the norm and individuals do not feel ashamed to admit to failure or a sense of inadequacy . . . relationships between staff who can and do help each other, provide one another with oases of calm in a long and frenetic day, set one another high but attainable standards for professional performance and provide a mutually supportive social environment, are characterised by: personal accessibility; plenty of opportunity for discussion; laughter; praise and recognition.

(pp.152–3)

Before deriving implications for teachers, we must be careful not to assume that increasing interaction among teachers is automatically a good thing. Little (1990) warns that there are many superficial examples of collaboration.

She suggests that several forms of collegiality involving assistance, sharing, storytelling, etc., represent 'weak ties' and are likely to be inconsequential and have little impact on the culture of the school. 'Joint work' involves deeper forms of interaction, such as joint planning, observation, and experimentation, and is dependent on 'the structural organization of task, time, and other resources in ways not characteristic of other forms of collegiality' (pp.14–15).

Little does not assume that joint work is automatically more appropriate:

> The content of teachers' values and beliefs cannot be taken for granted in the study or pursuit of teachers' collegial norms of interaction and interpretation. Under some circumstances, greater contact among teachers can be expected to advance the prospects for students' success; in others, to promote increased teacher-to-teacher contact may be to intensify norms unfavorable to children.
> (1990, p. 524)

And,

> Bluntly put, do we have in teachers' collaborative work the creative development of well informed choices, or the mutual reinforcement of poorly informed habit? Does teachers' time together advance the understanding and imagination they bring to their work, or do teachers merely confirm one another in present practice? What subject philosophy and subject pedagogy do teachers reflect as they work together, how explicit and accessible is their knowledge to one another? Are there collaborations that in fact erode teachers' moral commitments and intellectual merit?
> (p.525)

Hargreaves (1991) goes further. He distinguishes between 'contrived collegiality' and 'collaborative cultures'. Contrived collegiality

> is characterized by a set of formal, specific bureaucratic procedures. . . . It can be seen in initiatives such as peer coaching, mentor teaching, joint planning in specially provided rooms, formally scheduled meetings and clear job descriptions and training programs for those in consultative roles.
> (p.19)

Contrived collegiality can lead to the proliferation of unwanted contacts among teachers, which consume already scarce time. True collaborative cultures, according to Hargreaves, are 'deep, personal and enduring'. They are not 'mounted just for specific projects or events. They are not strings of one-shot deals. Cultures of collaboration are constitutive of, absolutely central to, teachers' daily work' (p.14).

In the same vein, Huberman (1990) observes:

> Collegiality is not a fully legitimate end in itself, unless it can be shown to affect directly or indirectly, the nature or degree of pupil development . . . by the same token, intensive collaboration – planning, exchanging materials, regulating pupil performance – does not automatically translate into observable changes in classroom practice and may, if pushed too hard, actually eat into time for ongoing instructional work in the class.
> (p.2)

Further, we cannot assume that autonomy is bad and collaboration is good. One person's isolation is another person's autonomy; one person's collaboration is another person's conspiracy. We must not lose sight of the importance of solitude. Flinders (1988) claims that for many teachers isolation is a strategy for getting work done because 'it protects time and energy required to meet immediate instructional demands' (p.25). . . . None of this is to deny that isolation can be a protection from scrutiny and a barrier to improvement but it does say that we must put the question of autonomy and collaboration in a perspective conducive to assessing the conditions under which each might be appropriate.

This debate has practical implications. Striving for school-wide consensus and conformity among teachers is not where one would start or even end. Consensus seeking may inhibit creativity and may result in the wrong solution. Instead of seeking widespread involvement in the use of a particular innovation, it may be more appropriate, especially in larger schools, to stimulate multiple examples of collaboration among small groups of teachers inside and outside the school. Huberman (1990, 1991) draws such a conclusion from his study of the career cycle of teachers. In its basic form, according to Huberman, we need to increase the number and quality of colleagues or experts to which individual teachers could turn in the course of experimentation in their classrooms. The goal is to expand the network of people working on similar problems. Louis and Miles' (1990) observation that subthemes may eventually coalesce is probably a more apt image than the concept that school-wide goals guide everyone's action. Paradoxically, school-wide efforts to implement single innovations may have less of an impact on the professional culture of schools (and thereby on the basic capacity of schools to improve) than would multiple focused collaborative networks that become 'deep, personal and enduring' in the service of improvement (see Hargreaves, 1989).

[. . .]

References

Ashton, P. and Webb, R. (1986) *Making a difference: Teachers' sense of efficacy and student achievement*. New York: Longman.

Firestone, W. and Rosenblum, S. (1988) *The alienation and commitment of students and teachers in urban high schools*. Washington, DC: Rutgers University and Office of Educational Research and Improvement.

Flinders, D. J. (1988) 'Teacher isolation and the new reform', *Journal of Curriculum and Supervision* **4**(1), 17–29.

Goodlad, J. I. (1984) *A place called school: prospects for the future*. New York: McGraw-Hill.

Hargreaves, A. (1989) *Curriculum and assessment reform*. Milton Keynes: Open University Press.

Huberman, M. (1990) 'The social context of instruction in schools'. Paper presented at the American Educational Research Association annual meeting.

Huberman, M. (1991) 'Teacher development and instructional mastery', in Hargreaves, A. and Fullan, M. (eds) *Understanding teacher development*. London: Cassell.

Little, J. W. (1982) 'Norms of collegiality and experimentation: workplace conditions of school success', *American Educational Research Journal* **19**, 326–40.

Little, J. W. (1990) 'The persistence of privacy: autonomy and initiative in teachers' professional relations', *Teachers' College Record* **91**(4), 509–36.

Louis, K. and Miles, M. B. (1990) *Improving the urban high school: What works and why*. New York: Teachers' College Press.

Mortimore, P. *et al.* (1988) *School matters: The junior years*. Somerset: Open Books.

Nias, J. (1989) *Primary teachers talking, a study of teaching as work*. New York: Routledge.

Rosenholtz, S. (1987) 'Workplace conditions that affect teacher quality and commitment: implications for the design of teacher induction programs', *The Elementary School Journal* **89**(4), 421–40.

Rosenholtz, S. (1989) *Teachers' workplace: The social organisation of schools*. New York: Longman.

Sarason, S. (1971) *The culture of the school and the problem of change*. Boston: Allyn & Bacon.

Werner, W. (1980) 'Implementation: the role of belief'. Unpublished paper, Center for Curriculum Studies, University of British Columbia, Vancouver.

Wilson, B. and Corcoran, T. (1988) *Successful secondary schools: Visions of excellence in American public education*. Philadelphia: Falmer Press.

Chapter 9

Performance review: opportunities for teachers in the early stage of their career

Anne Storey

Editors' Note: This chapter argues that, for teachers in the early stage of their career, performance management should hold few threats. If enacted correctly, it could offer a number of personal and professional development opportunities.

Appraisal – past and present

Appraisal or 'performance review' as it is now termed, is described as 'essential for effective performance management' (DfEE, 1999a: para. 8). This is a reshaped and tangibly different phenomenon from that of its earlier manifestation in the 1980s. Three controversial but quite different models of appraisal have been introduced during the last twenty years. Successive models have been criticised for moving further and further from the original focus on individual professional development; and for appearing to increase in an inexorable way, levels of anxiety, workload and bureaucracy (NASUWT, 2000). But a contrasting view is developed in this chapter. This is that the mandatory and systematic features of the current model of appraisal (DfEE, 2000) could actually work in favour of individual teachers, at an early stage of their career, by providing an entitlement to professional dialogue and the necessary support to achieve individual objectives within a performance management system.

The original pilot schemes, which operated in the 1980s, intended that appraisal should be a process that helped individual teachers with their professional development and career planning (ACAS, 1986). Its use then, during this period, can be characterised as developmental for individuals, full of potential for supporting professional growth but, ultimately, inconsistent in application.

By 1991, appraisal had been introduced into schools by legislation (DES, 1991) and national guidelines for what might be viewed as a second edition of the process were drawn up. Essentially, the regulations established a range of largely unthreatening elements: a system of recognition of teacher achievement and support for the extension of their skills and performance; the identification of potential career development of individual teachers; and the provision of guidance and counselling for teachers not performing well. The most controversial element, however, was the direct link made between appraisal, career promotion and professional discipline. Appraisal information could be used by head teachers in 'advising those responsible for taking decisions on the promotion, dismissal or discipline of school teachers or on the use of any discretion in relation to pay' (DES, 1991, Reg. 14(1)). Nevertheless, this model of appraisal clearly held to the notion of 'one professional holding him/herself accountable to him/herself in the presence of another' (Blandford, 2000, p.145). The focus remained on individual professional development.

Within five years, the TTA/OFSTED (1996) joint review of appraisal processes and outcomes had identified a range of key weaknesses. Among the catalogue of missed opportunities, described in the review, were: a lack of rigour; poor evaluation of impacts of appraisal (and professional development) upon teaching quality and standards; failure to secure the role of the line manager as appraiser; target setting which neglected a focus on improvements in teacher effectiveness; imprecise or unrealistic targets; and the low priority given to the appraisal process in schools. The clear implication (and fact) was that, despite pockets of good practice, the existing system had not worked. It was out of this recognition that a new government in 1997, with a reforming agenda in relation to education, rapidly developed a third variant of appraisal, termed 'performance management' (DfEE, 1999b, 2000).

This multifaceted appraisal and performance management scheme was designed to improve performance by 'attracting, motivating and retaining high-quality teachers' and to have in place a new, 'robust system' for appraising staff 'against clear objectives and outcomes' (DfEE, 1999a, para. 5). The essence of the proposals was that, 'Systematic performance management is key to achievement in organisations. In schools it motivates teachers to give of their best and provides school managers with the tools to deploy and develop their staff most efficiently' (DfEE, 1999a, para 4). What is worthy of comment is that the *private agenda* of appraisal for individual and professional growth, seen in the appraisal systems of the 1980s, is here replaced by a *public agenda* with a focus on management. Furthermore, this public agenda is officially declared in these documents as held in common by all those who have a stake in the quality, consistency and competitiveness of education experienced in Britain – predominantly, pupils, teachers, governors, LEAs, parents and employers.

Much of the brouhaha surrounding the performance management consultation proposals was directed at the proposed pay–performance links (Storey, 2000). There were real and deeply-held fears about a pay–performance equation, apparently targeted to pupil progress (or results) and also about the very concept of a performance–pay link; and to some critics of the proposals this merely represented a retrograde return to the payment-by-results scenario of a century earlier. But the point has been made elsewhere in this Reader (see Chapter 5) that teachers currently in the early stage of their teaching career may have felt much more sanguine than their more experienced colleagues when the performance management proposals were initially introduced. However partial and unhelpful such schemes might have been judged to be, nevertheless a widespread *belief* that they can be made to work (and that successful and committed professionals *should* be paid more than their less competent, less applied peers) is still strongly held in many spheres of work-life. Family members and friends of newer teachers, too, may be well acquainted with the warp and weft of such schemes which are still on the increase – at least in Britain and the USA and, to a much lesser extent, in continental Europe (IPD, 1998; Brown and Armstrong, 1999). Certainly, more recent entrants to teaching who have worked in other spheres will not be unfamiliar with such schemes. Moreover, as was noted above, a direct link between appraisal and promotion had been established in legislation some years earlier (DES, 1991).

Performance review and professional growth

In the context of a performance management system, which for some indicates the 'management' of teachers by the proponents of the scheme taking precedence over a shared openness and trust (NASUWT, 2000, p.8), what can performance review mean for individual teachers in the early phase of their careers? And what is the potential for *personal* professional growth through this process?

The regulations (DfEE, 2000) require that all teachers, on completion of induction, have an annual appraisal, usually carried out by their line manager or team leader. The basic process involves a cycle of objective setting (minimum 3), collecting evidence and review. All the objectives must focus on the teacher's job description and must include objectives linked directly to *pupil progress* and *developing and improving the teacher's professional practice.*

NASUWT guidance (2000) attempts to make the process as straightforward as possible, minimising bureaucracy, the impact on teacher workload and potential anxiety. They advocate a three-stage process.

Stage 1 Planning. At this stage, team leader and teacher meet to identify the three objectives, which must be clear, concise, realistic, achievable and measurable. Once the objectives have been identified, then the resources and support, which will be required to enable them to be met, will be discussed and agreed. A planning record, a confidential item, will then be produced, detailing the objectives, support and timescales. It is judged as helpful to record training and development needs separately as an annex to be passed on to those responsible for providing support.

Stage 2 Monitoring progress. At this point in the process, evidence is collected for the purposes of reviewing performance and the achievement of objectives. Classroom observation is seen as fundamental to this process and teachers should receive written feedback in relation to this. Teachers may be observed for up to three hours each year in order to achieve a balanced range of classes and curriculum taught (and to provide information for all aspects of appraisal within a performance management system). One observation is to be carried out by the team leader, as appraiser, but others may be part of the school's normal monitoring arrangements. Other evidence may be collected *in consultation* with the teacher.

Stage 3 Reviewing performance. At this annual review stage, evidence gathered is reviewed, strengths and achievements recognised and an outcome of the consideration of each objective is recorded on the review statement. New or revised objectives are agreed for the next cycle and development needs recorded.

There is much in this process that is encouraging for a teacher in the first phase of a teaching career.

- Performance appraisal when mandated as an annual cyclic process means that some of the more variable attributes of former schemes are avoided. This is more than an opportunity for professional development, it is an *entitlement* to go through a regular systematic cycle of target setting, action planning, support and review directly linked to personal professional growth.
- There exists an entitlement to have achievements recognised.
- There is in place an entitlement to support that will help teachers meet the set objectives and improve performance.
- It is a familiar practice, mirroring similar systems in initial teacher training and induction where there is an emphasis on reviewing progress against standards with the support of a mentor.
- The statutory requirement to identify objectives directly linked to pupil progress and developing and improving personal practice accords well with priorities for teachers at an early career stage (see Chapter 1).
- It may well lead to a better understanding of the individual's role, since the key elements of their job description, which have been discussed and agreed, are at the heart of the performance review.
- Key features, such as target setting, action planning, evidence collection and analysis, are common to models of practitioner action research and personal professional development (see Chapters 1 and 26). Working through the appraisal process could be helpful for professional development that focuses on a *personal* rather than a school-based agenda. There is also the possibility

of drawing the two processes more closely together and using evidence collected for appraisal to support other personal professional enquiry.

- Support is provided by an experienced teacher colleague. The opportunity to engage in professional dialogue is seen as critical to the development of learning organisations, communities of practice and the professional growth of teachers (Lave and Wenger, 1991; see also Chapters 29 and 10). Working with other teachers who can observe and give feedback, help identify strengths and weaknesses based on evidence, is a significant bonus, especially where they have received training for this role.
- Collecting evidence for review statements, year on year, could form the basis of the evidence required to determine whether a teacher meets the national standards for threshold assessment (NASUWT, 2000).
- Fast tracking, the possibility of an even earlier threshold application (point 5 has already been suggested), and the expanded numbers of Advanced Skills Teachers all require an evidence base and the professional development that might be an outcome of a systematic appraisal process.

Conclusion

Over the past two decades, different agendas have been operating in the context of appraisal – a government agenda for improving teaching and learning, accountability and management, and an individual teacher agenda for professional development for personal goals. From a government perspective, performance review might well be much more meaningful in terms of its capacity for improving classroom teaching and learning than has been the case. For the individual in the early stages of a teaching career, given the priorities expressed formally for professional growth in previous experiences ranging across ITT, induction and perhaps other employment, there may be particular advantages in this form of performance review system.

What lies ahead for the professional in the early years of teaching is, potentially, a supported environment as well as a challenging set of requirements. Elements of peer review in the performance review process (Wragg *et al.*, 1996), earlier leadership positions for recent entrants, better quality and more systematic CPD opportunities (DfEE, 2001) that mesh pupil need, personal professional growth and a national agenda of improved effectiveness and higher standards, will all contribute. So, too, will increased remuneration and a wider definition of what being an 'effective' teacher means (Hay McBer, 2000) in the cut and thrust of daily school life. The impact of all these may enable the review of performance to be a process shaped much more actively by the participating teacher-professional in the years ahead.

References

Advisory, Conciliation and Arbitration Service (ACAS) (1986) *Teachers' Dispute ACAS Independent Panel. Report of the Appraisal Training Working Group*. London: ACAS.

Blandford, S. (2000) *Managing Professional Development in Schools*. London: Routledge.

Brown, D. and Armstrong, M. (1999) *Paying for Contribution*. London: Kogan Page.

Department of Education and Science (DES) (1991) *School Teacher Appraisal*. Circular 12/91. London: DES.

Department for Education and Employment (DfEE) (1999a) *Teachers Meeting the Challenge of Change: Technical Consultation Document on Pay and Performance Management*. London: DfEE Publications.

Department for Education and Employment (DfEE) (1999b) *Performance Management Framework for Teachers: Consultation Document*. London: DfEE Publications.

Department for Education and Employment (DfEE) (2000) *The Education (School Appraisal) (England) Regulations*. London: DfEE.

Department for Education and Employment (DfEE) (2001) *Learning and Teaching: A Strategy for professional development*. Circular 71/2001. London: DfEE.

Hay McBer (2000) *Research into Teacher Effectiveness: Phase II Report A Model of Teacher Effectiveness*. London: Hay McBer.

Institute of Personnel Management (IPD) (1998) *Performance Pay Survey*. London: IPD.

Lave, J. and Wenger, E. (1991) *Situated Learning*. Cambridge: Cambridge University Press.

Office for Standards in Education (OFSTED) (1996) *The Appraisal of Teachers 1991–1996*. London: OFSTED.

National Association of Schoolteachers and Union of Women Teachers (NASUWT) (2000) *Performance Management – a practical guide for teachers and teamleaders*. Birmingham: NASUWT.

Storey, A. (2000) 'A leap of faith? Performance pay for teachers', *Journal of Educational Policy* **15**(5), 509–23.

Teacher Training Agency (TTA)/Office for Standards in Education (OFSTED) (1996) *Review of Headteacher and Teacher Appraisal by the TTA and OFSTED*, Summary Report. London: HMSO.

Wragg, E. *et al.* (1996) *Teacher Appraisal Observed*. London: Routledge.

Chapter 10

Working with others to develop professional practice

Hilary Burgess

Editors' Note: Schools should be learning communities for all: teachers as well as pupils. In this chapter Hilary Burgess focuses on the opportunities, methods and scope for creating such a 'learning school'.

> inexperience is an asset to be exploited. It is of use, however, only in the context of participation, when supported by experienced practitioners who both understand its limitations and value its role.
> (Lave and Wenger, 1991, p.117)

The inexperienced young teacher is the most valuable investment that a school can have in future achievement and success. This chapter will examine how young teachers can develop professionally through working with others in school contexts. It will do this through focusing on the school as a learning community and analysing the features of an effective community of practice. It will also explore the features of effective individual practice and how this can be supported through collaboration with other teachers, processes of appraisal, and mentoring and induction programmes. Professional development will be examined to explore a way forward for schools as learning institutions where the relationships of individuals, working with others or collaborating in groups, plays a central role. However, all these issues need to be located in the existing political context of professional development.

Opportunities and statutory obligations to undertake continuing professional development have been increasingly defined and resourced by central agencies in England since the 1988 Education Reform Act. This has raised many questions about the most appropriate means for professional development to take place, the role of the teachers' voice, the way professional judgement can be developed, and the role of higher education in supporting critical reflection on practice. From the mid-1990s funding was reduced and hence the opportunities for individual professional development have been restricted. Accompanying the reduction in funding was a shift towards the learning of teachers as a professional group and the collective needs of schools.

However, it has become evident in recent years that the lack of focus on individual professional development in schools has meant that many teachers have struggled to meet the challenges of the last decade.

The new strategy for professional development (DfEE, 2001a) brings an increase in resources and the requirement for providers to adhere to a code of practice (DfEE, 2001b). New funding can provide the impetus for innovative forms of professional development linking higher education and schools. However, addressing the needs of individual teachers in schools may require a range of strategies, for as Quicke argues, 'the knowledge base of professionals, the source of their previously much valued expertise, has become less secure' (Quicke, 2000, p.302). This problematic nature of the knowledge base of teachers, he suggests, is also intertwined with a lack of trust in professionals that stems from critique of the traditional knowledge base of teaching and criticisms of how professionals have operated in practice.

The national context, therefore, for developing professional practice in schools is not an easy one and may be fraught with tension and stress as teachers continue to meet the challenge of change. However, school contexts in terms of ethos, organisation and culture also play an important role in the developing practice and professionalism of teachers. Schools that are learning communities for all those who work in them – pupils, teachers, senior management staff, parent helpers and other administrative assistants – may provide the most support for continued professional development.

The learning community

What is a learning community? Blandford (Chapter 2) suggests that a learning community consists of individuals who have opportunities for learning available alongside the work tasks they perform. Such a community recognises the value of learning, which is managed by all the participants – individuals, teachers, helpers, team leaders, and managers. She argues that it is through recognising itself as a learning community that a school becomes a learning organisation, where the right of each member to learn is formally acknowledged. Learning communities are, therefore, reflective about how they manage the professional development of staff.

How can young teachers be inducted into communities of learning? Lave and Wenger (1991) suggest that individuals need to be sponsored if they are to have legitimate access to participate in the activities of a community. Legitimate participation, they argue, comes only diffusely through membership and legitimacy conferred by a sponsor is, therefore, more important for the newcomer. It is the practice of the community that provides the potential 'curriculum' to be learned by the new teacher who initially has only peripheral access to the activities in the school. Lave and Wenger distinguish between 'talking about' practice and 'talking within' practice. Each has a specific function linked to sharing practice through exchanging information about the progress of teaching activities or telling stories and sharing community folklore. In this way, newcomers learn to adopt the language of the community. They state:

> Moving toward full participation in practice involves not just a greater commitment of time, intensified effort, more and broader responsibilities within the community, and more difficult and risky tasks, but, more significantly, an increasing sense of identity as a master practitioner.
> (Lave and Wenger, 1991, p.111)

Learning communities, therefore, provide opportunities to learn how to learn, enabling young teachers to cope with issues as they emerge (Blandford, 2000). The ability to handle new situations and structure personal learning are important skills for teachers who have to identify their own needs for professional development and learn how to achieve objectives set through appraisal. Working to performance thresholds, such as those outlined by Hay McBer, will be more easily achieved where there is a learning community to support young staff. Indeed, some of the essential characteristics of effective teaching, outlined by Hay McBer, are specifically connected to working with others. For example, understanding the reasons for other people's behaviour, being able to work with others to achieve shared goals and the ability and drive to produce positive outcomes by impressing and influencing others (Hay McBer, 2000).

The relationship between professional development and organisational structure is reflected in the culture of a learning community. Such a culture is likely to be characterised by a high degree of collaboration and communication (Hargreaves, 1994). As Quicke argues:

> problems can only be resolved by the generation of shared knowledge constructed through dialogue between all parties in a particular context rather than through the 'top-down' application of a universal, 'objective' professional expertise.
> (Quicke, 2000, p.304)

The existence of a learning community, however, does not imply that there will be no problems or unresolved issues to deal with. New and experienced staff will discover differences and commonalities as they work together. Participating in the activities of teaching and learning they may feel both fulfilled and overwhelmed as they work to find strategies that will lead to an effective community of practice. What, though, might be the features of such a community?

Features of an effective community of practice

The concept of a community of practice is based on a view of learning as a social process that involves the whole person. In a community of practice, learners at first participate in activities in a very peripheral way. Gradually, as knowledge and experience deepens, there is increased involvement in the community of practice and greater understanding of the complexities of the work (Lave and Wenger, 1991).

Exploring what learning communities do will illustrate how they might operate and the ways teachers can work together effectively in supportive relationships. A list of what this might consist of has been devised by Holly (1994) who suggests that learning communities:

- look to the future by looking at their present;
- institutionalise reflection-in-action;
- treat planning and evaluation as learning;
- pace their learning and their development;
- attend to the new 'disciplines';
- learn from themselves;
- are lifelong learners.
    (From Holly, 1994, pp.132–6)

The implication for schools of such a list of characteristics is that an effective community of practice will be doing all of the above to a high standard. The criteria can provide schools with the overall aims for a learning community, but do not, necessarily, help teachers who are setting out to develop these features in their practice. However, it can be argued that where professional development is an integral component, situated in the context of the school, good practice will be reinforced through the creation of a learning environment (Blandford, 2000). This means that head teachers and other senior staff, as well as classroom practitioners, all need to be engaged in professional development, as it is up to the senior management team, Blandford argues, to create the conditions for effective learning in classrooms. In this way, head teachers and heads of departments will be able to provide role models of good practice, arrange specific guidance and training, and encourage reflection in their staff. Through sensitive delegation they will be able to promote initiatives and provide further information about developmental opportunities as they arise. Time committed to the professional development of teachers will be reflected in the learning outcomes of pupils. In the school that is operating effectively as a learning community there will be an emphasis on the development of individuals, and the professional development activities will be integrated into the school curriculum. Central characteristics of such a community will be negotiation, participation and collaboration.

There are, however, some dangers attached to working collaboratively where it is limited to unchallenging and non-threatening aspects of teachers' work (see Chapter 8). In these contexts, collaboration may reinforce existing practice and foster complacency (Hargreaves, 1994). The apparent growth of collaboration in primary schools and what this means for teachers' work has been examined by researchers on the PACE (Primary Assessment, Curriculum and Experience) Project (Osborn et al., 2000). They suggest that there are those who argue that primary schools are becoming more collaborative with a supportive ethos (Nias et al., 1989) while others consider it to be a contrived or imposed collegiality based mainly on rhetoric (Menter et al., 1997). Therefore, where constraints are placed on the collaborative process, teachers' situated knowledge of their own practice is prevented from further development (Quicke, 2000). What does the culture of a school have to be like to create a community of practice?

Hargreaves (1994) identifies five forms of teacher subcultures that can exist in schools. The first, individualism, denotes a teacher working in isolation and insulated from outsiders who avoids both support and blame. The second, collaboration, is where teachers spontaneously choose to work together without a controlling external agenda. The third is contrived collegiality where collaboration is imposed compulsorily by others in senior management or administrative roles. The fourth, balkanisation, occurs when small groups collaborate voluntarily and teachers are not isolated but neither are they working together as a whole school. This form of collaboration often happens in departments in secondary schools or with teachers working in infant and junior classes in one primary school. The fifth of Hargreaves' cultural forms, the moving mosaic, suggests the idea of teachers working together in a creative way with the aim of continuous learning and improvement. It is this last form of teacher subculture that appears to offer the most hope for understanding communities of practice. The moving mosaic offers flexibility and the opportunity for collaboration characterised by adaptable alliances and partnerships. It is responsive to both context and circumstance. Being part of the moving mosaic in a community of practice gives meaning to teachers working at every level in a school and has been summarised by Moon as follows:

- For *individuals*, it means that learning is an issue of engaging in and contributing to the practices of their communities.

- For *communities*, it means that learning is an issue of refining their practice and ensuring new generations of members.
- For *organisations*, it means that learning is an issue of sustaining the interconnected communities of practice through which an organisation knows what it knows and thus becomes effective and valuable as an organisation.

(Moon, Chapter 11)

These three ways of thinking about learning in schools point to the importance of collective approaches towards professional development in schools. They provide an opportunity for formal institutional structures to be reconciled with collegial activity where a wide range of inspirational leadership roles can be generated irrespective of status. In the remainder of this chapter I will be exploring how teachers can work together to achieve a community of learning that has these features. In particular, I will be focusing upon how individuals can work with others to engage in and contribute, in a confident and knowledgeable way, to developing professional practice in their school community.

Working together in a community of practice

In a school that operates as a community of practice the progress of pupils will be paramount. However, teacher learning is crucial to pupil learning. Teachers who have secure knowledge and skills, are happy and confident in their role as a teacher and comfortable with the ethos of the school, are more likely to motivate pupils (Stoll and Fink, 1995). Lifelong learning has to be a goal for both teachers and pupils in a school that operates as a community of learning. Achieving this goal can be helped by knowing how teachers learn, and the significance of events in teachers' lives (Goodson, 1992) and age and number of years in teaching (Oja, 1989). There is further discussion on this aspect of teacher development in Chapter 26 where the role of action research as a tool for teacher learning and sustaining improvement in schools is considered. However, action research is only one strategy for teacher learning and others that will be discussed in this chapter are induction and mentoring programmes, peer coaching, and systems of appraisal.

Induction

Induction into a school may be required for both newly qualified teachers and new appointments to a school. For those just beginning teaching there are statutory arrangements (DfEE, 1999) for a one year induction. Transitions from training to a place of work can cause uncertainties and successful induction will ensure the continued progress and development of teachers at the beginning of their careers. How induction is experienced by new teachers reveals how they see the nature and complexity of the task they have to face. It is also complicated by the shift from being a student to being a full-time teacher. This can include factors such as, changes in status and expectations of others, moving location, new school and curriculum content, getting to know new colleagues and isolation from other new teachers in their induction year. Developing new relationships with pupils and other teaching colleagues can seem a very individual and challenging experience as this comment from a newly qualified teacher shows.

> So I've got to be careful . . . she came into my lesson – she didn't comment on it to me, which I thought was a bit off, she went behind my back and commented on it to my head of department. And I thought, well, you know, I'm not a baby, I'm not a child – why don't you tell me?. . . . I feel less attached to these kids. I just see them once a week and they go out and I see them the next time. . . . On teaching practice I had less classes so I got to know more kids better, whereas here they just come in and they go out, it's rather like a conveyor belt system. And not having a registration class, again I just sort of get thrown in or go and see this class one day, this class another day. They just sort of come into the lesson and I give them the lesson, and then if they don't like it, they don't like it, if they do, they do. And I try hard to get them involved in that one lesson a week. I am sort of there and I am just sort of thrown in at the deep end; I'm not saying that nobody has made any special effort to say, 'Well, look out for this or look out for that' – I'm just there, and they haven't actually had (a newly qualified teacher) for a long time. I don't know, I'm not too taken up with the place. I don't feel that I belong at that school, I felt that I much preferred my teaching practice school, I think that is the main problem.
>   (Tickle, 2000, pp.133–4)

As this example illustrates, how induction is managed and perceived by the newly qualified teacher is going to affect the morale and hence the future progress and development of that teacher. Induction should ensure that all new teachers who are appointed feel supported and confident and willing to contribute. Clear details including full job descriptions, documentation stating the aims of the school, policies, reporting and assessment procedures, health and safety, staff handbooks and class lists should be provided. In addition, introductions to all members of the team and their role, that the new teacher is assigned to, as well as other school personnel, are essential.

The involvement of a variety of colleagues will help to promote the professional development of newly appointed colleagues (Blandford, 2000). The induction period is also when a system of mentoring, as a way of working together, can be introduced to new staff.

Mentoring

The major need expressed at the end of the first year by new teachers is continued personal support and encouragement from colleagues (Stoll and Fink, 1995). Mentoring provides the opportunity for experienced teachers to take on a leadership role as they work with less experienced colleagues. The mentoring relationship, however, is a complex one as it allows opportunities for both the mentor and the mentee to observe each other and reflect on their practice. For the mentor, this can be a disconcerting experience as learned skills and knowledge will have become embedded in his or her actions over a number of years and responses to pupils may often be at an instinctive or intuitive level (Burgess, 1987; Lazarus, 2000). Having an awareness of the role of intuition may bridge the gap between doing and knowing why one is doing. There are several intuitive ways of knowing that may be pertinent to mentors (Claxton, 2000). For example, most mentors are chosen because of their *expertise* and will therefore, have an intuitive grasp of many situations. However, they have to be able to step back from what occurred to explain why a particular strategy or technique was used. *Sensitivity* is required to know when it is the most appropriate time to offer advice, support or challenge the practice of the new teacher. Mentors need to rely upon objective criteria as well as their intuitive *judgements* when making assessments of mentees. Being aware of the intuitive strategies employed by mentees will help the mentor understand the *implicit learning* that student teachers and newly qualified teachers rely upon. The relevance of understanding the role of mentoring in this way becomes clear from recent research studies into mentoring in schools. Burgess and Butcher (1999) conducted a study of mentoring of primary and secondary students on the Open University PGCE programme. Their study explored how mentors articulated their knowledge base, the dialogue between mentor and student and the challenge of moving from novice to more experienced practitioner. Analysis showed that while most mentors were very supportive of their mentee, addressing challenge in the mentoring relationship was much more difficult. They argue that challenge as a mentoring strategy can trigger the kind of active mentoring through which learner needs can be confronted and met. One science mentor commented:

The weakest competence was in motivating pupils/empowering them. It is a difficult area to address . . . I counted the number of times the student smiled! . . . we talked about tone of voice/body language.
(Burgess and Butcher, 1999, p.37)

Other mentors employed less direct strategies such as the one described by this upper primary mentor.

Gave her varied experience on classroom management in other classes so that she was able to see that no one way is the right way and for her to establish her own way on managing the class and the curriculum.
(Burgess and Butcher, 1999, p.37)

The belief by mentors that young teachers need to develop their own style and the emphasis upon independent performance, means that too often mentors do not intervene and an opportunity for developing knowledge, skill or understanding is lost.

Knowing when is the appropriate time to offer challenge or offer support can depend upon the relationship between the mentor and mentee. Elliott (1995) carried out a study on six student teachers to explore significant instances of learning to teach in mentoring relationships. As part of his analysis he explored how the mentor/mentee believed that learning had occurred; the stimulus for learning; the perceived role played by both teachers and the outcomes of the development. In most of the cases the mentor relied upon the student to initiate her own learning and one commented 'She was really teaching herself more than what I was teaching her' (Elliott, 1995, p.252). In one instance where structured feedback was given the mentor indicated that this strategy strengthened the learning relationship through the significant amount of conversation that took place before and after the lessons. The structure allowed the mentor to focus upon very specific and substantial issues rather than the global form of feedback that other mentors used. For most of the students in this study, learning occurred through specific incidents in the classroom and not through direct intervention by the mentor. Most of these incidents were characterised by uncertainty and the students believed that they moved forward in their teaching skills when they felt comfortable in dealing with similar incidents in the classroom. Elliott concluded that the triggers for development were often unanticipated and signal periods when the mentee is ill at ease.

These studies have a number of implications for mentoring teachers in the early part of their career. The experienced teacher needs to ensure that sufficient time and emphasis is placed upon developing a mentoring relationship that inspires confidence and allows structured and appropriate communication about learning to take place. Elliott's finding, that triggers for development are signalled by unease, is valuable for the perceptive mentor who can then identify when to challenge, advise or support the new teacher. Such a finding also has implications for what mentors do as observation of teaching or working together collaboratively as a team is required in order to identify the developmental triggers. In these instances, conversation alone is not a substitute.

Peer coaching

Peer coaching is very similar to mentoring but involves a more equal partnership between the teachers concerned. Coaching relationships have been defined as those that are an extension of in-service training in schools as teachers try to implement new knowledge, skills and strategies (Joyce and Showers, 1982). Very often when teachers seek out professional development opportunities on their own and attempt to implement them without the support of other teachers their strategies are not successful. Research carried out by Showers and others (1987) has shown that peer coaching can be more powerful than other methods in terms of transferring training.

Peer coaching can operate in schools at a number of levels, department, group and one-to-one. It can include activities that take place inside and outside the classroom. Inside the classroom observation of teaching supported by pre-observation and post-observation meetings can provide opportunities to discuss, analyse and reflect. Outside the classroom, study groups, co-planning, problem solving and curriculum development activities are all strategies that peer coaching can employ (Swafford, 1998). Work groups that link across institutions can also provide another type of peer coaching and support. An illustration of work groups is provided by Estebaranz, Mingorance and Marcelo (1999), who discuss what they call 'Permanent Seminars'. In these seminars, work groups of teachers who may, or may not, belong to the same school, attempt to diagnose a teaching or administrative problem and set up a project to solve it. This approach, they argue, gives teachers the chance to gain confidence in introducing innovations and gather new information and share experiences. It also provides a practical opportunity to analyse classrooms in a variety of ways. Through communication, deliberation and reflection the teachers are able to learn together.

A variety of styles of peer coaching have been identified by Swafford:

- Technical coaching – for transference of specific teaching methods
- Expert coaching – uses specially trained teachers
- Reciprocal coaching – teachers who observe and coach each other

- Reflective coaching – involves dialogue about classroom practices to explore meanings
- Cognitive coaching – similar to reflective coaching.
  (From Swafford, 1998, p.55)

The form of coaching used will depend upon the needs of the individuals or groups of teachers. For peer coaching to work effectively, all those involved need to be committed to it as a strategy for furthering professional development in teachers. They also need to share the common goal that it will improve the quality of teaching in classrooms. It is important that there is whole school support in terms of administrative systems to facilitate peer coaching as well as teachers being actively involved in designing the programmes. However, Swafford argues, peer coaching is a voluntary, non-evaluative and non-judgemental activity.

Peer coaching can provide a valuable alternative to other types of staff development and encourage a collaborative environment in schools. In a community of learning, peer coaching provides teachers with the opportunities to investigate and explore alternatives, reflect on the effectiveness of their teaching, implement new strategies and reflect again.

Appraisal

Appraisal of teachers in English schools has been statutory for almost a decade although it remains a contentious issue (DfEE, 1998). However, I will not be focusing on the debate surrounding appraisal but rather how it can be used as a method for teachers to work together to identify and fulfil staff development needs. The statutory aims of appraisal set out in the 1991 regulations, are:

- To recognise the achievements of school teachers and help them to identify ways of improving their skills and performance.
- To help school teachers, governing bodies and local education authorities (as the case may be) to determine whether a change of duties would help the professional development of school teachers and improve their career prospects.
- To identify the potential of teachers for career development, with the aim of helping them, where possible, through appropriate in-service training.
- To help school teachers identified as having difficulties with their performance, through appropriate guidance, counselling and training.
- To inform those responsible for providing references for school teachers in relation to appointments.
- To improve the management of schools.
  (From DES, 1991)

Appraisals can be used to aid decisions on promotion, dismissal or discipline and in relation to discretionary pay awards. Appraisal has been defined by Blandford (2000) as one professional holding him/herself accountable to him/herself in the presence of another professional. Any staff appraisal scheme, therefore, should benefit staff by giving them a better understanding of their job, improving feedback and recognition and providing regular opportunities to consider their professional development needs. How effectively appraisal has operated in schools is demonstrated through the study by Stokes (1999) into primary teacher appraisal. Sixteen primary head teachers were interviewed about their own appraisal, the appraisal procedure in their schools and their perceptions of its effectiveness as a tool for improving their schools. Key features of effective appraisal were identified by Stokes as self-review and classroom observation. These should be embedded in development planning and staff development programmes, and clear, achievable targets should be set (see Storey, Chapter 9). In addition, she believes that all teachers should be appraised and there should be a commitment to time resource for the purposes of carrying out the appraisal. Her findings revealed that head teachers did relate their own appraisals to school issues such as communication and time management but not to initiatives in school development planning. Only one head teacher incorporated appraisal with staff development. In this school the appraisal discussion and targets related both to teaching skills and the teachers' contribution to management as subject coordinators. It is evident that appraisal introduced as a means of encouraging development both of individual teachers and the school is not yet well established. Appraisal could play a central role in the professional development of teachers, providing support and encouragement, particularly for young teachers who may need help to think through future promotion and career directions. In addition, appraisal can be a very powerful mechanism for promoting equal opportunity (Thompson, 1992) and provides perhaps one of the greatest challenges and greatest opportunities for restructuring the values of the teaching profession as a community of practice (see also Chapter 9).

Conclusion

This chapter has focused upon the ways in which teachers can work together to develop professional practice in a learning community. Induction, mentoring, peer coaching and appraisal, have all been considered as aspects of a learning community. Ways of adults working together will also include parents, governors and the wider community. The evidence from research studies reveals that induction programmes, mentoring and peer coaching have distinct possibilities for developing teachers professionally and in some schools have been used in imaginative ways. However, appraisal, which has the potential to be one of the most powerful tools for professional development when used in a supportive and collegial way, is much under utilised. In schools that are learning communities there are increased opportunities for self-development at all levels. Learning schools recognise the importance of social processes and relationships in deepening the knowledge and experience of teachers in the early years of their careers. Working together, young teachers will be able to play a greater role in their own professional development and contribute to understanding and knowledge about the complexities of teaching and learning.

References

Blandford, S. (2000) *Managing Professional Development in Schools.* London: Routledge.

Burgess, H. (1987) 'Springing free from formal assessment', in *Education 3–13* **15**(2), 11–16.

Burgess, H. and Butcher, J. (1999) 'To challenge or not to challenge: the mentor's dilemma', *Mentoring and Tutoring* **6**(3), 31–47.

Claxton, G. (2000) 'The anatomy of intuition', in Atkinson, T. and Claxton, G. (eds) *The Intuitive Practitioner: on the value of not always knowing what one is doing.* Buckingham: Open University Press.

Department of Education and Science (DES) (1991) *School Teacher Appraisal.* Circular 12/9. London: HMSO.

Department for Education and Employment (DfEE) (1998) *Teachers Meeting the Challenge of Change.* (Green Paper). London: HMSO.

Department for Education and Employment (DfEE) (1999) *The Education (Induction Arrangements for School Teachers) Regulations 1999.* London: DfEE.

Department for Education and Employment (DfEE) (2001a) *Learning and Teaching: a Strategy for professional development.* London: DfEE.

Department for Education and Employment (DfEE) (2001b) *Good Value CPD: A Code of Practice for Providers of Professional Development for Teachers.* London: DfEE.

Elliott, B. (1995) 'Developing relationships: significant episodes in professional development', *Teachers and Teaching: theory and practice* **1**(2), 247–64.

Estebaranz, A., Mingorance, P. and Marcelo, C. (1999) 'Teachers' work groups as professional development: what do the teachers learn?', *Teachers and Teaching: theory and practice* **5**(2), 153–69.

Goodson, I. (1992) *Studying Teachers' Lives.* Lewes: Falmer Press.

Hargreaves, A. (1994) *Changing Teachers, Changing Times: teachers' work and culture in the postmodern age.* London: Cassell.

Hay McBer (2000) *Research into Teacher Effectiveness*. London: DfEE.

Holly, P. (1994) 'Striving for congruence: the properties of a learning system', in Bayne-Jardine, C. and Holly, P. (eds) *Developing Quality Schools*. London: Falmer Press.

Joyce, B. R. and Showers, B. (1982) 'The coaching of teaching', *Educational Leadership* **40**(2), 4–10.

Lave, J. and Wenger, E. (1991) *Situated Learning: Legitimate peripheral participation*. Cambridge: Cambridge University Press.

Lazarus, E. (2000) 'The role of intuition in mentoring and supporting beginning teachers', in Atkinson, T. and Claxton, G. (eds) *The Intuitive Practitioner: on the value of not always knowing what one is doing*. Buckingham: Open University Press.

Menter, I. *et al.* (1997) *Work and Identity in the Primary School: a post-Fordist analysis*. Buckingham: Open University Press.

Nias, J., Southworth, G. and Yeomans, R. (1989) *Staff Relationships in the Primary School: A Study of Organisational Cultures*. London: Cassell.

Oja, S. N. (1989) 'Teachers: ages and stages of adult development', in Holly, M. L. and McLoughlin, C. S. (eds) *Perspectives on Teacher Professional Development*. Lewes: Falmer Press.

Osborn, M. *et al.* (2000) *What Teachers Do: Changing Policy and Practice in Primary Education*. London: Continuum.

Quicke, J. (2000) 'A new professionalism for a collaborative culture of organisational learning in contemporary society', *Educational Management and Administration* **28**(3), 299–315.

Showers, B., Joyce, B. and Bennett, B. (1987) 'Synthesis of research on staff development: A framework for future study and a state-of-the-art analysis', *Educational Leadership* **45**(3), 77–87.

Stokes, C. (1999) 'Appraisal in West Northshire: Primary Teachers' Practice'. University of Leicester, Working Papers in Education, No. 1. University of Leicester.

Stoll, L. and Fink, D. (1995) *Changing Our Schools*. Buckingham: Open University Press.

Swafford, J. (1998) 'Teachers supporting teachers through peer coaching', *Support for Learning* **13**(2), 54–8.

Thompson, M. (1992) 'Appraisal and equal opportunities', in Bennett, N., Crawford, M. and Riches, C. (eds) *Managing Change in Education: Individual and Organisational Perspectives*. London: Paul Chapman.

Tickle, L. (2000) *Teacher Induction: The Way Ahead*. Buckingham: Open University Press.

Section 2
Teaching for Learning

Chapter 11

Learning perspectives on the teachers' task

Bob Moon

Down through the centuries people have wondered about the nature of human learning. What is the relationship between the physical object we know to be our brains and the rich, informational and emotional world we know to be our mind? By what process of evolution did humankind develop capacities for thought? How did our mental strategies for dealing with the usual and the unusual evolve?

Creating the conditions for learning, observing learning, assessing learning are the key tasks of teachers. Yet learning is a misty territory. At the beginning of the twenty-first century we are still unsure quite how our minds work, or how the physical and mental processes within ourselves and between ourselves and the outside world create the conditions for learning. Numerous theories exist. At different periods in history particular ideas have often gained ascendancy but no one view of learning has ever gained universal approval.

Despite the uncertainties about how it happens the process of learning is a wonderful thing to behold. Two- or three-year-old children have minds far more complex than the most sophisticated computers. Their language recognition skills far outstrip the most advanced voice recognition technologies and appear likely to do so for a long time yet.

The challenge for formal teaching is how to transpose the extraordinary human capacity for learning, particularly in the young, to those artificial worlds we have created in schools and classrooms. I say artificial because much of our learning, and certainly all the early learning, occurs in far less structured places than schools. We are all voracious learners. It is estimated that the average adult has understanding of 75,000 words (Gopnick *et al.*, 1999) with the foundation for that vocabulary laid well before the years of formal schooling begin.

Learning is full of paradoxes. How come our linguistic skill at the age of five and the linguistic uncertainty, even embarrassment, in another language at the age of ten or twenty? By what means does a sight or smell conjure up memories that have lain dormant for decades or more? While there are theories about these sorts of phenomena, no one has definitive answers.

A few years ago Brazilian psychologists became intrigued by the numerical abilities of children who lived on the streets (Carraher *et al.*, 1985). These children, street traders by day and night, were found to have very high level mental computational skills, particularly when working with rapidly changing exchange rates. Yet in school their mathematics performance, especially in written exercises, was poor. Learning was clearly taking place, but not the sort schools expected or wanted, and certainly not using the rules and routines of school mathematics. Learning, therefore, is also influenced by context. Most people from personal experience will remember a time when they became passionately interested in some topic. Music, fashion, fishing or football might be examples from our teenage world. Learning about these things, fired by strong motivation, was almost effortless. What a contrast with some of the subjects we struggled with at school.

Controversies about learning have also been dominated by the nature–nurture debate. How much capability are we born with? How much do we acquire through our own efforts? There is now, however, a strong consensus that our intelligence and capacity for learning grows and develops given the right environment. Yes, there are some components that nature seems to provide. The ratio of nature to nurture, however, is unclear. Not the least because learning covers such a huge array of contents and contexts.

A great deal of evidence now shows intelligences to be a multifaceted and pliable concept; more flexible than suggested by pre-war psychologists who argued the case for fixed IQs. Yet the idea of 'born not made' is a strong one in the popular imagination.

The American psychologist, Howard Gardner, is an influential figure who has challenged the idea of a single and measurable intelligence (see Chapter 13). In a series of books he has argued the case for what he terms 'multiple intelligences'. Our minds, he suggests, are more complex than a singular notion of intelligence suggests. Gardner (1983) suggests at least seven types of intelligence that require different forms of encouragement and support:

- logical mathematical
- linguistic
- spatial
- bodily-kinaesthetic
- musical
- interpersonal
- intrapersonal.

Schooling, he argues, has tended to emphasise some forms of intelligence more than others and this is highly restrictive of full educational development. Gardner, mostly in the USA, has had the courage to put his ideas into practice (see Gardner, 1993) in seeking new forms of curriculum and school organisation that fosters the broad range of intelligences. It is too soon to pass judgement on the outcome of these experiments. There are, however, those who question the conceptual basis. John White, for example, in a critique (White, 1998) suggests that Gardner conflates ideas of physical and mental growth and he sees Gardner's own cultural context and values as heavily influencing a determination of intelligences that are claimed as universal.

In a similar way psychologists have increasingly focused on the way in which learning is very dependent on the situation in which it takes place. The phrase 'situated learning' is now used extensively by those working in this field. While not directly critiquing Gardner they point out the problems of theories that treat knowing as the manipulation of symbols inside the mind of the individual and learning as the acquisition of knowledge and skills applicable across a range of contexts (Putnam and Borko, 2000).

We are so accustomed to thinking of learning in individual terms that this can be a difficult concept to grasp. Essentially the argument is that learning always means engaging with some sort of other, outside ourselves, situation. This might be a book (with all the cultural associations that has for use) or a group of other learners in an impressively equipped science laboratory. You cannot think of learning without embracing a situation. Teachers, therefore, need to understand the significance of the contexts of learning every bit as much as they think about the organisation of knowledge or the receptivity of individual learners. In this context learning is a social process and the role of all the 'others' is crucial to effective learning.

There are some straightforward examples of how this works. Most people have had the experience of formulating an idea and hypothesis and then discovered that the first time they verbalise it to others it seems lacklustre and inadequate. The old adage 'the best way to learn is to teach' has some resonance here. Repeated verbalisation of ideas and concepts certainly can enhance learning and hence the vital role accorded to language in our understandings of teaching and learning. Hence, also over the past few decades, the interest in encouraging learners to articulate their ideas in pairs or groups – a mode of learning that worries some who would prefer a classroom with serried, silent ranks of children.

There is also another dimension to situated learning which goes under the term 'distributed'. This term emphasises the way that in most parts of everyday life, learning and human action is hardly ever 'wholly individual'. Most of the time we work with tools and others to create joint learning communities. This goes back to the beginning of social human activities.

The first time a flint or tree branch was used to supplement our individual prowess was the moment our learning became distributed across tools. The first groupings together to solve problems in our environment (hunting, fishing, agriculture) represented a distribution of learning across others. Often both tools and others work together in a learning environment.

Traditional school contexts often focus on individualistic learning. Learning with others and using tools (calculators, for example) may even be discouraged.

This is an interesting debate that continues. Over the last few decades, however, a professional consensus among psychologists and social psychologists has emerged that brings into question the notion of any overarching intelligence that embraces all human activity, including the range of activities played out in schools. Equally any idea that our capacities are limited at birth is now seen as flying in the face of all the evidence. Brain research, for example, is now demonstrating that our brains evolve and grow throughout most of our life, even if the early years, in establishing a conceptual understanding of the world, are particularly crucial. A consensus is also emerging that questions the dominance of highly individualistic approaches to understanding learning.

Implicit and explicit models of how our minds work do, however, have a strong influence on theories about how we learn. Numerous theories have been advanced and significant schools of thought exist that argue passionately for one approach rather than another. I have mentioned the work on multiple intelligence and situated learning. Etienne Wenger has usefully summarised the pedagogical focus of four psychological theories of learning (Wenger, 1998). The terms described often appear in the professional dialogue around teaching and learning.

- **Behaviorist** theories focus on behavior modification via stimulus-response pairs and selective reinforcement. Their pedagogical focus is on control and adaptive response. Because they completely ignore issues of meaning, their usefulness lies in cases where addressing issues of social meaning is made impossible or is not relevant, such as automatisms, severe social dysfunctionality, or animal training.
  (Skinner, 1974)
- **Cognitive** theories focus on internal cognitive structures and view learning as transformations in these cognitive structures. Their pedagogical focus is on the processing and transmission of information through communication, explanation, recombination, contrast, inference, and problem solving. They are useful for designing sequences of conceptual material that build upon existing information structures.
  (J. R. Anderson, 1983; Wenger, 1987; Hutchins, 1995)

- **Constructivist** theories focus on the processes by which learners build their own mental structures when interacting with an environment. Their pedagogical focus is task-oriented. They favor hands-on, self-directed activities oriented toward design and discovery. They are useful for structuring learning environments, such as simulated worlds, so as to afford the construction of certain conceptual structures through engagement in self-directed tasks.

    (Piaget, 1954; Papert, 1980)

- **Social learning** theories take social interactions into account, but still from a primarily psychological perspective. They place the emphasis on interpersonal relations involving imitation and modeling, and thus focus on the study of cognitive processes by which observation can become a source of learning. They are useful for understanding the detailed information-processing mechanisms by which social interactions affect behavior.

    (Bandura, 1977)

He goes on to suggest that some theories are moving away from the traditional exclusively psychological approach. One perspective, highly relevant to the world of schools, he cites are organisational theories. These concern themselves with the way individuals learn in organisation contexts and with the ways in which organisations can be said to learn as organisations. The pedagogical focus is on organisational systems, structures and politics and on institutional forms of memory (see Argyris and Schon, 1978; Brown and Duguid, 1991). Teachers joining a school, for example, can spend a considerable time coming to grips with the collective memory that is particular to any institution and that is crucial to their learning. In fact everything we say here about learning in general applies as much to teacher learning as it does to children.

Wenger himself takes a social perspective. In a number of influential publications, particularly the book co-written with Jean Lave (Lave and Wenger, 1991), he has argued that learning is a process of participation in communities of practice, participation that is at first legitimately peripheral but that increases gradually in engagement and complexity. The situation or context is crucial. It follows:

- For **individuals**, it means that learning is an issue of engaging in and contributing to the practices of their communities.
- For **communities**, it means that learning is an issue of refining their practice and ensuring new generations of members.
- For **organizations**, it means that learning is an issue of sustaining the interconnected communities of practice through which an organization knows what it knows and thus becomes effective and valuable as an organization.

Theories about learning have often become linked to social and political attitudes. Behaviourist ideas, for example, have been associated with more rigid, even totalitarian ways of organising society. Constructivist ideas have been linked to progressive, child-centred forms of organising teaching and learning. Protagonists for learning theories have, on occasions, brought to the debate the fervour associated with supporting a football team or a political party. Given the uncertainties in the field the wise teacher will draw eclectically from the range of insights provided by a range of ideas.

Jerome Bruner, another very influential figure over the last few decades, takes such a view (Bruner, 1996). He groups contemporary ideas about learning into two categories.

The first he terms the computational. The belief that you can devise a formal way of presenting any and all functioning systems that manage the flow of information. This is done in a way that produces foreseeable, systematic outcomes. In one manifestation this became what is termed artificial intelligence, the capability of systems outside the human mind to replicate our mental processes.

The second Bruner terms, culturalism, which takes its inspiration from the evolutionary fact that mind could not exist save for culture. For Bruner the culturalist conception sees mind as both constituted by, and realised in, the use of human culture. He sees the rules common to all information systems (the computational conception) as not covering the messy, ambiguous and context-sensitive processes of 'meaning making' as he terms it that most of us experience in most learning situations.

Bruner makes it clear that these two approaches are not necessarily in direct contradiction. Although he doubts that the computationalists will ever tame the messy or the ambiguous, he sees their efforts as interesting in shedding light on the divide between meaning making and information processing.

Why are these ideas about learning significant for teachers? There is plenty of evidence to suggest that the ideas we carry in our heads, implicit or explicit, about the nature of intelligence or the way the mind works, strongly influences the models of teaching that we adopt. A flexible, non-determinist perspective on learning might make us optimistic and ambitious for learners, even the struggling ones. An appreciation of the social context of learning will make us appreciate that a range of variables need taking account of in developing teaching and learning strategies. Acknowledging the importance of building on prior knowledge challenges the perception of the mind as a tabula rasa or blank slate upon which the imprint of learning can be made.

Such theories do not always offer the easiest way forward for teachers. We have all experienced the teacher who starts the year with a 'clean sheet' approach to the new class. Often this is with the best of motives in not wanting previous experience, successful or otherwise, to influence expectations. But the approach has limitations.

Most of us learn by making connections with our previous knowledge. We have all experienced the inspirational moment when 'things become clear' (going 'meta', as Bruner terms it) as the new frame of reference clicks in with our established ideas and understandings. The challenge for the teacher is orchestrating that over time, and mostly with twenty or thirty different pupils.

The importance of thinking about 'how pupils learn' lies in the way it will begin to influence patterns and styles of pedagogic practice. On a lesson-by-lesson basis it is not necessarily going to be in the forefront of teachers' minds. But as they reflect on the planning and implementation of their teaching, theories of learning can be influenced in a wide range of ways.

Anyone working as a teacher has a unique opportunity to observe and enquire about the process of learning. It is at the core of professional activity and in the decades to come new ideas, insights and empirical evidence will become available that may make existing theories appear naive or simplistic. Keeping abreast of ideas about learning, I am suggesting, is a significant part of the professional knowledge that needs to be updated, refined and questioned across a teaching career. I conclude with a quotation from a review by an American educationalist, Alison Gopnick (Gopnick *et al.*, 1999) who is optimistic about the way knowledge about mind may develop in the immediate future.

The history of education in the twenty-first century may turn out to be like the history of medicine in the nineteenth century. Both medicine and education have great moral urgency. Passing on what we know to our children is, after all, one of the few ways we have of genuinely defying death; medicine just postpones it. Both medicine and education invoke knowledge to justify their authority. Doctors have always justified their practices by claiming that they understand how our bodies work. Educators have always justified theirs by claiming that they understand how our children's minds work. But for most of history those claims were based on scarcely any systematic research. At best, they were pragmatic generalizations, the outcome of a long process of empirical tinkering.

During the last 150 years we have gradually begun to integrate real biological science into our medical practice. This has been one of the great scientific success stories. Surely even the most adamant postmodern critics of science believe that vaccinating babies is not just an exercise in patriarchal control. But our new biological knowledge has also told us that organisms and their illnesses are individual, variable, and complicated. And biology itself can't determine what kind of medicine is worth having, and how much we're willing to pay for it.

A similar story could unfold in education. In the last thirty years, we have begun to develop a science of children's minds. This new research might be the equivalent of the scientific physiology that has transformed medicine.

But it is unlikely to lead to some simple educational panacea. In fact, helping our children to be both smart and wise is likely to be just as difficult, as complicated and demanding, though just as valuable, as helping them to be healthy.

References

Anderson, J. R. (1983) *The Architecture of Cognition*. Cambridge, Mass.: Harvard University Press.

Argyris, C. and Schon, D. A. (1978) *Organisation Learning: A Theory of Action Perspective*. Reading, Mass.: Addison-Wesley.

Bandura, A. (1977) *Social Learning Theory*. Englewood Cliffs, NJ: Prentice-Hall.

Brown, J. S. and Duguid, P. (1991) 'Organizational learning and communication of practice: towards a unified view of working, learning and innovation', *Organisation Science* **2**, 40–57.

Bruner, J. (1996) *The Culture of Education*. Cambridge, Mass.: Harvard University Press.

Carraher, T., Carraher, D. W. and Schliema, A. C. (1985) 'Mathematics in the streets and in schools', *British Journal of Developmental Psychology* **3**, 21–9.

Gardner, H. (1983) *Frames of Mind*. New York: Basic Books.

Gardner, H. (1993) *Multiple Intelligences: The Theory in Practice*. New York: Basic Books.

Gopnick, A., Meltzoff, A. N. and Kuhl, P. K. (1999) *The Scientist in the Crib: Minds, Brains and How Children Learn*. New York: William Morrow.

Hutchins, E. (1995) *Cognition in the Wild*. Cambridge Mass.: MIT Press.

Lave, J. and Wenger, E. (1991) *Situated Learning: Legitimate peripheral participation*. Cambridge: Cambridge University Press.

Papert, S. (1980) *Mindstorm*. New York: Basic Books.

Piaget, J. (1954) *The Construction of Reality in the Child*. New York: Basic Books.

Putnam, R. T. and Borko, H. (2000) 'What do new views of knowledge and thinking have to say about research on teacher learning', *Educational Researcher* **29**(1), 4–15.

Skinner, B. F. (1974) *About Behaviourism*. New York: Knopf.

Wenger, E. (1987) *Artificial Intelligence and Tutoring Systems: Computational and Cognitive Approaches to the Communication of Knowledge*. San Fransisco: Morgan Kaufman.

Wenger, E. (1998) *Communities of Practice: Learning, Measuring, and Identity*. Cambridge: Cambridge University Press.

White, J. (1998) *Do Howard Gardner's multiple intelligences add up?* London: London Institute of Education series, Perspectives on Education Policy.

Chapter 12

What the most recent brain research tells us about learning

Alistair Smith

Editors' Note: Taking a more biological view of human learning, Alistair Smith presents a different perspective on the ideas presented in the previous chapter. In a similar way, however, he links what we know about the brain to practical strategies in the classroom.

Multisensory stimulation

A key question which will continue to perplex educationalists is the extent to which hereditary or environmental factors influence and shape brain development. Heredity and environment interact to produce neural networks which are complex and appear chaotic. Ligands, which are the basic body-wide units of a language used by cells to communicate with each other, associate with feelings, thoughts and learning behaviours and power our unique learning systems. The complex interaction of feelings, thoughts and learning behaviours shape personality characteristics and contribute to learning preferences and perhaps to learning styles.

So use it or lose it! The more we use our brain as we age, the more we encourage it to grow. With high levels of stimulus and challenge there are higher ratios of synapses (connections) to neurons. More synapses means more routes for higher order cognitive functioning. The optimal conditions for synaptic growth would include multiple complex connective challenges where, in learning, we are actively engaged in multisensory immersion experiences. Frequency of immediate feedback and opportunity for choice allows us to rehearse alternative strategies.

Marian Diamond's 1988 work described how an enriched environment where there was high sensory stimulation developed synaptic structures (connections between neurons) throughout the life span and into old age. We know that there is a proliferation of connections between neurons in the early years and that there are optimal 'windows' for developing sensory and motor functions which, if missed, can inhibit or remove the possibility of that development occurring.

The work of the British Institute for Brain Injured Children has shown that compensatory physical motor stimulation at a later stage in life can lead to remarkable developments in children who had previously been designated severely learning disabled and indeed 'beyond hope'. Their work utilises coordinated patterned physical movement which goes some way to compensate for the absence of such movements in what would have been the optimal developmental 'window' earlier in life.

Various parts of the brain develop at various rates. The neo-cortex, the part most actively engaged in higher cognitive processing, is fully developed between the ages of 16 and 25. However, the brain does not develop in an even continuum; it develops in spurts and plateaux. There may be as much as 18 months' developmental difference in the brains of youngsters of the same age in early teens. Researchers such as Alkon (1992) believe that experiences in the critical development periods of early childhood create neural networks and consistent neurological expectations which in turn create and reinforce behaviours, prejudices, fears and psychoneurological beliefs.

Lennenberg's work on supplies of minerals in the body demonstrated identified spurts of development corresponding to the presence of neurotransmitters (natural neural growth factors). He demonstrated their significance to walking and talking at around age two; reading, mathematical computation and writing at around age six and abstract reasoning at around age twelve. After this third spurt and because of the 'trimming' process it becomes harder to learn foreign languages. Precisely at the point where in the UK it becomes compulsory!

Learning, challenge and stress

The brain responds best to conditions of high challenge with low stress, where there is learner choice and regular and educative feedback. Multipath, individualised and thematic learning with the mental work of engaged problem solving enriches the brain. So does novel challenge and real-life experience.

The enemy of learning is stress. The optimal conditions for learning include a positive personal learning attitude where challenge is high and anxiety and self-doubt is low.

In the 1950s Dr Paul MacLean gave us his model of the triune or three-part brain and how the brain responded to stress. When challenge becomes unmanageable for a learner, stress develops. With stress comes a change in the chemical and electrical activity in the brain. Survival behaviours assume priority over logical and creative thinking, long-term planning and flexibility. We see the hardening of fight or flight responses, staying with the safe and familiar, anxiety over personal belongings and space. In these circumstances a student who is stressed cannot learn.

It is important to draw a distinction between challenge and stress. Stress includes both fear and anxiety and results from the desire to terminate or escape from a real or imagined negatively reinforcing experience. It coincides with a physiological change which, if not relieved, is harmful to the body and to health. When stress occurs we resort to fight, flight or flocking behaviours. The mid-brain floods with electro-chemical activity and higher order cognitive functioning associated with the neo-cortex is displaced. In stress we experience:

- constriction of the arteries with a rise in blood pressure – the heart rate goes from one to five gallons pumped per minute;
- activation of the adrenal gland assisting in the release of adrenalin and cortisol into the system to help us run and endure physical pain;
- enlargement of the vessels to the heart;
- constriction of vessels to the skin and digestive tract.

Ira Black (1991) reports that such stress responses 'of thirty to ninety minutes can result in a 200 to 300 per cent increase in enzyme activity for twelve hours to three days and in some cases for up to two weeks'. For many young learners whose lives are ones of constant stress, the classroom and the relationship with you as classroom teacher may be the only still point at the centre of a torrid existence.

The mid-brain is responsible for what have been labelled 'reptilian' behaviours. If a learner is experiencing stress or what is called 'induced learner anxiety' because of beliefs – real or imagined – about his or her ability to perform then don't be surprised to see the physiological responses listed above coincide with some or all of the following behaviours (Caine *et al.*, 1994):

- fight, flight, freezing or flocking;
- increased rigidity of behavioural response;
- preference for external motivation and increased adherence to rewards and punishment systems;
- preference for rote and ritualised activity;
- sensitivity to personal space and territoriality;
- status behaviours;
- inhibition of creativity;
- inhibition of the ability to form permanent new memories as a result of cortisol rush in the hippocampus;
- peer conformity.

Kotulak (1996), argues that stress turns on genes that leave a memory trace of a bad feeling and goes on to suggest that 'when reinforced, the feeling magnifies and the person "learns" to be difficult, depressed even epileptic'. Environments where risk taking is possible, is encouraged and is safe, presuppose accelerated learning. We are not talking of the obvious threat imposed by the overbearing attitude of some teachers but the pervasive background of fear which can characterise schooling inside and outside classrooms. Fear of authority, fear of the institution, fear of loss of independence, fear of failure, fear of physical confinement, fear of behavioural control within a confined physical space.

> (since) virtually all academic and vocational learning heavily involves the neo-cortex, it becomes plain that the absence of threat is utterly essential to effective instruction. Under threat, the cerebrum downshifts – in effect, to a greater or lesser extent, it simply ceases to operate.
>
> (Hart, 1983)

The Equal Opportunities Commission and MORI in England and Wales carried out some interesting research involving 15- and 16-year-olds. It pointed to the fear of psychological intimidation, ahead of physical bullying, among their prime safety concerns in schools and schooling. The Elton Report on Discipline in Schools suggested that 'schools which rely heavily on punishments to deter bad behaviour are likely to experience more of it'. Recent research into the brain and learning consistently points to the significance of creating an atmosphere of high challenge but low stress – what Lozanov called 'relaxed alertness'.

For many learners the comfort zone is where they prefer to be. They will happily copy out sections of text in a masquerade of note taking. Younger learners will 'copy out in rough, copy it out in neat, draw a coloured border around it, highlight the keywords in primary colours, draw you a picture'. But rote, repetitive comfort zone activity is not where real learning takes place. To engage in more complex forms of learning may require persistence amidst ambiguity and uncertainty. Doll (1989) pointed out that this can be, and can be made 'positively exciting'. For teachers it is a matter of taking learners beyond their comfort zone without undue threat.

Goleman, in his seminal book *Emotional Intelligence: Why it Can Matter More than IQ*, (1996) popularises the work of Joseph LeDoux on the brain and the primacy of the emotions. He describes the central role of the amygdala, which is part of the mid-brain, in routing signals to different areas of the brain including the neo-cortex. The amygdala plays a powerful role in acquiring, developing and retaining emotional responsiveness.

In essence his thesis is that emotions have primacy in responding to sensory data and thus emotion can overwhelm rational thought: sensory data is routed via an emotional response system before passing to the rational.

He describes the amygdala as an 'emotional sentinel' – 'the amygdala is the specialist for emotional matters . . . if the amygdala is severed from the rest of the brain, the result is a striking inability to gauge the emotional significance of events . . . the amygdala acts as a storehouse of emotional memory, and thus of significance itself; life without the amygdala is a life stripped of personal meanings'.

In arguing the case for a separate emotional intelligence from an understanding of neuroscience, Goleman goes on to describe the significance of self-knowledge and belief systems and the ability to defer immediate gratification and set purposeful personal goals. He argues for the 'schooling of the emotions' and goes on to show the impact of what is called learned optimism and chart the consequences and possible costs of 'emotional illiteracy'. His work provides a powerful argument for the key presuppositions underlying the Accelerated Learning in the Classroom model:

- create a positive, supportive learning environment;
- recognise the significance of limiting beliefs on performance;
- build and maintain positive self-esteem;
- develop the inter- and intrapersonal intelligences;
- encourage the setting of personal performance targets;
- recognise that external motivation systems – merits, points, stickers – are temporary and will mean less as learners mature;
- build and use affective vocabulary to allow young learners, particularly boys, to reflect meaningfully on the connections between behaviour, response and outcomes;
- develop reflective and meta-cognitive thinking as part of regular review activity.

Feedback and choice in learning

An underlying premise of accelerated learning is that given health, given the motivation, connection to a positive personal outcome and access to useful strategies, we can all learn. This does not mean we can all learn in the same way and to the same outcome but we can learn new skills and understandings and we can all be able to transfer them into new contexts.

As learners we will have different personal preferences for the strategies we use. These may vary by task and context but they will tend to show a consistency over time. Depending on our degree of self-knowledge and the opportunity to reflect on our own learning preference and compare with others, we may or may not become aware of exactly what our own preferred strategies are.

As teachers we may or may not be aware of our own personal learning preferences. We may or may not be aware that such preferences will influence our teaching. We may assume that how we make sense of and interpret data is how everyone makes sense of and interprets data. We may assume that the way we construct and reconstruct reality is how everyone does it. This is an unhelpful state of mind for the creation of powerful learning environments because our tools for understanding the preferred learning strategies of students in our classes are very limited. Our best option is to recognise that only a variety of approaches, reinforced by regular review and the opportunity for students to learn about their own learning will guarantee accessing all.

Do our students have any clue as to why they are learning what they are learning? Do we encourage them to be aware of the processes of learning? Do we utilise the positive power of peer feedback? Is our feedback frequent? Is it educative?

Positive reinforcement and carefully chosen words change the structure of the brain. An amine called serotonin plays a critical role in self-concept and self-esteem. Serotonin is one of a number of neurotransmitters in the brain which allows connections between neurons to be made. Serotonin is excitatory and is associated with sleep, appetite, pain and mood. It keeps aggression in line. The presence of serotonin encourages the electrical 'jump' across the synapse when connections are made. Where there is immediate positive reinforcement, such as the recognition of a challenge met or a task successfully achieved, serotonin is released simultaneously into the brain and intestines inducing a positive 'gut-feeling', a sense of well-being and security. This feeling coincides with the chemical conditions for enhanced neural networking and higher order thinking.

Reduced levels of serotonin are associated with clinical depression, loss of memory and low self-esteem and, according to Oliver James (1997), are found in people with the lowest status. Commercial drugs such as Prozac temporarily compensate for low levels of serotonin. Chocolate and alcohol have similar short-term effects. However, the continued absence of serotonin and other neurotransmitters can lead to impaired neural networking.

So reinforce success without dramatising failure! If you want to continue to build healthy brains catch the students being successful and let them know it! There is evidence that positive reinforcement impacts on the cellular structure of the brain strengthening the hippocampus and amygdala which are both associated with the emotions and memory. Harsh words and excess of stress can cause arrhythmia and the degeneration of neurons in the hippocampus. Indeed, as explained earlier in this section, under undue stress or anxiety, the mid-brain floods with chemicals prioritising survival behaviours of fight or flight, making creative problem solving, long-range planning and careful judgement impossible.

Research conducted by Hart, by Barzakov, by Schon and by Druckman and Swets points towards some key characteristics of giving and receiving feedback in the learning process.

Hart (1983) suggests that frequent and immediate feedback will help learners 'find out whether their pattern extraction and recognition is correct or improving'. The best feedback is also real rather than classroom based. So, in language learning it would be the feedback gained in successfully using the language with native speakers. In communications, it would be the ability to successfully make that telephone call to sell space in the school magazine. In science, the successful completion of a planned and researched experiment.

One of the ways in which suggestopaedic researchers such as Win Wenger (1996) suggest to boost thinking and intelligence is to utilise a strategy called 'pole-bridging'. This involves different areas of the brain in processing information as a task is undertaken. The brain connects information left and right, front and back simultaneously and this process can be encouraged deliberately by talking about or 'externalising' the experience as you do it. Wenger says, 'We go from regions of the brain weaving a tighter relationship and as you get more of what you reinforce, cumulatively, permanently you reinforce more and more onto line with immediate verbal consciousness those more distant regions of the brain, together with their resources and intelligence'.

Note taking which involves context as well as content works because of this 'pole-bridging' phenomenon. The fundamental psychological principle of 'you get more of what you reinforce' suggests that if we encourage learners to notice, pay attention to and in some way respond to their own immediate perceptions, however transitory, the behaviour of being perceptive is reinforced. Neurologically, this tightens underlying firing patterns between 'families' of neurons; weaving tighter relationships between regions of the brain. Wenger says that the 'most powerful way to support development of the brain and intelligence is to enrich and clarify feedback on the person's own actions'. This should be done in the here and now, and externally. Encourage the transmission of this external feedback on internal processing symbolically: 'storyboard your thinking', 'draw associated images – annotate and explain them', 'what metaphors come immediately to mind?'

Learners who describe what they are doing aloud as they do it; who reflect on their engagement with the task and their changing motivation; who speculate and hypothesise, achieve dramatically improved results. One commentator (Jensen, 1995) describes the outcomes of documented studies by Wenger as providing intelligence 'gains from one to three points per hour of pole-bridging practice' with some having 'increased intelligence up to 40 points in 50 hours of work'.

A simple strategy to improve performance is to add language to doing. Have students describe aloud what they are doing as they do it.

Encourage them to reflect on what has been done – aloud – and speculate on what is to come.

Both Barzakov in his work on 'educative' feedback and Schon in work on the reflective practitioner, see feedback as an essential part of a learning loop. Barzakov says that learners need educative feedback in a practical, evaluative and non-threatening form. Teachers would use phrases such as 'what might happen if you were to . . .?', 'In what other ways might this work?' 'How will you start to improve upon this?' 'What do you now know that you didn't before?' 'How might this best be taught to someone else?' The reflective practitioner learns through a cycle of plan, do and review – with review informing improvement and change. Through this process learners are being encouraged to incorporate inquiry and evaluation into their everyday working practice and thus into their thinking. It becomes a 'learned' approach where improvement depends on reflective analysis.

At Grace Owen Nursery School, Sheffield, a 'High Scope' style day was introduced in 1994/5. Children plan their activities, do what they have planned and review what they have done in small groups. The school describes the project as vital in raising achievement and say that children know far more about the classroom and even the youngest children thrive on it.

(Sheffield School Improvement Handbook)

According to Druckman and Swets (1988), peer feedback is as, or more, influential, than teacher feedback in obtaining lasting performance results. Excess of teacher feedback can be perceived as demotivating if it is too discouraging or 'plastic' or if it is too effusive. Apparently, the approval or disapproval of one's peers is the best reinforcer. This is contradicted by the pragmatic findings of some recent classroom research which points up the sensitivities young learners, particularly adolescents, have about peer feedback.

The most demotivating aspect was when teachers warned children in advance that they would not be able to mark their work. The obvious reaction was, 'why on earth should we bother to do it if it's not going to be marked?' Children also find it unpleasant and thankless to mark other children's work. They want teacher advice and approval. They do not like other children knowing how good or bad they are at their work.

(London Borough of Croydon, 1996)

We will vary in the degree in which we are convinced by Druckman and Swets but we can extract and apply the common principles on feedback:

- make it immediate, specific and educative;
- make it authentic whenever possible;
- the more often the better;
- remove it from threat and sanction;
- involve the learner peers and others;
- make it an essential part of a learning cycle.

Make action planning more than a termly ritual! The brain thrives on feedback – feedback that is educative and that can be acted upon. The brain also thrives on purpose. When we set ourselves a positive personal goal which has purpose for us, our brains actively filter data on behalf of the fulfilment of that goal. This would appear to be one of the functions of the reticular system – filtering and diverting data.

Goal and target-setting activities in schools should be brain-compatible. This would mean harnessing the power of positive visualisation.

Some of the major research findings on visual 'intelligence' suggest that the mind naturally thinks in images and that the most basic mental process is the ability to visualise (Samuels and Samuels, 1975) and that the mind can programme and reprogramme itself through visual images. Visual information is more readily accessed than semantic information and forms an 'inner guidance system' determining and controlling one's behaviour.

> Since the mind also operates by the process of inference, the mere creation of a mental image, similar to the real object, will cause it to react as if faced by the actuality. The image of an imagined object has mental effects that are in some ways very similar to the image of an object that is actually perceived. . . . If one is able to imagine something to be true, part of the mind appears to accept that imagined outcome as reality.
> (Harman and Rheingold, 1985)

A changed image can lead to a changed behaviour (Boulding, 1966) but it is an internal process. No other person can change those images and the process of selection for you. This is where affirmations become powerful: when a positive and desired state is created or recreated through a chosen visual image accompanied by a spoken message. Harmon of the Institute of Noetic Sciences, USA, (1986) suggests that 'whatever is vividly or energetically imagined or visualised by the mind, the brain believes to be true and current reality'.

For action planning to be more than the hollow exchange of banalities, encourage personal performance targets which are realisable and which do not make comparisons with others and in which a successful positive outcome can be visualised.

Whole-brain learning

fitful, irreverent, indulging at times in the grossest profanity (which was not previously his custom), manifesting but little deference for his fellows, impatient of restraint or advice when it conflicts with his desires, at times pertinaciously obstinate, yet capricious and vacillating.

(Physician's notes on Phineas Gage, 1848, R. H. S. Carpenter (1997) *Neurophysiology*, 3rd edn, Edward Arnold, Hodder & Stoughton Educational)

Starting a short section on whole-brain learning with a story about Phineas Gage exploits a pun which although awful, is also instructive.

Phineas Gage was an American Mining engineer who, in 1842 was tamping down dynamite with an iron crowbar, when the dynamite exploded and the bar shot through his left cheek and out his skull removing most of the frontal cortex of his brain. Gage survived and made a subsequent and precarious living out of exhibiting himself, fragments of his skull and the iron bar for many years afterwards. He also precipitated a rush of medical experiments on brain lesions and helped initiate a trend towards lobotomy which did not end until the 1960s. Gage's skull is in the Smithsonian Museum in Washington. The remarkable thing about Gage was that, despite the trauma of losing 30 per cent of his brain, his intellectual capacities were, according to his physician, 'apparently undiminished'. He endured a profound personality change but was able to continue to reason cognitively much as before.

Work with aphasics has from early times helped in an appreciation of hemispheric functions. Dr Samuel Johnson (1709–1784) left us a vivid account of what it is like to suffer a stroke.

I went to bed, and in a short time waked and sat up. I felt a confusion and indistinctness in my head that lasted, I suppose, about half a minute. I was alarmed, and prayed God, that however he might afflict my body, he would spare my understanding. This prayer, that I might try the integrity of my faculties, I made in Latin verse. The lines were not very good: I made them easily and concluded myself to be unimpaired in my faculties. . . . Soon after I perceived that I had suffered a paralytick stroke and that my speech was taken from me. Though God took my speech he left me my hand. In penning this note, my hand, I knew not how nor why, made wrong letters.

(Phineas Gage and Dr Samuel Johnson, R. H. S. Carpenter (1997) *Neurophysiology*, 3rd edn, Edward Arnold, Hodder & Stoughton Educational)

Just as we have a preferred hand, a preferred ear and a preferred eye we have a preferred or dominant hemisphere. After more than 20 years of research and from a database of over 500,000 people, Ned Hermann, creator of the Hermann Brain Dominance Instrument (HBDI), suggests that 30 per cent of this is genetically determined and the balance of 70 per cent or so determined by life experience. In 96 per cent of right-handed people it is the left hemisphere which dominates. In 65 per cent of left-handed people it is the right hemisphere which dominates. The Hermann Brain Dominance Instrument predicts whether an individual will have a right or left hemispheric preference and whether they favour cerebral or limbic processing. The prediction model, which Hermann describes as a 'metaphor', allows individuals to reflect on their dominant patterns and think of, and plan for, alternative developmental strategies.

In September 1997, Richard Wiseman of the University of Hertfordshire persuaded Yorkshire Television to help him with a simple hemispheric test involving viewers of the 'Tonight' programme. Presenter Carolyn Hodge told viewers she never had a pet when she was a child because she had asthma, then she said she loved pets and viewers were invited to guess whether she was telling the truth. There were over 5,000 calls with 1,564 left handers and 3,342 right handers. More than 72 per cent of the right handers guessed correctly but only 66 per cent of left handers guessed correctly. Apparently she had a guinea pig in her childhood. Professor Wiseman explained the consistency of the results: 'right handers tend to use the left hemisphere of the brain which is where linguistic information is processed . . . lots of the clues in the clips were to do with language . . . when the presenter was lying, there was little detail; when she was telling the truth there was lots of detail.'

Most brains are asymmetric. Sixty-six per cent have a larger left than a right hemisphere. There are differences in functional specialisms and dominance between left and right hemispheres and also in the processing of information and completion of tasks. The complexity of function and the fact that the brain is plastic, highly interconnected, situational and iterative should not be forgotten when we consider relative lateralisation. Some of the recognised specialisations are summarised in Figure 12.1.

A recipe for accelerating learning is to use strategies which connect left with right. Give the BIG picture first then chunk down. Pair students to have them describe in words (left) their learning map, graphs or charts (right). Have students visualise the desired outcome or learning goal (right) first before describing it orally (left). The strategies described in Chapter 15 continue to pay attention to the synergy of left and right connection.

There is evidence that *concrete* words are stored differently in the brain from *abstract* words. Concrete words may be stored within the visual system whereas abstract words may be stored via a semantic system. Concrete nouns

THE LEFT HEMISPHERE OF THE NEO-CORTEX	THE RIGHT HEMISPHERE OF THE NEO-CORTEX
● **LOGIC**	● **GESTALT**
● **PROCESSES INFORMATION CONVERGENTLY, RATIONALLY**	● **PROCESSES INFORMATION DIVERGENTLY, HOLISTICALLY**
● language: Broca's and Wernicke's areas	● perspective and dimension, depth and distance, perception
● likes words, symbols, letters	● likes forms and patterns, pictures, graphs, charts
● number and judgement of quantity	● spatial manipulation
● sequence	● images and pictures, face recognition
● linearity	● visualisation and pictorial representation
● words of a song	● tune of a song, melodies, musical chords, environmental sounds
● learning from the part to the whole	● learns whole first then parts
● more chemicals (neurotransmitters) involved in selective attention and concentration	● more chemicals (neurotransmitters) involved in arousal and inhibition of emotions
● dissociated information	● related information and relationships and connections in learning
● phonetic reading strategy	● whole language reading system
● propositional thinking	● lateral and divergent thinking

Figure 12.1 Recognised specialisations

produce mental images more readily than abstract nouns. For example 'potato' is more concrete than 'vegetable' which is more concrete than 'food' which is more concrete than 'nourishment'. The word 'potato' is easier to remember than 'nourishment'. Visual information is processed via the right hemisphere while linguistic information is predominantly via the left hemisphere.

Concrete words may be better remembered because they are recalled by left and right hemispheres. Left for the pattern of sounds and right for the visual image. You can see the object as you say the word.

The capacity to store and recall visual information is almost unlimited. Tests done with control groups and 10,000 pictures showed that a 90 per cent recognition level was possible and that this was retained up to three months after seeing the pictures only once (quoted in Higbee, 1996). Many studies have found that pictures of objects are remembered better than verbal descriptions of the objects. Jensen, in his book *Superteaching* (1995), claims that visual display placed above eye level in the classroom and sited so it can be read from anywhere in the room will reinforce long-term recall by as much as 70 per cent.

Patients who have had split-brain surgery often experience an inability to dream. Dreaming is a process involving visual imagery and so some investigators have speculated that it might be the responsibility of the right hemisphere. Split-brain patients are also reported as having a deficit in the ability to associate names with faces. The left hemisphere matches by function and the right by appearance. Interestingly, child and adult dyslexics consistently showed reversed or different hemisphere asymmetry with only 10 to 50 per cent of dyslexics having a larger left hemisphere than right. This may say something about the visual processing difficulties associated with dyslexia.

Different styles of music stimulate different hemispheres of the brain. According to research reported by Robertson (1993) and cited by Odam (1995), 'different styles of music will demand a more right or left brain approach both from the composer and the listener'. He goes on to give the examples of Gorecki, Part and Taverner accentuating right brain function through the use of tonality, concord and intuitive processes which cause strong emotional reactions in listeners, and the work of Boulez, Birtwhistle or Maxwell Davies conversely engaging the listener at an objective and intellectual level through its basis in left-brain processes – arhythmic and atonal properties and dissonance.

Consider this simple experiment. With a mixed group of males and females set up two tasks. In the first ask the whole group to mentally run through the alphabet and count the number of letters, including the letter 'e', that when pronounced contain the sound 'ee'. Next, ask the group to run through the alphabet mentally and count the number of letters that, when written as capitals, contain curves. In both instances the task is done in the head with no writing, speaking or physical manipulation! Which is harder?

The answer depends on whether you are male or female! Males are better with the shape task; females with the sound task. Why?

Male and female brains differ in some ways. These differences begin before birth and partly explain different behavioural patterns. Significant differences occur in the architecture of the brain – where functions are located, the chemistry of the brain – the presence of different levels of excitatory and inhibitory chemicals, and the interactivity of the brain – the capacity of different functional areas to communicate with each other, especially in times of high arousal.

Male and female brains differ in ways which include hemispheric organisation. To generalise, female brains communicate more effectively across the hemispheres. The corpus callosum which connects left and right is proportionately heavier, is thicker and has more fibres in female brains than in male brains and is less susceptible to shrinkage with age. Functional specialisms are more widely diffused in female brains. It is suggested therefore that women are better communicators – particularly under high levels of challenge – and are better at multitasking and in accessing intuitive experiences. Male brains are more specialised. They are more susceptible to permanent damage from strokes, especially with age, and are more likely to exhibit brain abnormality.

Lansdell's early work confirmed that language and spatial abilities are more bilateral in females, than males. In a piece of research by Witelson, reported in Springer and Deutsch (1998), the number of neurons per unit volume in the auditory cortex was 11 per cent greater in the brains of women in the sample than those of the men. In the auditory area women had more neural capacity to manipulate language.

Women are more attuned to detecting subtle changes of mood and body language: the left hemisphere develops earlier in baby girls than in baby boys. Girls speak earlier but are also more likely to have better internal connections to areas of the brain associated with language functions. Some researchers suggest therefore that emotional 'centres' are better linked to language functions. Baby boys will be better at an earlier age at manipulating themselves and objects through space. For most boys the right hemisphere – associated with depth perception, perspective and conceptualising spatial manipulation – develops earlier than in girls.

Some reported gender differences of interest to educationalists include those summarised in Figure 12.2.

Like many of the generalisations that have emerged about boys and girls, relative performance and about possible differences in preferred learning styles between boys and girls, the list in Figure 12.2 should be treated with caution and, where possible, reflected upon in the light of other research reported on the brain and learning. In brain research, like other areas of research, critical journals do not tend to report 'no difference' findings. Outcomes which are controversial if possibly tenuous are more attractive to editors!

There is a synergy of connections which comes with the attempt to create 'whole-brain' learning. Whether or not there is such a thing as whole-brain learning aside, teachers should heed the lessons from above and:

- be aware that your hemispheric preference – right or left – is not everyone's and challenge your own mental maps about the correct way to do things;
- present your material in ways which stimulate left and right brain and engage the senses; utilise visual display to reinforce learning points;

- aim for a balance of left and right hemisphere activity in classroom lessons and within individual pieces of work which you set;
- avoid rigid adherence to everyone doing the same thing at the same time; encourage learners to challenge themselves by doing some activities which feel uncomfortable;
- engage the emotions through role-play, empathising activities, discussion and debate.

[. . .]

MALES	FEMALES
• are better at spatial reasoning	• are better in grammar and vocabulary
• talk later (usually by age of four years)	• talk earlier (99 per cent by three years)
• have right hemisphere larger than left	• have left hemisphere larger than right
• talk and play more with inanimate objects	• read character and social cues better
• solve mathematical problems non-verbally	• talk while solving mathematical problems
• are three times more likely to be dyslexic	• are less likely to be dyslexic or myopic
• have better general mathematical ability	• have better general verbal ability
• are better at blueprint reading	
• enrol in more remedial reading (4:1)	• have better sensory awareness
• require more space	• perceive sounds better and sing in tune more
• favour right ear	• are slower to anger
• are less at ease with multitasking	• listen with both ears
• have shorter attention span	• handle multitasking more easily
• are more frequently left-handed	• have longer attention span
	• proportionately right- and left-handed
• differentiated hemispheres – hence right for mathematics and spatial skills, left for language	• less marked differentiation between hemispheres
• corpus callosum thinner and with fewer fibres	• corpus callosum thicker relative to brain size
• corpus callosum shrinks 20 per cent by age 50	• corpus callosum doesn't shrink
• reacts to pain slowly	• tolerates long-term pain better
• high tolerance of pain	

Figure 12.2 Gender differences (based on Moir and Jessell (1993) *Brain Sex: The Real Difference Between Men and Women*, Penguin)

Physical readiness for learning

'Our kids don't have very good attention spans, which means that more than ten minutes of talking to them is actually quite redundant, which in itself promotes good learning because you have to think of other ways of promoting learning rather than trying to pass over information from the front.'

(South Bristol Teacher, reported in Bath University, *Departments Adding Significant Value*, 1994)

Unless learners are in the appropriate learning state, it's time to stop everything and start changing their states.

(Jensen, 1996)

The brain is less than 2.4 per cent of body weight yet it accounts for 20 per cent of energy consumption at rest. To do this it needs oxygen and of all the organs in the body the brain is the greediest in fuel consumption. If it does without oxygen for just a few minutes it begins to die. If you are teaching in an airless room on a hot summer afternoon with the students immobilised behind desks then forget about them learning anything!

It doesn't need a neurologist to remind us about meeting basic needs before learning can begin. Abraham Maslow taught us that there is a 'hierarchy of needs' wherein lower level needs must be met before needs on the higher level

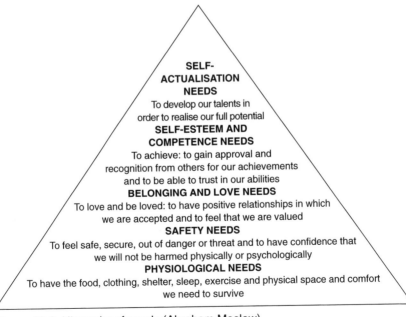

Figure 12.3 Hierarchy of needs (Abraham Maslow)

can begin to be met. He characterised it as a pyramid where movement to the next elevation required the previous level of need to have been satisfied (see Figure 12.3).

Maslow, a psychologist, argued that no matter what level we are currently operating on, all our energy will continually be drawn to any lower level for which we perceive an unmet need. For classroom teachers the message is simple. Students will not learn best when they are hungry, tired, too hot, too cold or too confined. Pay attention to the physical state of the learners in your class and intervene where possible if these factors are getting in the way.

Get them out from behind those desks! We are not designed to sit slumped behind a piece of wood for an hour and ten minutes at a time, nor are we designed to sit for three hours in front of a television screen or a computer terminal! Physical movement enhances learning! If you can learn or rehearse a new topic with accompanying movement it is more likely to be remembered. Furthermore, as you become more practised in a particular series of movements the brain changes its structure. Concert pianists use their brains differently from amateurs. Top sports players, like top musicians, use fewer brain cells than amateurs attempting the same moves and the cells used are more specifically located. Learning is underpinned by physical changes in neural pathways. Visualising or imagining the movements can have a similar effect. Mental rehearsal prepares the brain for learning.

Mobility, even simply standing up can boost learning. Dr Max Vercruysen of the University of Southern California discovered your body's posture affects learning. His research showed that, on the average, standing increased heartbeats. That sends more blood to the brain, which activates the central nervous system to increase neural firing. Researchers found that on the average, there's a 5–15% greater flow of blood and oxygen to the brain when standing. Psychologically, he says, standing up also creates more attentional arousal and the brain learns more.

(Jensen, 1996)

Physical activity, besides strengthening heart and muscles, improves the flow of blood to the brain and increases the connections between neurons. The cerebellum, responsible for movement, contains over half of the brain's neurons with more specific pathways into the rest of the brain than any other system. The simple expedient of insisting on rotating seating arrangements literally provides a different perspective of the classroom experience. Shea and Hodges did research to determine the effects of different types of seating – formal and informal – in the classroom. Shea found that students who preferred informal seating arrangements – comfortable chairs and choice of when to use them – performed significantly better in comprehension tests.

Highs and lows are how we are. In daytime we switch hemispherical dominance on cycles of roughly 90 minutes. In classroom lessons different learners will be on different stages within their natural cycle.

The idea of 'brain gym' is now less easy to deride when presented with evidence of links between movement and thinking skills. One of the most talked about ways of linking movement to brain development involves coordinating the left and the right sides of the body. For most of the population the right side of the brain will control many of the motor functions of the left side of the body and vice versa. Physical activity with coordinated cross-lateral responses will develop neural pathways across the two sides of the brain.

Build in frequent breaks and opportunities to reflect on the learning throughout lessons. Work on a rough guide of chronological age plus one. Twelve-year-olds should come out of task for some form of reflection activity every 13 minutes or so. Use such opportunities to build in review of content. Apply the six times rule – for new content the learners should have encountered it at least six times and in six different ways by the end of the lesson. Without review, recall can drop by as much as 80 per cent within 24 hours. The model recommended is shown in Figure 12.4.

Connecting is about accessing the previous related learning experience before giving the overview or BIG picture then onto task whatever that may be but patterned by frequent short and purposeful breaks known as 'diffusions'. Each diffusion space is an opportunity for physical stretching or brain gym with informal review activities, then back onto task. The brain needs time to assimilate new information, to integrate it and begin to make sense of it.

In addition to physical movement and a multisensory immersion learning environment, it is worth noting in summary what some researchers have found out about the environment and learning. Here is a selection. Read with caution! If you can apply the information do so . . .

- **Heat:** Overheating causes a decrease in all-round performance level in tasks requiring concentration, accuracy, physical dexterity and sensory acuity.
- **Hydration:** Dehydration leads to inattention, drowsiness and poor learning performance. The fluid to electrolyte balance in the body is adversely affected by dehydration and by some high sugar drinks. Put water fountains back in corridors and staffrooms.
- **Ionisation:** The more negatively charged the better. With emissions from smoke, dust, smog, pollutants, chemicals and heating systems the air becomes highly electrified with positive ions. Ionised air raises serotonin levels and stabilises alpha rhythms in the brain. Robert Ornstein (1997) reports that rats exposed to negative ionisation grew a 9 per cent larger cerebral cortex.

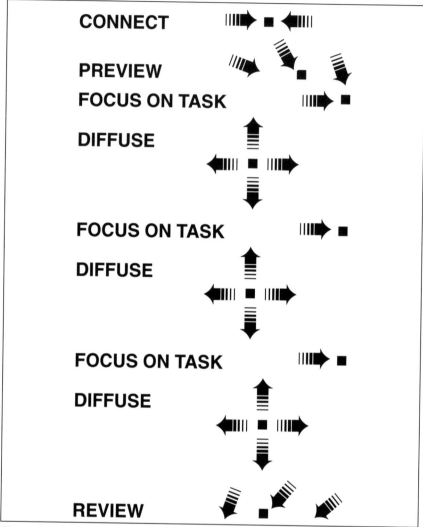

Figure 12.4 Learning model

- **Colours:** In *Color and Human Response* (1984) Faber Birren listed the different tendencies of human response to various colours:

  red – good for creative thinking, short-term high energy
  green – good for productivity, long-term energy
  yellow/orange – conducive to physical work, exercise, positive moods
  blue – slows pulse, lowers blood pressure, helps study and concentration
  light colours – provides minimum disruption across all moods and mental activity

Use light blue for worksheets! White paper with black print is more disruptive to smooth eye patterns.

- **Smell:** Females are more sensitive to odours than males. Most odours disrupt sleep: the heart rate increases and brain waves quicken. Smell, according to Charles Wysocki of the Monell Chemical Sense Centre in Philadelphia, is the only one of the five senses with direct linkage to the limbic system. Associate an experience with a smell and it is remembered for life! Lavender-chamomile scents reportedly reduce stress, lemon, jasmine and cypress induce a positive attitude. Gary Schwartz of the University of Arizona reports that within one minute, spiced apple scents yield more relaxed brain waves and an average drop in blood pressure of five millimetres per person (quoted Howard, 1994).

- **Sleep:** Milk products stimulate melatonin production which improves sleep. Simple sugars and fats decrease the oxygen supply to the brain, which decreases alertness and makes you sleepy. More physical interventions in the afternoon teaching slots! The amount of sleep we require is directly related to our body weight! People who nap consistently live longer and show a 30 per cent lower incidence of heart disease. Visualisation techniques have proved to be a big help in reducing or eliminating nightmares.

- **Lighting:** London conducted research on lighting and classrooms in 1988, involving 160,000 youngsters in his research. He found that on leaving primary school aged 11, over 50 per cent of the students had developed deficiencies related to classroom lighting. Students who were in class-rooms having full-spectrum lighting missed only 65 per cent of the school days missed by others in classrooms. He said, 'ordinary fluorescent light has been shown to raise the cortisol level in the blood, a change likely to suppress the immune system'.

Finally, in terms of physical readiness, be aware that in learning there are 'ah-ha' moments and 'ha' moments. There are occasional 'aaah' moments but there aren't enough 'ha-ha' moments!

Laugh! In his 1989 book, *Head First: the Biology of Hope*, Norman Cousins describes how tests of problem-solving ability yield better results when they are preceded by laughter. Laughter results in an increased number of immune cells and immune cell proliferation, an increased respiratory facility and increased endorphins. He says, 'laughter has a way of turning off posterior hypothalmic activity and freeing the cerebral cortex for stress free activity'. One of the most useful physical movements in the learning environment might be the belly laugh! Ha Ha!

[. . .]

How we store and receive information using three memory systems

How is it that one can walk from one room in the house to another to collect something, arrive in the room, forget what you've come for and have to go back to the original room before you remember?

Memory research has developed considerably in the last ten years. Whereas it used to be believed that memories were stored in specific areas of the brain and memory was regarded as accessing or re-exciting fixed sites, nowadays it is more likely to be described as a process which is both creative and inexact. The neurologists describe memory as learning that sticks. New synapses are formed and old connections are strengthened.

Metaphors for memory have tended to reflect the prevailing technology of the age. Memory does not, however, operate like a reference library, index-card system, filing cabinet or computer database. It is more complex. It is driven by perceived need, context, associations, the intensity and nature of the original experience and perhaps by the individual's preferred representational system. Memories are constructed from neural pathways that fire together in what Susan Greenfield calls a 'patterned neural assembly'. Such patterns are never the same as we constantly elaborate, modify and interpret.

A more useful metaphor for memory is that of the school fire drill. When the alarm sounds the students organise themselves from different lessons and from different places in or out of the building, at different speeds, in different degrees of readiness and with different individuals present or absent on the day. When the classes are assembled they are in roughly the same order but with subtle differences. With memory, the stimulus – the fire alarm – precip-itates a convergence of associated and connected strands of information which come together. The strands of information are like the individual students milling around with some awareness of how they work together to achieve the overall aim. The combination will be different in subtle ways each time dependent on the nature and the 'urgency' of the stimulus. It's never the same.

According to this particular model new learning becomes integrated into a patterning process and with each new integration the base reference points change. We integrate the memory of the memory. In teaching we build on the learner's prior knowledge and models of understanding irrespective of whether these are formally 'correct' or 'incorrect'.

Damasio (1994) shows how, as we are presented with new learning, the brain recalls past experience and references this to base data from different areas of the brain simultaneously. New information can thus be integrated into and thus change neural networks, so giving us an enriched template of experience. He says, 'Some circuits are remodelled over and over throughout the lifespan, according to the changes an organism undergoes. Other circuits remain mostly stable and form the backbone of the notions we have constructed about the world outside'.

Hannaford (1995) says that the reorganisation of base patterns becomes long-term memory and that 'we continue to elaborate and modify the patterning throughout our lives'. The model of memory which scientists are moving towards is one which is characterised by patterning, associations and context. Hannaford argues that the base patterns are 90 per cent in place by five years of age. The capacity to memorise seems to be fully developed by eight years of age. At this point we are able to recall one unit of information for every 100 we receive. A key point for educationalists here is to recognise the significance of teaching thinking and memory skills early.

Now that we have an understanding of how memory works at a neural level we ought not to forget the practical. Teachers need answers to the following questions about memory.

- What's the best way to remember complex information?
- How much information can be remembered by students at any one time?
- How can we improve students' capacity to remember?
- What is the ideal time spent on studying for recall?
- How much time should be spent on review?

Two models of memory are helpful here. The first describes the difference between immediate, short-term and long-term memory. The second three systems that operate within immediate, short- and long-term memory are categorical, procedural and sensory and contextual memory. In the prevailing research model, forming a memory can be described with a sheep pen metaphor.

You round up the sheep – *capturing them in the immediate memory*. Your sheepdogs chase them into a holding pen as you open and close a gate – *you capture them in the short-term memory*. You then transfer them into a larger, more secure pen, again as you open and close another gate – *you capture them in the long-term memory*. The round up is like the immediate memory with the sheepdogs acting like prompts or stimuli for recall. The holding pen, like short-term memory, has flaws. The fencing may be in disrepair and without more careful attention, the sheep may struggle out and need rounding up again. The permanent pen is like long-term memory. Once in, the sheep remain there. All you need to do is remember where the location of the pen is in the landscape.

Immediate memory is a capturing process where thousands of pieces of data can be held for two seconds or less. Here new information pushes out the old unless the old has conscious attention paid to it. The emotions, personal belief systems, context and perceived need direct conscious attention.

Short-term memory is like a holding pen but with gaps in the fencing. The hippocampus, sitting within the limbic system, appears to act as a gatekeeper, selecting chunks of data to remember. A chunk of information is defined as an unfamiliar array of pieces of information. Without conscious attention for a period of at least eight seconds or without rehearsal in an appropriate mode, information can be lost to short-term memory. The sheep escape through gaps in the fence. Try to remember a ten digit telephone number when you have placed your telephone book more than eight seconds away from your telephone and you will know what I mean! Strategies for recall help transfer the memory from the inadequate and temporary pen into the longer-term permanent pen.

Long-term memory involves a significant chemical response in the brain. The neurotransmitters epinephrine and norepinephrine, associated with arousal, are released and act like memory fixatives. James McGaugh, a psychobiologist at the University of California, showed that rats with low levels of epinephrine had poorer recall ability but when injected with epinephrine their ability to recall information to help them perform tasks improved. When we have strong experiences epinephrine seems to tell the brain to hold the information. Here again what seem to matter in directing the brain to hold the information are the emotions and the level of emotional arousal, personal belief systems, the context in which the information is apprehended and the perceived need for retaining it.

To get information into long-term memory be aware of the natural ways in which the brain assigns significance to experience. Here there is a hierarchy of memory systems. Sometimes described as categorical or semantic memory, procedural memory and contextual memory.

Categorical or semantic memory involves rehearsing information through an emphasis on content rather than context. Repetition, rote rehearsal and drilling are features of this recall system. Work done by George Miller in 1956 clearly demonstrated that there were limits to the amounts of information which could be retained by adults using this method. His famous seven plus or minus two formula also applies to younger learners: the younger the learner the fewer the chunks able to be retained. For adults the maximum amount of information which can be retained without chunking or categorising will be nine units.

The advantages of using this system include:

- it is readily understood and easy to manage;
- it provides immediate evidence of success or failure;
- it can combine with other strategies such as mnemonics, rhymes and pegging.

The disadvantages of using this system include:

- it requires high motivation and can be teacher dependent;
- it is short-term without regular rehearsal;
- it is context free and usually difficult to access and transfer;
- it is chunk limited and may require skill in categorising.

Procedural memory is sometimes called sensory memory and involves learning through sensory interaction, particularly movement. It requires little extrinsic motivation and generates physical associations. Research into the role of movement in learning shows that the density and number of neural pathways between the cerebellum – responsible for balance and some motor movement functions – and the cortex is proportionately greater than any other localised system and that movement plays a very important part in learning.

The advantages of using this system include:

- it is 'brain-compatible' with minimal extrinsic motivation;
- information is readily accessed and not necessarily limited by time;
- it is not chunk dependent or dependent on an ability to categorise.

The disadvantages of using this system include:

- sensory associations and opportunities for creating them are difficult in classrooms without preparation;
- it may need to interact with other methods of reinforcement so that a teacher can assess whether learning has occurred;
- some experiences are more difficult to readily recreate via a sensory approach, some classroom subjects will, by their nature – for example, philosophy – challenge the teacher to create opportunities for procedural or sensory learning.

Contextual memory is based on associative connections between location and circumstances in which the information or experience is accessed. It is natural and requires little extrinsic or intrinsic motivation. Sometimes described as state dependence this type of memory system is used by police forces all over the world to stimulate recall. 'People recall information more readily when they can remember the state in which they learned that information' (Howard, 1994). . . . Research cited by Goleman (1996) and by Howard demonstrated that groups performed better in memory test when they 're-created' the context of the original learning.

The advantages of using this system include:

- directly associated with events, circumstances or locations;
- can last for years with moderate review;
- utilises powerful visual storage systems in the brain;
- can be readily utilised by the classroom teacher through managing the learning environment, the nature of input, group-working, metaphor, class visits.

The disadvantages of using this system include:

- requires imagination and detailed pre-planning by teacher;
- poor at details over long-term unless connected with other systems;
- best achieved when new knowledge is built on thematically from what is already known and understood.

We acquire one or two bits of information per second during concentrated study. Decision theorist Herbert Simon says it takes about eight seconds of attention for a new 'bit' to be added to short-term memory. Our average brain capacity is 2.8×10^{20} bits or approximately ten million volumes of books at a thousand pages each.

Jensen (1995), reporting work by Pieron, describes the optimal time on task as 'chronological age plus one or two'. So for ten-year-olds the optimal time would be 11 or 12 minutes on task followed by an interval for reflection or review; for adults a maximum of 25 minutes before some sort of physical break and/or review activity.

The ideal study pattern may be one of **preview-focus-diffuse-focus-diffuse-focus-diffuse-review** (see Figure 12.4). Time spent on focus is age dependent. The younger the learner the shorter the focus time and the longer the time taken to review and integrate the new information.

A simple maxim is to apply the 'six-times rule'. By the end of the teacher–student involvement with the topic the student ought to have encountered the key learning points in at least six different ways. This could be in or out of the formal classroom, before, during or after the topic is covered in a lesson.

To optimise recall teachers should:

- at the beginning of a course go over the content and describe the processes they will use to teach the content;

- with a new unit of work detail the learning outcomes, specify the key words that learners will be able to spell and explain, and provide the questions they will be able to answer;
- start each lesson with a review of what's gone before and a preview of what's to come;
- use open questions to pre-process for student answers and to provoke extended thinking;
- during the lesson build in regular, spaced opportunities for students to review;
- utilise the review, input and memory techniques advocated throughout this chapter;
- at the end of the lesson pack up early and go over the material, preview the next lesson;
- at the end of the unit go over it asking students to memory map the key content; get the students to pair share and then test each other;
- at the end of each term spend the last lessons going over the material and highlighting key points.

References

Alkon, D. (1992) *Memory's Voice: Deciphering the mind-brain code*. New York: Harper Collins.

Birren, F. (1984) *Color and Human Response*. New York: Van Nostrand Rheinhold.

Black, I. B. (1991) *Information in the Brain: A Molecular Perspective*. Cambridge, Mass.: MIT Press.

Boulding, K. (1966) *The Image*. MI: University of Michigan Press.

Caine, R. N., Cane, G. and Cromwell, S. (1994) *Mindshifts: A Brain-Based Process for Restructuring Education*. USA: Zephyr Press.

Carpenter, R. H. S. (1997) *Neurophysiology*, 3rd edn. London: Edward Arnold, Hodder and Stoughton Educational.

Cousins, N. (1989) *Head First: the Biology of Hope*. USA: Penguin.

Damasio, A. (1994) *Descartes' Error: Emotion, Reason and the Human Brain*. New York: Grosset/Putnam.

Diamond, M. (1988) *Enriching Heredity: The Impact of Environment on the Anatomy of the Brain*. New York: Free Press.

Druckman, D. and Swets, J. A. (1988) *Enhancing Human Performance: Issues, Theories and Techniques*. Washington: National Academy Press.

Goleman, D. (1996) *Emotional Intelligence: Why it Can Matter More than IQ*. London: Bloomsbury.

Hannaford, C. (1995) *Smart Moves: Why Learning Is Not All In Your Head*. VA: Great Ocean Publishers.

Harman, W. and Rheingold, H. (1985) *Higher Creativity*. Los Angeles: JP Tarcher.

Hart, L. A. (1983) *The Human Brain and Human Learning*. New York: Addison Wesley Longman.

Higbee, K. L. (1996) *Your Memory: How it Works and How to Improve It*, 2nd edn. New York: Marlowe.

Howard, J. (1994) *The Ozoner's Manual for the Brain – Everyday Applications from Mind-Brain Research*. Texas: Bard Press.

James, O. (1997) *Britain on the Couch – Treating a low Serotonin Society*. London: Century.

Jensen, E. (1994) *The Learning Brain*. USA: Turning Point.

Jensen, E. (1995) *Brain-Based Learning and Teaching*. USA: Turning Point.

Jenson, E. (1995) *Superteaching: Master Strategies for building student success*. Brain Store Inc.

Jensen, E. (1996) *Completing the Puzzle: A Brain-Based Approach to Learning*. USA: Turning Point.

Kotulak, R. (1996) *Inside the Brain*. MO: Andrews and McMeel.

London Borough of Croydon (1996) *Pupil Motivation Research*. BRMB International.

MacLean, P. D. (1990) *The Triune Brain in Evolution*. New York: Plenum.

Moir, A. and Jessell, D. (1993) *Brain Sex: The Real Difference Between Men and Women*. London: Michael Joseph, Penguin Books.

Odam, G. (1995) *The Sounding Symbol: Music Education in Action*. Stroud: Stanley Thornes.

Ornstein, R. (1997) *The Right Mind: Making Sense of the Hemispheres*. New York: Harcourt Brace.

Samuels, M. and Samuels, N. (1975) *Seeing with the mind's eye: the history, techniques and uses of visualisation*. New York.

Springer, S. P. and Deutsch, G. (1998) *Left Brain, Right Brain: Perspectives from Cognitive Neuroscience*. New York: Freeman.

University of Bath (1994) *A Study of Departments Adding Significant Value*. University of Bath and Avon TVEE.

Wenger, W. (1996) *The Einstein Factor*. California: Prima Publishing.

Newspaper articles

Observer (1997) 'The blind shall see and the deaf hear – without a doctor', John Illman, London, 4 May.

Chapter 13

The theory of Multiple Intelligences

Howard Gardner

Editors' Note: This chapter explains in more detail ideas about 'Multiple Intelligences' which are mentioned in both Chapters 11 and 15. It draws on summaries of Gardner's (1983) book *Frames of Mind*.

Contrasting points of view

Two 11-year-old children are taking a test of 'intelligence'. They sit at their desks labouring over the meanings of different words, the interpretation of graphs, and the solutions to arithmetic problems. They record their answers by filling in small circles on a single piece of paper. Later these completed answer sheets are scored objectively: the number of right answers is converted into a standardised score that compares the individual child with a population of children of similar age.

The teachers of these children review the different scores. They notice that one of the children has performed at a superior level; on all sections of the test, she answered more questions correctly than did her peers. In fact, her score is similar to that of children three to four years older. The other child's performance is 'average' – his scores reflect those of other children his age.

A subtle change in expectations surrounds the review of these test scores. Teachers begin to expect the first child to do quite well during her formal schooling, whereas the second should have only moderate success. Indeed these predictions come true. In other words, the test taken by the 11-year-olds serves as a reliable predictor of their later performance in school.

How does this happen? One explanation involves our free use of the word 'intelligence': the child with the greater 'intelligence' has the ability to solve problems, to find the answers to specific questions, and to learn new material quickly and efficiently. These skills in turn play a central role in school success. In this view, 'intelligence' is a singular faculty that is brought to bear in any problem-solving situation. Since schooling deals largely with solving problems of various sorts, predicting this capacity in young children predicts their future success in school.

'Intelligence', from this point of view, is a general ability that is found in varying degrees in all individuals. It is the key to success in solving problems. This ability can be measured reliably with standardised pencil-and-paper tests that, in turn, predict future success in school (Cooley and Lohnes, 1976).

What happens after school is completed? Consider the two individuals in the example. Looking further down the road, we find that the 'average' student has become a highly successful mechanical engineer who has risen to a position of prominence in both the professional community of engineers as well as in civic groups in his community. His success is no fluke – he is considered by all to be a talented individual. The 'superior' student, on the other hand, has had little success in her chosen career as a writer; after repeated rejections by publishers, she has taken up a middle management position in a bank. While certainly not a 'failure' she is considered by her peers to be quite 'ordinary' in her adult accomplishments. So what happened?

This fabricated example is based on the facts of intelligence testing. IQ tests predict school performance with considerable accuracy, but they are only an indifferent predictor of performance in a profession after formal schooling (Jencks, 1972.) Furthermore, even as IQ tests measure only logical or logical linguistic capacities, in this society we are nearly 'brain-washed' to restrict the notion of intelligence to the capacities used in solving logical and linguistic problems.

To introduce an alternative point of view, undertake the following *Gedanken* experiment. Suspend the usual judgement of what constitutes intelligence and let your thoughts run freely over the capabilities of humans – perhaps those that would be picked out by the proverbial Martian visitor. In this exercise, you are drawn to the brilliant chess player, the world-class violinist, and the champion athlete; such outstanding performers deserve special consideration. Under this experiment, a quite different view of intelligence emerges. Are the chess player, violinist, and athlete 'intelligent' in these pursuits? If they are, then why do our tests of 'intelligence' fail to identify them? If they are not 'intelligent', what allows them to achieve such astounding feats? In general, why does the contemporary construct 'intelligence' fail to explain large areas of human endeavour?

In this chapter we approach these problems through the theory of Multiple Intelligences (MI). As the name indicates, we believe that human cognitive competence is better described in terms of a set of abilities, talents, or mental skills, which we call 'Intelligences'. All normal individuals possess each of these skills to some extent; individuals differ in the degree of skill and in the nature of their combination. We believe this theory of intelligence may be more humane and more veridical than alternative views of intelligence and that it more adequately reflects the data of human 'intelligent' behaviour. Such a theory has important educational implications, including ones for curriculum development.

The question of the optimal definition of 'intelligence' looms large in our inquiry. Indeed, it is at the level of this definition that the theory of Multiple Intelligences diverges from more traditional points of view. In a more traditional view, intelligence is defined operationally as the ability to answer items on tests of intelligence. The inference from the test scores to some underlying ability is supported by statistical techniques that compare responses of subjects at different ages; the apparent correlation of these test scores across ages and across different tests corroborates the notion that the general faculty of intelligence, 'g', does not change much with age or with training or experience. It is an inborn attribute or faculty of the individual (Eysenck, 1983).

Multiple Intelligences theory, on the other hand, pluralises the traditional concept. An intelligence entails the ability to solve problems or fashion products that are of consequence in a particular cultural setting. The problem-solving skill allows one to approach a situation in which a goal is to be obtained and to locate the appropriate route to that goal. The creation of a *cultural* product is crucial to such functions as capturing and transmitting knowledge or expressing one's views or feelings. The problems to be solved range from creating an end to a story to anticipating a mating move in chess to repairing a quilt. Products range from scientific theories to musical compositions to successful political campaigns.

MI theory is framed in light of the biological origins of each problem-solving skill. Only those skills that are universal to the human species are treated. Even so, the biological proclivity to participate in a particular form of problem solving must also be coupled with the cultural nurturing of that domain. For example, language, a universal skill, may manifest itself particularly as writing in one culture, as oratory in another culture, and as the secret language of anagrams in a third.

Given the desire of selecting intelligences that are rooted in biology, and which are valued in one or more cultural settings, how does one actually identify an 'intelligence'? In coming up with our list, we consulted evidence from several different sources; knowledge about normal development and development in gifted individuals; information about the breakdown of cognitive skills under conditions of brain damage; studies of exceptional populations, including prodigies, *idiots savants*, and autistic children; data about the evolution of cognition over the millennia; cross-cultural accounts of cognition; psychometric studies, including examinations of correlations among tests; and psychological training studies, particularly measures of transfer and generalisation across tasks. Only those candidate intelligences that satisfied all or a majority of the criteria were selected as bona fide intelligences.

In addition to satisfying these criteria, each intelligence must have an identifiable core operation or set of operations. As a neutrally based computational system, each intelligence is activated or 'triggered' by certain kinds of internally or externally presented information.

An intelligence must also be susceptible to encoding in a symbol system – a culturally contrived system of meaning, which captures and conveys important forms of information. Language, picturing, and mathematics are but three nearly worldwide symbol systems that are necessary for human survival and productivity. The relationship of a candidate intelligence to a human symbol system is no accident. In fact, the existence of a core computational capacity anticipates the existence of a symbol system which exploits that capacity. While it may be possible for an intelligence to proceed without an accompanying symbol system, a primary characteristic of human intelligence may well be its gravitation towards such an embodiment.

The Multiple Intelligences

(This section summarises descriptions and contains quotations from Gardner's (1983) book *Frames of Mind*.)

This analysis of a wider and more disparate set of data about human intellectual abilities suggests a minimum of seven distinct intelligences; logical-mathematical, linguistic, spatial, bodily-kinaesthetic, musical, inter-personal, and intrapersonal. A brief description of each of these intelligences is now presented.

Logical-mathematical intelligence

This intelligence can be understood as the ability, described in Piaget's theory of intellectual development, which involves the formal operation of symbols according to accepted rules of logic and mathematics. It is this intelligence that has been almost exclusively measured in 'intelligence tests'. Although it has been given pre-eminence in Western societies, there is no reason to believe that it is more fundamental than the other intelligences. There is more than one form of logic and each intelligence has an equally valid logic of its own.

Linguistic intelligence

There is strong neurological evidence for citing the existence of a separate linguistic intelligence. People with brain damage to a specific location in the left hemisphere have grave difficulty in forming grammatical utterances, although other thought processes are apparently unaffected. The linguistic intelligence makes use of rhetoric, for persuasion, allows us to develop semantic storage of information, and also to explain events, including its own operations.

It differs from logical-mathematical intelligence in having a strong auditory/oral component and in not being tied to the world of physical objects.

Spatial intelligence

This intelligence enables us to recognise faces, to find our way around a site, and to notice fine details. All these capacities are affected by damage to parts of the right hemisphere of the brain. Spatial intelligence is perhaps seen at its most developed among certain islanders who are able to navigate long distances by the stars.

> Central to spatial intelligence are the capacities to perceive the visual world accurately, to perform transformations and modifications upon one's initial perceptions, and to be able to re-create aspects of one's visual experience, even in the absence of relevant physical stimuli.
> (Gardner, 1983, p.173)

Bodily-kinaesthetic intelligence

This intelligence describes the abilities to use the body or parts of the body to solve problems or to produce worthwhile products or displays. It involves at its core the capacities to control bodily motions and to handle objects skilfully. In different forms and combinations it is exemplified by skilled dancers, athletes, surgeons, and instrumentalists. Again it is possible to identify these skills with a specific area of the brain, in this case the motor cortex.

Musical intelligence

It is possible that language and music evolved together as a single auditory–oral intelligence, but in the present day they appear to be separate, with many examples of people with high musical, but low linguistic, intelligences. Musical intelligence involves the capacities for imitation of vocal targets, for sensitivity to relative as well as absolute pitch, and for appreciating various kinds of musical transformations.

Interpersonal intelligence

> The core capacity here is *the ability to notice and make distinctions among other individuals* and, in particular, among their moods, temperaments,

motivations, and intentions. . . . Interpersonal knowledge permits a skilled adult to read the intentions and desires – even when these have been hidden – of many other individuals and, potentially, to act upon this knowledge – for example, by influencing a group of disparate individuals to behave along desired lines. We see highly developed forms of interpersonal intelligence in political and religious leaders . . . in skilled parents and teachers, and in individuals enrolled in the helping professions, be they therapists, counsellors, or shamans.

(Gardner, 1983, p.240)

Intrapersonal intelligence

The core capacity at work here is access to *one's own feeling life* – one's range of affects or emotions: the capacity instantly to effect discriminations among these feelings and, eventually, to label them, to enmesh them in symbolic codes, to draw upon them as a means of understanding and guiding one's behaviour. . . . One finds this form of intelligence in a novelist (like Proust) who can write introspectively about feelings, in the patient (or therapist) who comes to attain a deep knowledge of his own feeling life, in the wise elder who draws upon his own wealth of inner experiences in order to advise members of his community.

(Gardner, 1983, pp.239–40)

Of these seven intelligences, spatial, logical-mathematical, and bodily-kinaesthetic are all 'object related': they depend on relationships with the external physical world. Language and music are, in contrast, 'object-free'.

Finally, the personal forms of intelligence reflect a set of powerful and competing constraints: the existence of one's own person; the existence of other persons; the culture's presentations and interpretations of selves. There will be universal features of any sense of person or self, but also considerable cultural nuances, reflecting a host of historical and individuating factors.

(Gardner, 1983, p.278)

The unique contributions of the theory

As human beings, we all have a repertoire of skills for solving different kinds of problems. Our investigation has begun, therefore, with a consideration of these problems, the contexts they are found in, and the culturally significant products that are the outcome. We have not approached 'intelligence' as a reified human faculty that is brought to bear in literally any problem setting; rather, we have begun with the problems that humans *solve* and worked back to the 'intelligences' that must be responsible.

Evidence from brain research, human development, evolution, and cross-cultural comparisons was brought to bear in our search for the relevant human intelligences: a candidate was included only if reasonable evidence to support its membership was found across these diverse fields. Again, this tack differs from the traditional one: since no candidate faculty is *necessarily* an intelligence, we could choose on a motivated basis. In the traditional approach to 'intelligence', there is no opportunity for this type of empirical decision.

We have also determined that these multiple human faculties, the intelligences, are to a significant extent *independent*. For example, research with brain-damaged adults repeatedly demonstrates that particular faculties can be lost while others are spared. This independence of intelligences implies that a particularly high level of ability in one intelligence, say mathematics, does not require a similarly high level in another intelligence, like language or music. This independence of intelligences contrasts sharply with traditional measures of IQ that find high correlations among test scores. We speculate that the usual correlations among subtests of IQ tests come about because all of these tasks in fact measure the ability to respond rapidly to items of a logical-mathematical or linguistic sort; we believe that these correlations would be substantially reduced if one were to survey in a contextually appropriate way the full range of human problem-solving skills.

Until now, we have supported the fiction that adult roles depend largely on the flowering of a single intelligence. In fact, however, nearly every cultural role of any degree of sophistication requires a combination of intelligences. Thus, even an apparently straightforward role like playing the violin transcends a reliance on simple musical intelligence. To become a successful violinist requires bodily-kinaesthetic dexterity, and the interpersonal skills of relating to an audience and, in a different way, choosing a manager; quite possibly it involves an intrapersonal intelligence as well. Dance requires skills in bodily-kinaesthetic, musical, interpersonal, and spatial intelligences in varying degrees. Politics requires an interpersonal skill, a linguistic facility, and perhaps some logical aptitude. Inasmuch as nearly every cultural role requires several intelligences, it becomes important to consider individuals as a collection of aptitudes rather than as having a singular problem-solving faculty that can be measured directly through pencil-and-paper tests. Even given a relatively small number of such intelligences, the diversity of human ability is created through the differences in these profiles. In fact, it may well be that the 'total is greater than the sum of the parts'. An individual may not be particularly gifted in any intelligence; and yet, because of a particular combination or blend of skills, he or she may be able to fill some niche uniquely well.

Thus it is of paramount importance to assess the particular combination of skills which may earmark an individual for a certain vocational or avocational niche (Walters and Gardner, 1985).

Coping with the plurality of intelligences

Under the Multiple Intelligences theory, an intelligence can serve both as the content of instruction and the means or medium for communicating that content. This state of affairs has important ramifications for instruction. For example, suppose that a child is learning some mathematical principle but is not skilled in logical-mathematical intelligence. That child will probably experience some difficulty during the learning process. The reason for the difficulty is straightforward: the mathematical principle to be learned (the content) exists only in the logical-mathematical world and it ought to be communicated through mathematics (the medium). That is, the mathematical principle cannot be translated entirely into words (which is a linguistic medium) or spatial models (a spatial medium). At some point in the learning process, the mathematics of the principle must 'speak for itself'. In our present case, it is at just this level that the learner experiences difficulty – the learner (who is not especially 'mathematical') and the problem (which is very much 'mathematical') are not in accord. Mathematics, as a *medium*, has failed.

Although this situation is a necessary conundrum in light of the Multiple Intelligences theory, we can propose various solutions. In the present example, the teacher must attempt to find an alternative route to the mathematical content – a metaphor in another medium. Language is perhaps the most obvious alternative, but spatial modelling and even a bodily-kinaesthetic metaphor may prove appropriate in some cases. In this way, the student is given a *secondary* route to the solution to the problem, perhaps through the medium of an intelligence that is relatively strong for that individual.

Two features of this hypothetical scenario must be stressed. First, in such cases, the secondary route – the language, spatial model, or whatever – is at best a metaphor or translation. It is not mathematics itself. And at some point, the learner must translate back into the domain of mathematics. Without this translation, what is learned tends to remain at a relatively superficial level; cookbook-style mathematical performance results from following instructions (linguistic translation) without understanding why (mathematics retranslation).

Second, the alternative route is not guaranteed. There is no *necessary* reason why a problem in one domain *must be translatable* into a metaphorical problem in another domain. Successful teachers find these translations with relative frequency; but as learning becomes more complex, the likelihood of a successful translation diminishes.

While Multiple Intelligences theory is consistent with much empirical evidence, it has not been subjected to strong experimental tests within psychology. Within the area of education, the applications of the theory are even more tentative and speculative. Our hunches will have to be revised many times in the light of actual classroom experience. Still there are important reasons for considering the theory of Multiple Intelligences and its implications for education. First of all, it is clear that many talents, if not intelligences, are overlooked nowadays; individuals with these talents are the chief casualties of the single-minded, single-funnelled approach to the mind. There are many unfilled or poorly filled niches in our society and it would be opportune to guide individuals with the right set of abilities to these billets. Finally, our world is beset with problems; to have any chance of solving them, we must make the very best use of the intelligences we possess. Perhaps recognising the plurality of intelligences and the manifold ways in which human individuals may exhibit them is an important first step.

Note

This chapter is based on extracts from an article by J. Walters and H. Gardner (1984) published by and reprinted with the permission of the Association for Supervision and Curriculum Development, and on summaries from *Frames of Mind* by Howard Gardner (1983) published by Basic Books (New York).

References

Cooley, W. W. and Lohnes, P. R. (1976) *Evaluation Research in Education*. New York: Irvington Publications.

Eysenck, H. J. (1983) 'The nature of intelligence', in Friedman, M. P., Das, J. P. and O'Connor, N. (eds) *Intelligence and Learning*. New York: Plenum Press.

Gardner, H. (1983) *Frames of Mind*. New York: Basic Books.

Jencks, C. (1972) *Inequality: A Reassessment of the Effect of Family and Schooling in America*. New York: Basic Books.

Walters, J. and Gardner, G. (1985) 'The theory of multiple intelligences: some issues and answers', in Sternberg, R. and Wagner, R. (eds) *Practical Intelligence: Origins of Competence in the Everyday World*. Cambridge: Cambridge University Press.

Chapter 14

Dialogues for teaching and learning

Neil Mercer and Lyn Dawes

Editors' Note: The authors draw on their considerable research into the 'talk' used in classrooms to illustrate how teachers can 'scaffold' the learning of their pupils by the nature of the interactions with pupils and by skilfully arranging meaningful talk between pupils.

Introduction

In this chapter, we argue three main points: first, that one of the most important aims of education ought to be to develop children's capability in using language effectively as a tool for thinking collectively; secondly, that by the use of particular methods and strategies teachers can make a significant contribution to this development; and thirdly, that the development of children's use of language as a tool for collective thinking helps the development of their individual intellectual capabilities. To do so, we will first draw on research about parent–child interaction to discuss the relationship between children's engagement in dialogue and the development of their understanding. Shifting the focus then to schools, we consider education as a dialogic process in which both the talk between teachers and learners and talk among learners have important roles to play. We describe some classroom-based research which has enabled teachers to develop effective ways of encouraging the development of children's use of spoken language.

We also hope to show how such research can provide answers to some intriguing theoretical questions about the relationship between thought, language and social activity. The Russian psychologist Lev Vygotsky, who died in 1935, is now regarded as the founder of what is usually called 'sociocultural research'. This is an approach to the study of intellectual development and education which proposes that there is a close relationship between the use of language as a cultural tool (in social interaction) and the use of language as a psychological tool (for organising our own, individual thinking). Vygotsky also suggested that our involvement in joint activities can generate new understandings which we then 'internalise' as individual knowledge and capabilities. Although developmental psychologists have treated his claims about the connections between 'intermental' and 'intramental' activity with great interest, surprisingly little evidence has been offered to support or refute them. Towards the end of this chapter we will describe some classroom-based research which has provided such evidence.

Development from a sociocultural perspective

Most of Vygotsky's work was published posthumously in Russian, and only reached wider audiences through translation into English and other languages in the latter part of the twentieth century (e.g. Vygotsky, 1978; his distinctive contribution is discussed in Wertsch, 1985a). It is thus only in recent years that the sociocultural perspective on human intellectual development has been developed by other researchers. The central idea underpinning it is that individual development is integrated with the longer-term historical development of our species; and that language plays a vital role in achieving this integration. Psychological and anthropological studies of adult–child relations, observed in many cultures, support the view that growing up is an 'apprenticeship in thinking', an induction into ways with words and ways of thinking which is achieved through dialogue. (See for example, Heath, 1983; Rogoff, 1990, 1995; Wells, 1992.) This research has highlighted the importance of the role that parents and other people play in helping children learn, in the course of everyday joint activity. However, little of that research has been concerned with the activity of adults as self-conscious teachers or instructors, or in the ways children seek guidance or information to improve their understanding. Adults do not only allow children to participate in family activities, they also deliberately provide them with information and explanations and instruct them in ways to behave. And children, on their part, may take active roles in soliciting help or obtaining information and transforming what they are given into their own new understanding. They can also contest what they are told, by adults or other children, and gain understanding from engaging in argument. We can begin to illustrate these points through the following sequence of dialogue. It comes from a conversation between one of us and our daughter Anna, which happened when she was two years old. At that time, I (NM) was regularly recording our talk when I was looking after her. On this occasion, the topic of our conversation had continued from a little earlier the same evening, when for the first time she had seen bats flying round the house. I had pointed to the eaves, where I had said the bats slept.

Sequence 1: Bats in the roof

Me: What did you think of the bats?

Anna: What?

Me: Did you like the bats?

Anna: Yeh.

Me: Think of those bats now, they're out flying around now. Aren't they?

Anna: They not going – are they lying on the roof?

Me: What about them?

Anna: Lie on the roof.

Me: Oh yeh.

Anna: They not, but not inside.

Me: Yeh, I think they do go inside the roof.

Anna: But not in.

Me: You don't think so?

Anna: Not in!

Me: Not in the roof? I think they go inside the roof. That's where they go to sleep in the day.

Anna: *(sounding confused)* But they, they not going *in*side it.

Me: Why? *(laughing)* Why do you think that?

Anna: *(also laughing)* But they are not going *in*side it.

Me: They can get inside it. There are little kind of holes round the edge of the roof, at the top of the walls and they creep in there.

Anna: They go there to bye-byes now?

Me: Yeh- no, they go to bye-byes in the day. They're just coming out now.

Anna: Are they not going to bye-byes now?

Me: No, they go to bye-byes in the day, in the morning, and they fly around all night. They get up at night and go out.

It seems that our earlier conversation, while watching the bats, had left Anna with some intellectual dissatisfaction with what she had heard me explain about the lifestyle of the bats. This motivated her to ask whether the bats' habit was to sleep lying on the roof, thus questioning my own earlier statement that they slept inside it. As can be seen from the transcript, when I would not confirm her existing belief, she reiterated it four times, continuing to do so until I offered a more elaborated explanation of how the bats might enter the roof. She seemed to accept this explanation as reasonable, because in her next statement she asked if the bats were now going 'there' to sleep. As we continued on this topic, it became apparent to me that she did not understand that the bats were nocturnal, and so I tried also to explain this feature of their lifestyle.

The information children gain through language may sometimes be, or at least appear to be, incompatible with experience gained in other ways, or with their existing understandings which have been formed through past experience. Language provides both a means for generating a motivating kind of cognitive conflict and also a means for resolving it. Using language, children can actively test their understanding against that of others, and may use argument to elicit relevant information and explanations from adults and other children about what they perceive – and what they want to know.

The role of adults in the process of development

Research on the casual adult–child interactions of everyday life has revealed that adults often rely on particular techniques or guidance strategies for generating a common frame of reference during an episode of teaching-and-learning. For example, Wertsch (1985b) observed parents of young children using two techniques. The first, which he calls 'establishing a referential perspective', is when an adult responds to a child's apparent lack of comprehension by referring to other shared knowledge. Imagine, for instance, that while on a country walk a parent says to a child 'Look, there's a tractor'. If this reference fails (that is, the child doesn't seem to realise which object is being referred to), the adult may then say something like 'Can you see, that big green thing with enormous wheels?' In doing this, the adult is drawing on resources of common knowledge to build a shared contextual frame of reference, based on the reasonable assumption that the child's understanding of basic features like colour and appearance will help him identify the strange object in question. Coupled with this technique, adults use a kind of reverse process which Wertsch calls 'abbreviation'. This is when, over the course of time, an adult begins to assume that new common knowledge has been successfully established, and so when talking to the child makes progressively more abbreviated or cryptic references to what is being discussed. For example, the next time the same parent and child are out in the countryside, the parent may first point out 'another big green tractor', but then later just refer to 'the tractor'. In these ways, by creating common knowledge and then gradually assuming its existence, the adult first provides a 'scaffolding' to support the child's developing understanding and then dismantles it as the child becomes able to sustain his new understanding independently. It is important to note that from such experiences the child can gain not only a better understanding of the experience being discussed with the adult, but also of how language can be used effectively as a tool for describing and consolidating shared experience.

Research in schools has revealed that teachers also depend on the use of particular linguistic strategies for guiding, monitoring and assessing the activities they organise for their pupils (in ways described in Edwards and

145

Mercer, 1987; Mercer, 1995). All teachers ask their pupils a lot of questions. Most teachers also regularly offer their classes *recaps* – summaries of what they consider to be the salient features of a past event, which can help students to relate current activity to past experience. Teachers also often *elaborate* and *reformulate* the contributions made to classroom dialogue by pupils (for example in response to a teacher's questions) as a way of clarifying what has been said for the benefit of others, and also making connections between the content of children's utterances and the technical terminology of the curriculum (Lemke, 1990; Wells, 1999). These strategies seem to be in common use throughout the world, even though teaching styles and ways of organising class-rooms vary within and across cultures (see Edwards and Westgate, 1994 and Mercer, 1995 for a review of relevant research).

Of course, like the tools of any trade, teachers can use these common discursive strategies relatively well or badly. To make such an evaluation, we need to consider what their intended educational purpose might be. For a teacher to teach and a learner to learn, both partners need to use talk and joint activity to create a shared framework of understanding from the resources of their common knowledge and common interests or goals. Talk is the principal tool for creating this framework, and by questioning, recapping, reformulating, elaborating and so on teachers are usually seeking to draw pupils into a shared understanding of the activities in which they are engaged. We find it useful to think of this shared understanding as an 'intermental development zone' (IDZ) in which educational activity takes place. The IDZ is a dynamic frame of reference which is recon-stituted constantly as the dialogue continues, so enabling the teacher and learner to think together through the activity in which they are involved. If the quality of the IDZ is successfully maintained, misunderstandings will be minimised and motivations will be maximised. If this is successful, the teacher will be able to help the learner transcend his established capabilities and to consolidate his experience in the zone as improved capability and understanding. If the dialogue fails to keep minds mutually attuned, however, the IDZ collapses and the scaffolded learning grinds to a halt. The IDZ is a mutual achievement, dependent on the interactive participation and commitment of both teacher and learner; but a teacher must take special responsibility for its creation and maintenance. It is a continuing, contextualising framework for joint activity, whose effectiveness is likely to depend on how well a teacher can create and maintain connections between the curriculum-based goals of activity and a learner's existing knowledge, capabilities and motivations. (The relationships between the idea of the IDZ and the well-established sociocultural concepts of 'scaffolding' and the Zone of Proximal Development are discussed in Mercer, 2000, Chapter 6.) In the next section we will describe some strategies that teachers can use to successfully develop IDZs with their pupils and so help them make the most of their educational experience.

Some characteristics of effective teaching

For several years now, our research in primary schools in England has been linked with schools-based research in Mexico, led by Sylvia Rojas-Drummond at the Autonomous University of Mexico (UNAM). One focus of the Mexican research has been a comparison of teachers in state schools whose pupils had been found to develop particularly well in reading comprehension and mathematical problem solving, with teachers in similar schools whose pupils have not made such significant achievements. Using video recordings of class-room interactions, our analysis has tried to discover if the better teachers differed from those who were less successful in the ways they interacted with their pupils. Essentially, we have tried to see if the better teachers were pro-viding a more effective 'scaffolding' for their pupils' learning. We have also been interested in what kinds of learning teachers appeared to be encouraging.

Our analysis covered several features of classroom interaction, including teachers' uses of questions. We looked at the content of tasks, activities and discussions, at the extent to which teachers encouraged pupils to talk together, and the kinds of explanations and instructions teachers provided to pupils for the tasks they set them. The results of this time-consuming and complex analysis (described in detail in Wegerif, Rojas-Drummond and Mercer, 1999; Rojas-Drummond, 2000; Rojas-Drummond, Mercer and Dabrowski, in press) can be summarised as follows. We found that the more effective teachers could be distinguished by the following characteristics:

1. *They used question-and-answer sequences not just to test knowledge, but also to guide the development of understanding.* These teachers often used questions to discover the initial levels of pupils' understanding and adjust their teaching accordingly, and used 'why' questions to get pupils to reason and reflect about what they were doing.
2. *They taught not just 'subject content', but also procedures for solving problems and making sense of experience.* This included teachers demonstrating the use of problem-solving strategies for children, explaining to children the meaning and purpose of classroom activities, and using their interactions with children as opportunities for encouraging children to make explicit their own thought processes.
3. *They treated learning as a social, communicative process.* Most, if not all, teachers make regular use of a set of conventional dialogic techniques – question-and-answer sessions, recaps, reformulations and so on. The more effective teachers used these effectively to do such things as encouraging pupils to give reasons for their views, organising interchanges of ideas and mutual support among pupils and generally encouraging pupils to take a more active, vocal role in classroom events.

The findings of this research are in accord with those of other researchers (see for example Brown and Palinscar, 1989). Teachers have found their involvement in the research useful for examining their own practice. This suggests that it is useful for teachers to become aware of the techniques they use in dialogue and what they are trying to achieve through using them. Even very good teachers, who probably do these things without being aware that they do, seem nevertheless to appreciate gaining this kind of awareness.

As we suggested earlier, effective teaching does not simply depend on the use of particular interactive techniques, it depends on what they are used to achieve. The better Mexican teachers *and* those who were less effective were all using elicitations, recaps, reformulations and other conventional features of the everyday language of classroom life. The crucial difference between the two sets of teachers was how and when they used them, and what they used them to teach. They differed significantly in the extent to which they used dialogue to help children see the relevance of past experience and common knowledge, and in the opportunities they provided for children to explain their own understanding or misunderstanding. When setting up activities or reviewing them with children, the most effective teachers used language to support and guide the children's activity. They also encouraged more active and extended participation in dialogue on the part of the children. The extent to which the children themselves contribute to the establishment and maintenance of an IDZ is of course crucial. That is, the 'ground rules' of classroom interaction must offer them legitimate opportunities to express their uncertainties and reveal their confusions, and to request information and explanations from others who are more knowledgeable. The quality of children's educational experience is significantly affected by the extent to which their dialogue with the teacher gives what they are doing in class a continuity of meaning (so that activity is contextualised by the history of past experience) and a comprehensible and worthwhile purpose.

These findings suggest that a good primary school teacher is not simply the instructor or facilitator of the learning of a large and disparate set of individuals, but rather the creator of a particular quality of intermental environment – a 'community of enquiry' (Lipman, 1970; Wells, 1999) in which students can take active and reflective roles in the development of their own understanding. In such classrooms, the students are apprentices in collective thinking, under the expert guidance of their teacher. We will return to these matters shortly, after some consideration of talk among children when a teacher or other 'expert' adult is not involved.

Talk among learners

A sociocultural perspective helps us appreciate the reciprocal relationship between individual thinking and the collective intellectual activities of groups. We use language to transform individual thought into collective thought and action, and also to make personal interpretations of shared experience. Not only the intellectual development of early childhood but the whole of human life depends on the maintenance of a dynamic relationship between the social and the psycholological – the 'intermental' and the 'intramental'. So far, we have focused on how the pursuit of intermentality figures in the relationships between adults as 'experts' and children as 'novices'. But as well as learning from the guidance and example of adults, children (and novices of all ages) also learn the skills of thinking collectively by acting and talking with each other. Any account of intellectual development which was based only on the study of dialogues between older and younger generations of a community would of course be inadequate. Members of a younger generation use language among themselves to generate their own, shared understandings and to pursue their own interests. Each generation is active in creating the new knowledge it wants, and in doing so the communal resources of the language toolkit may be transformed. But it is worth noting that even the rebellious creativity of a new generation is, in part, the product of a dialogue between generations.

Language offers children a means for simulating events together in play, in ways which may enable the participants to make better sense of the actual experiences on which the play is based. The Dutch researcher Ed Elbers (1994) collected some interesting examples of children engaged in this kind of play activity. Like many children, when they were aged six and seven, his two daughters enjoyed setting up play 'schools' together with toy animals. They would act out scenarios in which, with one of them as the teacher, the assembled creatures would act out the routines of a school day. But Elbers noticed that one typical feature of their play school was that incidents which disrupted classroom life took place with surprising frequency. Here is one such example (translated by Elbers from the Dutch). Margareet is the eldest girl, being nearly eight years old, and here takes the role of the teacher. Elisabeth, her younger (six-year-old) sister, acts out the role of a rather naughty pupil.

Sequence 2: Play school

Margareet:	Children, sit down.
Elisabeth:	I have to go to the toilet, Miss.
Margareet:	Now, children, be quiet.
Elisabeth:	I have to go to the toilet.

Margareet:	I want to tell you something.
Elisabeth:	*(loud)* I have to go to the toilet!
Margareet:	*(chuckles)* Wait a second.
Elisabeth:	*(with emphasis)* Miss, I have to go to the toilet!!
Margareet:	OK, you can go.
Elisabeth:	*(cheekily)* Where is it? *(laughs)*
Margareet:	Over there, under that box, the one with the animals on, where the dangerous animals . . . *(chuckles)* under there.
Elisabeth:	Really?
Margareet:	Yes.

(Elbers, 1994, p.230)

In this sequence we can see a child appropriating an adult's way with words. 'Now, children, be quiet' is exactly the kind of teacher-talk that Margareet will have heard every day in 'real' school. But Elbers suggests we can also interpret this sequence as an example of children reflecting together on the rules which govern their behaviour in school, and how the robustness of these rules can be tested. They can play with ideas of power and control without risking the community sanctions which such behaviour would incur in 'real life'. Teachers normally have to be obeyed, and children are not meant to leave the class during lessons – but given the legitimate excuse of having to go to the toilet, how can a child not get her way? Sometimes, in setting up this kind of activity, the girls (out of role) would discuss how best to ensure that such disruptive incidents occurred. For example:

Sequence 3: Setting up the play school

Margareet:	You should choose four children who always talk the most; those children must sit at the front near the teacher. It'll be fun if they talk.
Elisabeth:	*(to one of the toy pupils)* You, you sit here and talk, right?
Margareet:	The desks are behind each other, then they can only . . . then I have to turn round all the time, if the children talk.

(Elbers, 1994, p.231)

These kinds of examples illustrate something important about how language use in play activities may contribute to children's development. Language can be used by them to simulate social life, to create virtual contexts in which they can practise using the genres of their culture to think together about their shared experience in the communities in which they are cultural apprentices. That is, language enables children to think together about social experience; and social experience enables them to acquire and practise using ways of using language to think collectively. For children, playing with discourses is an important way of assimilating the language resources of the community in which they are growing up.

Learning ways of using language to 'interthink'

In everyday life outside school, the 'ground rules' of everyday communication are usually taken for granted, and there is little meta-discussion or joint reflection on how things are normally done. This indicates a clear and useful role for schools, which are special institutional settings created for guiding intellectual development and understanding. Education should help children gain a greater awareness and appreciation of the discourse repertoire of wider society and how it is used to create knowledge and get things done. Some valuable, practical ways of using language may not be used much in the informal activities of everyday childhood life, and so children can hardly be expected to learn them. School life should give them access to ways of using language which their out-of-school experience may not have revealed. It should help them extend their repertoire of language genres and so enable them to use language more effectively as a means for learning, pursuing interests, developing shared understanding and – crucially – reasoning and solving problems together. That is, classroom activities should not only encourage children to inter*act*, but also to inter*think* (Mercer, 2000). However, the importance of language as a tool for 'interthinking' has not been acknowledged within most education systems, and it has not figured prominently in school curricula. In all levels of education, from primary school to university, students usually seem to have been expected to work the 'ground rules' of effective discussion out for themselves.

Classroom research has also shown that in most of the dialogue between teachers and pupils, it is rare for pupils to ask the teacher questions, and even less common for pupils to challenge explanations or interpretations of events that are offered by teachers. That is, the kind of interrogative exchange that took place between a father and daughter in Sequence 1 would be unlikely to occur in a classroom. Reasons for this, in terms of power relations and conventional norms of social behaviour, are not hard to find; but the fact is that teacher–pupil dialogues do not offer much opportunity for pupils to practise their use of language as a tool for reasoning more generally. A more suitable setting for productive argumentative dialogue, one might expect, would be collaborative activity among pupils without a teacher present. However, observational research in classrooms suggests that when pupils are asked to work together in groups most of their talk is either disputational or blandly and unreflectively cooperative, only involving some of the children and providing no more than a brief and superficial consideration of the relevant topics (Barnes and Todd, 1995; Bennett and Cass, 1989; Wegerif and Scrimshaw, 1997).

Since the early 1990s, with Rupert Wegerif, Karen Littleton and groups of primary teachers in the UK, we have been developing a practical programme for schools called *Thinking Together* (Dawes, Mercer and Wegerif, 2000). This consists of a set of ten 'Talk Lessons' which are designed with a careful balance of teacher-led and group-based activities. Each lesson begins with a teacher-led session which is used to establish explicit aims for each lesson, to raise children's awareness of how they talk together and how language can be used in joint activity for reasoning and problem solving. This then leads into a group-based task in which children have the opportunity to practise ways of talking and collaborating; and this in turn feeds back into a whole-class session in which the teacher and children reflect together on what has been learned. In this way, the children are given structured opportunities to practise their strategies for questioning one another, requesting information and reasons from one another, and negotiating a compromise and an agreed course of action. The group tasks include topics directly relevant to the National Curriculum for English, science and citizenship. The children work in mixed-ability, mixed-sex groups of three. One particularly important lesson in the teaching programme was Lesson 3, which focuses on 'ground rules for talk'. In this lesson, the class work together to devise a set of rules for talking together which all agree are sensible, and which when implemented should ensure that all voices are heard and relevant ideas are shared. These ground rules are displayed in the classroom, and are intended to become an important reference point for the children. The following notes by one of the teachers who has been closely involved in our project (Tara Lovelock) may help to explain how teachers set about putting the programme into practice.

My aims for the children in teaching the talk lessons

During class lessons, I wanted my class to feel part of a team, rather than individuals pulling in different directions. I felt that group work would help the children to achieve this spirit of cooperation, and so I began to incorporate group activities into science, maths and literacy. When observing and working with the children in their groups, I found that one or two of them would often take full control of the group. Other group members would underachieve, becoming frustrated because they could not find a way to get involved. And the typical, invisible child, often with many ideas, would simply give up and copy down the results of the other children. Discord was also created when the groups were asked to collect resources. Often, the children would return separately, each clutching the same resources, with no one in the group coordinating what was there and what was missing. Snatching of resources was evident and everyone talked at once, resulting in a heated, unhappy environment, the focus becoming group domination rather than the lesson objective.

It concerned me greatly that in a world where teams of people work together in many different areas of employment, the children in my class, however academically able, would be held back from progressing towards their chosen careers because they had no fundamental social skills. I was also aware that however much practice I gave them, putting the children to work in groups was not improving their team skills. I felt that in order for them to develop their full potential once they became adults, my pupils needed to be taught how to talk and listen as part of a team while they were children.

My main aims were therefore:

– to improve the children's learning skills when working as part of a group
– to improve the children's talking and listening skills
– to help the children to recognise that each individual has different qualities to offer to a working group.

Grouping the class for the talk lessons

The Year 4/5 children were grouped in single year groups and were split among four teachers. They were then organised into groups of three. Each teacher then carefully chose each child's role. To do this, I needed to know the children well, and so we waited until six weeks into the academic year before starting the programme. Once the groups were established, the teacher gave each child a role within the group. Each child knew that part of their value for the group was that they were a good listener, a good writer, or especially good at getting on with others. I made it clear to the children that equal value was placed on each of these roles. I also highlighted the personal qualities that were needed to take on these roles.

A particular lesson

The most effective lessons were set in contexts which the children saw as real life situations. In one particular lesson, 'Dog's Home', the children were given descriptions of six dogs, and descriptions of five families who wished to adopt a dog. The children then had to match each dog to a suitable owner. To make the situation more realistic, the unfortunate dog which was left over was scheduled to be 'put down'. This encouraged effective reasoning as the children had to convince each other of why each dog went with each owner.

They also had to justify 'putting down' the last dog (which actually got a reprieve at the end of the lesson). Finally each group presented its conclusions to the class, and everyone had the opportunity to talk together about how well their group had discussed the work. The children realised that not all groups came to the same conclusions, but that differences of opinion could be created by equally valid reasons; for example, one group placed the Great Dane with an old lady in a small flat. The group pointed out that the old lady would not have to bend down to stroke the dog.

Exploratory talk

The kind of language use the Talk Lessons were designed to encourage can be called 'exploratory talk', a way of using language which was first identified by the educational researchers Barnes and Todd (1995). Our own definition of this is as follows:

> *Exploratory talk* is that in which partners engage critically but constructively with each other's ideas. Relevant information is offered for joint consideration. Proposals may be challenged and counter-challenged, but if so reasons are given and alternatives are offered. Agreement is sought as a basis for joint decision making and action. Knowledge is made publicly accountable and reasoning is visible in the talk.

The kind of talk we call exploratory is illustrated in Sequence 4 below. It comes from our project data and is the talk of three children (aged 10) working together on a computer-based science activity (specially designed for our programme) called *Tracks*. This offers them a simulated environment in which weights are pushed along surfaces of material with different frictional qualities (ice, grass, carpet), and in which the sizes of the weights and forces can be varied systematically. In the sequence, the children are making predictions and carrying out experiments to test them.

Sequence 4: Tracks

Luke:	So one of those . . . no, one grass, and one ice. And the weight's the same, so two again, and both things on four.
Nicola:	Yes, two.
Luke:	Both on four. Yes.
Nicola:	Why don't you do one – oh, you have already! Now press 'ready'. The top weight will go faster.
Paul:	Would it?
Luke:	Yes, because it's smooth.
Nicola:	Yes. Because it's slippery, it'll go faster. Yes, it does.

Luke:	Why?
Paul:	Because if there was a rough surface and the bottom one was one ice . . .
Nicola:	If there was a rough surface, there's more friction, it would slow it down.
Luke, Paul:	Yes.

We see Luke, Nicola and Paul all offering opinions and giving reasons to support them. They seek each other's views and check agreement. Relevant information is made explicit. All the children are actively involved, their reasoning is often made explicit in the talk, and they come to agreement before taking joint action. These are all features of exploratory talk.

There are good reasons for wanting children to use this kind of talk in group activities, because it is a very functional kind of language genre, with speakers following 'ground rules' which help them share knowledge, evaluate evidence and consider options in a reasonable and equitable way. That is, exploratory talk represents a way in which partners involved in problem-solving activity can use language to think collectively – to 'interthink' – effectively, with their activity encapsulated in an intermental zone of their own construction. Other experimental and observational studies have demonstrated the value of talk of this kind in problem solving (Teasley, 1997; Lyle, 1993; see also Littleton and Light, 1999). Exploratory talk is embodied in some important social practices, such as those used in science, law and business, and it is reasonable to expect that education should help every child to become aware of its value and become able to use it effectively.

Effects of the Talk Lessons programme

Comparisons between the talk of the children before and after they had done the *Thinking Together* programme showed that the ways they used language had changed significantly. In a nutshell, the lessons led to the children using more 'exploratory talk', and the increased use of this kind of talk was associated with improved success in jointly solving problems. Moreover, as we mentioned at the beginning of this chapter, the results of this research also provided some evidence about Vygotsky's claims about the link between social, communicative activity and individual learning and development. We found that children who had experienced the Talk Lessons became significantly better at solving problems alone, when compared with control children who had not. That is, children's *individual* reasoning capabilities appeared to have been improved by taking part in the group experience of explicit, rational, collaborative problem solving.

Of course, we cannot be sure exactly what the target children learned from their experience that made the difference. It may be that some gained from having new, successful problem-solving strategies explained to them by their partners, while others may have benefited from having to justify and make explicit their own reasons. But a more radical and intriguing possibility is that children may have improved their reasoning skills by 'internalising' the ground rules of exploratory talk, so that they become able to carry on a kind of silent rational dialogue with themselves. That is, the Talk Lessons may have helped them become more able to generate the kind of rational thinking which depends on the explicit, dispassionate consideration of evidence and competing options. That interpretation is consistent with Vygotsky's claims about the link between the social and the individual; collective thinking has a shaping influence on individual cognition. In accord with this explanation, it is also worth noting that in the lead school in our project the Key Stage 2 SATs results achieved by children who had done the Talk Lessons were so improved compared with those of previous years that the school was specially congratulated by the Secretary of State for Education.

Conclusions

One of the strengths of bringing a sociocultural perspective to bear on education, we believe, is that it encourages us to recognise that the quality of education cannot be explained in terms of 'learning' or 'teaching' as separate processes, but rather in terms of the interactive process of 'teaching-and-learning'. We introduced the notion of an 'intermental development zone' (IDZ) to highlight the way that the success of education can be very dependent on partners creating and maintaining shared knowledge resources and a common frame of reference for their joint activity. For an applied researcher or teacher who is concerned with assessing and improving the quality of education, a sociocultural perspective helps avoid any tendency to attribute problems or solutions to the separate actions of teachers or learners, or to account for events without reference to the historical, cultural and institutional frameworks in which they take place.

A sociocultural perspective on educational practice may also help us transcend the tired old debate about whether teacher-led, whole-class teaching is 'better' than small group activities where children work together without constant teacher input. This is not a choice that has to be made, or which should be made. Group activities offer learners good opportunities to practise and evaluate ways of using language to think collectively, away from the teacher's authoritative presence. But they need first to be guided in how to talk and work together if these activities are to be of most benefit for their learning; and they may later need the intellectual leadership of a teacher to help them consolidate what they have learned from their joint efforts and relate it to the curriculum and other cultural reference frames. Thus in the Talk Lessons programme, teachers organise and lead activities, provide children with information and guidance and help them recognise and reflect on what they have learned. They talk explicitly with children about the goals of classroom activities. Each teacher models 'exploratory' ways of talking for the children in whole-class sessions – for example, asking 'Why?' at appropriate times, giving examples of reasons for opinions, and checking that a range of views are heard. The success of the Talk Lessons programme (which is now published as Dawes, Mercer and Wegerif, 2000) depends very much, we believe, on its careful balance between teacher-led, whole-class sessions and 'talk groups' in which children work and talk without constant teacher supervision. The organised continuity of this experience helps children to consolidate learning, gain educational benefit from their experience – and hopefully helps them understand better how language can be used, in many kinds of social situation, for thinking together and getting things done.

References

Barnes, D. and Todd, F. (1995) *Communication and Learning Revisited.* Portsmouth, NH: Boynton/Cook.

Bennett, N. and Cass, A. (1989) 'The effects of group composition on group interactive processes and pupil understanding', *British Educational Research Journal* **15**, 119–32.

Brown, A. and Palinscar, A. S. (1989) 'Guided, co-operative learning and individual knowledge acquisition', in Resnick, L. (ed.) *Knowing, Learning and Instruction.* New York: Lawrence Erlbaum.

Dawes, L., Mercer, N. and Wegerif, R. (2000) *Thinking Together: activities for teachers and children at Key Stage 2.* Birmingham: Questions Publishing.

Edwards, A. D. and Westgate, D. P. G. (1994) *Investigating Classroom Talk*, 2nd edn. London: Falmer Press.

Edwards, D. and Mercer, N. (1987) *Common Knowledge: the development of joint understanding in the classroom.* London: Methuen.

Elbers, E. (1994) 'Sociogenesis and children's pretend play: a variation on Vygotskian themes', in de Graaf, W. and Maier, R. (eds) *Sociogenesis Re-examined.* New York: Springer.

Heath, S. B.(1983) *Ways with Words: language, life and work in communities and classrooms.* Cambridge: Cambridge University Press.

Lemke, J. (1990) *Talking Science: language, learning and values.* Norwood, NJ: Ablex.

Lipman, M. (1970) *Philosophy for Children.* Montclair, NJ: Institute for the Advancement of Philosophy for Children.

Littleton, K. and Light, P. (eds) (1999) *Learning with Computers: analysing productive interaction*. London: Routledge.

Lyle, S. (1993) 'An investigation in which children talk themselves into meaning', *Language and Education* **7**(3), 181–96.

Maybin, J., Mercer, N. and Stierer, B. (1992) '"Scaffolding" learning in the classroom', in Norman, K. (ed.) *Thinking Voices*. London: Hodder and Stoughton.

Mercer, N. (1995) *The Guided Construction of Knowledge: talk amongst teachers and learners*. Clevedon: Multilingual Matters.

Mercer, N. (2000) *Words and Minds: how we use language to think together*. London: Routledge.

Rogoff, B. (1990) *Apprenticeship in Thinking: cognitive development in social context*. New York: Oxford University Press.

Rogoff, B. (1995) 'Observing sociocultural activity on three planes: participatory appropriation, guided participation and apprenticeship', in Wertsch, J. W., del Rio, P. and Alvarez, A. (eds) *Sociocultural Studies of Mind*. Cambridge: Cambridge University Press.

Rojas-Drummond, S. (2000) 'Guided participation, discourse and the construction of knowledge in Mexican classrooms', in Cowie, H. and van der Aalsvoort, D. (eds) *Social Interaction in Learning and Instruction: the meaning of discourse for the construction of knowledge*. Oxford: Elsevier.

Rojas-Drummond, S., Mercer, N. and Dabrowski, E. (in press) 'Collaboration, scaffolding and the promotion of problem solving strategies in Mexican pre-schoolers', *European Journal of Psychology of Education*.

Teasley, S. (1997) 'Talking about reasoning: how important is the peer group in peer collaboration?', in Resnick, L. *et al.* (eds) *Discourses, Tools and Reasoning: Essays on Situated Cognition*. Berlin: Springer Verlag.

Vygotsky, L. S. (1978) *Mind in Society: the development of higher psychological processes*. Cambridge, Mass.: Harvard University Press.

Wegerif, R. and Scrimshaw, P. (eds) (1997) *Computers and Talk in the Primary Classroom*. Clevedon: Multilingual Matters.

Wegerif, R., Rojas-Drummond, S. and Mercer, N. (1999) 'Language for the social construction of knowledge: comparing classroom talk in Mexican pre-schools', *Language and Education* **13**(2), 133–50.

Wells, G. (1992) *The Meaning Makers: children learning language and using language to learn*. London: Hodder and Stoughton.

Wells, G. (1999) *Dialogic Inquiry: towards a sociocultural practice and theory of education*. Cambridge: Cambridge University Press.

Wertsch, J. V. (ed.) (1985a) *Culture, Communication and Cognition: Vygotskian perspectives*. Cambridge: Cambridge University Press.

Wertsch, J. V. (1985b) 'Adult-child interaction as a source of self-regulation in children', in Yussen, S. R. (ed.) *The Growth of Reflection in Children*. Orlando, Fla: Academic Press.

Chapter 15

The strategies to accelerate learning in the classroom

Alistair Smith

Editors' Note: Drawing on Gardner's notion of Multiple Intelligences, and also work on preferred learning styles, this chapter offers practical ideas and techniques to support pupil learning.

Connecting the learning

> We have got to do a lot fewer things in school. The greatest enemy of understanding is coverage. As long as you are determined to cover everything, you actually ensure that most kids are not going to understand. You've got to take enough time to get kids deeply involved in something so they can think about it in lots of different ways, and apply it – not just at school, but at home and on the street and so on.
>
> (Gardner, 1997, *Educational Leadership*)

Connecting to what the learner already knows and understands is an essential prerequisite for accelerating learning. The brain constantly seeks patterns of meaning based on those patterns which are already known and understood and its capacity to recognise and learn new patterns. Leslie Hart (1983) said of this propensity, 'recognition of patterns accounts largely for what is called insight, and facilitates transfer of learning to new situations or needs, which may be called creativity'.

Recognising and building on this innate pattern-making facility is a powerful starting point when we commence teaching or learning new material. The deliberate priming of the learners as to what is to come not only alerts the brain to search for familiar patterns and connections but also directs attention to the possibility of new ones. So too is the recognition that students come to us with existing knowledge and with mental models for making sense of that knowledge. We need to find out what they already know and understand and build upon it. In some cases this may involve undoing some flawed understandings and challenging their existing mental models before we can build onto more solid foundations. Teaching has never been and never will be about the transfer of information.

Take, as an example, this short excerpt from an English language comprehension text cited by Susan Kovalik in her 1994 book, *Integrated Thematic Instruction*, with the questions which follow:

> *Cayard* forced *America* to the left, filling its sails with 'dirty' air, then tacked into a right hand shift . . . . That proved to be the wrong side. *America*, flying its carbon fibre/liquid crystal main and hand sails, found more pressure on the left. *Cayard* did not initiate a tacking duel until *IL Moro* got headed nearly a mile down the leg. . . . *Cayard* did not initiate a jibing duel to improve his position heading downwind and instead opted for a more straight-line approach to the finish.
>
> 1. Who forced *America* to the left?
> 2. What kind of air filled *America*'s sail?
> 3. Which boat had carbon fibre liquid crystal main and head sail?

It is correctly pointed out that 'does answering the questions successfully mean you understand what the paragraph is saying?' The example correctly suggests that the questions could be answered successfully without any understanding of the context, without a capability of generalising based on new learning and without any ability to apply new learning to a different context. In other words it is quite possible to successfully answer the questions without having a clue as to what's going on!

If we continue to transfer information without checking for understanding, without relating to the existing mental models which allow or disallow the student to integrate the new information, without relating the new information *to their world*, then we build in failure from the outset.

Basic mathematics provides a good example of how this could be done. I asked a lower school maths teacher what the very basic things *every* child, irrespective of ability, should be able to do in maths before leaving school. What should they be able to do, remember and transfer into everyday situations, without which they would be seriously disadvantaged in life? How should it be taught so it would be remembered *forever*? Here is an extract of *some* of the things which were described:

Addition and subtraction – four basic rules for working without a calculator and practised through giving and receiving change.
Recognising number – a sense of the relative size of numbers emphasised through simple games like 'What is bigger?' and 'Is it better to have? . . .'.

Tables – how to make sense of information presented in this format; practice on football tables.

Basic multiplication and division – exchanging money on holiday abroad; estimating what your car does to the litre or gallon.

Area – estimation of floor area for a new carpet for your bedroom.

Interest rates and percentages – borrowing money on credit for a new stereo system; calculating VAT.

Metric and imperial units – how to get a good 'feel' for amounts.

Rough conversions – travelling.

24 Hour clock – what it means in real time.

Income and expenditure – working out whether the wages for a new job leave you better off or not.

Household finance – where your money is going.

Tax, National Insurance and Superannuation – what is it for and where does it go?

And here are some of the ways in which these were taught, bearing in mind the need to connect to what is already known and the innate tendency to look for recognisable patterns of meaning.

Understanding the rough amounts in metric and imperial units. 'It was as important that children should have a good "feel" for what each unit corresponded to so I used:

mm – the thickness of a 1p

cm – the length of your thumb nail

metre – a "big" step, we'd march around saying "big, step, metre"

km – we would choose somewhere near to the school and march them there singing kilometre, kilometre, kilometre" as we went

litre – bottle of coke

gram – £5 note

kilogram – bag of sugar.

I used similar examples with imperial units and I also made them visual. We had a teaspoon of sugar for an ounce, then two packs of butter for a pound and a cat for a stone. Then I'd get them to remember feeding the cat on 16 teaspoons of sugar and 14 pounds of butter. We'd make up songs that they had to practice like "just a teaspoon of sugar makes the ounces go down" and do "fun tests" and competitions constantly.'

Remembering the significance of tax, National Insurance and Superannuation and understanding what it is for. 'Here I always used a story to combine the three things and what they paid for. The story was about a student who has been taken in a taxi from hospital and is going 30 kilometres to prison handcuffed to a police officer for fiddling the unemployment benefit. On the journey he passes Buckingham Palace and sees the Queen in an army uniform. Tax at 30p in the pound pays for education, health, police, prisons, royal family, defence and pensions but not taxis as one lad put in his exam one year! With Superannuation, I'd say it sounded like supergran and all grannies are different and some of us don't have one so there was no standard rate, it varied and you may not even pay it.'

The five key principles for connecting the learning follow:

1. Always give the BIG picture overview before chunking down into content.
2. Always use participative review strategies to connect to what has already been covered and prime the new learning.
3. Build out from examples which learners can readily recognise.
4. Encourage independent, predictive and speculative thinking.
5. Develop meta-cognitive awareness by describing and using 'connecting' learner tools.

We will say more about the significance of the BIG picture in the next section and how it can build into and from connecting activities. Participative review activities are designed to allow every student to participate in a non-threatening way. They keep the retention of information high. They allow the possibility of the retained information being transferred to novel contexts. Most importantly they aid learners to build new knowledge onto what they already know and understand.

Participative review strategies include:

- **'Three things'**
  'I'd like you to describe three things that you remember as significant about the last lesson. Then swap your three things in pairs. Try to get at least five significant things between you.'

After a minute on their own, allow two or three minutes in pairs then solicit contributions from the whole group. Encourage participation and prompt contributions by asking them to describe what they have been talking about, not what they remember. Reinforce with praise and humour. Variations and extensions on this can include:

'three most important/three most useful/three things to teach someone else'

'three important questions which someone should be able to answer'

'agree what the keywords were – use them in a sentence to show understanding'.

- **'One, Two, Four, Eight'**
  'Think of one significant piece of information from the work we did last time. Now take your one thing and swap it with someone else so that you have two pieces of significant information. Now swap your two again so that you are left with four. Finally, go for eight or as near to eight as you can manage!'

- **'Interview mapping'**
  'Interview at least three others and from each find out what three things they considered most important about the work we did last time. Then review your findings in pairs.'

To lead out from the participative review we would encourage speculative thinking about either the content, or the nature, of the input to come, or both.

Providing the big picture

I begin first by becoming aware of the overall length of the work, then of how it will divide itself into sections (perhaps movements), and then of the kind of texture or instruments that will perform it. I prefer not to look for the actual notes of the composition until this process has gone as far as possible. Finally the notes appear.
  (Michael Tippet, 1963, quoted in Odam, 1995)

At St John the Baptist RC School, Woking, providing the BIG picture at the beginning of lessons is now part of school policy. Included in the Staff Handbook are ten recommended strategies for improving the quality of learning. Every teacher begins his or her lesson with an overview of what they are to do, how it connects with what went before and how it will connect with what is to come. Review at the end of lessons is also school policy.

Lorraine Barker, Deputy Head Teacher at Mirfield Free Grammar School, helps staff and students understand the significance of providing the BIG picture through what she calls 'The White Socks Rule'. She says it directs the focus of attention without being directive, it's like 'sending students out for a break mid-morning and when they come back in twenty minutes later asking them how many others there are wearing white socks. Or for a more useful approach, signalling **before** they go out that they might like to be aware of how many others there are wearing white socks'. This principle is known as pre-processing and is based on the fact that the brain constantly searches out patterns of meaning and does so as part of learning.

The 'photoreading system' developed by Paul Scheele utilises the principle of pre-processing to activate the unconscious pre-processing structures of the brain. It is argued that the brain has a strong facility for processing visual information without engaging conscious attention. Typically, the method would encourage scanning pages smoothly yet very quickly without attempting to 'read' or to consciously assimilate and engage with the material. Utilising our peripheral vision we work through and get a sense of structure and glean the main points. Scheele (1993) argues that on any page, 4 to 11 per cent of the words carry the meaning. Look for these 'trigger' words and we effectively cue our understanding before actively and consciously engaging with the text.

By providing the questions at the beginning of a unit that learners will be able to answer by the time they reach the end of the unit, we pre-process. By encouraging the learners to quickly scan text to familiarise themselves with its physical structure and organisation we pre-process. An extension of this is to get them to quickly isolate 'trigger words' from the text before reading for detail and with only these trigger words encourage speculation as to what the text is about: then we read for detail.

At both Lutterworth Grammar and Community School, Leicestershire, and the Sir William Nottidge School, Kent, students encounter the 'white socks principle' through different types of pre-processing activities. Teachers are encouraged to provide an overview of each syllabus and chunk it down into shorter learning units.

At Lutterworth, each subject area has been encouraged to break down its syllabus into modules which can be taught in discrete time units. For each module, students are given a pre-briefing paper which outlines exactly what they are going to do and what the learning objectives are. At Sir William Nottidge each unit of work has a summary provided to each student at the beginning. The summary specifies the unit of work, the learning objectives, the keywords used and the questions the students will be able to answer by the end of the unit. In each category there is a section for students to tick whether they know and understand before and after.

Cris Edgell is Deputy Head of Upper School and Coordinator of Key Stage 3 Science at Sacred Heart School, South London. An understanding of the principles of good classroom practice underlies his coordination of the teaching of KS3 Science. This is his BIG picture of the dramatic improvement in results achieved this year.

After a year developing detailed differentiated work schemes in response to the Dearing Report we were at last in a position to concentrate our energies more fully on teaching strategies. Meetings were devoted to reviewing each unit in order to share best practice within the team. In particular we attempted to diversify our teaching methods to access the learning preferences of our students. Science lends itself very well to VAK (Visual, Auditory and Kinaesthetic) delivery but teachers often need reminding of their own bias. Team teaching and peer observation helped to redress this. Sometimes teachers became unnerved by the sheer weight of the syllabus but I insisted that they take all the time necessary to teach concepts thoroughly – 'doing the syllabus' is not the same as teaching science!

Poor SATs results for the previous two years meant that our expectations of students had fallen too low. We agreed to teach each class to a standard about one level higher than their pedigree might suggest. The result of this simple exercise was an immediate raising in self-esteem and a revision of personal goals. Frequent and accurate feedback on tests, quizzes and assessments meant that students could plot real progress throughout the year. They were trained in the skills of drawing together apparently disparate concepts or information in order to complete the big picture. With the approach of the SATs, students were armed with checklists and revision guides and were confident enough to fill in gaps in their knowledge on their own.

The 1997 SATs results confirmed that a total frame shift in expectation had led to a comprehensive rise in achievement. There had been an increase from 35 to 56 per cent of students attaining L5 and above and for the first time ever, the school celebrated Level 7 students (5.3 per cent). Not a single child scored below Level 3.

Among the success factors which the school identified as contributing to the dramatic improvements were:

- improved teaching strategies;
- effective use of comprehensive and differentiated schemes of work;
- provision of textbooks for all Y9 classes;
- frequent testing and immediate feedback;
- accurately set classes;
- high academic and behavioural expectations;
- careful monitoring of groups and individuals;
- development of effective SEN materials;
- matching teachers' strengths to particular classes when timetabling;
- plenty of exam practice;
- revision classes;
- provision of revision checklists and guides.

A learner working on his or her own needs the BIG picture first so that all the subsequent learning experiences can be ordered and assigned a level of significance. Some of the best ways of beginning to work on a text are summarised below. Let us assume the student has to use a large and unwieldy textbook for study purposes. This method is better suited to older learners. This is how he or she might get the BIG picture and begin to extract the information needed:

1. **Step One.** Before starting, quickly note down some questions you seek answers to. Outline some of the questions on cards or post-its and have these nearby – perhaps on a wall – as you begin. Ask yourself again, to what use do you wish to put the information in the book?

2. **Step Two.** Future-base – by the end of reading this book what outcome do you wish for yourself? Envisage the successful achievement of that outcome. What do you see yourself doing, hear being said and how do you feel? Then relax, breathe deeply, make yourself comfortable and continue . . .

3. **Step Three.** Survey the book first – flick through the pages to get a 'feel' for its content and layout – do this quickly and simply scan for visual information and as you do so you will begin to notice certain key words; look at all sections including the index and appendices. Do this several times quickly. Refer back to the original questions you noted down. You will already have begun to get a sense of the book's order and layout and what can be found where.

4. **Step Four.** Relax again before 'photoreading' the book. Move through a page at a time taking in the visual information from all of the page. Soften the focus of your eyes so that all of the information is available. Spend about a second or two on each page. Relax and don't linger on any page. The method is not to 'read' in the conventional sense but to absorb information to help with your next stage.

5. **Step Five.** Formulate questions for those sections you wish to use. This is where you begin to search more closely for the information you need. Again, do this quickly and smoothly. Before returning to those sections and scanning down the centre of the page, dip into the text for more focused reading, finding cues which will begin to answer your questions. If it is your book use a highlighter pen to note key paragraphs – they will often be the opening paragraphs or the first few sentences from the opening paragraphs – and alongside the highlighted marks note in pencil why it is of use or interest. Relax again. Take a break if necessary.

6. **Step Six.** Rapid read those areas of the text which the cues have alerted you to. Read for meaning and comprehension at this stage and only read the sections which you have identified as of real significance, before finally going to:

7. **Step Seven.** From the pencil comments you have made on the relevant pages and the detailed reading of the significant sections, go back and build up a memory map or text and context notes. Review your map or the notes as they build up by referring to your original questions.

Specifying outcomes

A little girl came up to me one day and said, 'Mr Jensen, Mr Jensen, look at my paper'. She showed me her paper and every single word on it was mis-spelled. I looked at her and said, 'Maureen I really like your paper – the margins are nice and neat and your printing is clear and readable'. And she said, 'Thank you, Mr Jensen – I've really been working hard on it. Next, I'm going to work on my spelling'.

(Jensen, 1995, *Brain-Based Learning and Teaching*)

The literature of management development abounds with metaphors, particularly from the animal kingdom. In the last year I've read or heard about herds of buffaloes and flights of geese in the context of leadership and followership, about habituation and boiling frogs, about blind men holding on to different parts of an elephant and training dolphins by differentiation! My favourite involves whales.

Some years ago there was a Safari Park at Windsor, England. Before it closed down and became a Lego theme park it contained 'wild' animals who, for a small entrance fee, would come and defecate on your car and remove your windscreen wipers. It also had a marine pool. In this pool you could watch the antics of sea-lions, dolphins and a large killer whale. As you walked to your seat in the marine pool you passed a plated glass window below surface level. This would be your first sight of the whale. He was on one side of the plate glass with his eye up against it looking at you; you were on the other side looking at him. Later he would leap out of the water, crash back down again and you would wish you'd sat further back. The question everyone asks is how do you train a ten ton killer whale to jump over a rope six feet above the water in return for a bucket of sprats?

The way it is done is to take the rope and place it well under the surface of the water. When the whale passes over it it is rewarded. The rope is raised six inches at a time and each time the whale passes over it it gets its reward. A little at a time the rope is raised out of the water. Each successful leap is rewarded with a bucket of sprats. The principle is to chunk it down into realisable units and reward success on each achievement. You motivate a whale in much the same way as you might motivate an intransigent Y9 student!

The story of the whale reminds us of the difference between goals, targets and tasks and the difference between short-, medium- and long-term aspirations. A goal is 'a dream with a timescale'; it is aspirational and at the outer edge of performance. Targets are journey points along the route to the goal. They can be specified in terms of detailed outcome. Sometimes the acronym SMART is applied here: Specific, Measurable, Agreed, Realistic and Time based. Tasks are what you do to meet targets.

It also reminds us that we may need to differentiate and certainly encourage learners to adopt personal targets. Dolphins are encouraged to perform through a slightly more sophisticated reward structure and one which is differentiated. To get a dolphin to do more than leap over a rope and eat sprats, the trainer rewards performance and then changes the pattern. Sometimes when the dolphin leaps there is no reward. Then the dolphin leaps again: no reward. After a third leap without reward the dolphin changes its strategy. It leaps but it twists or it leaps twice with spins or it leaps backwards. This time the innovation is rewarded with the sprats. The dolphin has learned to perform at a different level for an improved reward!

In classrooms be specific about outcomes. When setting work, be specific about what a successful piece would look like. Encourage discussion around this and have students describe in advance the sort of finished product they seek.

In working with targets, they must be differentiated. The best way to differentiate the target is to start with the learners' own aspirations. Their Radio WIIFM (What's In It For Me). To get to this we have progressed through informal personal performance targets for short-term performance improvement or maintenance to formal medium-term targets which are written, negotiated and reviewed. Five ways of enhancing this process are described below. They are time-lines, future-basing, templates, anchoring and affirmations.

Time-lines and time-line therapy has a heavy industry of subscribers to the practice. Used in therapy and counselling, it works on the premise that we have a concept of time which can be delineated in space. For some it takes the form of a line angled with the future laid out in front or to the side and the past behind or to the other side. The present is where we stand in the middle. Stepping up and down is to step back and forwards on the time-line. Examples of practical applications include projecting forward to a given point and experiencing what it is like to be successful – perhaps to have achieved the personal goal – there. Or, going back and examining an experience 'as though you were there' and considering the consequences of actions taken there. In a learning situation it can be used to project forward to a point where a goal has been successfully achieved. What is it like there? What are you feeling, saying and doing? How are others responding to you? Stay there for a moment and enjoy the feeling of success, now walk back down the time-line to the present and give yourself advice about how to get to your goal successfully.

Future-basing develops time-lining into a problem-solving tool. It works by starting from the position of having successfully achieved an outcome rather than confronting the desired outcome as a problem or challenge. It is like being at the top of the hill looking down, rather than being at the bottom looking up, where all is effort and difficulty. In schools it is highly successful in planning and I have seen it used for three-year development plans, for departmental improvement plans, to successfully introduce schemes of work and, in one case, to introduce a new learning tutor system across year groups.

It works best in pairs. Physically step forward to the future base and record what happens there on large sheets of paper. Have separate sheets for each academic term working back to the present. Act as if success has been achieved. Write the date and the successful outcome down. 'It is . . . and we have . . . all students are . . .' and continue building up a picture of success. With the partner writing down the outcomes everything is described in terms of success. Somehow it creates an energy and the positive and desired outcomes flow out! Then, for each written success project back down the time-line. Ask questions which continue to keep you in the future base and presume success. Work hard at this. Questions like, 'do you remember when we had the previous system? What was the first thing we did back then to change it?' What happened as a consequence? Then what happened? How did we overcome that difficulty? Stay in the future base literally looking back! Build up a sequence of actions and consequences for each itemised success outcome. Gradually come forward, itemising each action as you come. Once the process is complete, then and only then do we step out of the future base and critique what is written. At this point logistical detail is added and the timescales can be shifted up or down.

Templates work best in situations where they are a prompt for speculation and reflection. They are a prompt for dialogue and where they are 'real' they are highly motivational. The speculation comes with projecting forward, 'What do I want? What would a successful outcome look and feel like? How would I know I had achieved it? How would others know?' The reflection is part of assessing the resources – inner and outer – the learner has for working towards the goal. Goals which are written and discussed become more concrete when they are described in specifics. The brain identifies and recognises concrete images more easily than abstract 'desires'. Get the students to conceptualise their desired outcomes in VAK. It is brain-compatible!

We have all got successes in our lives which when remembered seem to evoke a 'warm glow of satisfaction'. Why is this? Why should our physiology change at the point of recapturing that earlier experience? The NLP (Neuro Linguistic Programming) technique of anchoring does not come with an explanation of the neurological phenomenon but it does operate on the principle that we can access positive states of mind as and when we need them.

Anchoring involves choosing a particular state you wish to access and then using the technique with such effectiveness that you can access that state of mind at any time and under any circumstances. Let us say that the state of mind the student desires is 'confidence'. Firstly we ensure that everyone in the group is relaxed and comfortable, working in pairs and with the physical surroundings. Then we invite the students to think of a state of mind which would be helpful to them – [give examples] – then have them think about a moment in their lives when they felt that way. For our student, she accesses a time in her life when she was confident. Then with her partner alongside as observer, at the point when she begins to feel a 'state change' – feeling slightly more positive and perhaps experiencing a physical warmth – she steps forward into the magic circle and as she does so she says one word that is significant for her – 'yes!' or 'now!' or something similar – while at the same time squeezing a finger or clenching a fist or some other easily replicable gesture. This is repeated again then again. The observer can give feedback on anything he or she observed. Eventually, with this tool it is possible just to make the gesture and the associated feeling of confidence and control comes. The gesture and the state of mind have become anchored. This technique will work with young children and can be particularly useful when anxieties are beginning to inhibit performance.

Affirmations are sometimes described as 'brain convincers'. The process of affirming the positive is a direct intervention to counter the little voice which comes with limiting personal beliefs. Repeated sufficiently, affirmations are intended to confuse and contradict our internal belief systems and eventually displace negative and limiting beliefs with more positive ones. It is a method used in counselling. It is particularly powerful when used alongside positive personal goals and anchoring.

Encourage the students to reframe negative and limiting beliefs they may have about themselves into positive beliefs. Positive, unconditional statements in the present tense repeated regularly especially in moments of self-doubt such as: 'I am good at . . .' and 'I will . . .'. They need to be said aloud or listened to. Get students to repeat these positive messages to themselves regularly. The Arsenal and England soccer player, Ian Wright, uses a specially recorded tape with positive affirming messages from friends and family interspersed with his favourite pieces of music. The purpose of the tape is to get him into the correct mental state before important matches.

It's all about putting the power of positive thinking into my game. I've had a special compilation tape made up of things that are designed to make me feel positive and encourage me to concentrate on the good aspects. The tape includes some of my favourite bits of music and messages from one or two people close to me . . . it's all about surrounding myself with positive things and shutting out the negative vibes.

(Ian Wright interviewed in *The Daily Mirror* by Mike Walters, August 1997)

Wright is Arsenal's all time top goal scorer.

The combination of a stated positive personal outcome with anchoring and affirmations can provide the 'mind technology' to make a lifelong difference!

Input via VAK

Learning first comes in through our senses. As we explore and experience our material world, initial sensory patterns are laid down on elaborate nerve networks. These initial sensory patterns become the core of our free-form information system that is updated and becomes more elegant with each new novel experience. These initial sensory patterns become our reference points and give us the context for all learning, thought and creativity. From this sensory base we will add emotions and movement in our lifelong learning dance.

(Hannaford, 1995, *Smart Moves: Why Learning Is Not All In Your Head*)

To ensure that the information you present has the most impact, use VAK.

An airline pilot explains how he learns complex sequences of drills and checks. Each six months his licence, and therefore his living, depends upon him being able to remember all these drills in sequence and apply them in a test situation. In this case the test situation is in a simulator and among the many compulsory drills to be tested is a simulated engine failure during take-off. It is a situation, imagined or real, of high stress. Seventy per cent of all airline accidents occur as a result of human error. Lives depend, not only on his ability to remember, but on his ability to perform the remembered tasks in sequence while accounting for other, unanticipated, variables. Does he remember and learn to perform to this level by being told about it as he sits at a desk and takes notes? Does he remember by reading and rereading the manual? Does he remember by sitting a written exam? Completing a multiple choice paper? Writing an essay on the psychology of human response? The answer in every case is no.

The flight deck of a modern airliner is organised so that the systems controlling the aircraft can be managed effectively and systematically. You would expect it to be so. Flight instrumentation gives visual feedback on all operating systems. The crew are required to talk through agreed procedures and affirm their completion: it is aural. As they engage a control or operate a switch the pilots point to or physically touch the instrument: it is physical. In the unlikely event of a stall or being too close to terrain a warning system operates. Lights flash, a loud warning signal repeats and a recorded voice warns of the danger, the control column 'shakes'. It is visual, auditory and kinaesthetic.

How does a pilot learn the complex systems? Yes, there are manuals. Yes, there are updates and briefings. Yes, there are simulator courses, feedback from supervisory captains working with you on the job and regular tests. But, ultimately, it requires the individual on his or her own to learn the mass of material.

So, the airline pilot explains how he does it. Firstly, he takes the systems notes provided by the official manual and, for learning purposes, reconstructs the essential areas into his own notes. These are more maps than notes. Comprising flow charts, highlighted keywords, and the actions sequenced and attached to a mnemonic. Each complex procedure is broken down into structured elements following the same formula. Each separate 'map' is referenced to others and placed in a file. A summary map is placed on the wall above the study desk. Alongside the summary map is a black and white layout plan of the controls in the airline flight deck. To learn the drills, the pilot looks at his flow chart, says the action described there aloud as he reaches forward and touches the switch or control as suggested by the layout plan on the wall. It is visual, auditory and kinaesthetic. It is rehearsed until there is no need for the props and prompt cards. Finally, he is able to say the action described, see – in his mind's eye – the position of the switch or control, move left or right hand and operate the switch or control before moving on to the next action. Again, it is visual, auditory and kinaesthetic. The learning is being rehearsed in three different sensory modalities. The new knowledge is reviewed formally and informally and at regular intervals to keep the retention high.

The significance of visual, auditory and kinaesthetic learning has become more than just common sense in recent years. The discipline of NLP concerns itself with observing the subtleties of human behaviour and particularly how we communicate with others and ourselves. The work of the pioneers of NLP, Richard Bandler, John Grinder and Michael Grinder has now been progressed to such a degree that we are able to identify three distinct communication and learning preferences. Because we take in data about the world around us through our senses it makes 'sense' to pay attention to those senses and our modes of utilising them.

- **Visual.** Some of us prefer to learn by seeing. We will enjoy communicating through pictures, graphs and visual artefacts. We may at an early age show an ability to visualise remembered or constructed scenes. Our spelling and memory strategies may utilise pictures rather than sounds.
- **Auditory.** Some of us enjoy communicating with and learning by sound including the spoken word. Discussion, audiotape, radio programmes, lectures, debates, orals, spoken language exercises will suit those of us with an auditory preference. It may also be that we remember names rather than faces and we spell by recalling the patterns of sounds. When we remember our telephone numbers we will chunk it into three and repeat and become familiar with the pattern of sounds.
- **Kinaesthetic.** Some learners prefer to engage with the experience physically. In communication we will model our point with our hands and bodies and become animated as we do so. We learn through experience, movement, modelling and feel frustrated more readily with other forms of learning. Learners of this sort are most critically disadvantaged by schooling which requires physical stasis for extended periods of time.

We do, to some extent, utilise all three. But just as we each have a hand preference, an ear preference, an eye preference and a brain hemisphere preference, we also have a representational system preference.

The leading practitioners in NLP have spent many years characterising the 'typical' attributes of visual, auditory and kinaesthetic learners. This work is not research based. It is pragmatic and based on detailed elicitation and modelling. It also recognises that in using language we select and describe the world and our experiences in it, based on that process of selection. The language we use therefore reflects the way we make sense of everyday experience.

Visual learners

'I use pictures and the visual dimension in work more readily now. I also use the visual dimension for note-taking and it frees up associations and ideas which linear note-taking cannot do. The students work better in this format too.'
(Andrew Duncan, Technology teacher)

Visual learners . . .

- will have very good visual recall and be able to visualise remembered scenes, objects or faces many years later;

- will enjoy and benefit from visually presented information such as graphs, charts, peripheral posters, keyword display, memory and concept mapping;
- will utilise a visual spelling strategy and thus 'see' the words, their letters and constituent shapes as they spell them;
- will look upwards when accessing remembered information;
- upward eye movements to the left indicate the access of remembered sights or scenes; upward eye movements to the right indicate the access of constructed visual scenes – what an imagined scene may look like;
- visualisation is characterised by shallow breathing high in the chest;
- visual learners will speak rapidly, possibly with high-pitched tonality;
- will use lots of pointing gestures with hands outlining or describing the imagined shape or outline of the argument or information presented;
- prefer to 'map out' instructions using a layout plan; when giving directions will make lots of references to what you will 'see';
- will use visual predicates: 'I see what you mean', 'it looks good to me', 'just imagine', 'I can't quite picture it', 'let's shed some light on this', 'it has the appearance of being right', 'it's not a view I share', 'the future looks hazy', 'someone to look up to', 'do I make myself clear?', 'it has all the signs of success', 'there's light at the end of the tunnel', 'I'm still in the dark', 'she's very bright' and 'look at it from my perspective'.

Auditory learners

'I have always used short role-plays but I will tend to use it more and with a better awareness of sound as a stimulus for learning – for example, reading Macbeth with half the class emphasising the reading of verbs and the other half the reading of adjectives in a soliloquy. This helps to highlight keywords in an auditory context and stimulates understanding. It also helps them remember it better.'
(Mandy Reddick, English teacher)

Auditory learners . . .

- will have good auditory recall and be able to rehearse or anticipate situations by 'hearing' them played out in one's head;
- will enjoy and benefit from discussion activity, lectures, orals, interviewing, reading and hearing stories, sound recordings and language games;
- use an auditory spelling strategy which involves remembering the patterns of sounds made as words are spelled;
- when accessing auditory information, will often adopt a 'head-cocked' position accompanied by eye movements which are level;

- level eye movements to the left indicate the access of remembered sounds; level eye movements to the right indicate the access of constructed sounds – how to say things, anticipating what they may sound like;
- even breathing in the diaphragm or with the whole chest and with a typically prolonged exhale indicates auditory accessing;
- auditory learners will utilise an even, rhythmic tempo when speaking with skilled patterning and modulation of sounds to clarify and enhance meaning;
- the use of accompanying hand gestures to emphasise meaning – counting out points on the fingers, chopping the air for emphasis – is typical of auditory learners;
- prefer to give and receive instructions verbally with emphasis on sequence, repetition and summary;
- will use auditory predicates: 'I hear what you are saying', 'it sounds great to me', 'alarm bells started sounding for me', 'it has the ring of truth about it', 'suddenly it clicked', 'everyone's talking about it', 'this idea has been rattling around in my head', 'let me sound you out', 'I'm in tune with your thinking', 'something tells me not to', 'it struck a chord', 'a resounding victory' and 'I don't like your tone'.

Kinaesthetic learners

'I use the idea of writing in the air . . . and I get the class to repeat words and phrases as they do so with their eyes shut. We use shouts and whispers and high and low voices. I use large cards with questions written on and we physically move them around – blu-tacked to the board – to make matching pairs. I also used cards with sentences summarising a literary text which had to be physically moved around to make sense, thus instilling a "picture" of the sequence of events in the students' minds.'
   (Susan Short, Languages teacher)

Kinaesthetic learners . . .

- will remember events and moments readily and will also recall their associated feelings or physical sensations;
- will enjoy and benefit from physical activity; modelling; body sculpture; field trips; visits; learning by 'doing';
- may spell best when able to replicate the physical pattern of the letters of the words either by writing or by moving the writing hand or by rehearsing such movements as the letters are spelled out;
- may be characterised by use of accompanying hand and body gestures

while talking but not to reinforce meaning; often it will be a physical and repetitive patterning of small movements as one talks or listens;

- will fidget and need regular breaks when learning;
- will give instructions by demonstration or modelling with the body or with gestures; when giving directions would be more inclined to take you there;
- will use kinaesthetic predicates: 'It feels good to me', 'Can you handle this?', 'I feel touched by what you say', 'she's got a solid understanding of this material', 'I've changed my stance on this', 'does this grab you?', 'I don't follow', 'it was a deeply moving experience', 'it's a weight off my mind', 'I felt backed into a corner', 'we are making great strides together'.

Teachers can dramatically increase their impact by exploiting opportunities for their input to be visual, auditory and kinaesthetic.

Examples of visual input include:

- use of peripheral display posters;
- keyword display;
- visualisations;
- video, demonstration, OHP;
- memory mapping, collage, posters, flow charts, story-boards;
- lively and engaging texts;

Examples of auditory input:

- teacher instruction;
- paired and group discussion;
- active listening roles;
- debate and presentations;
- music for relaxing, energising, review;
- raps, rhyme, chants, verse, dramatic readings;
- balance of groupings to promote use of language.

Examples of kinaesthetic input:

- design and make activities;
- continuity lines;
- physical modelling;
- visits, field trips;
- body sculpture, mime, learned gestures;
- accompanying learned physical movements;
- regular break-states and brain gym.

References

Gardner, H. (1997) 'Teaching for Multiple Intelligences', *Educational Leadership* **55**, September.

Hannaford, C. (1995) *Smart Moves: Why Learning Is Not All In Your Head.* VA: Great Ocean Publishers.

Hart, L. A. (1983) *The Human Brain and Human Learning.* New York: Addison Wesley Longman.

Jensen, E. (1995) *Brain-Based Learning and Teaching.* USA: Turning Point.

Kovalik, S. (1994) *Integrated Thematic Instruction: The Model*, 3rd edn. SKA.

Odam, G. (1995) *The Sounding Symbol: Music Education in Action.* Stroud: Stanley Thornes.

Scheele, P. R. (1993) *The PhotoReading Whole Mind System.* Learning Strategies Corporation.

Chapter 16

Effective teaching: practical outcomes from research

Alma Harris

Editors' Note: This chapter draws on the considerable evidence of the last 30 years to synthesise what is known about the behaviour, skills and teaching styles of effective teachers.

Introduction

[. . .]

The term 'effective teaching' is used in this review in a much broader sense than simply teacher behaviour or what teachers are seen to do in the classroom. While teaching behaviour is acknowledged to be important, the underlying processes, principles and practice of effective teaching are equally significant. Consequently, this review considers the managerial and organisational aspects of effective teaching, as well as the pedagogical processes.

The research on effective teaching has considered the topic from various methodological positions. However, despite the diversity of approach, there is a degree of consensus about the generic features of effective teaching (Good and Brophy, 1980; Rosenshine, 1983; Bickel and Bickel, 1986; Walberg, 1986, 1990; Bennett, 1988; Wang *et al.*, 1990; Wang, 1991; Bennett and Carre, 1993). The sheer breadth of the work carried out in so many different contexts and ways compensates for any methodological differences or weaknesses in particular studies.

Over the years, research into effective teaching has been approached in a number of different ways and there are many different perspectives on the theme of effective teaching. In order to provide an introduction to the research this chapter will adopt an organisational format acknowledging the various perspectives. This format, initially conceptualised by Hopkins *et al.* (1994, 1997), describes three broad perspectives.

The first perspective is that of 'teaching effects', which encompasses sets of teaching behaviours or teaching skills. Teaching is viewed as a complex task, which can be analysed in order to examine individual elements of the teaching process. Consistently high levels of correlation have been found between student achievement scores and teaching behaviours or skills. The second perspective concerns the acquisition of a repertoire of 'models of teaching' or distinct teaching approaches. Here, models of teaching are defined in terms of distinct pedagogical and operational specifications. Within this literature there is some consideration of teaching styles as a sub-set of teaching models. The third perspective is that of 'artistry', where teaching is seen as being a highly creative activity involving the use of sophisticated repertoires of responses and the ability to reflect upon practice. Within this final perspective, the literature focuses upon sustained professional development.

Using these three perspectives it is possible to refine and categorise the literature on effective teaching a little further, into the following areas: teaching behaviours, teaching skills, teaching styles, teaching models and teacher artistry. These categories will be used to organise this review of research in the field. However, it is important to emphasise that in using this approach certain crude distinctions will be made. It is also important to acknowledge that the categories are not mutually exclusive but offer just one possible way of analysing the vast literature on the subject of effective teaching. The research evidence summarised within each of the categories is only part of a substantive empirical base upon which to consider the various dimensions and facets of effective teaching.

Effective teaching behaviour

The earliest research studies of teacher effectiveness focused upon the personality of the teacher. Indeed, the literature on personality characteristics of teachers is immense. In the first *Handbook of Research on Teaching*, Getzels and Jackson (1963) devoted an entire chapter to teachers' personality traits and their relationship to student achievement. In 1988 Borich similarly provided a comprehensive overview of frequently studied teacher personality characteristics, while earlier research gave an insight into the relationship between teacher attitudes and student achievement. However, this research was criticised as being too far removed from actual classroom events to be a good predictor of effective classroom behaviour (Gage, 1963; Getzels and Jackson, 1963). Despite this particular limitation, research on teacher qualities and effective instruction has continued (e.g. Stones, 1992).

After this early research came studies that concentrated on what the effective teacher might do in the classroom, rather than his or her personality. Actual teaching behaviour in classrooms was described and a search for the behavioural characteristics of effective teachers was started. The research paradigm dominating this type of enquiry was termed 'process-product', which investigated the correlation between certain teaching behaviours (the process) and student achievement (the product) (Brophy and Good, 1986). This approach sought teacher behaviours that predicted or preferably caused growth in student knowledge and skills.

At first many of these early studies were of a descriptive nature, but later statistical and experimental studies, which introduced certain behaviours and checked their effects on students, were performed (Gage and Giaconia, 1983). Process-product studies overwhelmingly dominated research on effective teaching in the 1970s (Flanders, 1970; Wright and Nutall, 1970; Hughes, 1973; Nutall and Church, 1973; Eggleston *et al.*, 1976). This led to the creation of a massive database from which many of the characteristics of effective teaching behaviours have been derived (Gage, 1972; Brophy and Good, 1974; Dunkin and Biddle, 1974; Good *et al.*, 1975).

Initially the focus of the 'process-product' studies was almost exclusively on the instructional activities of teachers. Kounin (1970) then introduced a distinction between management and instructional behaviour. *Instructional* behaviour is ultimately directed at the individual learning behaviour of students, whereas *management* behaviour is directed at the students as a group, with maintenance of a learning situation being the main focus of the teacher. Several researchers subsequently undertook comprehensive studies of classroom management activities in relation to student achievement (Kounin and Gump, 1974; Kounin and Doyle, 1975; Reiss, 1982).

While there are recognised shortcomings of 'process-product' studies (Rosenshine, 1971; Dunkin and Biddle, 1974; Doyle, 1986; Kyriacou, 1986), they nonetheless provided some interesting insights into the practice of effective teaching. For example, many of the research studies undertaken in the 1970s revealed a positive relationship between the effective management of academic time and higher student achievement. Research by Stallings *et al.* (1978) found that students who spent most of their time being instructed by teachers or working independently under teacher supervision, made greater gains than those who spent a lot of time in non-academic activities or who were expected to learn largely on their own. Similarly, Soar and Soar (1979) established that pupils learned more in classrooms where teachers established clear structures and routines. Furthermore, their research highlighted the fact that the teachers who exerted greater control generally elicited higher student achievement.

A major research study conducted by Powell (1980) found that the largest adjusted gains for students occurred in classes where teachers were well organised, maximised time devoted to instruction and minimised time for presentation and who spent most of their time actively instructing the students. Other research studies also reinforced the importance of structuring subject content through clear presentation, providing feedback and effective questioning (Clark *et al.*, 1979; Bennett *et al.*, 1981; Smith and Land, 1981; Wragg, 1984).

Pupils achieve more, when a teacher does the following:

- emphasises academic goals;
- makes them explicit and expects pupils to be able to master the curriculum;
- carefully organises and sequences the curriculum;
- clearly explains and illustrates what pupils are to learn;
- frequently asks direct and specific questions to monitor students' progress and check their understanding;
- provides pupils with ample opportunity to practise;
- gives prompts and feedback to ensure success;
- corrects mistakes and allows pupils to use a skill until it is over-learned or automatic;
- reviews regularly and holds pupils accountable for work.
    (Doyle, 1987, p.95)

Figure 16.1

The research on teacher effectiveness repeatedly emphasises *direct instruction* as a route to higher student achievement. This is described as explicit, step-wise instruction, emphasising student learning and cognitive achievement (Rosenshine, 1983). It is suggested that students achieve more when teachers employ such a structured approach to their teaching. The features of structured teaching are summarised in Figure 16.1.

Teachers promote student learning by: structuring and organising their teaching tightly; by explaining to students what they are to learn; by providing continuous feedback. The research evidence has consistently demonstrated that teachers achieve higher learning outcomes from pupils using such approaches in the classroom.

In their major review of the research on teacher effectiveness Brophy and Good (1986) conclude: to maximise student achievement the teacher should focus upon the *quantity and pacing of instruction*. This is the most consistently replicated of the research findings. The main features of quantity and pacing of instruction according to Brophy and Good (1986) include:

- emphasis upon academic instruction as a major part of the teacher's role;
- high engagement rates (ensured by organising and managing the classroom efficiently);
- use of activities of appropriate difficulty, suited to achievement levels and needs.

In another major review of the literature Porter and Brophy (1988) suggest that effective teachers are semi-autonomous professionals who possess certain characteristics, summarised in Figure 16.2.

Effective teachers:

- are clear about their instructional goals;
- are knowledgeable about their content and the strategies for teaching it;
- communicate to their students what is expected of them – and why;
- make expert use of existing teaching materials in order to devote more time to practices that enrich and clarify the content;
- are knowledgeable about their students, adapting teaching to their needs and anticipating misconceptions in their existing knowledge;
- teach students 'meta-cognitive strategies' and give them opportunities to master them;
- address higher as well as lower level cognitive objectives;
- monitor students' understanding by offering regular, appropriate feedback;
- integrate their teaching with that in other subject areas;
- accept responsibility for student outcomes;
- are thoughtful and reflective about their practice.
    (Porter and Brophy, 1988)

Figure 16.2

The literature on effective teaching is replete with such cues and tactics necessary for effective teaching. Brophy and Good (1986) reviewed the research on teaching behaviours and found that those most associated with student achievement gains were as follows:

Content coverage. Students learn more when their teachers cover more material.

Time allocated to instruction. Students learn more when teachers allocate available class time to academic activities.

Engaged time. Students learn more when on task a high proportion of the time.

Consistent success. Students learn more when their success rates are high.

Active teaching. Students learn more in classes where their teachers spend most of their time actively teaching, rather than students working on their own without direct supervision.

In summary, the majority of the research studies exploring teacher behaviour, consistently endorsed a 'structured' or direct mode of instruction as being most effective in the classroom.

Effective teaching skills

In addition to the extensive research on teaching behaviour, much has been written about effective teaching skills (see for example Perrott, 1982). Yet the various research studies reveal a number of perspectives on the skills used in teaching. Leinhardt and Greeno (1986) argue that teaching is a complex cognitive skill based on knowledge about how to construct and conduct a lesson and about the content to be taught. Similarly, Wragg (1984) views teaching skills as strategies that teachers use which facilitate pupils learning, not to be seen in isolation. Research into teaching skills has shown that three important elements are discernible:

1. Knowledge, comprising the teacher's knowledge about the subject, curriculum teaching methods, the influence on teaching and learning of other factors and knowledge about one's own teaching.
2. Decision making, comprising the thinking and decision making which occurs before, during and after a lesson, concerning how best to achieve the educational outcomes intended.
3. Action, comprising the overt behaviour by teachers undertaken to foster pupil learning (Kyriacou, 1991).

Kyriacou (1986) and other writers have highlighted the *active* or *interactive* nature of teaching skills. Clark and Peterson (1986) note how teachers' effectiveness in the classroom seems to depend on how well they modify and change their strategies as lessons proceed. Furthermore, Calderhead (1986) suggests that it is useful to define effective teaching skills in an interactive way as possessing certain features:

- they are intended to achieve a particular goal;
- they take into account the particular context;
- they require precision and fine tuning;
- they are performed smoothly;
- they are acquired through training and practice.

While the research literature contains many lists of teaching skills, Mortimore (1994) has summarised the skills that modern teachers need in order to be effective. These are reproduced in Figure 16.3 on p. 184. This list is similar to that proposed by Kyriacou (1991) in his comprehensive study of essential teaching skills. It also reflects those teaching skills consistently identified as being important by Her Majesty's Inspectorate (HMI, 1977, 1990).

Effective teaching styles

The question *how best to teach* has been most typically formulated in the

---

Effective teaching skills

Organisational – to sort out materials and sources of information.
Analytical – to break down complex sources of information.
Synthesising – to build ideas into arguments.
Presentational – to clarify complex information without harming its integrity.
Assessing – to judge the work of pupils so that appropriate feedback can be given.
Managerial – to coordinate the dynamics of individuals, groups and classes.
Evaluative – to improve teaching continually.
  (Mortimore, 1994)

Figure 16.3

literature in terms of what teaching method is best. Research by Bennett (1976) and Galton *et al.* (1980) explored the relative effectiveness of different 'teaching styles', or approaches. Bennett's research looked at pupil gains in standardised tests of reading, mathematics and English and involved two polarised teaching styles, namely a 'traditional' and a 'progressive' style. His findings showed that teachers representative of the 'traditional' or 'formal' teaching style were generally more effective. However, the findings from this research have been considerably qualified following a re-analysis of the data (Aitken *et al.*, 1981; Bennett, 1987, 1988).

Another well-known study of teaching styles in primary classrooms was that of Galton *et al.* (1980). This study concluded that teaching approaches which involved close teacher control and effective classroom management were most prevalent in the primary classroom. The study did not reach a conclusion concerning the optimum teaching style, but instead underlined the complexity of relating teaching styles directly to pupil learning outcomes. Subsequent research studies which considered teaching styles in the primary sector, such as that by Steedman (1980), similarly exposed the difficulty of identifying 'effective' teaching styles.

At secondary school level there have been fewer studies focusing directly upon teaching styles. The major study, conducted by Rutter *et al.* (1979), into secondary school effectiveness commented upon different teaching styles and pupil learning. However, the study also noted the difficulty associated with defining teaching styles and relating them directly to pupil outcomes. Other subject-focused studies at secondary school, e.g. within science (Eggleston *et al.*, 1976) and within mathematics (Heene and Schulsman, 1988), reached similar conclusions.

In summary, whatever the relative merits of different teaching approaches or styles, the research findings reveal little concrete evidence in favour of one teaching style in terms of overall effectiveness. Indeed, several authors have highlighted the difficulty of establishing a direct link between particular aspects of teacher effectiveness and students' learning (Coker *et al.*, 1988; Mortimore and MacBeath, 1994). The major problem in looking at the effectiveness of different teaching styles with any precision is due to the sheer diversity of teaching situations and contexts.

The research concerning teaching styles, therefore, is very much of a hortatory nature, with little recourse to clear empirical evidence. Despite the extensive literature of theories and investigations (e.g. Anthony, 1979) it seems that a mixture of approaches or styles suited to the learning context is preferable. The National Evaluation of TVEI (Technical and Vocational Education Initiative) concluded that 'a teacher who mixes his/her methods as appropriate to the topic is doing as much as we would commonly ask' (Hazelwood, 1988, p.71).

Effective teaching models

At the core of the effective teaching process is the arrangement of a *learning environment* within which pupils can interact and study how to learn (Dewey, 1916). Joyce and Weil (1996) suggest that there are *models of teaching* which describe particular types of learning environment and approaches to teaching. This research views teaching in terms of several distinct models designed to bring about particular kinds of learning. Unlike the early research on teaching behaviour, models of teaching are not premised on matching behaviour to student outcomes. The work on teaching models underlines the need for teachers to adopt a wide repertoire of teaching approaches which foster different types of pupil learning.

The most extensive work on developing effective teaching models has been carried out by Bruce Joyce and various colleagues (Joyce *et al.*, 1987; Joyce and Showers, 1988, 1991; Joyce and Weil, 1996). The most recent review of teaching models was conducted by Joyce *et al.* (1997). This book suggests that there are *four* families of models of teaching based upon the types of learning they promote and on their orientation of how people learn. The four families of models of teaching are as follows.

The information processing family

Information processing models emphasise ways of organising data, sensing concepts and generating solutions to problems. Some models in this family provide the learner with information and concepts, some emphasise concept formation and hypothesis testing by the learner and other models generate creative thinking. The information processing models help pupils learn how to construct knowledge, as they focus directly upon intellectual capacity.

Social family models of teaching

This family of models is premised upon the importance of working together within a social context. The social models of teaching are constructed to take advantage of cooperative relationships in the classroom and to produce integrative and productive ways of interacting which support vigorous learning activity. The social family of models help pupils learn how to sharpen their own cognition through interaction, how to work productively with individuals and how to work as a member of a team.

Personal family models of teaching and learning

The personal models of teaching begin from the perspective of the self-hood of the individual. They attempt to shape education so that individuals can come to understand themselves better, to take responsibility for individual development and can be more sensitive and creative in the search for high quality lives. The cluster of personal models of teaching pays great attention to the individual perspective and seeks to encourage productive independence, so that individuals can become increasingly self-aware and responsible for their own destiny.

Behavioural systems family of models of teaching and learning

This set of models are also known as behaviour modification, behaviour therapy and cybernetics. These models are based on the idea that we learn through feedback and adjustment. The most famous studies in this area became known as 'stimulus and response' studies, with psychologists like Skinner (1953) organising task and feedback structures to make it easy for human beings to self-correct and to learn.

Joyce and Weil (1996) argue that the development of a model of teaching is the process of submitting an educational idea to repeated testing until it can guarantee a learning effect. Consequently, for over 30 years the research on models of teaching has inquired into the effects of teaching the underlying model of learning. The concept of effect size (Glass, 1982) is used to describe the magnitude of gains from any given change in educational practice and thus to predict what can be gained. The research into effect size and models of teaching has consistently shown that there are substantial gains in learning from using different models of teaching. The relationship between different models of teaching and their effect size is summarised in Figure 16.4.

Teaching models

Advance organisers and mnemonics are models from the **information processing family** and yield modest to substantial effect sizes. These effects have been shown to be long lasting.

Cooperative learning approaches are models from the **social family** and yield effect sizes from modest to high. The more complex the intended outcomes, i.e. higher order thinking, problem solving, social skills and attitudes, the greater the effects.

'Synectics' and non-directive teaching are models from the **personal family** and increase student creativity and enhance self-concept as well as affecting student achievement in areas such as recall of information.

Direct instruction is a model from the **behavioural systems family** and yields modest effect and has been shown to increase general aptitude to learn.

(From Joyce, Calhoun and Hopkins, 1997)

Figure 16.4

The research evidence shows that when these models and strategies are combined they have even greater potential for improving pupil learning and making teaching more effective.

Teacher artistry

This final dimension of the research on effective teaching is of a different order from that associated with teacher behaviour/skills and teaching styles/models. Within this research tradition there is the central recognition that teaching involves creativity and is carried out in a highly personalised way. This model emphasises the personal responsibility for creating the conditions for effective learning undertaken by the teacher. While effective learning *can* take place in the absence of effective teaching, optimum results will occur when there is a good match of the two. The ability to match these two has been characterised as 'artistry'. Artistry characterises a highly personalised and individualistic approach to the study of teaching (Hopkins *et al.*, 1994). The idea of artistry in teaching was summarised by Rubin (1985):

> There is a striking quality to fine classrooms. Pupils are caught up in learning; excitement abounds; and playfulness and seriousness blend easily because the purposes are clear, the goals sensible and an unmistakable feeling of well-being prevails. Artist teachers achieve these qualities by knowing both their subject matter and their students; by guiding the learning with deft control – a control that itself is born out of perception, intuition and creative impulse.
>
> (p.v)

Artistry incorporates the recognition that teaching is a highly creative and personal activity. Unlike the previous research on teacher behaviour and models, the research evidence here does not lend itself to specifications or lists of features. Yet this perspective on teaching is one which has received belated attention (Armstrong, 1980; Rowland, 1984; Gray, 1990; Louden, 1991). The importance of a good and vital interrelationship with students is at the core of artistry. Being an effective teacher involves the capability to engage with and turn to advantage events and responses that could not have been anticipated.

Conclusion

A number of conclusions can be drawn from this review of the effective teaching literature. Firstly, effective teaching is highly dependent upon the nature of the educational outcomes and goals that the teaching is aiming to foster. Secondly, there are central qualities, skills and behaviours necessary for effective teaching. Thirdly, an extensive repertoire of teaching models or styles is an essential prerequisite of effective teaching. Finally, effective teaching is linked to reflection, enquiry and continuous professional development and growth. Effective teaching requires teacher commitment to be effective. In order to foster such commitment in schools teachers should feel that their work is respected, valued and appreciated. Furthermore, teachers need to feel that they are part of a professional community in which it is recognised that the quality of teaching is linked to professional development and growth.

While the conclusions from these research studies are valuable, questions about the process of teaching which these studies have raised remain. There are some areas of this field which remain largely unexplored. One area is that of differential teacher effectiveness. Why is it that the same teachers are highly effective in one classroom or school and not in another? Similarly, there are questions about differential effectiveness of teachers within the same departments that require further investigation (Sammons et al., 1995; Harris et al., 1995).

Another area little touched on by existing studies is that of ineffective teaching practices. Is it the case that the characteristics of the ineffective teacher are simply the reverse of those of the effective teacher? At present there is insufficient empirical evidence to demonstrate that this is or is not the case. Finally, one of the most important areas neglected by existing research is the consideration of exactly *how* teachers become more effective. With the exception of the work of Joyce et al. (1987, 1997) and researchers within the field of school improvement, much of the work on effective teaching has been concerned with describing, analysing and categorising practice. There is little to suggest that these type of research findings lead to more effective teaching. Consequently, within the current climate of competition, raising standards and achievement, there is an urgent need for more studies of teaching which focus on *improving* rather than *describing* effective teaching classroom practice.

References

Aitken, M., Anderson, D. and Hind, J. (1981) 'Statistical modelling of data on teaching styles', *Journal of Royal Statistical Society* **144**, 419–61.

Anthony, W. (1979) 'Progressive learning theories: the evidence', in Berbaum, G. (ed.) *Schooling in Decline*. London: Macmillan.

Armstrong, M. (1980) *Closely Observed Children*. London: Writers and Readers.

Bennett, N. (1976) *Teaching Styles and Pupil Progress*. London: Open Books.

Bennett, N. (1987) 'Changing perspectives on teaching – learning processes in the post-Plowden era', *Oxford Review of Education* **13**(1), 67–79.

Bennett, N. (1988) 'The effective primary school teacher: the search for a theory of pedagogy', *Teaching and Teacher Education* **4**(1), 19–30.

Bennett, N. and Carre, C. (eds) (1993) *Learning to Teach*. London: Routledge.

Bennett, N. *et al.* (1981) *The Quality of Pupil Learning Experiences: Interim Report*. Lancaster: University of Lancaster Centre for Educational Research and Development.

Bickel, E. and Bickel, D. D. (1986) 'Effective schools, classrooms and instruction: implications for special children', *Exceptional Children* **52**(6), 489–500.

Borich, G. D. (1988) *Effective Teaching Methods*. Columbus, OH: Merrill.

Brophy, J. and Good, T. L. (1974) *Teacher–Student Relationships: causes and consequences*. New York: Holt, Rinehart and Wilson.

Brophy, J. and Good, T. L. (1986) 'Teacher behaviour and student achievement', in Wittrock, M. (ed.) *Handbook of Research Teaching*, 3rd edn. New York: Macmillan.

Calderhead, J. (1986) 'A cognitive perspective on teaching skills'. Paper presented at the British Psychological Society Education Section Annual Conference, Nottingham.

Clark, C. M. and Peterson, P. L. (1986) 'Teachers' thought processes', in Wittrock, M. (ed.) *Handbook of Research Teaching*, 3rd edn. New York: Macmillan.

Clark, C. *et al.* (1979) 'A factorial experiment on teacher structuring, soliciting and reacting', *Journal of Educational Psychology* **71**(4), 534–52.

Coker, H., Medley, D. and Soar, R. (1988) 'How valid are expert opinions about effective teaching?', *Phi Delta Kappan* **149**, October, 131–4.

Dewey, J. (1916) *Democracy and Education*. New York: Macmillan.

Doyle, W. (1986) 'Research on teaching effects as a resource for improving instruction', in Wideen, M. and Andrews, I. (eds) *Staff Development for School Improvement*. Lewes: Falmer Press.

Dunkin, M. J. and Biddle, B. J. (1974) *The Study of Teaching*. New York: Holt, Rinehart and Winston.

Eggleston, J. F., Galton, M. J. and Jones, M. E. (1976) *Processes and Products of Science Teaching*. London: Macmillan.

Flanders, N. (1970) *Analysing Teacher Behaviour*. Reading: Addison-Wesley.

Gage, M. L. (1963) *Handbook of Research on Teaching*. Chicago: Rand McNally.

Gage, M. L. (1972) *Teacher Effectiveness and Teacher Education: the search for a scientific basis*. Palo Alto, Calif.: Pacific Books.

Gage, M. L. and Giaconia, R. (1983) 'Teaching practices and student achievement causal connections', *New York University Education Quarterly* **12**(3), 2–9.

Galton, M., Simon, B. and Croll, P. (1980) *Inside the Primary Classroom*. London: Routledge and Kegan Paul.

Getzels, J. W. and Jackson, P. W. (1963) 'The teacher's personality and characteristics', in Gage, M. L. (ed.) *Handbook of Research on Teaching*, 506–82. Chicago: Rand McNally.

Glass, G. V. (1982) 'Meta-analysis: an approach to the synthesis of research results', *Journal of Research in Science Teaching* **19**(2), 93–112.

Good, T. L. and Brophy, J. (1980) *Educational Psychology: a realistic approach*, 2nd edn. New York: Holt, Rinehart and Winston.

Good, T. L., Biddle, B. J. and Brophy, J. (1975) *Teachers Make a Difference*. New York: Holt, Rinehart and Winston.

Gray, J. (1990) 'The quality of schooling: frameworks for judgement', *British Journal of Educational Studies* **38**, 203–23.

Harris, A. (1998) 'Improving the effective department: strategies for growth and development', *Educational Management & Administration*.

Harris, A., Jamieson, I. M. and Russ, J. (1995) 'A study of effective departments in secondary schools', *School Organisation* **15**(3), 283–99.

Hazelwood, R. (1988) in Hopkins, D. (ed.) *TVEI at the Change of Life*. Bristol: Multilingual Matters.

Heene, J. and Schulsman, K. (1988) 'Teacher's effectiveness: the greybox', in McAlpine, S. *et al.* (eds) *New Challenges for Teachers and Teacher Education*. Amsterdam: Swets and Zeitlinger.

Her Majesty's Inspectorate (HMI) (1977) *Ten Good Schools*. London: HMSO.

Her Majesty's Inspectorate (HMI) (1990) *Standards in Education 1988–89*. London: DES.

Hopkins, D., Ainscow, M. and West, M. (1994) *School Improvement in an Era of Change*. London: Cassell.

Hopkins, D. *et al*. (1997) *Creating the Conditions For Classroom Improvement*. London: David Fulton Publishers.

Hughes, D. (1973) 'An experimental investigation of the effects of pupil responding and teacher reacting on pupil achievement', *American Educational Research Journal* **10**(1), 21–37.

Joyce, B. and Showers, B. (1988) *Student Achievement through Staff Development*. New York: Longman.

Joyce, B. and Showers, B. (1991) *Information Processing Models of Teaching*. Aptos, Calif.: Booksend Laboratories.

Joyce, B. and Weil, M. (1996) *Models of Teaching*, 4th edn. Englewood Cliffs, NJ: Prentice-Hall.

Joyce, B., Showers, B. and Rolheiser-Bennett, C. (1987) 'Staff development and student learning: a synthesis of research on models of teaching', *Educational Leadership* **47**(2), 11–23.

Joyce, B., Calhoun, E. and Hopkins, D. (1997) *Models of Teaching Tools For Learning*. London: Oxford University Press.

Kounin, J. S. (1970) *Discipline and Group Management in Classrooms*. New York: Holt, Rinehart and Winston.

Kounin, J. S. and Doyle, P. H. (1975) 'Degree of continuity of a lesson's signal system in the task involvement of children', *Journal of Educational Psychology* **67**, 159–64.

Kounin, J. S. and Gump, P. (1974) 'Signal systems of lesson settings and the task related behaviour of pre-school children', *Journal of Educational Psychology* **66**, 554–62.

Kyriacou, C. (1986) *Effective Teaching in Schools*. Oxford: Basil Blackwell.

Kyriacou, C. (1991) *Essential Teaching Skills*. Oxford: Basil Blackwell.

Leinhardt, G. and Greeno, J. G. (1986) 'The cognitive skill of teaching', *Journal of Educational Psychology* **78**(2), 75–95.

Louden, W. (1991) *Understanding Teaching*. London: Cassell.

Merson, M. (1990) 'The problem of teaching style in TVEI', in Hopkins, D. (ed.) *TVEI at the Change of Life*. Bristol: Multilingual Matters.

Mortimore, P. (1994) 'School effectiveness and the management of effective learning and teaching', *School Effectiveness and School Improvement* **4**(4), 290–310.

Mortimore, P. and MacBeath, J. (1994) 'Quest for the secrets of success', *Times Educational Supplement*, 25 March, 14.

Nutall, G. and Church, J. (1973) 'Experimental studies of teacher behaviour', in Channan, G. (ed.) *Towards a Science of Teaching*. London: NFER.

Perrott, E. (1982) *Effective Teaching*. London: Longman.

Porter, A. C. and Brophy, J. (1988) 'Synthesis of research on good teaching:

insights from the work of the Institute for Research on Teaching', *Educational Leadership* **46**, 74–85.

Powell, M. (1980) 'The beginning teacher evaluation study: a brief history of a major research project', in Denham, C. and Leieberman, A. (eds) *Time to Learn*. Washington, DC: National Institute of Education.

Reiss, V. (1982) *Influencing Educational Outcomes*. Frankfurt: Peter Lan.

Rosenshine, B. (1971) *Teaching Behaviours and Student Achievement*. Windsor: NFER.

Rosenshine, B. (1983) 'Teaching functions in instructional programs', *Elementary School Journal* **83**(4), 335–51.

Rowland, S. (1984) *The Enquiring Classroom*. London: Falmer Press.

Rubin, I. (1985) *Artistry and Teaching*. New York: Random House.

Rutter, M. *et al*. (1979) *Fifteen Thousand Hours: secondary schools and their effects on schoolchildren*. Somerset: Open Books.

Sammons, P. *et al*. (1995) 'Understanding school and developmental differences in academic effectiveness: findings from case studies of selected outlier secondary schools in inner London'. Paper presented to the International Congress for School Effectiveness and Improvement, Leeuwarden, The Netherlands.

Skinner, B. F. (1953) *Science and Human Behavior*. New York: Macmillan.

Smith, L. and Land, M. (1981) 'Low inference verbal behaviours related to teacher clarity', *Journal of Classroom Interaction* **17**(1), 37–42.

Soar, R. S. and Soar, R. M. (1979) 'Emotional climate and management', in Peterson, P. and Walberg, H. (eds) *Research on Teaching Concepts: Findings and Implications*. Berkeley, Calif.: McCutchan.

Stallings, J. *et al*. (1978) *A Study of Basic Reading Skills Taught in Secondary Schools*. Menlo Park, Calif.: SRI International.

Steedman, J. (1980) *Progress in Secondary Schools*. London: National Children's Bureau.

Stones, E. (1992) *Quality Teaching: a sample of cases*. London: Routledge.

Walberg, H. J. (1986) 'Syntheses of research on teaching', in Wittrock, M. (ed.) *Handbook of Research Teaching*, 3rd edn. New York: Macmillan.

Walberg, H. J. (1990) 'Productive teaching and instruction: assessing the knowledge base'. *Phi Delta Kappan* **71**, 470–78.

Wang, M. C., Haretel, G. D. and Walberg, H. J. (1990) 'What influences learning? A content analysis of review literature', *Journal of Educational Research* **84**(1), 30–43.

Wang, M. C. (1991) 'Productive teaching and instruction: assessing the knowledge base'. *Phi Delta Kappan* **71**(6), 470–78.

Wragg, E. C. (ed.) (1984) *Classroom Teaching Skills*. London: Croom Helm.

Wright, C. and Nutall, G. (1970) 'Relationships between teacher behaviours and pupil achievement in three experimental science lessons', *American Educational Research Journal* **7**(4), 447–91.

Chapter 17

Research into teacher effectiveness

Hay McBer

Editors' Note: The DfEE commissioned research from Hay McBer to provide a framework describing effective teaching. This chapter is a heavily abridged version of their report.

[. . .]

Three factors

This chapter is a summary of the main outcomes from our work. It is intended to be of practical use to teachers and head teachers who are interested in what we found to be important in effective teaching.

Our research confirms much that is already known about the attributes of effective teaching. It also adds some new dimensions that demonstrate the extent to which effective teachers make a difference for their pupils. We found three main factors within teachers' control that significantly influence pupil progress:

- teaching skills
- professional characteristics
  and
- classroom climate.

Each provides distinctive and complementary ways that teachers can understand the contribution they make. None can be relied on alone to deliver value-added teaching.

The measures of teacher effectiveness

The three factors (Figure 17.1) are different in nature. Two of them – professional characteristics and teaching skills – are factors which relate to

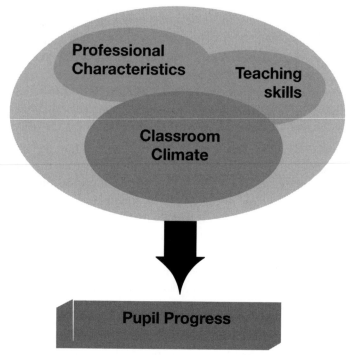

Figure 17.1

what a teacher brings to the job. The professional characteristics are the ongoing patterns of behaviour that combine to drive the things we typically do. Among those things are the 'micro-behaviours' covered by teaching skills. Whil teaching skills can be learned, sustaining these behaviours over the course of a career will depend on the deeper-seated nature of professional characteristics. Classroom climate, on the other hand, is an output measure. It allows teachers to understand how the pupils in their class feel about nine dimensions of climate created by the teacher that influence their motivation to learn.

So, for example, a teacher may have – among other things – the professional characteristic of Holding People Accountable, which is the drive and ability to set clear expectations and parameters and to hold others accountable for performance. Such a pattern of behaviour could make it more natural for this teacher to exhibit teaching skills like providing opportunities for students to take responsibility for their own learning, or correcting bad behaviour immediately. And the impact of these teaching skills, regularly exhibited, might be that pupils feel that there is a higher degree of Order in their class, or that there is the emotional Support needed to try new things.

It should be noted, however, that this is only an example. In other circumstances, with different pupils, in a different context, other approaches might have been more effective. There is, in other words, a multiplicity of ways in which particular patterns of characteristics determine how a teacher chooses which approach to use from a repertoire of established techniques in order to influence how pupils feel.

A summary of how the model works

All competent teachers know their subjects. They know the appropriate teaching methods for their subjects and curriculum areas and the ways pupils learn. More effective teachers make the most of their professional knowledge in two linked ways. One is the extent to which they deploy appropriate teaching skills consistently and effectively in the course of all their lessons – the sorts of teaching strategies and techniques that can be observed when they are at work in the classroom, and which underpin the national numeracy and literacy strategies. The other is the range and intensity of the professional characteristics they exhibit – ongoing patterns of behaviour which make them effective.

Pupil progress results from the successful application of subject knowledge and subject teaching methods, using a combination of appropriate teaching skills and professional characteristics. Professional characteristics can be assessed, and good teaching practice can be observed.

Classroom climate provides another tool for measuring the impact created by a combination of the teacher's skills, knowledge and professional characteristics. Climate is a measure of the collective perceptions of pupils regarding those dimensions of the classroom environment that have a direct impact on their capacity and motivation to learn.

Taken in combination, these three factors provide valuable tools for a teacher to enhance the progress of their pupils.

Factors that do not contribute

On the other hand, we found that biometric data (i.e. information about a teacher's age and teaching experience, additional responsibilities, qualifications, career history and so on) did not allow us to predict their effectiveness as a teacher. Effective and outstanding teachers came from diverse backgrounds. Our data did not show that school context could be used to predict pupil progress. Effective and outstanding teachers teach in all kinds of schools and school contexts. This means that using biometric data to predict a teacher's effectiveness could well lead to the exclusion of some potentially outstanding teachers. This finding is also consistent with the notion that pupil progress outcomes are affected more by a teacher's skills and professional characteristics than by factors such as their sex, qualifications or experience.

We used start-of-year and end-of-year pupil attainment data to underpin our assessment of relative effectiveness based on value added. Using this knowledge and the outcomes from our research described below, we have been able to model the impact teachers have on the classroom climate, how that climate affects pupil progress and what aspects of teaching skills and behavioural characteristics had most impact on climate.

Our findings suggest that, taken together, teaching skills, professional characteristics and classroom climate will predict well over 30 per cent of the variance in pupil progress. This is very important for teachers because it gives them a framework for assessing how they achieve their results and for identifying the priorities for improvement.

So we show that teachers really do make a difference. Within their classrooms, effective teachers create learning environments which foster pupil progress by deploying their teaching skills as well as a wide range of professional characteristics. Outstanding teachers create an excellent classroom climate and achieve superior pupil progress largely by displaying more professional characteristics at higher levels of sophistication within a very structured learning environment.

Teaching skills

Teaching skills are those 'micro-behaviours' that the effective teacher constantly exhibits when teaching a class. They include behaviours like:

- involving all pupils in the lesson;
- using differentiation appropriately to challenge all pupils in the class using a variety of activities or learning methods;
- applying teaching methods appropriate to the national curriculum objectives;
- using a variety of questioning techniques to probe pupils' knowledge and understanding.

The 35 behaviours we looked for are based on research conducted by Professor David Reynolds and other colleagues. They are clustered under the seven OFSTED inspection headings for ease of use (see Figure 17.2).

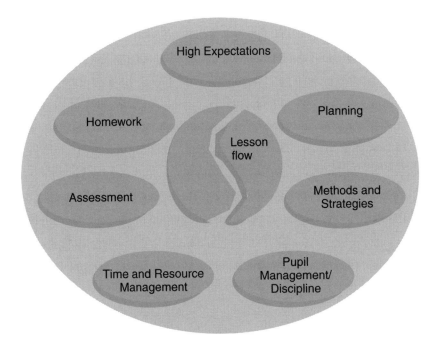

Figure 17.2 The teaching skills

In addition to the micro-behaviours under the seven inspection headings (Figure 17.2), teaching skills can be observed in terms of the way the lesson is structured and flows, and the number of pupils who are on task through the course of the lesson.

In primary schools, the outstanding teachers scored higher on average in four out of the seven clusters: High Expectations, Time and Resource Management, Assessment, and Homework. In secondary schools there was stronger differentiation covering all clusters, but it was particularly evident in High Expectations, Planning, and Homework.

Our lesson observations revealed that in classes run by effective teachers, pupils are clear about what they are doing and why they are doing it. They can see the links with their earlier learning and have some ideas about how it could be developed further. The pupils want to know more. They understand what is good about their work and how it can be improved. They feel secure in an interesting and challenging learning environment. And they support one another and know when and where to go for help. The research shows the criticality of the teacher in the pupil learning process. The effective teachers whom we observed and studied were very actively involved with their pupils at all times. Many of the activities were teacher-led. They created maximum opportunities to learn and no time was wasted. The environment was very purposeful and businesslike. But at the same time there was always a great deal of interaction between teacher and pupils.

One factor that led to this purposeful learning environment was the range of effective teaching skills and techniques deployed by the teacher in the classroom. The following paragraphs describe these skills and techniques in detail.

High expectations

Effective teachers set **High expectations** for the pupils and communicate them directly to the pupils. They challenge and inspire pupils, expecting the most from them, so as to deepen their knowledge and understanding. The most effective teachers determine the appropriateness of objectives for pupils by some form of differentiation. At its lowest level, this means expecting different outcomes from pupils of varying ability. At a more sophisticated level teachers know and use an extensive repertoire of means of differentiation – so that they are able to cope with the needs of more and less able pupils. But within these parameters effective teachers are relentless in their pursuit of a standard of excellence to be achieved by all pupils, and in holding fast to this ambition. These expectations are high, clear and consistent.

[. . .]

Planning

Effective teachers are good at **Planning**, setting a clear framework and objectives for each lesson. The effective teacher is very systematic in the preparation for, and execution of each lesson. The lesson planning is done in the context of the broader curriculum and longer-term plans. It is a very structured approach beginning with a review of previous lessons, and an overview of the objectives of the lesson linked to previous lessons and, where appropriate, the last homework assignment. Where homework is set (normally in secondary schools and for older primary pupils), the teacher often spends 5 to 10 minutes reviewing what pupils have learnt from it.

The effective teacher communicates the lesson content to be covered and the key activities for the duration of the lesson. Material is presented in small steps, with opportunities for pupils to practise after each step. Each activity is preceded by clear and detailed instructions. But the planning also takes into account the differing needs of pupils, including those with specific learning difficulties. For pupils, there is clarity of what they are doing, where they are going and how they will know when they have achieved the objectives of the lesson.

Effective teachers create the time to review lesson objectives and learning outcomes at the end of each lesson. Some teachers employ a Tactical Lesson Planning approach which describes both the content of the lesson and the learning objectives, and the methods to be employed. But the focus of the planning activity is on pupil learning outcomes.

In some schools, particularly special schools, the highly effective teachers involve support staff in the preparation of the curriculum/lesson plans, and outline to them the role they are expected to play.

[. . .]

Methods and strategies

Effective teachers employ a **Variety of teaching strategies** and techniques to engage pupils and to keep them on task. In our observations we saw effective teachers doing a great deal of active teaching. Many of the activities were led by the teacher. The teachers presented information to the pupils with a high degree of clarity and enthusiasm and, when giving basic instruction, the lessons proceeded at a brisk pace. Nevertheless, there was, in the majority of the classes, a range of teaching approaches and activities designed to keep the pupils fully engaged.

Individual work and small group activities were regularly employed as ways of reinforcing pupil learning through practice and reflection. However, it was evident that when the effective teachers were not actively leading the instructions they were always on the move, monitoring pupils' focus and understanding of materials. Content and presentation were varied to suit the needs of the class and the nature of learning objectives.

So what we saw effective teachers doing was a great deal of direct instruction to whole classes, interspersed with individual and small group work. But the active style of teaching does not result in passive pupils. Rather, there is a great deal of interaction between teacher and pupils. Effective teachers ask a lot of questions and involve the pupils in class discussion. In this way the pupils are actively engaged in the lesson, and the teacher is able to monitor pupils' understanding and challenge their thinking by skilful questioning. It is evident that effective teachers employ a sophisticated questioning approach – ranging from asking many brief questions on main and supplementary points to multiple questioning of individuals to provide greater understanding and challenge.

[. . .]

Pupil management/discipline

Effective teachers have a clear strategy for **Pupil management**. A sense of order prevails in the classroom. Pupils feel safe and secure. This pupil management strategy is a means to an end: allowing maximum time for pupils to be focused on task, and thus maximising the learning opportunity. Effective teachers establish and communicate clear boundaries for pupil behaviour. They exercise authority clearly and fairly from the outset, and in their styles of presentation and engagement they hold the pupils' attention. Inappropriate behaviour is 'nipped in the bud' with immediate direct action from the teacher. Some effective teachers employ a 'catch them being good' policy whereby pupil behaviour which is appropriate and on task is recognised and reinforced by praise. One outstanding teacher referred to the importance of the 'lighthouse effect' – being fully aware of everything that is going on in the classroom and having 360° vision.

In those schools where there was a likelihood of a high incidence of pupil misbehaviour, the effective teachers employed a very structured behavioural approach to each lesson, e.g. standing at the door to greet pupils; commanding attention at the beginning of the lesson; taking action on latecomers; taking direct and immediate action on inappropriate behaviours. The most effective teachers had a longer-term strategy of getting to know the pupils with behavioural problems. In other words the highly effective teacher is able to create an environment in which all pupils can learn by employing direct means of pupil management to ensure that disruption to pupil learning is minimised and pupils feel safe and secure.

[. . .]

Time and resource management

Effective teachers **Manage time and resources** wisely. The effective management of pupils, time, resources and support promotes good behaviour and effective learning. Effective teachers achieve the management of the class by having a clear structure for each lesson, making full use of planned time, using a brisk pace and allocating his or her time fairly among pupils. The effective teachers start their lessons on time and finish crisply with a succinct review of learning.

Where they are able to do so, pupils are encouraged to manage their own time well and to achieve what is required in the time available. The classrooms are effective learning environments in which activities run smoothly, transitions are brief, and little time is lost in getting organised or dealing with disruptions. In our observations we found that highly effective teachers managed to get well over 90 per cent of the pupils focused on task over the course of a lesson.

In those schools where support and/or parental help was available, the effective teachers involved helpers in the lesson planning stage and in the execution of the lessons. In some instances, support staff were trained in aspects of pupil management, reading support and computer skills.

[. . .]

Assessment

It is evident that effective teachers employ a range of **Assessment** methods and techniques to monitor pupils' understanding of lessons and work. These could be tests, competitions, questioning or regular marking of written work. The effective teachers look for gains in learning, gaps in knowledge and areas of misunderstanding through their day-to-day work with pupils. Also, effective teachers encourage pupils to judge the success of their own work and to set themselves targets for improvement. They also offer critical and supportive feedback to pupils.

[. . .]

Homework

An important part of the assessment process is the regular setting and marking of **Homework**, particularly in secondary schools. The effective teachers ensure that homework is integrated with class work, is tailored to individual needs and is regularly and constructively marked.

[. . .]

Time on task and lesson flow

Overall, effective teachers had well over 90 per cent of the pupils on task through the lesson, and their lessons flowed naturally to achieve an appropriate balance between:

- whole class interactive
- whole class lecture
- individual work
- collaborative group work
- classroom management
  and
- testing or assessment.

The full observation schedule used in our research has since been adapted by the DfEE as a standard observation tool which has been offered to all schools as part of the new performance management arrangements.

Professional characteristics

Professional characteristics are deep-seated patterns of behaviour which outstanding teachers display more often, in more circumstances and to a greater degree of intensity than effective colleagues. They are how the teacher does the job, and have to do with self-image and values; traits, or the way the teacher habitually approaches situations; and, at the deepest level, the motivation that drives performance.

From the in-depth interviews (behavioural event interviews) with the teachers in our sample we found that 16 characteristics contribute to effective teaching. Strength in five clusters is required. Certain different combinations of characteristics within these clusters can be equally effective. This is not a static 'one-size-fits-all' picture. Effective teachers show distinctive combinations of characteristics that create success for their pupils.

The dictionary of characteristics and the descriptions of different levels for each characteristic were not part of a pre-existing model. They are defined by the data we collected from teachers. (See Figure 17.3.)

[. . .]

Figure 17.3 The model of professional characteristics

Professionalism cluster

The driver for teachers is a core of strongly held and enacted values which, taken together, are a powerful basis for professionalism. There are four characteristics which describe this cluster or group of characteristics.

Respect for Others underpins everything the effective teacher does, and is expressed in a constant concern that everyone should treat pupils and all members of the school community with respect. Effective teachers explicitly value others, and value the diversity in the school community, and retain their respect of others even when sorely tried. Outstanding teachers take a number of steps over time to create a feeling of community in the class or in the school. Effective teachers also provide **Challenge and Support** – a 'tough caring' where they not only cater for pupils' needs for physical and psychological safety but, crucially, repeatedly express positive expectations and build pupils' self-esteem and belief that they can succeed, as learners and in life. Threshold and outstanding teachers do everything in their power to ensure *all* pupils get the best deal possible from their education.

Effective teachers show **Confidence** in most situations, expressing optimism about their own abilities and making an active contribution in meetings.

203

Over time this confidence grows, so that a teacher sees him or herself as a fully rounded professional, able to succeed in most circumstances. Effective teachers take a full part in moving the school forward and improving its effectiveness, drawing on their experience to help shape policies and procedures.

They have emotional resilience in dealing with challenging pupils and situations where, because they have a range of professional skills and have already experienced similar challenges, they are able to keep calm. This ability is fuelled by a conviction about the importance and value of what they are doing as highly effective practitioners in shaping the future of their pupils. They identify with the job and see the challenge of an increasingly 'front line' role as part of the territory. The very best go even further, rising to stretching challenges and expressing a belief that they will succeed against the odds.

Effective teachers are consistent and fair, **Creating Trust** with their pupils because they honour their commitments. They are genuine, and generate the atmosphere where pupils can venture to be themselves, express themselves and not be afraid of making mistakes – an important starting point for learning. They are a dependable point of reference in what, for many pupils, is a turbulent world. As they progress in the profession, increasingly they live up to their professional beliefs.

These characteristics, taken together, result in an underlying concern for pupils and their achievement. Effective teachers are quite evidently there to support their pupils, and their sense of vocation is at the heart of the model of effective teaching.

Characteristic definitions:
Challenge and Support: A commitment to do everything possible for each pupil and enable all pupils to be successful.
Confidence: The belief in one's ability to be effective and to take on challenges.
Creating Trust: Being consistent and fair. Keeping one's word.
Respect for Others: The underlying belief that individuals matter and deserve respect.

Thinking cluster

The **Thinking** that effective teachers bring to the job is characterised by **Analytical Thinking** – the drive to ask why, to see cause and effect and think ahead to implications; and **Conceptual Thinking** – the ability to see patterns in behaviour and situations and, at the level of outstanding teaching, to adapt creatively and apply concepts, ideas and best practice. Effective teachers plan individual lessons, units and programmes of work soundly based on data and evidence-led assessment of pupils, and evaluation of results. They attend to what is actually happening and have a logical, systematic approach to the job, looking after the details in order to achieve success for all pupils. Outstanding teachers are able to analyse many more variables in a complex situation, and have the ability to trace many possible causes and effects.

Characteristic definitions:
Analytical Thinking: The ability to think logically, break things down, and recognise cause and effect.
Conceptual Thinking: The ability to see patterns and links, even when there is a lot of detail.

Planning and setting expectations cluster

By adopting a professional approach, teachers' energy can be channelled into **Planning and Setting Expectations**, targeting the key elements which will make the most difference to their pupils, and the results they are able to achieve. Teaching is a demanding role and the pace of change rapid. Effective teachers are committed to meeting the needs of all pupils and to including everyone in the class. This means carefully prioritising and targeting their efforts so that all pupils get their fair share of attention and everyone achieves good results. There are three characteristics which group together in this cluster of the model.

In terms of **Drive for Improvement**, all effective teachers want not only to do a good job but also to set and measure achievement against an internal standard of excellence. Threshold teachers seek to do everything they can to improve the attainment of their pupils, to make the school itself more effective in raising achievement, and to reflect on and improve their own professional practice. Outstanding teachers continuously set and meet ambitious targets for themselves and their pupils. They refer regularly to visible, quantifiable and tangible measures; and they focus on whether they and the school really are making a difference and adding value to pupils.

Information Seeking works with this drive for results. All effective teachers ask questions to get a first-hand understanding of what is going on. At threshold level teachers dig deeper to find out more about their pupils and their classes, so they can set differentiated programmes of work, and targets that start from an understanding of prior attainment and potential perfor-mance. Outstanding teachers continually gather information from wider and more varied sources and use their own systems progressively to do so.

All effective teachers use their **Initiative** to seize immediate opportunities and sort out problems before they escalate, and are able to act decisively in a crisis situation. Pupils in their classes will be aware of the 'lighthouse effect', the habitual scanning by which effective teachers appear to pick up everything that is going on. Threshold and outstanding teachers show a stronger ability to think and act ahead, to seize a future opportunity or to anticipate and address future problems: for example, to enrich the curriculum or to bring additional resources into the school.

Characteristic definitions:

Drive for Improvement: Relentless energy for setting and meeting challenging targets, for pupils and the school.

Information Seeking: A drive to find out more and get to the heart of things; intellectual curiosity.

Initiative: The drive to act now to anticipate and pre-empt events.

Leading cluster

In terms of delivery of effective teaching and learning, teachers take a role in **Leading** others. There are four characteristics in this cluster of the model.

In their drive to motivate and provide clear direction to pupils, all effective teachers are adept at **Managing Pupils**. They get pupils on task, clearly stating learning objectives at the beginning of a lesson and recapping at the end, and giving clear instructions about tasks. They keep pupils informed about how the lesson fits into the overall programme of work, and provide feedback to pupils about their progress. Threshold teachers are more consistently able to make every lesson effective and remove any barriers to the effective working of the class and groups within it. Outstanding teachers go further, going out of their way to get extra materials or extra resources they need. Many of them are able consistently to enthuse pupils in their classes and achieve full involvement, creating a positive, upbeat atmosphere to secure the results planned.

All teachers demonstrate a **Passion for Learning** by providing a stimulating classroom environment, giving demonstrations, checking understanding and providing whole class, group and individual practice in using and applying skills and knowledge. They consistently differentiate teaching and learning when it is appropriate to do so, to help all pupils learn and to tailor opportunities to practise, embed and extend new learning to each pupil. Outstanding teachers are able to go further in the extent to which they are consistently able to support all pupils in their classes to think for themselves, and to deepen their understanding of a subject or a skill.

Effective teachers show a high degree of **Flexibility**. Not only are they open to new approaches and able to adapt procedures to meet the demands of a situation, but they are also flexible in the classroom and outside.

At threshold level, when they need to change direction they do so fluently. If they are not getting through to a pupil or a class they approach things from another angle, accessing a wide repertoire of teaching techniques and methods to do so. They are also able to deviate from and return to a lesson plan, to take advantage of an unexpected occurrence or to pursue something in which pupils show particular interest.

Because effective teachers are determined that pupils will achieve good results, they are committed to **Holding People Accountable** – both pupils and others with whom they work in the school. They set clear expectations of behaviour and for performance, and contract with pupils on these, setting clear boundaries for what is acceptable. In this way they provide a clear framework, routines and security in which work can take place. Teachers at threshold level go further, in that they constantly keep pupils and others up to the mark and get them to do what they had undertaken to do. Outstanding teachers consistently and successfully confront poor performance, taking timely and decisive action to ensure performance recovery.

Characteristic definitions:
Flexibility: The ability and willingness to adapt to the needs of a situation and change tactics.
Holding People Accountable: The drive and ability to set clear expectations and parameters and to hold others accountable for performance.
Managing Pupils: The drive and the ability to provide clear direction to pupils, and to enthuse and motivate them.
Passion for Learning: The drive and an ability to support pupils in their learning, and to help them become confident and independent learners.

Relating to others cluster

Underpinning their leadership role, effective teachers are good at **Relating to Others**. In this cluster there are three characteristics. Effective teachers have strengths in **Understanding Others**, working out the significance of the behaviour of pupils and others, even when this is not overtly expressed. Outstanding and threshold teachers have a deep insight into the reasons for the ongoing behaviour of others: why pupils and others act the way they do. They have an insight into what will motivate others, or what may be obstructing learning.

It also means they can use their ability to **Impact and Influence** pupils to perform. All effective teachers use several different logical arguments to persuade. At threshold level, teachers are able consistently to calculate what will appeal to pupils – and others – so that learning can be vivid, memorable and fun. Outstanding teachers go further in their use of indirect influence, with and through others, to bring about positive educational outcomes. This, together with their own deep understanding of and enthusiasm for their subject or specialism, works as a strong influencing factor on pupils and how they engage with learning.

Finally, all effective teachers are good at **Teamworking**. Not only do they provide help and support to colleagues, but they also seek and value their ideas and input. Outstanding teachers are active in building team spirit and the 'feel good' factor, so that people in the school feel part of the team, identify with it, and are proud of what it is doing to support pupils in achieving their full potential, as learners and in life.

Characteristic definitions:

Impact and Influence: The ability and the drive to produce positive outcomes by impressing and influencing others.

Teamworking: The ability to work with others to achieve shared goals.

Understanding Others: The drive and ability to understand others, and why they behave as they do.

Classroom climate

Classroom climate is defined as the collective perceptions by pupils of what it feels like to be a pupil in any particular teacher's classroom, where those perceptions influence every student's motivation to learn and perform to the best of his or her ability.

Our research shows that effective teachers use their knowledge, skills and behaviours to create effective learning environments in their classrooms. They create environments which maximise opportunities to learn, in which pupils are well managed and motivated to learn. From the pupils' perspectives, they are mostly looking to the teacher to create a sense of security and order in the classroom, an opportunity to participate actively in the class and for it to be an interesting and exciting place.

Each climate dimension represents an aspect of how the pupils feel in that classroom. They are defined as follows:

1. **Clarity** around the purpose of each lesson. How each lesson relates to the broader subject, as well as clarity regarding the aims and objectives of the school.
2. **Order** within the classroom, where discipline, order and civilised behaviour are maintained.
3. A clear set of **Standards** as to how pupils should behave and what each

pupil should do and try to achieve, with a clear focus on higher rather than minimum standards.

4. **Fairness:** the degree to which there is an absence of favouritism, and a consistent link between rewards in the classroom and actual performance.
5. **Participation:** the opportunity for pupils to participate actively in the class by discussion, questioning, giving out materials, and other similar activities.
6. **Support:** feeling emotionally supported in the classroom, so that pupils are willing to try new things and learn from mistakes.
7. **Safety:** the degree to which the classroom is a safe place, where pupils are not at risk from emotional or physical bullying, or other fear-arousing factors.
8. **Interest:** the feeling that the classroom is an interesting and exciting place to be, where pupils feel stimulated to learn.
9. **Environment:** the feeling that the classroom is a comfortable, well organised, clean and attractive physical environment.

[. . .]

Chapter 18

Learning more about learning improves teacher effectiveness

John Munro

Editors' Note: John Munro describes a study which supports the view that when teachers make their knowledge of the learning process explicit, it has a direct impact on their effective teaching.

Recent examinations of the factors influencing school effectiveness identified variables associated with teacher–learner interactions. The existence of this factor is hardly surprising since a major function of schools is to create environments in which students can learn, and the more successfully these interactions are managed, the more effective the school is likely to be. While organisational aspects of schools provide the necessary preconditions for effective teaching, it is the quality of teacher–student interactions that determines it (Caldwell and Spinks, 1992).

It is reasonable then, to expect a strong nexus between teacher effectiveness and school effectiveness. Successful learning requires learner activity in several areas. Contemporary social-constructivist theories of learning (Voight, 1994; von Glaserfeld, 1988) develop the notion of learners constructing knowledge during social interactions by changing what they already know. The interactions foster various 'learning functions' that have an impact on a learner's existing knowledge in various ways. Examples of learning functions include having a purpose or reason for learning, being in a state of 'cognitive conflict', having an impression of the outcome or goal of the learning, reviewing what has been learnt, encoding the change in knowledge in long-term memory and integrating it with what is known. These functions can be implemented either spontaneously by learners, or they can be initiated, managed, and directed by the teaching.

Teachers, through their selective and systematic use of a range of teaching procedures, can activate the use of these functions. The likelihood of learning and the quality of the learning outcome is determined by teachers' activation. The extent to which teachers provide the opportunity for students to be challenged by a novel set of ideas and to link them with their existing knowledge determines in part student motivation to learn these novel ideas.

The extent to which teachers provide the opportunity for students to encode ideas in long-term memory determines in part how well the students will recall these ideas later. For teaching to be optimally effective, teachers need to create the opportunity for the learning functions to be used.

It seems reasonable then, to expect that teacher knowledge about learning may influence the effectiveness of a school. A review by Scheerens (1992) supports this expectation. Factors that influenced effectiveness included structured teaching, use of learning time, provision of the opportunity to learn, monitoring student progress, students' self-perceptions as learners, and attitudes to school and high expectations (Holdaway and Johnson, 1993; Mortimore, 1993; Scheerens, 1992; Stoll and Fink, 1994). One might expect that the likelihood of provision of these conditions would depend in part on a teacher's knowledge of learning. Changing teacher knowledge about learning may be expected to change teacher and hence school effectiveness.

[. . .]

Teacher knowledge about learning can be examined from various perspectives. The present investigation considers two: quality and relevance and availability of use. In terms of its quality, it has been noted with increasing frequency recently that teacher knowledge about learning is referenced on inappropriate theories (Brown, 1994).

[. . .]

For most teachers, knowledge about learning is organised principally as complete episodes that encapsulate their set of experiences (Munro, 1994). Experience .. . guides subsequent teaching actions. Actions taken and decisions made in classrooms are more likely to be justified on the basis of having worked in the past rather than being supported by specific learning propositions. This type of knowledge is appropriate in similar future situations where the goal is to implement previously learnt regimes. However, experience by itself is insufficient in situations in which transfer of knowledge to substantially different situations, and a capacity to initiate and respond effectively to change are required. It is also insufficient in situations that focus on debate about theories of effective teaching or learning.

For effective teaching, teachers need to restructure their knowledge into explicit theories of learning that are based on their personal experiences. These theories generate testable propositions that can be investigated in teaching practice. These theories need to be compared with appropriate 'public' domain theories of learning so that they can benefit optimally from current cultural knowledge of learning. The present study examines whether teacher engagement in this type of restructuring activity leads to an increase in teaching effectiveness.

[. . .]

The present investigation used a structured professional development activity that combines aspects of direct instruction, peer coaching and reflection to facilitate the restructuring process. Teachers engaged in a systematic analysis of their existing knowledge of learning and of their beliefs about learning. They tested these against empirical data collected by them and their colleagues in teaching and against contemporary theories of learning. They mapped their theories into teaching procedures and put these to trial in their classes.

Assumptions were made about the nature of the theories of learning that individual teachers can be assisted to construct. It was assumed that teacher theories of learning are personal, derive from unique experiences, and are transient in the sense that they are modifiable. It was also assumed that they can be seen to be comprised of a number of key components. Each component was thought of as a 'mental hook' on which learning concepts can be hung. Together, these components form a scaffold for organising a person's knowledge about learning. Each component was mapped onto an area of enquiry by the professional development activity.

The first component related to the nature of the learning process. It included a consideration of definitions, beliefs and attitudes learners have of learning, the structures of different types of learning outcomes, the conditions under which learning is more likely, and the actions learners use to learn. The second component addressed variation in the ways in which learners learn, and the implications of these for effective teaching. The third component examined the process by which learners show what they know, its influence on further learning, the relationship between this and assessment, the opportunities learners perceive they have for this, and teaching implications such as ways of broadening and automatising the ways learners have to show what they know.

The remaining components addressed strategies for learning new content knowledge, ways of learning, positive attitudes to learning, the use of working memory space during learning, learning by reading, writing and listening, long-term retention of knowledge, learning in different sociological contexts (individually, in small collaborative groups, and in large groups), and students learning to organise themselves as learners and monitoring their progress in learning. The various components were integrated into a scaffold or framework used by teachers to examine and restructure their implicit knowledge about learning.

The present investigation made assumptions about the means by which the restructuring could be facilitated within the context of the contemporary school community. It was assumed that teachers would be more likely to explicate their implicit knowledge when they (1) had a reason for doing this (that is, they were supportively challenged), (2) had an opportunity to engage in learning and change processes (that is, activities such as researching and evaluating their teaching, critical reflection of practice, responding to challenges, collecting classroom data and reflecting on it were demonstrably legitimised and valued in their teaching contexts), and (3) had the opportunity to implement change in their classrooms. These assumptions mirror the components identified as necessary for teacher change (Fullan and Pomfret, 1977; Grant, 1984; Schon, 1987).

Six main conditions were identified as necessary for teacher change: when teachers (1) had the opportunity to learn through active construction processes, (2) saw that their existing implicit knowledge about learning was valued, (3) framed up goals or challenges for learning, (4) had the opportunity for individual and collegiate collaborative activities, (5) engaged in self-direction and systematic reflection of their practice, and (6) explored and demonstrated new teaching procedures in their classrooms.

[. . .]

The professional development activity directly encouraged teachers to frame up challenges in relation to learning and teaching.

Teachers, like other learners, differ in their preparedness to engage in change and the rate at which they implement it. This preparedness is related to teachers' implicit models of and beliefs about teaching and learning, and their relevant conceptual knowledge (Joyce et al. 1992). The professional development programme recognised the need to take account of a range of attitudes, from those who resist efforts to change their classroom practice, through those who are positive to small 'practical' change, to those who are willing and prepared to change.

Change is more likely when teachers have the opportunity for both collegiate collaborative activities (discussion, team teaching, mutual observation of teaching, joint problem solving; Glatthorn, 1987) and individual participant activity, engaging in self-direction and systematic reflection (Glatthorn, 1987; Wells and Chang, 1986). The change programme used recognised this need.

The focus on school effectiveness in the present investigation is at the microscopic level, on the teaching behaviours displayed by individual teachers. . . . The present study examines a mechanism for increasing the frequency of display of teaching behaviours that bring about these instructional outcomes.

Identifying teaching behaviours most likely to characterise effective teaching is no less difficult than defining effectiveness more generally. The present study used the learning principles identified by Brown (1994) for the community of learners, that is, a social-constructivist view of learning (Voight, 1994). To provide these types of learning contexts the following teaching behaviours needed to be displayed; behaviours that (1) facilitated the efficient use of student attention and thinking while learning, (2) facilitated the display of positive attitudes towards content area learning and learning behaviours, (3) provided students with a range of options for learning an idea and for showing what they had learnt, (4) helped pupils to learn to organise themselves more efficiently as learners, (5) developed learner-oriented behaviour management strategies such as on-task redirection strategies, (6) helped students improve how they learn, (7) assisted students to manage their learning in collaborative relationships and that (8) encouraged students to monitor their progress as learners. These areas of teaching behaviours provided a set of criteria for the evaluation of teaching.

The present investigation examined the prediction that exposure to a systematic exploration of the learning process by teachers increases the display of effective teaching behaviours and attitudes to learning.

Design of the present investigation

Participants

Participants were 32 qualified secondary teachers from three state and independent co-educational schools in eastern metropolitan Melbourne, teaching the entire range of secondary subjects.

[. . .]

Prior to their involvement in the professional development activity, participants' knowledge of contemporary theories of learning and their personal theory of learning were assessed using an open-ended survey. Knowledge of contemporary theories of learning was assessed by asking teachers to outline their understanding of theories of learning. This was scored as; 0 if teachers displayed no knowledge, 1 for a display of vague, unrelated ideas, (for learning theories, for example, 'Didn't Piaget test conservation'), 2 for a display of partial knowledge, or 3 for a display of a substantial, integrated body of knowledge.

Personal theories of learning were assessed by teachers selecting and justifying five recent decisions they had made in their teaching in relation to students' learning on the basis of what they believe about learning. Each decision was scored on the following scale; 0 if teachers justified their use in terms of earlier experience (for example, 'I know that it always works' or 'It worked in the past'), 1 for the display of a superficial explanation, and 2 for an integrated explanation in terms of a contemporary theory of learning. The score for each teacher was averaged over the five decisions.

The professional development programme

The professional development programme used was Facilitating Effective Learning and Teaching (Munro and Munro, 1992). This programme provides a framework whereby teachers work through a reflective study of the learning process, examine at first hand key aspects of learning in their classes, and identify the implications for them as teachers. The nine components of learning that were used as focus for self-reflection are:

1. *The process of learning* examined the following influences on learning; personal definitions of learning, beliefs about learning and one's self as a learner, the cognitive and meta-cognitive strategies used, learner assumptions about the nature or the outcome, the areas of learner existing knowledge activated, the goals and challenges framed by the learner, the personal metaphors learners have of the learning process and, the social-cultural group in which the learning occurs.
2. *Individual ways of learning* examined the range of dimensions that explain alternative ways of learning and their implications for teaching.
3. The process of *students displaying what they know* examined the knowledge display process in the classroom, students' differences in this process, students' understanding of and beliefs about this process, the role of feedback, the display process and assessment, the opportunities students have for showing what they know in the classroom.
4. *Learning new ideas* examined the learning of conceptual and procedural knowledge, thinking and problem-solving procedures and strategies, and attitudinal learning.
5. *Managing concentration* examined the concept of the thinking space as the site for learning, attentional short-term working memory processes in learning, and their implications for teaching.
6. *Facilitating remembering* examined types of long-term memory processes (semantic, episodic, etc.), and teaching strategies to help students to use these processes more efficiently.
7. *Learning by reading/writing/listening* examined the influence of the format of information input on the learning, and the development of

strategies to optimise efficient learning and to interact with emerging instructional technologies.

8. *Learning in different contexts* examined the influence of different sociological contexts of learning (learning in a large group, small group interaction, solo learning) the advantages and limitations of each, and the most effective learning strategies for each.

9. *Students' knowledge about learning and about themselves as learners* examines self-management of the learning process and includes managing one's self as a learner, monitoring progress, developing action plans and the learning episode as a personal model of learning, managing attitudinal knowledge, achievement motivation, and learner attribution styles.

Each of these components was investigated in a three-phase teaching format. . . . It proposed that learning is more likely when learners have the opportunity to learn through active construction processes, see that their relevant existing learning is valued, frame up authentic goals or challenges for learning, have the opportunity for individual and collaborative learning activities, for engaging in self-direction and systematic reflection of the learning, and for exploring and transferring the learning outcomes. These were mapped onto the following format for the professional development activity:

1. Pre-session activity in which teachers researched and reflected on aspects of the component in their teaching. The pre-session investigative questions for the first component were:
   (a) What beliefs do your students have about learning?
   (b) What do they think learning means?
   (c) What conditions do your students see as most effective for learning?
   (d) What are the factors that they believe explain success or failure in learning?
These research activities directed teachers to analyse their purposes for using particular teaching procedures and the assumptions and beliefs underlying their practices.

2. A seminar-workshop session in which teachers analysed collaboratively the component of learning from the perspectives of contemporary theories of learning and the data they have collected in the pre-session research. In most sessions they worked through learning activities that exemplified the component. They examined what the component meant for their teaching practice, and developed sets of teaching procedures for further research. . . .

3. Post-session activity in which the teachers further put to test aspects of each component in their teaching, and reported ongoing evaluation in terms of whether they perceived students learning more efficiently at subsequent seminar sessions.

In summary, the programme involved teachers framing up challenges in relation to learning in their classes, researching these in their classrooms, discussing and analysing their findings collaboratively, re-orienting their action plans and gradually explicating their personal theory of learning.

Monitoring changes in teacher effectiveness

Changes in teacher effectiveness following participation in the programme were monitored in several ways:

1. Changes in the display of effective teacher behaviours consistent with a social-constructivist model of learning (Brown, 1994; Voight, 1994) were monitored for each participant by analysing twelve lessons; four successive lessons in a particular subject area with the same class taught prior to involvement in the professional development activity, four taught within a school term of the programme completion, and four taught two terms after the completion of the programme. All lessons were audiotaped. The types of teaching behaviours monitored were those:

    (a) Facilitating the efficient use of student attention while learning, for example, encouraging students to automatise content knowledge and, cueing the use of attention-allocation strategies such as 'Tell yourself what you will do first, second . . .', 'Plan how you will . . .', or 'Imagine what the final outcome of learning will be like'. Statements that instructed students to 'pay attention' or to 'think more carefully' without cueing functional student behaviours were not categorised as positive instances of this type.

    (b) Facilitating the display of positive attitudes towards content area learning, for example, valuing partially correct ideas, encouraging risk taking in learning, exploring, asking questions.

    (c) Providing students with a range of options for learning an idea particularly when they had difficulty learning, for example, cueing students to visualise, to talk to themselves about ideas, to ask elaborative questions.

    (d) Providing students with a range of options for showing what they have learnt.

    (e) Helping pupils to organise themselves more efficiently as learners.

    (f) Using learner-oriented behaviour management strategies such as on-task redirection strategies, providing options for unacceptable behaviours.

    (g) Providing students with the opportunity to learn more about how they learn.

(h) Providing students with the opportunity to manage their learning in collaborative relationships.

(i) Encouraging students to monitor their progress as learners.

The number of instances of each behaviour in each four lesson period was recorded. The difference in mean number of instances before the programme, immediately after and two terms later was examined using planned comparisons for repeated measures procedures.

2. Changes in perceived ability to facilitate learning in classes was monitored using questionnaire and individual interview procedures. Teachers nominated areas in which they perceived their knowledge of teaching to have improved by the change programme. The percentage of teachers reporting each area was calculated.

Monitoring changes in student learning

Calibrated tasks that permitted comparison with a standard population were not available in several of the subject areas. Change in performance over time for groups of students in a subject was inappropriate, because content taught in the intervening period may have contributed to the change. Change in teacher knowledge over the course of the programme may have led to change in learning evaluation criteria.

Student outcomes were evaluated by having participants compile a set of criteria to assess the quality of matched learning outcomes for each student in each subject area at each grade level. The criteria were subject specific and in most cases already included in the subject area curriculum, so that the preparation of the set of criteria involved minor modification of criteria that were already in use. The student outcomes included projects, models, sets of mathematics tasks, essays, pieces of art. Participants calculated a mean grade score for each subject taught before and after the professional development activity. In addition, participants recorded their perceptions of changes in how individual students and groups learnt.

Outcomes of the investigation

First, changes in the display of effective teaching behaviours consistent with a constructivist model of learning and in teacher knowledge and beliefs about learning will be examined.

Changes in teacher behaviour

The mean number of instances of effective teaching behaviours increased on completion of the programme. The increase in display of all types of effective teacher behaviours following the professional development activity was significant and was maintained two terms after the completion of the involvement. The mean number of instances of each type of teaching behaviour across content areas is shown in Table 18.1.

Table 18.1 Mean number of instances of each type of teaching behaviour for each lesson, across teaching areas and teachers

Types of general purpose teaching behaviours	Before	After	2 terms later
Facilitating the efficient allocation of student attention while learning	0.2	8.6	8.2
Facilitating the learning of positive attitudes towards content area learning	0.5	6.3	5.8
Providing students with a range of options for learning an idea particularly when they find learning difficult	0.3	7.1	8.9
Providing students with a range of options for displaying what they know or have learnt	0.4	7.6	9.4
Helping pupils to organise themselves more efficiently as learners in their subjects	0.3	5.1	5.8
Using learner-oriented behaviour management strategies such as using on-task redirection strategies	0.7	11.8	10.5
Providing students with the opportunity to learn more about how they learn	0.2	4. 8	4.9
Providing students with the opportunity to take control of their learning in a more collaborative relationship	0.6	7.6	9.4
Providing students with the opportunity to monitor their own learning and to see themselves progressing	0.3	6.8	7.9

None of the teacher variables of age, level of qualifications, gender, or length of teaching experience influenced the display of teaching behaviours. The lack of influence of these variables suggests that the targeted types of teaching outcomes are not likely to be acquired only through 'teaching experience' per se.

Improvement was greatest in those areas associated with teachers analysing their teaching in terms of learning and implementing alternative strategies. In the area of classroom management, they were more likely to implement learner-oriented behaviour management strategies such as using on-task redirection strategies and providing student options for instances of unacceptable behaviour, rather than targeting the instance of unacceptable behaviour as separate from the learning activity.

Teachers were more likely to implement teaching procedures consistent with helping students to use more efficiently their attention while learning. They were more likely to cue students to use a range of self-instruction strategies such as 'What does the task say to do? What will the outcome be like? What is it like that you already know? What will you do first, second, etc.?' When students were required to learn by reading, they were reminded to clarify their purpose for reading, what they knew about the topic already, and how they would organise the information as they learnt it. At the conclusion of a learning activity teachers were more likely to cue students to allocate attention to encoding the ideas learnt in long-term memory.

Following participation, the teachers provided students with a wider range of options for displaying what they had learnt. This increased the likelihood of students receiving positive feedback from teacher and peers for what they knew and, in all probability, motivated in turn further learning. Teachers also provided a greater range of options for learning an idea. Teachers were more likely to cue students to visualise and verbalise ideas, to recode ideas from episodic or experiential to more abstract verbal-propositional form, and to make multiple links between new ideas and their existing knowledge.

Opportunity for students to manage their learning in collaborative relationships with teachers and peers increased. This was displayed in the increase in less-directive teacher and peer responses to students' ideas ('Why do you think . . .? But what about . . .? Where would . . . fit in?') as well as more-directive feedback in convergent learning, the opportunity for creative more-opened development of ideas and the development of 'group knowledge' as a resource in learning contexts.

Teachers provided more opportunities for students to monitor their learning and to see themselves making progress. At the beginning of lessons, teachers were more likely to indicate how student knowledge might change during the lesson. They negotiated ways of observing these changes with their class. At the end of lessons teachers were more likely to have students review how their knowledge had changed. Students were encouraged to implement their own 'action pathways' for monitoring their learning.

Changes in teacher knowledge

Prior to the professional development programme, participants' knowledge of contemporary theories of learning and their personal explicit theory of learning was comparatively undeveloped. . . . None displayed more than a vague understanding of contemporary theories of learning. Few displayed evidence of a personal explicit theory of learning; 85 per cent of the explanations provided to justify teaching decisions were of earlier experiences (for example, 'I know that it always works', or 'It worked in the past').

Following the programme, participant knowledge in these areas increased. . . .

Teachers reported that the programme improved their knowledge and beliefs about learning (the learning process and the types of learning actions that they needed to foster and encourage by their teaching) and improved their perceived ability to facilitate learning in their classes and their understanding of meeting individual ways of learning in their teaching. Teachers believed that the programme led to an improvement in the delivery of classroom teaching in the school. These data are discussed in greater detail in Munro (1993). The areas of gain most frequently identified and the percentage of teachers reporting each are shown in Table 18.2.

Teachers were more likely to perceive their teaching effectiveness improve in areas over which they had greatest control (for example teaching pupils to reflect on how they learnt, catering for a range of ways of learning in their teaching and using a range of cueing strategies). They perceived themselves as being least able to actually change pupils' dispositions to learning (for example, helping students to use a concept of the 'learning episode' in their ongoing learning or to organise themselves more efficiently in their subjects). Several felt unsure about reporting improvement in this area because they were either not sure of precisely what students would be doing when they had improved, or needed more time to be assured of changes in the general learning of students. These data suggest that teacher effectiveness change programmes may need to assist participants to identify what students will be doing when they are learning.

These outcomes support the direction of change in effective teaching behaviours shown in Table 18.1. Change was greatest in areas in which teachers were encouraged to interpret classroom events differently. Interpreting instances of inappropriate behaviour as possibly due to a mismatch between the learning demands made by a teaching procedure and students' preferred ways of learning, or as a lack of opportunity for students to display outcomes that would be valued by the peer group or teacher were most readily assimilated into teachers' repertoires.

Change was least (though still significant) in areas in which teachers were required to implement activities from the perspective of learners, for example, procedures that assisted students to organise themselves more efficiently as learners in their subjects or that provided them with the opportunity to learn more about how they learn.

Table 18.2 Areas of gain most frequently identified by teachers

Teacher understanding	% of teachers reporting the area
Learning to analyse the demands their teaching style and content taught made on learning	83
Teaching pupils to reflect on how they learn and helping them learn more effective learning strategies	76
Developing ways of monitoring and evaluating the effectiveness of their teaching	69
Catering for a range of ways of learning in their teaching	65
Learning to use a range of cueing strategies as part of their regular teaching	64
Using students' existing knowledge in a range of ways, tapping into knowledge in episodic memory as well as semantic memory	62
Giving students a range of options for displaying what they knew	61
Understanding the role of attention in learning, helping students learn to use it most effectively when learning	59
Learning ways of researching particular teaching innovations in their classes	48
Distinctions between different types of learning outcomes (such as deep and surface learning) and to teach for each type of outcome	46
Helping pupils learn more positive attitudes towards learning	45
Giving students a range of options when they are learning, particularly when they find learning a particular idea difficult to learn, modality switching	45
Becoming aware of the concept of learning and teaching models and the expectations attached to each and how these influence the actual learning programme	43
Helping students to use a concept of the 'learning episode' in their ongoing learning	37
Helping pupils to organise themselves more efficiently in their subjects	34

Changes in student learning outcome

Mean student gain scores were calculated by each teacher for each subject at each grade level. Of the 127 gain scores collated, 73 per cent indicated a substantial gain in the quality of learning outcome.

This gain was not restricted to particular teachers, subject areas or year levels. Explanations of the distribution of this gain are complex. First, in the majority of the classes, some students achieved at a high level prior to their teacher's involvement in the programme. Improving teacher effectiveness was less likely to impact on the performance of these students on the criteria used. The performance of the lowest achievers improved. Improving teacher effectiveness led to increased performance for many of the underachieving students.

[. . .]

Aspects of the change programme identified as facilitating change

The identification of the aspects of the change programme that were most likely to facilitate change is important both for understanding the change in teacher effectiveness and for implementing future effectiveness improvement programmes. The monitoring of teacher change over the course of two semesters led to the identification of conditions under which change was most likely. The conditions most frequently reported by teachers were when they:

1. Reflected on and made explicit their own models of learning and teaching. Providing pre-organised teaching procedures based on 'sound teaching practice' was seen as insufficient. Teachers valued the opportunity to explicate and evaluate the implications of their beliefs about learning and teaching, to gather first-hand data from their students about aspects of learning, to have the opportunity to reflect on these data and relate them to their beliefs, to discuss them with colleagues, to use them to plan a course of action and then to trial the inferences. Teachers who reported trialing their own inferences and courses of action were more likely to report changing their approach to teaching.

2. Were able to observe teaching procedures that facilitated learning being practised in their own classes. Teachers noted that a valuable component of the change programme was the opportunity to imagine how new procedures might be implemented in the context of content they would teach during the following weeks. They also valued the opportunity to role-play a teaching strategy or to implement it with a small group of students first.

3. Were using teaching procedures to solve temporary problems or challenges that were confronting them in their classes at that time. The recommended change in teaching procedure needed to be seen to assist in solving current problems. Teachers are more likely to adopt new teaching procedures that can potentially solve existing problems. Professional development and teacher change programmes need to recognise this and to include, as a major aspect of the programme, the opportunity for teachers to explicate and explore solutions to existing problems.

4. Experimented with the new procedure soon after seeing it. An optimal duration seemed to be two weeks.

5. Observed student change in learning behaviour and outcome as a result of a teaching modification. Teachers who had identified specific student behaviours likely to suggest change were more likely to engage in further experimentation and more sustained change. Using an audiotape recorder or having a 'mirror' or a coach monitor it, as well as being able to discuss its success with the colleague group, contributed to the likelihood of teacher change.

6. Initiated comparatively small changes initially. Not surprisingly, teachers noted small changes at the practical level were easier to handle successfully by an individual teacher than larger changes.

7. Observed the change to be beneficial to a majority of students in their classes. Changes in teaching procedures that were useful or necessary for only one or two students in a class were more likely to be forgotten, and certainly less likely to be integrated within the teacher's repertoire of teaching strategies.

8. Had the opportunity to evaluate the teaching procedures. Teacher evaluation of the effectiveness of the procedure was identified as important by several of the teachers.

9. Saw that it was possible to predict and anticipate how students might learn.

10. Felt confident that their peers validated the notion of change and research in the classroom. They knew that colleagues were prepared to countenance the need to change when they heard colleagues discuss positive outcomes.

In summary, the findings support the prediction that involvement in a systematic exploration of the learning process, in which teachers explicate their knowledge of learning, impacts directly on the display of effective teaching behaviours and teacher attitudes to learning. The assumption that practising teacher knowledge of learning is usually represented episodically was supported. This knowledge becomes more generally useful when it is recoded into an explicit personal theory, tested against a practical data base (the classroom), and mapped into teaching procedures. A key issue in the recoding was the provision of a conceptual framework or scaffold that teachers used to develop their personal explicit theory of learning.

[. . .]

References

Brown, A. L. (1994) 'The advancement of learning', *Educational Researcher* **23**, 4–12.

Caldwell, B. and Spinks, J. M. (1992) *Leading the self-managing school.* London: Falmer Press.

Fullan, M. G. and Pomfret, A. (1977) 'Research on curriculum and instruction implementation', *Review of Educational Research* **47**, 335–97.

Glatthorn, A. (1987) 'Cooperative professional development: peer-centred options for teacher growth', *Educational Leadership*, November, 31–5.

Grant, C. A. (1984) *Preparing for reflective teaching.* Boston: Allyn and Bacon.

Holdaway, E. and Johnson, N. A. (1993) School effectiveness and effectiveness factors', *School Effectiveness and School Improvement* **4**, 165–88.

Joyce, B., Weil, M. and Showers, B. (1992) *Models of Teaching*, 4th edn. Boston: Allyn and Bacon.

Mortimer, P. (1993) 'School effectiveness and the management of effective learning and teaching', *School Effectiveness and School Improvement* **4**, 290–310.

Munro, J. (1993) *FELT and Teacher Change.* Melbourne: MERA.

Munro, J. (1994) 'Episodic and procedural: the models of learning underpinning the work of teachers and principals'. Keynote paper presented at the Biennial Conference for Principals and Senior School Staff, Townsville, Queensland, August.

Munro, J. and Munro, K. (1992) 'Learning styles: the way forward in the twenty-first century', *Australian Journal of Remedial Education* **22**, 6–12.

Scheerens, J. (1992) *Effective schooling: Research, theory and practice.* London: Cassell.

Schon, D. A. (1987) *Educating the reflective practitioner.* San Francisco: Jossey-Bass.

Stoll, L. and Fink, D. (1994) 'School effectiveness and school improvement: voices from the field', *School Effectiveness and School Improvement* **5**, 149–77.

Voight, J. (1994) 'Negotiation of mathematical meaning and learning mathematics', *Educational Studies in Mathematics* **26**, 275–98.

von Glaserfeld, E. (1988) 'Environment and communication'. Paper presented at the Sixth International Congress on Mathematics Education, Budapest.

Wells, G. and Chang, G. L. (1986) *Effecting educational change through collaborative research.* Toronto: OISE.

Chapter 19

Matching teaching to learning

John Beresford

Editors' Note: In this chapter, John Beresford describes his research into how successfully teaching strategies were matched to learning styles in eight secondary schools in England.

French with Year 10, last lesson, Friday, May. The school is set in the middle of a huge council estate. It has poor examination results, and an equally poor reputation within the town. The usual pushing and shoving by the boys as they wait for the teacher. He wants me to look at two students during the lesson, one a quiet girl and the other one of the boisterous boys. The teacher arrives. He is surprisingly young- and fragile-looking. The boys rush to the front of the classroom, where chairs are laid out in three rows.

The teacher speaks French throughout the lesson, and even cracks jokes in French. There are no complaints from anyone about not understanding. He uses an OHP acetate as an initial focus for the students' attention. He lectures, questions and makes students repeat after him. He then mimes an action, and invites students to identify the action. Shortly afterwards, the students leave their seats and break up into groups, where they do their own mimes to each other. There is little surface noise above the excited chatter of random guesses.

The students resume their seats, and play a memory game led by the teacher. After this they quietly take their seats and form a semi-circle. They play a paired game, the rules of which they clearly already know. The teacher joins the semi-circle as a participant and, because his presence makes the total of participants odd, a puppet is placed in one of the seats. At the end of a fixed length of time, one of each pair joins up with a new partner. The puppet is a shared class joke, and no one seems self-conscious in conversation with it.

At the end of the activity students pick up their chairs and return in an orderly way to the front of the classroom. The last three minutes of the hour-long lesson are taken up with students scoring their participation in the lesson on a scale of 1 to 5, with 5 indicating full participation and 1 indicating poor and spasmodic participation. The teacher records the scores in a book, and occasionally challenges a score, though he doesn't change it if the student remains adamant. The boisterous boy I have been observing scores himself 4: I scored his on-task behaviour as 87 per cent. The quiet girl has been taken ill during the lesson, and doesn't give a score: I scored her at 73 per cent on task. The teacher tells me after the lesson that the level of scores has risen gradually since September, and so has his perception of levels of student participation in lessons.

All day with Year 8, Tuesday, June. The school is set in fields on the edge of a large city in the Midlands. It has a growing local reputation matched by its improving examination results.

I'm looking at two fairly able students to try to map what kinds of learning experiences they have in a typical school day. The first lesson is English. After the register is taken the teacher organises the class into groups, and they brainstorm a topic for about ten minutes. There is a hum of purposeful activity, and the students are clearly conversant with the technique. The richness of their responses in the subsequent plenary confirms this impression. In the course of the 45-minute lesson the class breaks up into groups on two more occasions. The next lesson is humanities, where students work quietly in pairs over a hand-out. In the science lesson which follows they undertake a practical activity in pairs, then move quietly into a large circle to discuss their work. The teacher seems to play little part beyond chairing the circle and organising the order of speakers.

Art consists mainly of individual work. The second science lesson contains another brainstorming session, and more group work looking at and evaluating health education leaflets. The last lesson of the day consists of individual work using maths textbooks. I ask the deputy head about the versatility of the teachers in their teaching and the students in their learning. He tells me that there has been extensive school-based INSET on using various teaching strategies in the classroom, and that Year 7 students have an induction course lasting five days in the effective use of these strategies at the beginning of the academic year. The two students observed have been exposed to twelve different teaching strategies in the course of the day, and have both been in excess of 80 per cent on task.

What is striking in these two vignettes is not merely the range of strategies used by the teachers, but the versatility of the students in responding to them. The teachers have, in terms of retaining the attention of the students under observation, effectively applied a wide range of teaching strategies.

The students, in terms of their observed responses, have shown themselves able to respond to these strategies and to participate fully in the concomitant activities. Effective teaching and learning appear to have taken place.

Introduction

The relation between the application of a wide range of teaching strategies and effective learning in the classroom has been the subject of periodic but fierce debate during the last thirty years. This has been for a number of reasons. First, there was an extensive debate about the efficiency as well as the effectiveness of various strategies, particularly in the primary sector, following the publication of the Plowden Report in 1967. The report recommended, *inter alia*, 'a combination of individual, group and class work' in primary schools, and welcomed 'the trend towards individual learning' (DES, 1967, 474). The subsequent debate had an added poignancy, taking place as it did in a period of public expenditure cuts and a 'Great Debate' about priorities in education (Beresford, 1995). It both questioned the efficiency of attempting to provide such a wide range of strategies (see, for example, Cox and Boyson, 1977), and rehearsed the comparative benefits of what were polarised into 'formal', whole-class strategies and 'informal', group- and child-centred ones (see Bennett and Entwistle, 1977; Aitkin *et al.*, 1981).

Second, the prescriptive content of the National Curriculum now taught in schools has meant that teachers have not always been able to rely upon the intrinsic interest of what they teach in order to retain the interest of all students in their classes. Teachers have sought a variety of ways of presenting similar materials and topics. Inextricably linked with this quest on the part of teachers has been a growing interest in and concern for the interests and opinions of the students themselves about their learning. The advice of academics like Rudduck in Britain and Levin in Canada is increasingly being followed in schools:

> Pupils' accounts of experience should be heard and should be taken seriously in debates about learning.
> (Rudduck *et al.*, 1996, p.2)

> Working to motivate students would seem necessarily to require that their ideas and interests be taken seriously . . . that they have significant influence (which is not to say total control) over what they study, how they study, and when they study.
> (Levin, 1994a)

Finally, the thrust of central government since the early 1990s to improve examination and test results has driven schools to look at various ways of enhancing their performance. One of these ways has been to encourage teachers to look at alternative ways of delivering the curriculum to groups of students who have formerly been regarded as marginal within their schools (see Southworth, 1996). The subsequent debate about the most appropriate teaching strategies to be used has again largely centred on the primary sector, and has this time involved the government and other related bodies (Alexander, 1991; DES, 1991; Alexander *et al.*, 1992; Woodhead, 1992; OFSTED, 1995a; DfEE, 1997). The debate has once more focused on the relative merits of whole-class, group and individual teaching, and has drawn on evidence from the schools of our more successful industrial competitors overseas (Reynolds and Farrell, 1996). It has again spilled over into a general debate about cost-effectiveness in education, and whether the size of classes is an important factor in effective teaching (OFSTED, 1995b; NAHT/University of Nottingham, 1996; Labour Party, 1997). The government has taken the unprecedented step of effectively prescribing teaching methods, in the delivery of the 'Literacy Hour' in its primary schools (DfEE, 1998).

While it has been suggested that the 'complex pedagogy' employed results in 'a wide variation between the levels of quality' in our schools (Reynolds and Farrell, 1996, p.58), this criticism of too wide a range of teaching strategies being used by teachers has been comparatively rare. The debate has tended to concentrate more on the overuse of particular teaching strategies in the delivery of the curriculum. Thus the report of the so-called 'Three Wise Men' into primary classroom practice, commissioned by the DES, noted that

> the substantial body of research which now exists about primary school teaching methods endorses what common sense would expect: that the debate about the relative effectiveness of traditional and progressive methods ignores the fact that different organizational strategies and teaching techniques are needed for different purposes. Teachers need to evaluate the strengths and weaknesses of different approaches in order to make informed choices and, when necessary, should be prepared to learn new skills in the interests of effective teaching and learning.
>
> (Alexander *et al.*, 1992, p.27)

OFSTED reported, in its findings on class size in 1995, that

> appropriate variety of methods, including well-directed, whole-class teaching and activity, featured strongly in those lessons judged by inspectors to be successful.
>
> (OFSTED, 1995b, p.40)

The philosophical justifications for the provision of a range of teaching strategies in classrooms has been largely client-centred. Their fundamental tenet has been that the employment of such a range is likely to impact upon a greater number of students than the use of a more limited number of such strategies. Corno and Snow, for example, have suggested that students each have learning aptitudes which comprise

> propensities for processing information in certain ways that develop around ability – personality intersections.
> (Corno and Snow, 1986)

For them the process of teaching involves either the development of these aptitudes by instruction in cognitive skills, or the circumvention of and compensation for students' lack of aptitude by adaptive teaching through the provision of individual help, guidance and information. They conclude that

> since learner aptitudes and inaptitudes are multiple in virtually any group, adaptive teaching always requires the provision of alternative routes to common goals.
> (Corno and Snow, 1986)

Kolb, using a similar construct of learning styles based upon the personality of the learner (Kolb, 1984), suggests that the incongruency of the learning environment provided by the teacher and the learning styles favoured by individual students can lead to anomie and alienation in the classroom. The implication is that the consistent failure to address the learning styles of groups of students can lead to forms of classroom disruption that themselves can affect the learning of others.

What is being advocated is the construction of what Elliott has called 'a common stock of professional insights' (Elliott, 1984) in order to maximise the degree of student accessibility to learning in the classroom. The 'Accelerated Schools' project in America is an example of this paradigm:

> Lessons use a variety of techniques such as experimentation, exploration, peer tutoring and trial and error on the part of the child. Children are encouraged to take risks. The children discover, construe, collaborate and discuss rather than simply reading, writing, copying and memorizing.
> (Hague and Walker, 1996)

Seminars involving teachers in participating schools have enabled one teacher 'to share my knowledge on how to incorporate students of all learning styles and levels' (Hague and Walker, 1996). In the course of acquiring an extensive teaching repertoire, teachers are urged to develop that repertoire in directions which will engage the learning styles of their students.

Matching teaching and learning

The introduction to this chapter has presented a brief view of the context for the current interest in teachers' repertoires, and has looked at some of the literature which provides the philosophical justification for providing a wide range of teaching strategies in the classroom. For several years I have been involved with a number of colleagues, both in Cambridge and Nottingham, in a project which, in part, has been committed to extending the teaching armoury of its participant schools.

IQEA (Improving the Quality of Education for All), in common with a number of school improvement projects throughout the world, has sought to develop the capacity of schools to accommodate and use external change in order to maximise student outcomes. The initial work, based at the Cambridge Institute of Education, sought to develop the management conditions of its client schools (for further detail see Hopkins *et al.*, 1994). Drawing from the already extensive literature on effective teaching (see, for example, Brophy and Good, 1986; Joyce and Weil, 1986; Joyce *et al.*, 1987), and the burgeoning school effectiveness literature (see, for example, Sammons *et al.*, 1995), subsequent school-based research has suggested to us that there is a set of classroom conditions which also need developing in order for effective teaching and learning to take place (West *et al.*, 1995; Hopkins, *et al.*, 1997; Hopkins *et al.*, 1998).

One of the conditions identified has been the teaching repertoire of staff:

> Effective teachers have a range of learning activities, tasks or experiences for pupils which they know are successful in bringing about certain types of pupil learning . . . . In practice, more effective practitioners have a range of teaching skills, styles, models and approaches which comprise a teaching repertoire.
>
> (Hopkins *et al.*, 1997, p.60)

I have argued elsewhere (see Beresford, 1996) that there is a complementary set of student conditions that need to be developed in order that effective learning can take place. Sharing the belief expressed elsewhere that 'models of teaching are in fact models of learning' (Joyce *et al.*, 1997, p.8), I have argued that students need to be conversant with the learning techniques required by the teaching methods employed in lessons in order to take best advantage of them. Stated simply, students who know how to work effectively in groups will learn better when teachers organise group work than those who do not have the necessary skills. For an extension of teachers' repertoire to be most effective, there needs to be a concomitant extension of their students' learning repertoire. The growing interest in students' views highlighted earlier would also suggest that some consideration ought to be paid to extending staff's teaching repertoire in response to students' stated learning preferences.

There is already an extensive literature on the component parts of effective teaching (see, for example, Rosenshine and Stevens, 1986; Gipps, 1992; Harris, 1995), but less on the process of matching teaching strategies to students' learning styles. There have been a number of instruments designed, mainly in the form of questionnaires or interview schedules, to try to discover the learning preferences of discrete groups of students: of secondary science students (Cunliffe,1995); for students excluded from school (De Pear, 1997); for 8- to11-year-olds (Norwich, 1998); and for Year 10 students (Barnett, 1985). However, much of the matching of teaching and learning styles has been extremely speculative, based upon the premise that if a sufficient variety of strategies is employed, then a catch-all effect will apply:

By offering a range of learning opportunities, including those that use their strengths, teachers are more likely to provide a learning experience that students feel good about.
(Faccenda and Fielding, 1992)

If teaching excludes or dissuades those who learn in ways other than that of the subject specialist involved . . . entitlement is denied.
(Fielding, 1994)

Increasing the range of learning experiences provided in our schools increases the likelihood of more students becoming more adept learners.
(Joyce *et al.*, 1997, p.15)

The need for some form of dialogue between teachers and students about teaching and learning methods in the classroom has been recognised by a number of writers (see, for example, Levin, 1994b; Hord, 1997; Hubbard, 1997) and, increasingly, by a number of the schools in the IQEA project. These schools have shown themselves willing to interrogate students on their views about what constitutes effective teaching. It is also clear that they regard some acknowledgement of student learning preferences, in the teaching which takes place within their classrooms, as an element of effective teaching in its own right. They have also called for a research instrument, easy to administer, which can both help them match what goes on in classrooms more closely to the preferences of their students, and provide clues about where to develop the teaching repertoire of their teachers and the learning repertoire of their students.

In 1996 I was approached by an IQEA school in Essex, concerned about its performance in public examinations, to undertake an audit of the teaching strategies used in its classrooms and a survey of students' views on those strategies. I consulted a colleague at Cambridge, Michael Fielding, who directed me to the work of David Kolb. The socio-psychological and epistemological theories underpinning Kolb's conceptualisation of the learning process are too complex to be adequately dealt with within the confines of this chapter. However, some background knowledge may be useful in order to appreciate the principles behind the derived instrument.

Kolb's seminal work, *Experiential Learning* (1984), effectively reconceptualises Piaget's work on developmental learning in the light of subsequent neurological research findings. What Piaget regarded as four sequential phases of learning (sensory-motor, representational, concrete operational and formal operational) are redefined by Kolb into four distinct and authentic learning styles, with no implicit hierarchical structure. These four learning styles can be represented as quadrants in a grid where the two dimensions of perceiving and processing information have been juxtaposed (see Figure 19.1).

Kolb gives useful descriptors of each learning style, which I have summarised in Table 19.1. He further illuminates the four approaches by applying each to the playing of pool. I have found, in relating Kolb's work to English audiences, that the less culture- and gender-specific example of learning how to use a computer has been more apposite.

LEARNING STYLES

SENSING/FEELING
Concrete experiences

Accommodators	*Divergers*
DOING	WATCHING
Testing implications of concepts in new situations	Observation and reflections
Convergers	*Assimilators*

THINKING
Formation of abstract concepts and generalisations

Figure 19.1 Kolb's four learning styles (adapted from Fielding, 1994)

Table 19.1 Characteristics of Kolb's four learning styles (adapted from Kolb, 1984, pp.77–8)

Learning style	Dominant learning orientations	Greatest strengths	Best learning situations	Organisation of knowledge	Learner characteristics
Accommodative	Concrete experience Active experimentation	Doing things Carrying out plans, tasks Getting involved in new experiences	Opportunity seeking Risk taking Action	Adaptation to changing, immediate circumstances Scepticism of theory	Intuitive Trial-and-error approach Reliance upon others for information At ease with people Sometimes impatient, pushy
Divergent	Concrete experience Reflective observation	Imaginative ability Awareness of meaning and values	Generation of alternative ideas and implications	Adaptation by observation rather than action Viewing concrete situations from many perspectives	Interested in people Imaginative Feeling-oriented
Convergent	Abstract conceptualisation Active experimentation	Problem solving Decision making Practical application of ideas	Conventional intelligence tests Problems with single correct answer	Hypothetical-deductive reasoning Focus on specific problems	Controlled expression of emotion Preference of technical tasks to interpersonal issues
Assimilative	Abstract conceptualisation Reflective observation	Inductive reasoning Creation of theoretical models	Assimilating disparate observations into integrated explanation	Logically sound and precise theories Re-examines facts if they don't fit	Concern with ideas, abstract concepts Less concerned with people

Someone with an accommodative learning style will sit at the keyboard and try out different methods, in a hit-and-miss way, of achieving the same end. They will listen to advice from others, but will trust their own intuition at least as much as the information derived from others. Divergent learners will want to watch others working on a computer, and will want to discuss their experience with them before trying a variety of alternative approaches themselves. Assimilative learners will also want to watch and listen, but will make their own notes and design their own method of working, which they will then test out. Convergent learners will consult the manual, and approach learning how to use the computer in a logical way, on their own.

Clearly most people will learn to use the computer using a mixture of these approaches. However, Kolb's typology recognises the integrity of each learning style as a way of accessing and processing information. He argues that an individual's approach to a learning situation will be strongly oriented to one of these approaches. The research literature suggests that the range of teaching strategies and learning opportunities operational within the school context needs to cater for each of these learning styles in order that significant numbers of students are not excluded from the learning process.

Kolb's work concentrates mainly on university students, and his 'Learning Style Inventory', derived from his four models of learning, is intended more for individual adult learners. The inventory does not lend itself easily to an analysis of group needs and preferences. However, much of what Kolb writes about learning environments is applicable to English secondary school classrooms, and much of what he says about learning styles can be used in a broad-brush way to assess group as well as individual needs. The value of such an approach has been acknowledged elsewhere:

> There is no one theory or model which fully describes learning differences or offers a panacea for teachers. Working with one of the models can help teachers to recognise powerfully the extent of the differences in the way that people learn and the fact that there is no single best way to teach. They can provide teachers with a powerful tool to help them examine and develop their practice.
> (Scottish Consultative Council on the Curriculum, 1996)

In addition, Fielding had usefully identified a range of classroom activities and strategies associated with each of the four learning styles (see Fielding, 1994). The most striking feature of this list is the unevenness of the numbers of strategies identified with each learning style. There are, for example, only six accommodative strategies identified, compared to fourteen convergent ones. While Fielding does not explain this imbalance, the list does reflect the difficulty in articulating a range of strategies associated with each learning style which could be recognised by practising teachers. More important than this, however, is the use to which the list can be put in order to compare directly the strategies used by teachers with those preferred by students.

Using Fielding's list, I produced an observation schedule which could be used to record the incidence of these various activities in a lesson. The schedule has been reproduced elsewhere (Beresford, 1998a), and appears here as Table 19.2. Each activity is coded according to the learning style for which it caters. As each activity occurs in the lesson, its incidence is noted. There is no assessment attempted regarding the effectiveness of the various strategies within the context of the lesson. At the end of the period of observation the different number of strategies and learning activities employed by the teacher is totted up and recorded, in the boxes provided, against the appropriate learning style. Hence the lesson can be said to have a particular profile corresponding to the combination of numbers in the boxes. These can be converted into percentages of the total number of strategies and activities used. Table 19.3 shows a sheet which has been filled in. The experience of such observations over three years suggests that a 20-minute observation provides sufficient evidence of the likely profile of lessons.

In order to assess students' preferences for these characteristic teaching activities, I originally drew up a similar schedule on which students were asked to indicate which of the activities they preferred. This original schedule is also reproduced elsewhere (Beresford, 1998a). This schedule has subsequently been refined (Table 19.4) in order to make the nature of the various activities more explicit to students, and thus to reduce the amount of time needed for elaboration by the teacher or researcher prior to students completing the schedule. This schedule consists of a list of classroom activities directly related to the teaching strategies listed in the observation schedule (Table 19.2). So, for example, the classroom activity associated with 'Gut feelings asked for' is 'one where the teacher asks us for our feelings about something'. The associated activities are listed in the same order as the teaching strategies, in order to expedite their analysis. I further refined the instrument by introducing 'Don't like', 'Don't mind' and 'Like' categories of response. This allowed for a Likert-type scoring of responses, and ultimately enabled comparisons between different-sized groups to be made more easily. The activities are not coded on the student schedule in order to reduce the amount of explanation required. Students take on average ten minutes to fill this in.

By scoring 'Don't like' responses as 0, 'Don't mind' as 1 and 'Like' as 2, and adding the total for each of the learning style categories, a profile similar to that derived from lesson observations can be derived for each student. By adding the totals of all students in a particular group, a group profile can be obtained. These profiles indicate individual and group learning style

Table 19.2 Observation schedule of teaching strategies, based on Kolb's four learning styles

Date:		Lesson:

Teaching strategies		*Incidence*
Accuracy stressed	C	
Accurate recall	As	
Action planning	As	
Brainstorming	D	
Case-study	As	
Choice of activities	C	
Classwork	As	
Clear goals expressed	C	
Comprehension	C	
Data collection	As	
Demonstrations	As	
Discussion	D	
Group interaction	D	
Group work organised	Ac	
Gut feelings asked for	Ac	
Hand-outs	As	
Investigations	D	
Lecture	As	
Mistakes allowed	Ac	
Note taking	C	
Open-ended questions asked	D	
Paired work	D	
Planning of work by pupils	C	
Practising skills	C	
Problem solving	C	
Reflection on experience	D	
Relevance of work explained	C	
Reporting back methods varied	Ac	
Role-play	D	
Scientific experiments	C	
Simulations used	Ac	
Specialisms tapped	As	
Testing	C	
Thoroughness stressed	C	
Variety of approaches	Ac	
Video	As	
Working alone	C, As	
Worksheets	C	

Ac – Accommodative   D – Divergent
C – Convergent   As – Assimilative

Table 19.3 Completed observation schedule of teaching strategies, based on Kolb's four learning styles

Date: 22.10.96   Lesson: Spanish, Year 8

Teaching strategies	Incidence	
Accuracy stressed	C	
Accurate recall	As	✓
Action planning	As	
Brainstorming	D	
Case-study	As	
Choice of activities	C	
Classwork	As	✓
Clear goals expressed	C	✓
Comprehension	C	
Data collection	As	
Demonstrations	As	✓
Discussion	D	
Group interaction	D	
Group work organised	Ac	
Gut feelings asked for	Ac	
Hand-outs	As	
Investigations	D	
Lecture	As	✓
Mistakes allowed	Ac	
Note taking	C	
Open-ended questions asked	D	✓
Paired work	D	✓
Planning of work by pupils	C	
Practising skills	C	
Problem solving	C	
Reflection on experience	D	
Relevance of work explained	C	
Reporting back methods varied	Ac	
Role-play	D	
Scientific experiments	C	
Simulations used	Ac	
Specialisms tapped	As	
Testing	C	✓
Thoroughness stressed	C	
Variety of approaches	Ac	
Video	As	
Working alone	C, As	✓
Worksheets	C	✓

Ac	0 (0%)	D	2 (18%)	
C	4(36%)	As	5 (45%)	

Table 19.4 Refined schedule

Please tick which box best fits your feelings about the use of these activities in the teaching of _____

Description of activity	Don't like	Don't mind	Like
One where accuracy is important			
One where I'm asked to recall information accurately			
One where the teacher involves me and the class in the planning of our work			
One where we are asked to brainstorm ideas and facts			
One where we look at case-studies and other real-life examples			
One where we are given a choice of activities to learn the same thing			
One where we are taught as a class, and all do the same work			
One where the teacher makes the goals of the lesson clear			
One where we have to interpret information given to us			
One where we have to collect information and data ourselves			
One where the teacher demonstrates something			
One where we have a group or class discussion			
One where we can work things out in groups			
One where the teacher organises group work			
One where the teacher asks us for our feelings about something			
One where the teacher gives us information on printed sheets			
One where we have to undertake investigations			
One where the teacher gives us information through teaching in front of the class			
One where I'm allowed to make mistakes			
One where I take notes			
One where lots of different answers are possible			
One where I work in pairs			
One where I plan my own work			
One where we practise skills			
One where we have to solve a problem			
One where I'm asked to think about my experiences			
One where the reason I'm doing something is clear to me			
One where we can report back our findings in different ways			
One where we have role-play			
One where we do experiments			
One where we have to deal with simulated, real-life situations			
One where I can use my particular skills			
One where we are being tested			
One where I have to be thorough and careful in my work			
One where the teacher uses different teaching methods			
One where we have a video			
One where I work alone			
One where worksheets are given out			

I am in Year _____   I am male/female
(ring correct one)

Thank you for taking time to fill in this questionnaire

preferences. The schedule is versatile inasmuch as it can be used to gauge individual learning preferences as well as group ones. Students' preferences in individual subjects can be assessed as well as their general learning preferences.

[. . .]

The schools

(Editors' Note: Beresford conducted an analysis of teaching strategies across eight schools.)

[. . .]

The lesson profiles show a reasonable balance between doing and watching orientations in all of the subject categories, but a marked imbalance between sensing and thinking orientations, except in drama and a few other isolated lessons. In creative arts, the profiles suggest a strong element of teacher instruction and direction in art and music, and less surprisingly a strong element of social interaction and learning in drama. English lessons show a marked lack of accommodative activities, and a general emphasis on the use of convergent and assimilative ones. Teachers in RE, geography and history lessons depend heavily upon convergent and assimilative activities: the two exceptions in the lessons observed were teachers teaching general humanities rather than specific humanities subjects. Teachers in all seven modern languages lessons largely ignored accommodative and divergent activities, as did all but one of the science teachers observed.

The combined data suggest a quite stunning uniformity of teaching diet in the classrooms of the eight schools. Art and music teachers are employing the same activities and strategies as science, English and French teachers. All six schools, irrespective of their catchment areas and examination performances, cater overwhelmingly for students with convergent and assimilative learning styles.

This picture is reflected in the research of others. Newton and Harwood observed 126 lessons in three secondary schools, and noted that 82 per cent of them used primarily didactic methods of teaching (Newton and Harwood, 1993). A similar survey of 40 social studies classes indicated that 92 per cent of them used didactic and problem-solving approaches to learning (Hacker and Carter, 1987). The assertion that

academic studies socialize teachers into distinct subgroups that display different orientations towards knowledge and the nature of teaching
(Yaakobi and Sharan, 1985)

seems largely unproved. It would appear that most of the teachers observed in the 74 lessons rely upon a restricted repertoire characterised by largely didactic teaching methods.

Students' learning preferences

[. . .]

The overriding impression of the school learning profiles is one of uniformity. Accommodative scores vary by only three points, convergent by four, assimilative by five and divergent by seven. Subject-specific group profiles show slightly greater variance: divergent scores in particular show a 12-point spread. Another striking feature is the difference between schools' teaching and learning profiles. While students' learning preferences still show a bias towards assimilative and convergent activities, they demonstrate a desire for a far greater proportion of accommodative and divergent activities than their teachers are offering. Three schools, for example, offer their students a diet of four parts convergent and assimilative activities to one part accommodative and divergent: their students would prefer a 3:2 ratio. One school offers a 9:1 ratio of similar activities: their students, with an interesting conservatism compared to their peers in the three other schools, would prefer a 2:1 ratio.

Gender differences tend to be subsumed within the breadth of activities characteristic of each learning style. . . . The girls show a preference for concentrating on written work and getting on by themselves rather than interrelating in the learning activities favoured by accommodators and divergers. . . .

[. . .]

The instrument was created with the intention of providing schools with a broad-brush picture of the teaching activities and strategies used by teachers, and of the learning preferences of their students. The derived data were intended to provide a focus for a discussion between staff and staff and, perhaps, staff and students about teaching methods. This has generally been the case. In one school for example, the results confirmed staff's fears about the lack of opportunities provided for independent learning in its 11–16 classes, a lack which they felt partly explained their comparatively disappointing A-level results. The school has since provided more of these activities, including cooperative group learning, and has been provided with audit sheets in order to monitor whether such learning is taking place. The community studies department in another school has tried to integrate more accommodative and divergent activities into its curriculum, and has involved students in evaluating the activities (see Beresford, 1998b). Teachers in a third school have learnt how to organise inductive learning sessions using paired and group work techniques, and have involved staff and students in an evaluation of the effectiveness of the teaching model.

Discussion

The instrument has exposed the discrepancy between what the eight schools offer in terms of teaching strategies and activities, and what their students would prefer them to offer. This did not come as a surprise to many of the teachers with whom I discussed the results. Their general responses can be summarised under the following four headings.

Accommodative and divergent activities are more enjoyable for students, therefore they will prefer them. Some suggested that accommodative and divergent activities were generally more enjoyable for students, and did not involve as much 'hard work' as convergent and assimilative activities. It is true that such activities do not involve as much writing as assimilative and convergent activities, and my own research, as well as that of others (see, for example, Rudduck *et al.*, 1996), suggests that students in particular regard writing as 'hard work'. There is a substantial literature, however, that suggests that social learning techniques are among the most effective known (see, for example, Slavin, 1993). Sweden is sufficiently convinced of its efficacy to make an element of group work mandatory in all lessons in its schools (Beresford, 1999). The most effective group work is often hard work for students. There are few teachers who would argue that effective learning should not be fun.

Accommodative and divergent learning processes take longer than the two others, and teachers cannot afford to allocate time to associated activities. Some teachers argued that convergent and assimilative activities were more time- and cost-efficient. Teachers of students in Years 9 to 13 in particular suggested that the pressures of coverage of options and exam syllabuses meant that they were less adventurous in their teaching than they were when taking Years 7 and 8. Yet within the IQEA network we are able to identify schools where students have been thoroughly versed in a variety of learning techniques as soon as they have arrived at the school, and where social learning techniques and opportunities are exploited by staff beyond Year 8 and in exam classes.

Teachers are able to keep better control of the class during convergent and assimilative activities. This sentiment is expressed in the research of others (Hacker and Carter, 1987; Newton and Harwood, 1993; Budge, 1997). However, much of the classroom disruption which I have observed during lessons involving an element of group work has been the result of poor planning, or a set of students unskilled in working in groups. I observed little disruption in Swedish classrooms, where group work is commonplace.

It is more difficult to assess the group work characteristic of accommodative and divergent learning than the individual work characteristic of convergent and assimilative teaching activities. This would be a reasonable argument to avoid social learning situations if students were advocating a diet which consisted exclusively of group work. The data included in this chapter suggest this is not the case.

The arguments rehearsed above represent a mixture of prejudice and pragmatism. They do not provide a rationale for the limited range of strategies and activities being provided in the schools which have been the subject of this article. There is no reason to suggest that these schools are exceptional in terms of the limited range of activities being offered by their teachers. Where they are exceptional is in their willingness to address the issue. It is clear that where schools do not address the issue, and do not attempt to match the teaching offered more closely to their students' learning preferences, they will continue to suffer the consequences of student alienation and anomie to which the learning incongruency described by Kolb and Fielding contributes. For effective learning to take place, teachers need to be knowledgeable about the learning repertoire of their students, and mindful of the need both to cater for and to expand that repertoire.

References

Aitkin, M., Bennett, S. N. and Hesketh, J. (1981) 'Teaching styles and pupil progress: a re-analysis', *British Journal of Educational Psychology* **51**, 170–86.

Alexander, R. (1991) 'Primary education in Leeds. Briefing and summary'. Leeds: School of Education, University of Leeds.

Alexander, R., Rose, J. and Woodhead, C. (1992) 'Curriculum organisation and classroom practice in primary schools. A discussion paper.' London: DES.

Barnett, T. (1985) 'Pupil personality and styles of teaching', *Pastoral Care* **3**(3), 207–15.

Bennett, N. and Entwistle, N. (1977) 'Rite and wrong: a reply to "A chapter of errors"', *Educational Research* **19**(3), 217–22.

Beresford, J. (1995) 'Teacher union perspectives on the management of professionals', in Busher, H. and Saran, R. (eds) *Managing Teachers as Professionals in Schools*, chap. 5. London and Philadelphia: Kogan Page.

Beresford, J. (1996) 'Adaptation of technique six to student conditions'. Mimeo, University of Cambridge School of Education.

Beresford, J. (1998a) *Collecting Information for School Improvement*. London: David Fulton Publishers.

Beresford, J. (1998b) 'Target practice', *Managing Schools Today* **7**(4), 22–5.

Beresford, J. (1999) 'Some reflections on the conduct and reporting of inspections in England and Sweden'. Paper presented to ICSEI 99, San Antonio, January.

Brophy, J. and Good, T. L. (1986) 'Teacher behavior and student achievement', in Wittrock, M. C. (ed.) *Handbook of Research on Teaching*, 3rd edn, chap. 12. The Project of the AERA. New York: Macmillan.

Budge, D. (1997) 'Deprived pupils left to read alone', *Times Educational Supplement*, 27 June.

Corno, L. and Snow, R. E. (1986) 'Adapting teaching to individual differences among learners', in Wittrock, M. C. (ed.) *Handbook of Research on Teaching*, 3rd edn, chap. 21. New York: Macmillan.

Cox, C. B. and Boyson, R. (eds) (1977) *Black Paper 1977*. London: Maurice Temple Smith.

Cunliffe, A. (1995) 'How do my students believe they learn?' Paper presented at Conference of Australian Science Teachers' Association.

De Pear, S. (1997) ' "Excluded pupils" views of their educational needs and experiences', *Support for Learning* **12**(1), 19–22.

Department of Education and Science (DES) (1967) *Children and their Primary Schools. Volume 1: The Report*. London: HMSO.

Department of Education and Science (DES) (1991) *News,* 4/12/91. Primary Education – A Statement by the Secretary of State for Education and Science, Kenneth Clarke, 3 December.

Department for Education and Employment (DfEE) (1997) *Excellence in Schools*. Cm 3681. London: The Stationery Office.

Department for Education and Employment (DfEE) (1998) *The National Literacy Strategy*. London: DfEE.

Elliott, J. (1984) 'Improving the quality of teaching through action-research', *Forum* **26**(3), 74–7.

Faccenda, J. and Fielding, M. (1992) *Learning Styles in FE*. Model-making Colleges Pack, Sussex University.

Fielding, M. (1994) 'Valuing difference in teachers and learners: building on Kolb's learning styles to develop a language of teaching and learning', *The Curriculum Journal* **5**(3), 393–417.

Gipps, C. (1992) *What We Know about Effective Primary Teaching*. London: The Tufnell Press.

Hacker, R. G. and Carter, D. S. G. (1987) 'Teaching processes in social studies classrooms and prescriptive instructional theories', *British Educational Research Journal* **13**(3), 261–9.

Hague, S. A. and Walker, C. (1996) 'Creating powerful learning opportunities for all children: the development and use of a self-monitoring checklist for teachers'. Paper presented at AERA Annual Conference, New York.

Harris, A. (1995) 'Effective teaching'. *SIN Research Matters 3* (Summer). London: Institute of Education.

Hopkins, D., Ainscow, M. and West, M. (1994) *School Improvement in an Era of Change*. London and New York: Cassell.

Hopkins, D. *et al.* (1997) *Creating the Classroom Conditions for School Improvement*. London: David Fulton Publishers.

Hopkins, D., West, M. and Beresford, J. (1998) 'Creating the conditions for classroom and teacher development', *Teachers and Teaching: Theory and Practice* **4**(1), 115–41.

Hord, S. M. (1997) 'Speaking with high school students in the southwest', in Restructuring Collaborative, *Look Who's Talking Now. Student Views of Learning in Restructuring Schools,* Chapter 4. Portland: Regional Educational Laboratory Network.

Hubbard, G. (1997) 'Pupil-managed co-operative learning: why and how pupils interact and co-operate'. Paper presented at BERA Conference, York, September.

Joyce, B. and Weil, M. (1986) *Models of Teaching*, 3rd edn. Englewood Cliffs, NJ: Prentice-Hall.

Joyce, B., Calhoun, E. and Hopkins, D. (1997) *Models of Learning – Tools for Teaching*. Buckingham and Philadelphia: Open University Press.

Joyce, B., Showers, B. and Rolheiser-Bennett, C. (1987) 'Staff development and student learning: a synthesis of research on models of teaching', *Educational Leadership* **45**(2), 11–23.

Kolb, D. A. (1984) *Experiential Learning. Experience as the Source of Learning and Development*. Englewood Cliffs, N J: Prentice-Hall.

Labour Party (1997) *New Labour. Because Britain Deserves Better*. London: Labour Party.

Levin, B. (1994a) 'Improving educational productivity: putting students at the center', *Phi Delta Kappan,* June, 758–60.

Levin, B. (1994b) 'Improving educational productivity through a focus on learners', *Studies in Educational Administration* **60**, 15–21.

National Association of Head Teachers (NAHT)/University of Nottingham (1996) *Class Size Research and the Quality of Education*. London: NAHT.

Newton, P. and Harwood, D. (1993) 'Teaching styles and personal and social education: how far have "Active Learning" strategies permeated the secondary curriculum?', *Pastoral Care* **11**(1), 36–42.

Norwich, B. (1998) 'Developing an inventory of children's class learning approaches', *Educational Psychology in Practice* **14**(3), 147–55.

Office for Standards in Education (OFSTED) (1995a) *Teaching Quality. The Primary Debate*. London: OFSTED.

Office for Standards in Education (OFSTED) (1995b) *Class Size and the Quality of Education*. London: OFSTED.

Reynolds, D. and Farrell, S. (1996) *Worlds Apart? A Review of International Surveys of Educational Achievement involving England*. London: HMSO (for OFSTED).

Rosenshine, B. and Stevens, R. (1986) 'Teaching functions', in Wittrock, M. C. (ed.) *Handbook of Research on Teaching*, 3rd edn, chap. 13. New York: Macmillan.

Rudduck, J., Chaplain, R. and Wallace, G. (eds) (1996) *School Improvement: What Can Pupils Tell Us?* London: David Fulton Publishers.

Sammons, P., Hillman, J. and Mortimore, P. (1995) *Key Characteristics of Effective Schools: A Review of School Effectiveness Research*. London: London Institute of Education (for OFSTED).

Scottish Consultative Council on the Curriculum (1996) *Teaching for Effective Learning*. Dundee: Scottish CCC.

Slavin, R. (1993) 'Co-operative learning in OECD countries: research, practice, and prevalence'. For the Centre for Educational Research and Innovation, Organization for Economic Co-operation and Development: Johns Hopkins University.

Southworth, G. (1996) 'Improving primary schools: shifting the emphasis and clarifying the focus, *School Organization* **16**(3), 263–80.

West, M., Hopkins, D. and Beresford, J. (1995) 'Conditions for school and classroom development'. Paper delivered at ECER, Bath, September.

Woodhead, C. (1992) 'Raise the standard bearers'. *Guardian*, 11 February.

Yaakobi, D. and Sharan, S. (1985) 'Teacher beliefs and practices: the discipline carries the message', *Journal of Education for Teaching* **11**(2), 187–99.

Chapter 20

Pupils' voices: discerning views on teacher effectiveness

Jane Devereux

Editors' Note: Jane Devereux considers the opinions people hold about what constitutes 'good' teaching. In particular, she reports on the views of the least powerful group – the pupils.

Introduction

> There are signs of change with a growth of recognition that consulting pupils about teaching and learning is worthwhile and that inviting pupil participation in this way can help to build a more positive learning culture.
>
> (Doddington, *et al.*, 2000, p.46)

But how is this done and what are the benefits? In exploring pupils' views on teachers, and on teaching and learning, we consider the characteristics shared across all phases as well as examining differences between the opinions of primary and secondary pupils, and between boys and girls.

'Nobody forgets a good teacher' was the catch-phrase of the first publicity campaign by the Teacher Training Agency (TTA) to encourage more people from different walks of life to enter the teaching profession. In the advertisement, famous people named someone they thought was a good teacher. What was not clear from the advert were the criteria each personality used to judge their favourite teacher. Analysis of the different dimensions of good teachers and teaching identified by 'the great and the good', would no doubt list some common features. Whether these would all accord with current literature on effective teaching, and school improvement is unlikely. But some of their criteria would almost certainly accord with current *pupils'* perspectives on what makes a good teacher.

A recent study by Hay McBer (2000) (see Chapter 17), for the DfEE, into teacher effectiveness opens with the following description of a good teacher written by Year 8 pupils.

A good teacher:

> *is kind*
>
> *is generous*
>
> *listens to you*
>
> *encourages you*
>
> *has faith in you*
>
> *keeps confidences*
>
> *likes teaching children*
>
> *likes teaching their subject*
>
> *takes time to explain things*
>
> *helps you when you're stuck*
>
> *tells you how you are doing*
>
> *allows you to have your say*
>
> *doesn't give up on you*
>
> *cares for your opinion*
>
> *makes you feel clever*
>
> *treats people equally*
>
> *stands up for you*
>
> *makes allowances*
>
> *tells the truth*
>
> *is forgiving.*

It is likely that all of those celebrities in the TTA advert would agree with many of the notions of a good teacher on the Year 8 pupils' list.

Close examination of teachers' work and reflections on their practice have tended to explore dimensions of the classroom life from the teacher perspective, but other groups also have views on what should take place in the classroom. Parents, the community, school senior management, inspectors and LEAs have their own opinions and theories about what makes for effective teaching and learning. In the recent years of intensive curriculum change, many of these groups have been consulted on the nature of effective teaching and learning in an attempt to raise standards. This chapter considers data gathered on what pupils say about their teachers, the match between pupil comments and studies on teacher effectiveness, and finally the implications of this for teachers in the classroom.

Pupil voices

Over the last twenty years an increasing interest in exploring pupils' perspective on schooling has begun to emerge. It extends the many studies looking at teachers' practice from their viewpoint. The ability of pupils to discern effective teaching, tacitly acknowledged by the TTA recruitment campaign, has been openly acknowledged by the Hay McBer study (2000). So what are pupils' views of what makes for an effective teacher and what is their opinion of effective teaching and learning in school? (See Thiessen, Chapter 25, p. 323, **Teachers and students** for discussion on the role of students in teacher development.

Researchers and educators (such as Wragg, 1984; Rudduck *et al.*, 1996; Wragg and Wood, 1984; Harris *et al.*, 1996; Brown and McIntyre, 1993; Woods, 1990; Younger and Warrington, 1996) have been at the forefront of exploring what pupils think. Pupils from all phases, stages and experiences have been involved in expressing their opinions on good teaching. As Rudduck *et al.* (1996) say

> the voices of all pupils should be listened to and not just those who are more academically and socially confident, for it is the less effective learners who are most likely to be able to explore aspects of the system that constrain commitment and progress; these are the voices least likely to be heard and yet most important to be heard.
>
> (p.177)

According to Clark (1995), pupils' thoughts and stories about good teachers concern four fundamental human needs, namely:

– to be known
– to be encouraged
– to be respected
– to be led.

Words like 'listens' and 'cares', from the introduction to this chapter, indicate that 'knowing' aspects are valued by pupils.

> The ideal – teacher student – model which enables teachers to communicate 'caring' without inadvertently 'parenting', is dialogue.

Repeatedly interviewees mention certain teachers who **knew** them, who would **talk to** and **explain things** to them, and who would **listen**. Knowing students in this way implies that the teachers have the ability to assume the student's perspective.
(Pomeroy, 1999, p.477)

Pupils' voices can be mapped into areas associated with respect and trust on the one hand and inspiring and enabling on the other.

Respect and trust

Pupils often cite the more undesirable qualities of teaching and teachers in their accounts.

Hardly surprisingly, students often cite public humiliation, especially shouting, as one of the most negative teacher–student interactions (White and Brockington, 1983; Woods, 1990; Chaplain, 1996; John, 1996; Rudduck et al., 1996). In this study teacher behaviour patterns that were found to be antagonistic and humiliating included shouting, telling students to 'shut up', responding sarcastically, putting young people down and name-calling. These actions were often perceived to communicate a message to the students that they are not valued as students and, often, that they are not liked as individuals.
(Pomeroy, 1999)

Much of this negativity can be expressed by the following:

Michael: well, when I go up and talk to her, go, 'can you explain this?' and that, she'll go, 'Explain what? You've been doing it all, like'all term. This is what you've been taught'. And I don't understand what I'm doing . . .
(Pomeroy, 1999, p.471)

One of Soo Hoo's (1993) student researchers commented 'if they (the teachers) have an attitude I don't know how they expect us to learn'.
Cullingford (1995) in exploring young children's perceptions of teaching and learning, highlighted how children valued those teachers who involved them in formulating some aspects of classroom practice, such as behaviour expectations. Primary school children understood the difference between being taught *how* to learn as opposed to *what* to learn, and knew when teachers were helping them with their learning.

250

Most students believe learning to be a valuable activity and the teacher's failure to facilitate learning is what is criticised.

Being listened to, having your views and ideas taken seriously, making decisions on matters affecting your life and well-being: these are fundamental rights in any democratic society.
(Doddington *et al.*, 2000)

Inspire and enable

Pupils are able to recognise the quality of a good teacher but earlier concerns about the achievements of girls and the recent concern about boys' attainment falling behind girls raises the question of whether boys and girls have different perceptions of good teaching and of their own learning styles.

Younger and Warrington's (1999) study explored gender differences among GCSE pupils and showed that girls are willing to take more responsibility for their own learning than are boys. Boys expect teachers to take greater responsibility for generating enjoyment and motivation in lessons. In their discussions with groups of Year 11 boys and girls some shared perceptions of a good teacher and good teaching were identified, namely:

- students of both sexes enjoyed teachers who were knowledgeable and enthusiastic about their subject and were willing to go beyond the syllabus;
- good lessons were characterised as enjoyable, fun and interesting and good personal relations between students and teachers were stressed as important;
- teachers who showed clear commitment to the class and individuals, who offered extra help and who were sensitive to the needs of the individual were also appreciated greatly;
- variety in teaching strategies, was also seen as important by both girls and boys.

Head (1996) described the difference between girls and boys.

males tend to develop a defence mechanism of attributing success to their own efforts and failure to external factors. Girls show the reverse tendency. The pedagogic implications is that girls may sink into . . . 'learned helplessness' in which the perception of failure inhibits subsequent performance. By contrast boys have to learn to take responsibility for their poor work.
(p.63)

From the study by Younger and Warrington (1999, pp.231–341) girls' liking for subjects affected the way in which they responded to lessons and the students themselves crucially affected the teaching and learning situation. Boys were much more likely to participate in lessons if they were fun and well presented and valued a relaxed atmosphere more than girls. Girls felt it was much better to be able to talk while working as it helped thinking and contributed to learning.

Younger and Warrington (1999) found that both girls and boys valued working in groups but boys preferred mixed groups because they thought girls were better at having an overview of issues whereas a proportion of girls preferred single sex groups as they often felt pushed out by boys. Boys felt that control of behaviour was the teachers' responsibility and none of the groups mentioned self-discipline.

Boys consistently spoke of the need for encouragement but this had to be positive and not negative. Praise, real praise, was seen as a vital part of this gaining respect and showing that teachers understood individuals and the class. However, some boys spoke of wanting the praise to be given quietly as they did not want to be seen to be doing well as it did not fit in with peer culture. Praise was seen as important to building self-esteem by both groups but particularly disaffected pupils as it helped them to grow in their own esteem but it also helped

> to establish an accepting and supportive classroom environment.
> (Younger and Warrington, 1999)

Boys liked teachers to talk about things other than work with them but some girls were not so happy as they resented the intrusion into their lives and too much friendliness. They wanted teachers to be approachable, helpful and friendly and were critical of those teachers who were moody and unpredictable but were not concerned whether the teacher was male or female.

Some students were concerned that many teachers were only interested in those who would gain grade 'C' and above. Students said good teachers recognised the achievements of all students and gave them encouragement; brought their subjects alive, believed in the importance of the subject and could communicate it to the students. In sum, in this most demanding of professions, a good teacher:

> Is not unfair to anyone. The lessons (are) always interesting and he makes it funny, we always seem to do more work than we think we're doing, and we learn a lot as well.
>
> Doesn't treat anyone unequally. He tries to give the class a good go, and

we get on well with him. He knows his stuff. He knows your weaknesses and strengths, and he'll sit down and talk to you the whole lesson to explain something. He'll go round and you learn more then. He's a very good teacher.

(Younger and Warrington, 1999, p.239)

Wragg (1993), in talking to primary pupils about what they felt allowed to do in the classroom, found that they knew they could:

– work
– talk to each other
– play when finished work
– choose something you want to do
– walk freely in the classroom with a reason.

Wragg noted that five-year-olds said they couldn't talk, but by Year 6 pupils said they could talk if it was related to work. The implications are that teachers should spend more time developing the skills younger children need in order to talk about their work and their learning.

Doddington *et al.* (2000) listed the following perceptions of primary school children on aspects that promoted or hindered learning. They were:

– pupil–teacher relationships
– disruptive behaviour
– being praised for work well done
– ownership and responsibility in learning.

Pupils also mentioned organisational systems such as classroom layout, materials and displays as possibly affecting their work.

Teacher effectiveness

How do the comments pupils make relate to other studies on teacher effectiveness? In exploring pupil perceptions of effective teaching Ramsden (1991) identifies seven characteristics of effective teaching that students see as crucial and link closely to the characteristics of a good teacher described by the Year 8 pupils at the start of this chapter. They are that an effective teacher:

– provides understandable explanations
– provides good feedback
– encourages independent thought

- is organised
- stimulates students' interest
- is focused on student needs
- sets clear goals.

In his work examining change in teacher effectiveness Munro monitored nine components of learning for teacher reflection (see Chapter 18, pp. 215–6). One component relates to the students' knowledge about learning, and about themselves as learners. The finer detail entailed looking at self management of the learning process including managing one's self as a learner, monitoring progress, developing action plans and the learning episode as a personal model of learning, managing attitudinal knowledge, achievement motivation, and learner attribution styles. Although students were not directly asked for their opinions, assumptions were made, from the data collected, that the significant rise in achievement had been because teachers used a wider range of skills and took more account of the effect on students. These included providing clear guidelines and expectations for each task, helping students to reflect on their successes and to identify action plans for individuals. As a result of the project teachers were more likely to provide opportunities for pupils to work collaboratively and at the end of lessons were more likely to have students review how their knowledge had changed (see Chapter 18, pp. 219–20).

By offering a range of learning opportunities, including those that use pupil strengths, teachers are more likely to provide a learning experience that students feel good about (Faccenda and Fielding, 1992). Student gain in Munro's study showed a 73 per cent increase and – particularly for those in the lowest quartile – a clear indication that clarifying ways of working and defining learning intentions can have a significant effect. Listening more carefully to pupils and incorporating their ideas into a developing personal knowledge of teaching and learning can only be beneficial to pupils. School effectiveness according to Munro will improve in parallel with any change in teaching effectiveness.

Beresford's work (see Chapter 19) in which he used a version of Kolb's Learning styles (1984) to observe and classify the work of several teachers in a range of schools, showed clearly that the teaching styles offered by schools did not match that desired by pupils. This suggests that we might need to consider in more detail the preferred learning styles of pupils. For the secondary teachers, this may be easier as older pupils are able to describe their ideas and desires more clearly. But for the primary teacher it can pose a problem, as children are not always able, because of age, stage and experience, to articulate their preferred learning styles. However, teachers can and should spend time exploring what children like doing, what seem to be effective sessions and analyse these so that they can use a variety of strategies to better effect. If schools ignore student views on their preferred learning styles then they will continue to have a higher proportion of students who are alienated from learning.

Effective teachers in primary school, according to Hay McBer (see Chapter 17) showed particular strengths in the following categories of high expectations, time and resource management, assessment and homework, whereas in secondary school there was

> a stronger differentiation across all clusters but it was particularly evident in high expectations, planning and homework.
>
> (p.197)

The range and variety of skills used by an effective teacher are wide and are skilfully deployed to take account of the needs and interests of the pupils. The care and consideration of pupil needs results in a constructive classroom climate that exists to meet and extend pupils' perspectives on teaching and learning. This care is summarised by Hay McBer, suggesting

> that taken together teaching skills, professional characteristics and classroom climate will predict well over 30 per cent of the pupil variance in pupil progress.
>
> (p. 196)

Managing and working with pupils to achieve a climate conducive to learning is not something that comes naturally to every teacher. The standards for initial teacher training, while they contain a great deal on effective teaching, are not able to ensure that all newly qualified teachers (NQTs) have clear understandings of all the issues raised about effective teaching. The recent professional development initiatives for NQTs and the new proposals for the continuing professional development (CPD) of teachers, with the particular focus on the early years of teaching, provide exciting opportunities to support young professionals (DfEE, 2001).

Garner (1995) highlights that teachers, rather than the curriculum, are the crucial element in stimulating pupils and creating a learning culture in any lesson or classroom. While this study focuses on the secondary stage, the findings are valid in primary but the nature and way they might work will be different. Skilled teachers at all stages are able to identify potentially volatile situations and behaviours and take measures to defuse or de-escalate tensions. Providing a space for individuals to go if they feel the need, providing the opportunity to talk through problems are just two of the many aspects of care and consideration that marks out effective teachers.

There is one particular aspect of effective teaching that is essential to learning and the development of individual pupils. It is the provision of feedback to individuals that they themselves find useful.

A small-scale research project undertaken by Burrell and Bubb (2000) which built on work by Tunstall and Gipps (1996) found that the kind of feedback given to very young children at the start of school has long-lasting effects on progress and attainment of pupils. Black and Wiliam (1998) comment that pupils who have difficulties with tasks and do not succeed are often led to believe, by the feedback given, that it is their fault and they turn their backs on learning, or as Black and Wiliam say, 'retire hurt'. They go on to say that in helping students to overcome short-term obstacles, offering feedback which they appreciate and which helps them make sense of their own learning, is an essential part of the formative assessment role of effective teaching.

> pupils should be trained in self assessment so that they can understand the main purposes of their learning and thereby grasp what they need to do to achieve.

In another context, Cullingford (1995) says an effective school depends on dialogue and this operates at all levels within the school but is of particular importance to the end user – the pupil.

Pupils' voices and implications for effective teaching

Although the literature highlights the crucial importance of the pupil's voice in classroom practice, the question always lingers as to whether the voice of the pupil should have as much authority as the voice of the teacher. It could be argued that, while important to them, certain perceptions held by students may not be in their best interests and that the experience, authority and training of teachers outweighs the pupils' demands. This would be to negate much of the research on teacher effectiveness. The effective teacher may well set the main agenda, but this agenda is informed by the voices of those he or she teaches. The learning agenda is one in which the relationship is not one of master or mistress over servant, but one of partnership, not necessarily an equal one, with child and teacher serving the higher task, namely, that of extending learning and understanding.

If we wish to improve the educational outcomes of the pupils we teach, we must take seriously the profound insights shown by all the pupils in these studies and think about how we support teachers and pupils as learners in our schools. A fundamental conclusion is that there must be:

mutually respectful treatment between individuals in a working relationship. The model recognises that the roles and responsibilities of the two actors are different and unequal, but maintains that this difference does not form a justifiable basis for interactions which transmit a message of disrespect or de-valuing. In addition, the inherent inequalities in the relationship should not result in dialogue being precluded from the relationship. Rather, dialogue, which attempts to understand different perspectives, is a central characteristic of the ideal model of the student–teacher relationship.

This ability to create a sense of trust with pupils brought about by honouring their commitments, by being genuine and allowing pupils to be themselves, to take risks and not be laughed at, are professional attributes that all contribute to the creation of a trusting environment. An underlying concern for pupils' welfare and progress as well as the skills to support their pupils are indicative of good teachers.

(Pomeroy, 1999, p.480)

Effective teaching leaves both teacher and pupil magnified by the transaction feeling positive, excited, and conscious of their growing skills, confidence, knowledge and attitudes.

References

Black, P. and Wiliam, D. (1998) *Inside the Black Box*. London: Kings College.

Brown, S. and McIntyre, D. (1993) *Making Sense of Teaching*. Milton Keynes: Open University Press.

Burrell, A. and Bubb, S. (2000) 'Teacher feedback in the Reception class: associations with children's positive adjustment to school', *Education 3–13*, October.

Chaplain, R. (1996) 'Making a strategic withdrawal: disengagement and self-worth protection in male pupils', in Rudduck, J., Chaplain, R. and Wallace, G. (eds) *School Improvement: what can pupils tell us?* London: David Fulton Publishers.

Clark, C. M. (1995) *Thoughtful Teaching*. London: Cassell.

Cullingford, C. (1995) *The effective teacher*. London: Cassell.

Department for Education and Employment (DfEE) (2001) *Learning and Teaching*. London: DfEE Publications.

Doddington, C., Flutter, J. and Rudduck, J. (2000) 'Taking their word for it: can listening, and responding to pupils' views give new directions for school improvement?', *Education 3–13*, October.

Faccenda, J. and Fielding, M. (1992) *Learning Styles in FE.* Model-making Colleges Pack, Sussex University.

Garner, P. (1995) 'Schools by scoundrels: the views of "disruptive" pupils in mainstream schools in England and the United States', in Lloyd-Smith, M. and Davies, J. (eds) *On the Margins: the educational experience of 'problem' pupils.* Stoke: Trentham Books.

Harris, S., Rudduck, J. and Wallace, G. (1996) 'Political contexts and school careers', in Hughes, M. (ed.) *Teaching and Learning in Changing Times.* Oxford: Blackwell.

Hay McBer (2000) Research into Teacher Effectiveness. London: Hay Group/DfEE.

Head, J. (1996) 'Gender identity and cognitive style', in Murphy, P. F. and Gipps, C. V. (eds) *Equity in the Classroom: towards effective pedagogy for girls and boys.* London: Falmer Press.

John, P. (1996) 'Damaged goods: an interpretation of excluded pupils' perceptions of schooling', in Blyth, E. and Milner, J. (eds) *Exclusion from School.* London: Routledge.

Kolb, D. A. (1984) *Experiential Learning. Experience as the Source of Learning and Development.* Englewood Cliffs, NJ: Prentice-Hall.

Pomeroy, E. (1999) 'The teacher student relationship in secondary schools: insights from excluded students', *British Journal of Sociology of Education* **20**(4).

Ramsden, P. (1991) 'A performance indicator of teaching quality in higher education: the course experience questionnaire', *Studies in Higher Education* **16**, 129–50.

Rudduck, J., Chaplain, R. and Wallace, G. (1996) *School Improvement: what can pupils tell us?* London: David Fulton Publishers.

Soo Hoo, S. (1993) 'Students as partners in research and restructuring schools', *The Educational Forum* **57**, 386–92.

Tunstall, P. and Gipps, C. (1996) 'Teacher feedback to young children in formative assessment: a typology', *British Educational Research Journal* **22**(4), 389–404.

White, R. and Brockington, D. (1983) *Tales Out of School: consumers' views of British Education.* London: Routledge and Keegan Paul.

Woods, P. (1990) *The Happiest Days?: how pupils cope with school.* London: Falmer Press.

Wragg, E. C. (1993) *Primary Teaching Skills.* London: Routledge.

Wragg, E. C. and Wood, E. K. (1984) 'Teachers' first encounters with their classes', in Wragg, E. C. (ed.) *Classroom teaching skills.* London: Croom Helm.

Younger, M. and Warrington, M. (1996) 'Differential achievement of girls and boys at GCSE: some observations from the perspective of one school', *British Journal of Sociology of Education* **17**, 299–314.

Younger, M. and Warrington, M. (1999) '"He's such a nice man, but he's so boring, you have to really make a conscious effort to learn": the views of Gemma, Daniel and their contemporaries on teacher quality and effectiveness', *Educational Review* **51**(3), 231–41.

Chapter 21

Vernacular pedagogy

David McNamara

Editors' Note: This article first appeared in 1991. It has much to say about the importance of a study of 'pedagogy' and shows that such concerns are not new.

Introduction

There has been a welcome resurgence of interest in and emphasis upon the study of pedagogy in recent years. On this side of the Atlantic, Simon[1] has argued that the concept of pedagogy, which he defines as 'a science of teaching embodying both curriculum and methodology', is alien to the manner in which educationists and teachers regard teaching and learning and he articulates the case for focusing upon pedagogy in order to establish teaching and learning upon a credible intellectual foundation in order to promote the development of all children. For him this entails 'importing a definite structure into teaching, and so into the learning experiences provided for the pupils'.[2] Stones[3] has elaborated how his notion of *psychopedagogy*[4] can inform the theory and practice of teacher education since pedagogy is particularly relevant to practice and has the potential for ensuring that practical teaching is informed by theory and research. In a similar vein Galton[5] has drawn upon Simon's thesis when criticising the somewhat theoretical nature of primary teacher training and proposed that the study of pedagogy could be used to develop more consistent and rigorous teacher

1. B. Simon, 'Why no pedagogy in England?', in B. Simon, *Does Education Matter?*, (London: Lawrence and Wishart, 1985), p. 80.
2. Ibid., p. 99.
3. E. Stones, 'Pedagogical studies in the theory and practice of teacher education', *Oxford Review of Education* **15**(1) 1989, pp. 3–15.
4. E. Stones, *Psychopedagogy: Psychological Theory and the Practice of Teaching*, (London: Methuen, 1979).
5. M. Galton, 'Primary teacher-training: a practice in search of pedagogy', in V. A. McClelland and V. P. Varma (eds), *Advances in Teacher Education*, (London: Routledge, 1989), pp. 34–57.

education programmes. In the USA a seminal event was Shulman's presidential address to the American Educational Research Association.[6] The flavour of Shulman's thesis and agenda are indicated in the following quotation:

> How does the successful college student transform his or her expertise in the subject matter into a form that high school students can comprehend? When this novice teacher confronts flawed or muddled textbook chapters or befuddled students, how does he or she employ content expertise to generate new explanations, representations, or classifications? What are the sources of analogies, metaphors, examples, demonstrations and rephrasings? . . . What pedagogical prices are paid when the teacher's subject matter competence is itself compromised by deficiencies of prior education or ability?[7]

While Shulman's proposals have provoked professional discussion and debate, for example Sockett[8] claims that he has a narrow vision of the purposes of education, his distinctive contribution has been to foster a series of empirical investigations which focus researchers' attention upon an essential purpose of education which is the passing on of knowledge, however defined, from teacher to children.[9] The contributions of educationists working in cognate areas[10] give added impetus to pedagogical studies and enhance their appeal for the practising teacher because their research has recognised that the teaching of subject matter must be set within the context of (a)

---

6. L. S. Shulman, 'Those who understand: knowledge growth in teaching', *Educational Researcher*, **15**(2), 1986, pp. 4–14, and elaborated in L. S. Shulman, 'Knowledge and teaching: foundations of the new reform', *Harvard Educational Review* **57**(1), 1987, pp. 1–22.

7. L. S. Shulman, 'Those who understand: knowledge growth in teaching', op cit., p. 6.

8. H. T. Sockett, 'Has Shulman got the strategy right?', *Harvard Educational Review* **57**(2),1987, pp. 208–19.

9. See, for example, D. L. Ball, 'Prospective teachers' understandings of mathematics: what do they bring with them to teacher education?'. Paper presented at the annual meeting of the American Educational Research Association (New Orleans, 1988). D. L. Ball and S. Feiman-Nemser, 'Using textbooks and teachers' guides: a dilemma for beginning teachers and teachers' educators', *Curriculum Inquiry*, **18**(4), 1988, pp. 401–23. R. Marks, 'What exactly is pedagogical content knowledge? Examples from mathematics'. Paper presented to the American Educational Research Association, (San Francisco, 1989). R. E. Orton, 'A study of the foundations of mathematics teachers' knowledge'. Paper presented to the annual meeting of the American Educational Research Association (San Francisco, 1989). D. C. Smith and D. C. Neale, 'The construction of subject matter knowledge in primary science teaching', *Teaching and Teacher Education*, **5**(1), 1989, pp. 1–20.

10. See, for example, M. Buckman, 'The flight away from content in teacher education and teaching', *Journal of Curriculum Studies*, **14**(1), 1982, pp. 61–8. W. Doyle, 'Content representation in teachers' definitions of academic work', *Journal of Curriculum Studies*, **18**(4), 1986, pp. 129–49.

organising children and materials in busy classrooms with limited resources and (b) the management of learning tasks.

The systematic study of pedagogy is probably best established within the Soviet Union[11] and *glasnost* has made Soviet work in the field more freely available. Setting aside the distinct ideological thrust of Soviet pedagogy, it has many connections with work now being undertaken in the West. Within the Soviet work there are emphases upon the process of instruction, the manner in which subject matter material is presented, the setting of tasks and guiding of work and assessing how well children have assimilated knowledge – all of which are echoed in the American research.[12]

The study of pedagogy has, in the past, held an important place in the training of teachers and informed teaching practices. It was, for example, central to Dewey's[13] educational writings and has an honoured place in the Continental educational tradition;[14] however, there has been a prejudice against it in both Britain[15] and the USA.[16] In what follows I aim to identify the distinctive contributions which current pedagogical thinking and research may make to the study of teaching, especially within the context of teacher education and training, but also suggest that we must treat this potential contribution with a measure of circumspection concerning its capacity to inform classroom practice. This is because commentators have failed to appreciate that class teachers are, in effect, already practising pedagogues. Teachers are a valuable source of practically useful pedagogic knowledge, as is recognised in the Soviet Union.[17] It will be necessary to meld formal pedagogical knowledge (which I define as that pedagogical knowledge generated by systematic and rigorous research) and vernacular pedagogical knowledge (which I define as the working pedagogical

---

11. See, for example, E. I. Monoszon, 'The establishment and development of Soviet pedagogy, Excerpts (I)', *Soviet Education*, **30**(11), 1988, (M. E. Sharpe, New York). E. I. Monoszon, 'The establishment and development of Soviet pedagogy, Excerpts (II)', *Soviet Education*, **30**(12) 1988, (M. E. Sharpe, New York). E. I. Monoszon, 'The establishment and development of Soviet pedagogy, Excerpts (III)', *Soviet Education*, **31**(1) 1989, (M. E. Sharpe, New York).
12. Notably in M. A. Danilov and B. P. Esipov, *Didaktika* and M. A. Danilov, *The Process of Instruction in Soviet Schools*, substantial extracts of both are contained in E. I. Monoszon, 'The establishment and development of Soviet pedagogy, Excerpts (II), op cit.
13. J. Dewey, 'The Relation of Theory to Practice in Education, National Society for the Scientific Study of Education', Third yearbook, Part I, (1904) reprinted in R. D. Archambault (ed.) *John Dewey on Education: Selected Writings*, (University of Chicago Press, 1964), pp. 313–38.
14. Simon, 'Why no pedagogy in England?' op. cit.
15. Ibid.
16. J. S. Hazlett, 'In defence of pedagogy', *Contemporary Education*, **57**(3), 1986, pp. 154–5.
17. E. L. Monoszon, 'The establishment and development of Soviet pedagogy, Excerpts (IIT), op. cit., pp. 67ff.

knowledge developed by teachers through their experience) if the study of pedagogy is to have an important contribution to make in developing more effective teaching within the particular circumstances of ordinary classrooms.

The contribution of pedagogy

There are a number of ways in which the systematic and rigorous study of pedagogy may make a contribution to teaching and learning and while they are, to a significant degree, interrelated they will, for the purposes of exposition, be identified separately and discussed seriatim.

Emphasis on content

The essential purpose of teaching is passing on to learners subject matter content, be it knowledge, skills or attitudes (what constitutes a subject or how it is passed on need not concern us at this stage). For Shulman[18] the central pedagogical question is how beginning teachers transform their knowledge of subject matter into forms and practices which pupils can comprehend. He argues that in order to do this teachers must first acquire knowledge of a subject. In addition they must also develop *pedagogical content knowledge* (which is information germane to a subject's teachability, namely the ways of representing and formulating a subject so as to make it comprehensible to pupils and what makes learning specific topics easy or difficult) and curricular knowledge (which includes an understanding of the full range of ways available for teaching a subject, the instructional methods available, different mediums of instruction and their advantages and disadvantages and information about how ways of teaching may be modified in practice). Shulman has set out an agenda for researchers and teacher educators which is being attended to.[19] The thrust of this work is to develop coherent conceptual frameworks and pursue empirical studies which have some demonstrable benefit in terms of enhancing teachers' ability to ensure that children learn content.

[. . .]

---

18. Shulman, 'Knowledge and teaching: foundations of the new reform', op. cit.
19. See, for example, investigations cited under Note 9 and also: T. P. Carpenter, 'Teachers' pedagogical content knowledge of students' problem solving in elementary arithmetic', *Journal of Research in Mathematics Education*, **19**(5), 1988, pp.385–401. P. Ernst, 'The knowledge, beliefs and attitudes of the mathematics teacher: a model', *Journal of Education for Teaching*, **15**(1), 1989, pp.13–33. P. C. Peterson *et al.*, 'Teachers' pedagogical content beliefs in mathematics', *Cognition and Instruction*, **6**(1), 1989, pp.1–40. P. Tamir: 'Subject matter and related pedagogical knowledge in teacher education', *Teaching and Teacher Education*, **4**(2), 1988, pp. 99–110.

Promoting reflective teaching

[. . .] In many ways teachers' autonomy and professional independence have been eroded and they are increasingly subject to state control[20] and this process may be accelerated by the statutory requirements for the National Curriculum. However, despite initiatives such as the literacy and numeracy hours, for most of the curriculum teachers are still in a position to decide how to teach; teaching method and style is still the teacher's responsibility. In this respect also pedagogical studies have a crucial role to play in promoting reflective teaching[21] and in requiring teachers and teacher educators to ask searching questions about, for example:

i) *Their own understanding of subject matter and what they need to know about a subject, or area of studies in order to translate what they know into forms which facilitate children's learning.* For instance pedagogical studies which have investigated student teachers' knowledge of basic mathematical concepts reveal that their understanding is often wrong or confused thus creating problems when they seek to help children comprehend; they are more likely to resort to reinforcing practice routines which produce the right answer, rather than tackle children's fundamental learning difficulties.[22]

ii) *The nature of materials which encapsulate content and make it available for pupils, such as textbooks, schemes of work and computer software.* Teachers must critically assess the value of teaching materials and aids as pedagogical devices which are claimed to assist in facilitating learning as exemplified, for example, by Newton and Gott's[23] exposure of the inadequate notions of process-based approaches to science teaching contained within science textbooks. There is, for example, no necessary reason why the use of advanced technologies enhance the presentation of information or subject matter in ways which promote learning. While the computer may have a significant contribution to make to children's learning it must be evaluated in a hard-headed and critical manner.[24]

iii) *The quality and nature of the learning tasks which children are required to undertake and how these actually shape children's understanding.*

---

20. J. Ozga (ed.), *Schoolwork: Approaches to the Labour Process of Teaching*, (Open University Press, 1988).
21. See, for example, L. Rubin, 'The thinking teacher: cultivating pedagogical intelligence', *Journal of Teacher Education*, **40**(6), 1989, pp. 31–4.
22. See, for example, Ball, op. cit. and Orton, op. cit.
23. D. P. Newton and R. Gott, 'Process in lower school science text books', *British Educational Research Journal*, **15**(3), 1989, pp. 249–58.
24. See, for example, the articles contained in the special issue of *Teachers College Record*, **89**(3), 1988 devoted to Computing and Education.

The work of Doyle[25] and his colleagues[26] is of particular interest in demonstrating that whatever teaching method is employed and whatever the teacher's aspirations for a lesson there comes a point at which children will be required to engage in tasks (which may, for example, focus on their knowledge, skills or attitudes and involve different activities and products). From the point of view of the child it is probably the nature of the specific tasks set which shape his or her learning and understanding, rather than the overt content of the lesson or the teacher's exposition. For example, teachers will often require young children to engage in practical activities so that they may learn and better understand formal mathematical procedures, but as one commentator[27] has demonstrated, the gap between the two types of experience is not easily bridged. Alternatively, educationists and teachers claim that classroom discussion among children and with the teacher has an important part to play in developing children's basic skills and success in mathematics; however, the educational theory upon which these claims rest has yet to be tested rigorously and the real time and resource constraints of busy classrooms make it extremely difficult for teachers to introduce these practices.[28] In addition, such factors as children's readings of the teacher's attitude to tasks (will they be marked and will the marks 'count'?) and how the teacher is perceived to value tasks by children (does the teacher really give marks for tidiness and spelling or creativity?) affect learning and attitudes towards it.

[. . .]

Professional responsibility

Pedagogy requires us to focus upon teachers' professional responsibility to promote learning and thereby explore the links between teaching and learning. The considerable literature stemming, in the main from analytical philosophy, has failed to elicit precisely what teaching is and its conceptual links with learning.[29] To some degree learning must be accepted as the

25. See, for example, W. Doyle, 'Academic Work', *Review of Educational Research*, **53**(2), 1983, pp. 159–99.
26. See, for example, W. Doyle and K. Carter, 'Academic tasks in classrooms', *Curriculum Inquiry* **14**(2), 1984 , pp. 129–49.
27. K. Hart, 'There is little connection', in P. Ernst (ed.), *Mathematics Teaching: The State of the Art*, (Falmer Press, 1989), pp. 138–42.
28. C. Desforges, 'Classroom processes and mathematical discussions: a cautionary note', in Ernst, op. cit., pp. 143–50.
29. See, for example, W. A. Hart, 'Is teaching what the philosopher understands it to be?', *British Journal of Educational Studies*, **24**, 1976, pp.155–70. E. L. Pincoffs, 'What can be taught', in R. T. Hyman (ed.) *Contemporary Thought on Teaching*, (Prentice-Hall, 1971), pp. 239–51. D. M. Senchuk, 'The polymorphous character of teaching', *Educational Theory*, **34**(2), 1984, pp. 183–90.

independent achievement of the learner[30] but, nevertheless, it is part of our commonsense understanding and certainly the assumption of the lay public that teachers should in part be responsible for children's learning and that the transmission of knowledge, skills and attitudes lies at the heart of their work. Unfortunately a major problem with the 'educational disciplines' approach to educational theory is not so much that it is unrelated to practice but that it has provided teachers with a series of psychological and sociological 'myths' whereby they can explain away any failure on their part to promote children's learning by invoking deficiencies in the individual child's mental abilities or home background.[31] Educational theory derived from the social sciences confers some academic distinction upon the study of teaching but it tends not to address the central purposes of teaching except in so far as it provides explanations for the failure to learn.[32] Educational theory based upon pedagogical studies, on the other hand, stresses the content of instruction and learning and while it does not provide the teacher with information which enables her to legislate for learning, it offers the potential for providing the teacher with information which should enable her to maximise the child's learning in so far as the dispositions, ability and circumstances of the child permit. It certainly focuses upon promoting success in learning rather than explaining failure. In this central respect pedagogy provides the context in which the work of the professional teacher may be distinguished from that of other professional groups, some of whom are also interested, in part, in fostering children's learning such as social workers, medical practitioners and librarians. Teaching involves promoting children's learning within the particular constraints of classrooms[33] where circumstances such as lack of resources, ratio of one teacher to many learners, and the organisation of time often make it difficult to encourage the effective learning of content which children may not be naturally disposed to want to learn.

The limitations of formal pedagogy

Educationists' contributions to the study of pedagogy are rooted within

30. G. Ryle, *On Thinking*, (Blackwell, 1979), ch. 4, pp. 65–78.
31. D. H. Hargreaves, *Interpersonal Relations and Education*, (Routledge and Kegan Paul, 1972), pp. 66ff.
32. D. R. McNamara, 'The outsiders' arrogance: the failure of participant observers to understand classroom events', *British Educational Research Journal*, **6**(2), 1980, pp. 113–26.
33. For discussion of these themes see, R. Dreeben, 'The school as a workplace', in R. M. W. Travers (ed.) *Second Handbook of Research on Teaching*, (Rand McNally, 1973), pp.450–73. C. Desforges and A. Cockburn, *Understanding the Mathematics Teacher: A Study of Practice in First Schools*, (Falmer Press, 1987).

classroom practice, however, it does not follow that the products of the formal study of pedagogy can be applied directly in the classroom or that there is an easy transfer from theory to practice, as Valli and Tom[34] have demonstrated in their critique of Shulman's seminal paper which they claim does not meet the *adequacy criteria* which would help teachers bring knowledge to bear on practice. If the usual pitfalls in the hiatus between theory and practice are to be avoided the limitations of formal pedagogy, given the current state of the art, must be acknowledged and addressed.

The lack of a comprehensive knowledge base

On the basis of a limited number of analytical exercises and empirical studies it is, at present, possible to provide interesting and telling examples which illustrate the potential which the systematic study of pedagogy has for informing teaching. However, we are nowhere near the stage where there is a comprehensive knowledge base which extends across all areas of the curriculum and age phases. It is one thing, say, to provide intending primary teachers with information drawn from a few studies in elementary arithmetic processes in order to show what is possible and to illustrate ways in which they can think analytically about their teaching and their pupils' learning difficulties; it will be quite another matter to reach the stage where teacher educators have a coherent corpus of pedagogical knowledge about merely, say, the primary mathematics curriculum. Pedagogical studies have identified a formidable agenda for research and development but the available corpus amounts to little more than a preliminary exercise. Meanwhile class teachers must continue with their teaching.

Conservative teaching

When focusing upon the transmission of subject matter the available empirical studies usually have an implicit or explicit notion of knowledge which is conventional and conservative and which does not necessarily map onto teachers' notions of good practice. The curriculum is invariably couched in terms of conventional subject headings and while this is not necessarily a criticism it must be recognised that even within the context of the National Curriculum primary phase teachers are enabled and encouraged by the non-statutory guidelines for the core subjects to integrate their teaching of subject

---

34. L. Valli and A. R. Tom, 'How adequate are the knowledge based frameworks in teacher education?' *Journal of Teacher Education*, **39**(5), 1988, pp. 5–12.

matter using topics or themes. To date pedagogical investigations can offer no advice to teachers about how they should tackle the teaching of content in ways that seek to break down or cut across conventional subject boundaries.

There must, in addition, be a measure of concern that in practice pedagogical studies are likely to lag behind curricular innovation and change which has been shaped by technological or political factors. For instance major innovations such as the introduction of microcomputers and information technology or the establishment of GCSE examinations have clear implications for pedagogy which teachers must work through in practice. The systematic study of pedagogy is likely to follow rather than inform curriculum implementation. This should be seen as a matter to note, rather than a major criticism since, especially as far as primary education is concerned, various studies have demonstrated the enduring consistency of teaching practices which in the majority of schools exemplify more traditional and subject-centred approaches to teaching.[35] Whatever the rhetoric of primary education, empirical investigations suggest that the majority of primary teachers continue to teach conventional subject matter in conventional ways and pedagogical studies have a part to play in informing their current practices (but probably will not offer the impetus to inform more fundamental change).

Practical constraints

Even though pedagogical studies address teaching and learning within the context of classrooms it must be remembered that findings must be codified in written documents and that this information must be acquired by teachers prior to their introducing it into the concrete and particular circumstances of their classrooms.[36] It is very difficult for teachers to make use of formal information within the context of the real time constraints of interactive teaching, which include lack of resources and pressure of time, and thereby teach as they would prefer.[37] Moreover, teachers are rarely, for instance, in a

---

35. See, for example, I. Cuban, *How Teachers Taught: Constancy and Change in American Classrooms 1890–1980*, (Longman, 1984). M. Galton, 'Change and continuity in the primary school: the research evidence', *Oxford Review of Education*, **13**(1), 1987, pp. 81–93. K. A. Sirotnik, 'What you see is what you get: consistency, persistency, and mediocrity in classrooms', *Harvard Educational Review*, **53**(1), 1983, pp. 16–31.

36. J. J. Schwah, 'The practical 3: translation into curriculum, *School Review*, **81**, 1973, pp. 501–22.

37. C. Desforges, 'Teachers' perspectives on classroom interaction', in C. W. Desforges (ed.) *Early Childhood Education, British Journal of Educational Psychology* Monograph Series No. 4, (Scottish Academic Press, 1989), pp. 158–66.

position to make, say, informed pedagogical decisions about the merits of competing textbooks or schemes of work. Their professional task, all too often, is to make the best use of what is currently available in the classroom. It may be the case that the contribution of pedagogical studies could be that they engender in teachers a disposition to reflect upon their teaching but not provide them with the wherewithal to actually change their practices.

Vernacular pedagogical knowledge

These three factors, the lack of a comprehensive knowledge base, the conventional representation of subject matter, and the practical constraints of class teaching may make it difficult for pedagogical knowledge to have a worthwhile and extensive impact upon practice in the near future but there is one overriding factor which has not been mentioned so far and which is neglected as a specific issue in the pedagogic literature. It is that teachers are already practising pedagogues. Moreover, while it may not be explicitly articulated, they will have a repertoire of pedagogical knowledge which 'works' within the exigencies of classrooms. This is not to comment on the quality of teachers' pedagogical knowledge or to say that it is necessarily effective in fostering pupils' learning; what 'works' may be nothing more than a coping strategy. Setting aside this caveat it is demonstrably the case that many teachers are exemplars of good, working, pedagogical practices and that teachers can acquire valuable pedagogical knowledge through their classroom experience.

If progress is to be made in the development of those forms of pedagogical knowledge which can be established in the classroom then I suggest that the formal study of pedagogy must be linked with what I term teachers' vernacular pedagogical knowledge. I use the term vernacular because it carries with it connotations of belonging to the people, of being rooted within the local community and environment, of being concerned with the practical and having a sense of purpose, of having a sense of modest appropriateness, and not being dressed in ornamental language.[38] These are characteristics which, at their best, describe class teachers' *pedagogical* knowledge; for instance it is rooted within the particular circumstances of classrooms and is concerned with the everyday purpose of teaching in the particular environment of those classrooms and it acknowledges that at the point of contact between teacher and child the teacher must talk to children and impart

---

38. Here I am following the discussion on vernacular architecture in A. Raistrick, *The Pennine Dales*, (Arrow, 1968), pp. 147ff.

content using everyday language which they understand. As Hazlitt[39] recognised so long ago we must recognise the familiar and understand and write about it without affectation.

An essential part of the task of developing pedagogical knowledge must be to value and make use of the important contribution which practising teachers' pedagogical knowledge can make to developing a representative corpus of pedagogical knowledge. It must be stressed that this is not to say that the 'outsider' does not have a contribution to make or that teachers' pedagogical knowledge exemplifies good practice – quite often it will need to be challenged. It is to say that vernacular pedagogical knowledge is an important matrix in the development of pedagogy and that the essential role of the educator is to collect examples of this knowledge and subject them to critical scrutiny before vernacular pedagogy can be passed on to, say, beginning teachers as a set of guides or proposals for good practice. Here a clear distinction must be made between (a) collations of samples of practice acquired by outsiders visiting classrooms, examples of which are the HMI series *Aspects of Primary Education*,[40] based upon HMI inspections of primary schools and (b) serving teachers' accounts of how they actually engineered the examples of good practice. The HMI Reports illustrate good practice but procedures for accessing vernacular pedagogy are required in order to provide accounts of how good practice can be achieved within busy classrooms.

Procedural and methodological implications

It is not enough to nominate teachers' vernacular pedagogical knowledge as a focus for investigation; it is also necessary to consider the problems entailed in assessing such knowledge and then codifying it so as to establish a corpus of material which may be introduced into initial or in-service teacher training courses. The notion of vernacular pedagogical knowledge carries with it connotations of subjectivity and of being tied to the particular exigencies of time and place. How, then, can such knowledge be researched and organised as information which may inform teachers' professional practices? Issues of this sort are currently being addressed by the research community and it is being recognised that if the activities of educational researchers are to have an impact upon classroom practice then research must be conducted and justified

---

39. W. Hazlitt, *Selected Writings*, (Penguin, 1970), pp. 187ff.
40. DES (1989) *The Teaching and Learning of Mathematics*, (HMSO, 1989). DES (1989) *The Teaching and Learning of Science*, (HMSO, 1989). DES (1990) *The Teaching and Learning of Language and Literacy*, (HMSO, 1990). Note that the series is being extended to cover the curriculum.

according to criteria other than those conventionally accepted such as validity, reliability and generalisability. It is essential to listen to the voice of the teacher and invoke other criteria such as verisimilitude and transferability so as to make the expertise of individual class teachers available to others.[41] Appropriate methodological procedures are being established for acquiring evidence from teachers which examine their professional practice within the real time constraints of classrooms.[42] The change in approach is epitomised by Eisner:[43]

> Educational researchers are beginning to go back to the schools, not to conduct commando raids, but to work with teachers as colleagues in a common quest and through such collaboration to rediscover the qualities, the complexities, and the richness of life in classrooms. We are beginning to talk with teachers, not only to teachers.

Such an approach may have practical beneficial consequences for participating teachers also. Recent work by Huberman[44] indicates that teachers find it more satisfying to engage in small-scale research and that participation with research of this kind is more likely to affect their practice than being involved with radical educational reform. Cultivating one's private garden, pedagogically speaking, seems to be preferred and to have more practical impact than being involved with collective attempts to reshape institutional practices. In addition, Popper's[45] distinction between World 2 and World 3 knowledge offers an heuristic for moving from the acquisition of teachers' vernacular pedagogical knowledge to the systematic codification of that knowledge; it provides a content for the shift from the private world of subjective knowledge to the public world of codified knowledge. Codified knowledge is knowledge which is written down or recorded in some way so that it exists as a permanent artefact which can be made freely available to others. It no longer exists only in the private mind of the individual as his or her personal, subjective knowledge. It is accessible to colleagues and can therefore be communicated to them and they can evaluate and appraise it.

---

41. F. M. Connelly and D. J. Clandinin, 'Stories of experience and narrative inquiry', *Educational Researcher*, **19**(5), 1990, pp. 2–14. M. Cochran-Smith and S. L. Lytle, 'Research on teaching and teacher research: the issues that divide', *Educational Researcher*, **19**(2), 1990, pp. 2–11.

42. For example, Connelly and Clandinin, op. cit. and notably, G. Leinhardt, 'Capturing craft knowledge in teaching', *Educational Researcher*, **19**(2), 1990, pp. 18–25.

43. E. Eisner, 'The primacy of experience and the politics of method', *Educational Researcher*, **17**(5), 1978, p. 19.

44. M. Huberman, 'The professional life cycle of teachers', *Teachers College Record*, **91**(1), 1989, pp. 31–57.

45. K. Popper, *Objective Knowledge: An Evolutionary Approach*, (Oxford, Clarendon, 1972).

Once teachers' vernacular pedagogical knowledge enters the realm of codified knowledge there is the potential to develop a corpus of systematic pedagogical knowledge. The crucial shift from subjective experience to codified knowledge is not an automatic process. It requires deliberate intervention by a sensitive observer to ensure that teachers' subjective skill and experience become codified as permanent records of practice. Once this transition has been made it becomes possible to examine critically and interpret codified records of practice so that they can be established as formal knowledge.

Since it is essential to codify teachers' classroom skills as they are actually practised the information must be collected from active teachers whose daily work is in the classroom and whose professional conduct is to some degree shaped by the exigencies and constraints of typical classrooms. The most appropriate, indeed probably the only way in which it is possible to proceed with the codification of professional skill is for a third party to observe teachers at work and then talk to them about their practice.[46] The third party must, among other things, be sensitive to the pedagogical dilemmas faced by the teacher between what she is expected to accomplish and the inner struggle about how to do her job according to her values.[47] The ultimate aim of this endeavour is not, in the words of Rorty[48] to seek a spurious objective understanding but to offer accounts of situations which may help others to decide what to do.

As the adage has it[49] school is about the moment between someone not knowing something, and then knowing it and pedagogy lies at the heart of that moment. My aim has been to suggest that the study of vernacular pedagogy is central to improving the quality of the teaching and learning which takes place within the idiosyncratic and particular circumstances or ordinary, busy classrooms. Such an endeavour must involve and value the distinctive contribution which teachers' professional expertise can bring to the task, if it is to have any enduring impact upon practice.

46. Adopting methodological procedures such as those described by Cochran-Smith and Lytle, op. cit., Connelly and Clandinin, op. cit., Leinhardt, op. cit.
47. M. Lampert, 'How do teachers manage to teach', *Harvard Educational Review*, **55**(2), 1985, pp. 178–194.
48. R. Rorty, *The Consequences of Pragmatism*, (The Harvester Press, 1982), p. 197.
49. F. Sedgewick, 'Thank God it's Friday', *Times Educational Supplement*, (8 December, 1989), p. 20.

Section 3
The Classroom Teacher and School-based Research

Chapter 22

Teaching as an evidence-based profession

Elizabeth Bird

Editors' Note: In this chapter, Elizabeth Bird provides a comprehensive overview of the current debate on teaching as an evidence-based or evidence-informed profession. She argues that access to a breadth of evidence, which can be tested out by teachers in their specific teaching context, is fundamental to improving teaching and pupil learning. Important comparisons are made between the way medical practitioners and teachers advance their own professional development.

> Research and evidence can help teachers to teach better, to enhance learning and raise the status of the profession.
> (Cordingley, 2000, p.1)

Hargreaves' 1996 lecture to the Teacher Training Agency called for teaching to become an evidence-based profession. The concept arises, at least in part, from moves in the medical profession that have sought to establish a situation in which the actions of practitioners are informed by the evidence of research. The aim of this is to improve practice – but there is also a clear element of making doctors accountable for the decisions that they take, and of requiring them to be able to justify their actions not only in terms of their own localised knowledge, but also in terms of the wider sources of knowledge in their field. Evidence-based education is similarly conceived as meaning:

> the support for and promotion of practices and policies that are based on good evidence about their effects (i.e. costs and benefits).
> (Coe *et al.*, 2000, p.2)

integrating individual teaching and learning expertise with the best available evidence from systematic research on educational interventions and practice.
(Davies, 2000, p.374)

The move towards evidence-based practice in medicine was assisted by the production of syntheses of research data, such as systematic reviews and meta-analyses. (For an account of the different types of research synthesis, see Davies (2000).) The development of such reviews and analyses was seen as fundamental to its success. Systematic reviews are different to the kinds of academic review publication (narrative reviews) that we may be used to from educational journals, which tend to review a selection of the available literature around a topic, often from a particular author perspective. A selective review of this sort is inadequate for a clinical practitioner attempting to find the best evidence on which to base his or her action. Systematic reviews, on the other hand, attempt to consider all of the relevant studies, which will include, where possible, so-called 'grey' and unpublished work. These studies are then assessed against robust and transparent criteria. In the case of meta-analysis, the aim is to go one step further, and to combine a number of (usually randomised controlled[1]) trials, taking into account their different contexts, in order to produce an overall indication of the result. While this method was developed for use in combining quantitative studies, there have been developments that attempt to apply a similar approach to studies that are more qualitative in nature. The key to the use of research syntheses is their accessibility to practitioners, and these reviews are freely available to the medical profession through the international Cochrane collaboration and, in the United Kingdom, the National Health Service Centre for Reviews and Dissemination.

Hargreaves' concept of an evidence-based profession has sparked considerable debate (see, for example, Hammersley (1997)). A number of, sometimes conflicting, arguments have been presented, such as:

1. A substantial and useful body of educational research already exists, but it has not been effectively disseminated to practitioners or policy makers. It is therefore essential to improve access by the creation of accessible databases and systematic reviews.

   Research does exist which would be of use to classroom teachers if it could be made more accessible.
   (TTA, 1996, p.3)

---

1. Trials in which two or more groups are treated differently, with subjects being assigned to the groups at random.

2. The majority of existing research is not useful,[2] and large-scale,[3] cumulative, quantitative studies (randomly controlled trials or as near to them as possible) are needed if we are to find what is effective in practice.
3. Even large trials are unlikely to provide definitive answers for what will or will not work in all cases.

> One of the arguments sometimes put forward against Evidence-Based Education is that activities like teaching are too complex, too dependent on the particular context and moment, too much the result of subtle interactions among people . . . for anything so crude and simplistic as a randomised controlled trial to be of any use.
> (Coe *et al.*, 2000, pp.4–5)

Hammersley (1997) points out that research may not be able to indicate

> what is the appropriate technique to use in a particular situation, or even what are the chances of success in a technique in a particular type of situation. The nature of the contribution may be closer to the enlightenment model, involving the provision of information that corrects assumptions and alters the context in which teachers view some aspect of their situation.
> (Hammersley, 1997, p.148)

4. Existing research does not address the real concerns of teachers, but is carried out by researchers who are remote from the classroom. The solution is a predominance of school-based action research, with researchers acting in partnership with teachers to investigate those areas which most closely address the day-to-day concerns of the practitioners.[4]
5. Research should be directed towards studies that relate directly to classroom practice and the agenda for research should be defined by a national forum.

> A National Educational Research Forum needs to be established to develop an overall research strategy and framework, and co-ordinate and monitor developments.
> (Hillage *et al.*, 1998, p.xii)

6. Fundamental and 'blue-skies' research carried out by researchers are still/are not of great importance.

> Curiosity-driven, long-term 'basic' and 'blue-skies' research is as vital in education as in any other scientific field.
> (Hargreaves, 1996, p.8)

---

2. See the Tooley critique of educational research (Tooley and Darby, 1998). This report has, however, been much criticised.
3. Or multiple, small-scale experiments (see Centre for Evaluation and Measurement (2000)).
4. For an examination of what these issues might be, see Everton *et al.* (2000).

> There must be a place for the fundamental 'blue skies' research which thinks the unthinkable.
>> (Blunkett, 2000, p.14)

There is an extent to which all of these arguments have already been taken cognisance of, and, in view of which, policy changes are being made which will impact on what an evidence-based profession comes to mean for both practitioners and policy makers.

What is evidence?

Some writers use the term evidence-based practice, while others refer to research-based practice. In most cases these two terms seem to be used interchangeably. Whether or not we accept that these two terms have the same meaning depends on what we consider to constitute research or, indeed, what we consider to constitute evidence.

Educational research is clearly one form of evidence. For some, this implies working to the 'gold standard' of the random controlled trial. Others would disagree with this, and point to the value of small-scale, classroom-based action research projects. Whatever our view on this, both of these fall clearly within the 'traditional' understanding of educational research, and form part of the evidence base available. However, even the question of whether or not all research constitutes evidence is contentious.

> The only worthwhile kind of evidence about whether something works in a particular situation comes from trying it out. . . . In the language of research, that means doing well controlled field experiments.
>> (CEM, 2000, Sources of evidence, p.1)

On this basis, Coe *et al.* claim that school effectiveness research, such as the Hay McBer Report (DfEE, 2000a), for example, is description rather than intervention (Coe *et al.*, 2000, p.30). Thus it does not provide 'good evidence': that is to say that it provides no indication as to whether copying the described behaviour of effective teachers will bring about improvements. Only research which has evaluated the effects of such 'copying' (i.e. an intervention or change in practice) would be able to do this.

> 'Evidence' from surveys or correlational research is not a basis for action. This is not to say that these kinds of research are worthless; far from it.
>> (CEM, 2000, Evidence-based policies and Evidence-based practice, p.1)

Such descriptive research, while it may not provide a recipe for improving practice, does, nevertheless, provide evidence of a sort, and, moreover, evidence which can *inform* practice.

> Evidence-based education should be conceived as context-sensitive education. This requires systematic reviews, and single study findings, of the best available evidence from ethnographic studies, sociological observational studies, and the whole range of qualitative studies in educational and social scientific research.
> (Davies, 2000, p.374)

Equally, there is much other evidence available to teachers, such as OFSTED data, which may or may not be classed as research, but which may be a useful source of information to be taken into account when making decisions about practice, or which may suggest avenues to explore.

What does evidence-based education mean for policy makers?

There is a clear recognition that, to date, most educational policy changes have not been evidence-based. The government has an explicit aim to move away from this situation towards one in which policy is based on firm evidence of what is effective in practice.

> We need a revolution in the relations between government and the research community. . . . We need to be able to rely on social science and social scientists to tell us what works and why, and what types of policy initiatives are likely to be most effective.
> (Blunkett, 2000, pp.14, 15)

The idea of evidence-based education, and the arguments around this have, in some ways, markedly different aspects when policy is considered as opposed to the practice of the individual teacher. The reasons for this are clear. Research, even on a very small scale, can indicate the outcomes of an intervention or describe practice in a particular educational context, and this evidence may be of use to an individual practitioner wishing to improve his or her practice within a very similar context. Policy makers, in contrast, are required to deal with aspects of education over a very broad range of different contexts. Nevertheless, research evidence may enable policy makers to make recommendations. Where policy involves compulsion and regulation, the issues are much more serious:

There is an important difference between the kind of evidence that may justify advocating something as 'good practice' and requiring it as policy. In the former case, teachers can make a judgement about whether something is applicable to their context or can adapt it to be most effective. In the case of policy, however, where all schools are compelled to change what they are doing, the evidence to support it must be much stronger.
(CEM, 2000, Evidence-based policies, p.1)

While some writers argue that properly carried out experimental trials can lead to evidence of effective practice across all educational contexts, and even Hammersley (1997, p.92) cautiously states that 'I would not want to dismiss the possibility of universal laws of social phenomena', many seem to agree that

Educational research shares with research in the other social sciences the problem that, because it is social, i.e. about human beings, it inevitably embraces a multitude of variables. This precludes the making of scientific generalisation.
(Bassey, 2001, p.20)

This raises questions about the extent to which educational policy can be evidence based. But while it may not be possible, at least in most cases, to *base* policy on unequivocal evidence, it must, nevertheless, be the case that those making policy decisions can use the available evidence to suggest the likely outcomes of their decisions. Bassey's (2001) concept of the 'Fuzzy generalisation'[5] is of particular value here. Decisions should, at least, be *informed* by the best available evidence. As Hargreaves suggests:

To avoid any implication that teachers or educational policy makers should not, in making decisions, take account of (i) the quality and strength of the research evidence and (ii) the contextual factors relating to that decision, we should, I suggest, speak of evidence-informed, not evidence-based, policy or practice.
(Hargreaves, 1999b, p.246)[6]

Likewise, Bassey points out that:

Managers and policy-makers seek predictions of what may be the consequences of policies they are operating, or proposing to introduce.

---

5. 'A fuzzy generalisation is one that is neither likely to be true in every case, nor likely to be untrue in every case; it is something that may be true. In consequence it is important for the researcher who enunciates a fuzzy generalisation to endeavour to explore the conditions under which it may, or may not, be true.' (Bassey, 2001, p.10)
6. See also Sebba, 1999, p.4.

They know – or if they do not, they need to learn – that research can only guide their actions, it cannot tell them what to do. Research can inform decision-making, not determine it.

(Bassey, 2001, p.12)

What does evidence-based education mean for practitioners?

Pendry and Husbands (2000) investigated research and practice in History teacher education. In their research, they asked student teachers about their understanding of the phrase 'teaching as a research-based profession'. The authors developed three categories of student response, which they describe as the *producer* view, the *consumer* view, and a third view which is a hybrid of these two. These categories are interesting not only because of their relationship to practice, but also because of the ways in which they relate to the different recommendations and arguments around the whole issue of evidence-based education.

The producer view

The understanding that Pendry and Husbands identified as the producer view is typified by these student responses:

> constantly evaluating your performance in the classroom and analysing the results of this.

> it refers to a reflective teaching approach – that teachers should critically evaluate their teaching.
> (p.329)

In this view, the students' descriptions entail recognition of the individual teacher's action within the context of her own classroom, working to develop and improve her own practice. It encapsulates the most fundamental level at which teachers can be considered both to carry out research and to make use of evidence in their own practice. However, the implication of the students' descriptions above is that this is not a formalised process. It is what Hargreaves (1999a, p.130) refers to as 'tinkering'.

Leach and Shelton Mayes (1998), report on a small-scale study that looked at the evaluations being carried out by staff within a school. This study found that all of the teachers interviewed recognised that they regularly undertook informal evaluations such as 'reflection on an incident in a lesson or discussion of the success of a worksheet with a colleague over coffee in the staff room', but that

60 per cent did not consciously think of such activity as evaluation.

and

There was no evidence to suggest that this informal evaluation had led to any significant change in classroom practice.
(p.99)

In addition to this informal evaluation, there are increasing requirements for teachers (and, also, governors) to use evidence more formally. On an individual basis, teachers are required to provide evidence of their own competence, making explicit areas of their own practice. This requirement to provide evidence starts in initial teacher training, continuing through induction and threshold assessment. For example, threshold assessment requires teachers to provide evidence of pupil progress as indicated in Figure 22.1; not only providing evidence from their own context, but also comparing this with external data.

---

3. Pupil progress

This standard requires evidence that, as *a result of the teacher's teaching:*

their pupils achieve well relative to the pupils' prior attainment, making progress as good or better than similar pupils nationally. This should be shown in marks or grades in any relevant national tests or examinations, or school based assessment for pupils where national tests and examinations are not taken.

Teachers can demonstrate the progress of pupils using a wide variety of assessment data. For pupils taking external examinations, teachers should compare National Curriculum test results, GCSE, GNVQ and AS and A level grades with pupils' prior attainment. Other information which may be useful includes the charts in the DfEE's 'Autumn Package', local authority data, other school data, performance indicator systems, nationally derived value added data such as YELLIS and commercial test results.

Figure 22.1 Extract from Threshold Application Guidance Notes (DfEE, 2000b)

On a departmental or whole-school basis, schools are increasingly required to look at the wider picture.

> The idea of 'self-evaluation', using only one school's data, is one likely to lead to disappointment and confusion. What is needed is a large set of data from many schools so that we will be able to make fair comparisons, comparing like with like.
> (Fitz-Gibbon, 1996, p.12)

Schools are required to compare their own achievements with those of other schools, to account for their performance, and to set targets. For example, school PANDA (Performance and Assessment) and PICSI (Pre-Inspection Context and School Indicator) reports give information about pupils' results compared to national averages and also their results as compared to the schools in the same benchmark group.[7] The 2000 PANDA Report (OFSTED, 2000) states:

> This PANDA report has been sent to your school to aid self-evaluation and the development of your plans to raise standards.
> (p.1)

> Benchmarking your school's performance helps you to understand your school's performance in relation to the range of performances achieved by similar schools nationally.
> (p.A2)

It is clear that in the current climate, teachers and all those involved in schools are expected to move beyond an informal, reflective approach to using evidence. In the study reported by Leach and Shelton Mayes (1998), 50 per cent of the teachers interviewed were involved in formal evaluation activities. However, that study concluded that despite these clearly focused evaluations, no departmental or whole-school initiatives had been identified as arising from them (p.99). Of the respondents, 85 per cent were

> aware of the need to place evaluation activities within a more formal process of ongoing evaluation and review to produce improvements.

Schools are required to collect, analyse and use evidence more explicitly, and

---

7. 'Similar' schools, which are defined on the basis of the number of pupils known to be eligible for free school meals and the average prior attainment of pupils at a school.

to justify their planning and actions on the basis of this evidence. This is a part of evidence-based education, but the concept is much broader still.

Many of those who have been critical of the existing body of educational research regard the key to an evidence-based profession to be the involvement of teachers in researching their own practice in a much more formalised way, and in extending the influence of that research far beyond the insular context of the individual classroom, or of the individual school. This is summarised by Coe *et al.* (2000, p.8):

> Many teachers and schools already develop their practice continuously by trying new things. This kind of experimentation is at the heart of a 'problem-solving' approach to education. Moreover, if adequate feedback is available it can provide a very quick way to learn what works. Involving teachers in 'research', therefore, is just an extension and formalisation of existing good practice.

> However, there is a bit more to it than this. . . . It is easy to get it wrong when trying to evaluate whether something has worked or not. It is hoped that the use of more rigorous forms of evaluation would reduce this danger. Also there is a good deal to be gained by the pooling of results from different teachers in different schools all of whom have experimented in much the same way.

Hargreaves (1999a) sees teachers' engagement in research as an important element in what he calls 'knowledge creation':

> This may be seen as a more systematic form of tinkering. . . . School-based research, and school-based research consortia as pioneered by the Teacher Training Agency, are important here . . . [as they will] typically lead to internal and external networking; and such collective tinkering promotes knowledge creation and its effective transposition and transfer.
> (p.133)

However, the involvement of teachers in researching their own practice, thereby acting as producers of evidence, only represents one side of the coin. The consumer view reflects the other.

The consumer view

The responses identified by Pendry and Husbands (2000) as representing the consumer view included:

teaching is informed by a consideration of current development and studies – using this when thinking about how to develop one's own teaching.

> I take this to mean that the strategies and practices adopted in both the classroom and at senior management level are intended to be based on research into pupils' learning behaviour and attitudes.
> (p.329)

These reflect an understanding of teachers making use of external research to inform the decisions they make in their practice. In this way the teacher is seen as a consumer of externally produced evidence.

> While teachers' professional craft knowledge is necessarily developed by individuals in their own distinctive contexts and in interaction with other individuals in these distinctive contexts, the quality of that knowledge depends on individual practitioners having and using opportunities for learning about high quality new ideas which they might be able to use in developing their practice: and one valuable source for such high quality new ideas is from disciplined educational research.
> (Counsell *et al.*, 2000, p.467)

The use of evidence such as national assessment data has already been mentioned above. Teachers will also be encouraged and expected to make use of research findings. It is pertinent to note, in this respect, the expectation of advanced skills teachers:

> ASTs focus on helping colleagues to raise teaching and learning standards in their own and other schools.

> Activities can include: . . . spreading good practice based on educational research.
> (DfEE, 2000c)

The hybrid view

> Teaching . . . can significantly improve if informed by research and review carried out at national and school level. It means teachers need to think carefully about their teaching and evaluate it from several points of view.
> (Pendry and Husbands, 2000, p.329)

The third view of research-based practice as identified by Pendry and Husbands is a hybrid between the consumer and producer views. I would argue that only a hybrid of these views, and, indeed, an extension of them, can fully reflect what is meant by evidence-based teaching in the context of individual practice. Such a hybrid sees practitioners as both consumers of externally produced evidence, and also as producers of evidence themselves.

Using evidence in practice

The University of Oxford's Master's Programme in Evidence-based Health Care represents evidence-based practice as a cyclic process (CASP, 1999, p.2; see Figure 22.2).

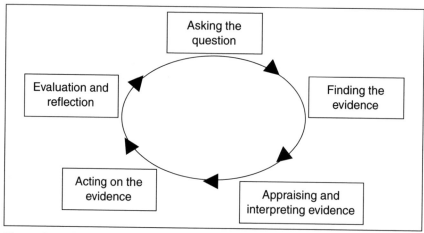

Figure 22.2 Steps in evidence-based health care

The starting point is seen as the identification of a problem within practice that leads to defining a question. It is then necessary to find research evidence that may be helpful in answering that question, and to appraise that evidence. The next stage in this model is the application of those findings to practice. The application must then be evaluated. Thus, the individual teacher needs to be able both to find and interpret external evidence, and to research and evaluate changes in his or her own practice.

I have suggested elsewhere, Bird (2000), that it may be useful to consider another model that requires a different approach to evidence. I have called this a **monitoring** approach (see Figure 22.3) on p.285, and see this as evidence-led, rather than the question-lead **search** model represented in Figure 22.2.

The **monitoring** approach to evidence-based practice has a different starting point; that of information, which leads to the identification of a problem or suggests an innovation in practice. This requires practitioner

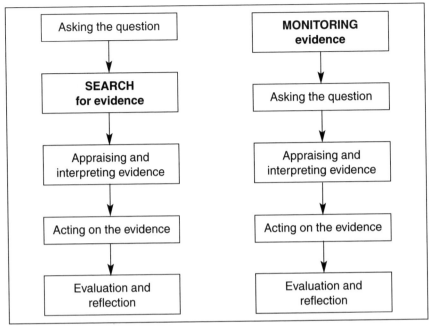

Figure 22.3 Search and Monitoring patterns in evidence-based practice

awareness of up-to-date research and other evidence, some of which may throw new light on their practice or suggest changes to their practice even where a problem (or information gap) had not previously been identified. This level of 'keeping in touch' requires a different approach to evidence – an ongoing monitoring of publications, rather than a search related to a specific question.

These two patterns are interrelated; in particular, the identification of a question within the monitoring pattern may then lead to the adoption of a search pattern as further research evidence is sought. Nevertheless, the distinction is a useful one in terms of the types of access to evidence that are required.

These two models suggest that evidence-informed practice requires practitioners to be able to:

– search for evidence
– monitor evidence
– appraise evidence
– apply evidence
– evaluate intervention.

The TTA's (2000a) statement agrees with this, that:

Teachers who use research and evidence effectively in order to improve their practice and raise attainment:

Know how to find and interpret existing, high quality evidence from a range of sources, such as research reports, other schools' experience, OfSTED inspection and performance data as a tool for raising standards.

Interpret external evidence confidently, in relation to pupil or subject needs, rather than viewing it as a threat.

Searching for evidence

Searching requires easy practitioner access to evidence. While some evidence, such as OFSTED and school performance data, is readily available, research evidence may be harder to find. The Hillage Report identified, as an issue in the dissemination of research, the 'absence of time and intermediary support available to both policy-makers and practitioners to help them access research' (Hillage *et al.*, 1998 p.xi). Ideally, for the practitioner, the initial step should not be to search for primary evidence in the form of published research reports, but to consult systematic reviews, meta-analyses and other research syntheses prepared to provide teachers with rapid access to the evidence they require (Chapter 16 is an example). In terms of access to research evidence, it is certainly true that, to date, as Davies (1999) points out,

Educational research has lacked a centralised data-base for preparation, maintenance and dissemination of systematic reviews of education such as the Cochrane collaboration.
(p.116)

In the absence of systematic reviews, search for information requires teachers to locate primary sources of research evidence.

Both identifying and obtaining primary sources present problems for the practitioner. Few educational research journals are likely to be found in the school itself, or even in most public libraries, and hand-searching of research journals within a university library is a time-consuming task, inappropriate for the busy classroom teacher. A more suitable approach to identifying relevant literature is the use of on-line databases but this remains problematic, since, in many cases, on-line databases are not currently available without subscription.

Obtaining primary evidence is also problematic, although books and documents can be obtained through document delivery services. The problem is greatly reduced where journal articles and other publications can be accessed on-line in full text, but this is generally only available to subscribers or at a cost. All of these options have financial implications.

There are dangers in the access of primary research as the initial move by practitioners, which have been well illustrated by Dobby (1999). The main danger is that, given the constraints under which the teacher is working, retrieval of research studies is likely to be incomplete and selective. This may result in the study of a report which asserts a positive response to a particular intervention, while other papers may exist, unknown to the teacher, which show that this same intervention has no effect or, worse, a deleterious effect in a context closer to that of the teacher carrying out the search. Truly systematic review should go some way to removing this danger but, even then, the process is complicated by more extensive reporting and publication of those studies which indicate positive impacts.

In the UK the situation is changing in response to the call for better dissemination and accessibility of research evidence. Websites such as those of the TTA and DfEE already carry reports of research findings in areas of national concern. The DfEE's commissioned Evidence for Policy and Practice Information and Coordinating Centre (EPPI Centre) aims to make a comprehensive database accessible to all education practitioners and policy makers, and has registered review groups of researchers and users to undertake systematic reviews of educational research. The Economic and Social Research Council (ESRC) is establishing a Coordination Centre for Evidence-based Policy and Practice, and the Campbell collection, sister to the Cochrane collaboration, has been established for education, criminal justice and social work and welfare. Thus, in the UK, meta-data should become increasingly available to the profession.

Systematic research reviews will also identify for teachers those primary sources whose context may seem particularly relevant to their own. The practitioner will need to consult these primary reports before making changes in his or her own practice, and the problem of obtaining the primary source may still be a real one.

Monitoring evidence

Rather than seeking out research related to a particular issue, the monitoring approach involves maintaining a general awareness of evidence, including up-to-date knowledge of research. This can occur in a number of different ways. Examples of this monitoring approach include the scrutiny of pupil performance data and of official publications that are sent into schools such as DfEE, OFSTED and TTA documents. The regular reading of journals and the *Times Educational Supplement* also constitutes a form of monitoring. In a study by Everton *et al.* (2000), 76 per cent of responding teachers stated that they relied upon official publications to gain information about educational research. In the same study, an even higher proportion of teachers saw INSET courses as a source of research information.

Monitoring of this sort can be systematic, either on an individual or on a group basis, with routine dissemination within the school. Individual staff can be responsible for monitoring particular publications on a regular basis (whether their own subscription or a school subscription), and for reporting back to other members of staff. Whether this takes place within the whole school, year team, faculty, or other group will depend on the school itself. However, even systematic monitoring of this sort is unlikely to provide the sort of coverage of the research literature that is required if a staff is to remain fully informed of current research findings. In particular, in secondary schools, Hannan *et al.* (1998) suggest that most of the journals to which teachers or departments subscribe are likely to be subject related rather than general education publications, so that a whole body of evidence may be missed.

An additional way of monitoring, but one that may involve greater time commitment from an individual, or from all individuals within a staff team, is to use alerting services which mail contents pages of periodicals to list members.

Monitoring of research can take place in a highly organised fashion. Hannan *et al.* (1998) report on an infant school where:

> recent and relevant research was apparently reviewed by the staff as a whole on a regular basis, with meetings of the staff and in-service events focused on research findings.
> (p.11)

Activities at this school included books being 'dished out' to staff for them to read, and to offer critiques at staff meetings. All members of staff were involved, including support staff. Staff coordinators had a role in reading incoming materials and in disseminating relevant information to staff, both in written form and at staff meetings.

Attendance at conferences may be another way of keeping in touch with the research evidence or of searching for the answer to particular questions. In recent years, dissemination of findings has assumed much greater importance among research funders, and most research proposals are required to define clear dissemination strategies at their outset. Frequently, stakeholder involvement in research design is also encouraged.

> Funding agencies insist more and more on policy relevance, on negotiation by researchers with prospective 'users', on explicit plans for dissemination designed to maximise impact.
> (Hammersley, 1997, p.141)

Thus, conferences used by researchers to disseminate their findings are likely to become an increasing source of practitioner information. Yet again, however, conference attendance has cost implications, especially when supply cover has to be paid for. Conference attendance resulting in teacher absence is also likely to impact on pupils' learning. Both of these considerations may severely restrict this type of activity.

A further possibility worth mentioning here is the use of networks in monitoring. National or local teacher networks can provide a forum for teachers to share the research evidence of which they have become aware. Facilities of this sort can be especially valuable in sharing the findings of school-based action research projects. As Hargreaves writes:

> ICT provide opportunities for networking for professional knowledge creation, shared tinkering, and concurrent dissemination on a scale and at a rate that has hitherto been unimaginable.
> (Hargreaves, 1999a, p.139)

Appraising evidence

If teachers are to be able to make use of research and other evidence, they need to be able to interpret the data and critically appraise the research reports they read. This is especially the case in which primary data is sought. Hill (2000) writes:

> Critical appraisal skills are at the heart of evidence-based practice. . . . Critical appraisal helps the reader decide three things:
> Whether the reader can trust the results
> What the results mean
> Whether they are relevant to the reader's situation.
> (p.249)

The provision of systematic reviews may reduce the burden of critical appraisal. Nevertheless, the individual teacher must still assess the extent to which a particular change may be appropriate to the specific context within which he or she works. It is precisely because a strategy that is successfully employed in one context may not be able to be successfully transferred to another context (see Hargreaves 1999a), that the teacher should now take on the role of producer, applying an intervention in his or her own context and producing evidence of its success or otherwise.

Applying evidence

Applying evidence to practice does not mean

> picking up research findings and automatically translating them
> into . . . practice. . . . Presented with evidence, some teachers will mediate
> or process the findings according to the specific context (pupils, resources,
> staffing) in which they are teaching.
> (Sebba, 1999, p.4)

Cordingley and the National Teacher Research Panel (2000) refer to 'the
difficult and extended business of interpreting, adapting and acting upon
proposals from research' (p.4), while the TTA (2000a) points out that

> taking messages from new evidence from research, from OfSTED and
> from target setting data into account is complex. It means making routine
> and often implicit practices, explicit so that they can be evaluated and
> developed in the light of new information. It also means teachers
> interpreting the implications of research findings and evidence for their
> own specific context.
> (p.4)

All of these suggest that the application of research findings to practice is by
no means a simple process, and those advocating teacher action research
recognise the development of practitioner research skills as an important
dimension. The learning of these skills as a part of teachers' professional
development has been an area of some discussion, and is considered below.

Evaluation

Where the teacher makes a change in her practice as a result of this process,
the next step is evaluation of the impact on her practice. While this evaluation
may be informal, it may also be more formal in terms of the evidence
collected and the way in which it is used. Indeed, the process of evaluating the
effects of a change in practice may be formalised as action research, the
results of which can be disseminated to extend the knowledge base on which
other teachers can build. This is particularly important given the highly
context-specific nature of teaching, where those searching for evidence may
be looking for information about the extent to which a particular intervention
is successful in a context close to their own. The possible role of teacher
networks in disseminating evidence of this kind has already been mentioned.

This evaluation is important, as this is the evidence on which the teacher must make, and justify, decisions about her practice. Does the intervention have a positive impact, and should it be continued? Does this raise further issues requiring a search for further information? How can effectiveness be further improved?

Teacher professional development

Evidence-based, or evidence-informed, education requires skills from practitioners, and these skills need to be learnt. It is very clear from the literature in this area that study for higher level education courses has, to date, been a key element in stimulating teachers' interest in using research, in developing their skills in accessing and appraising research, and leading them to carry out research into their own practice: moving beyond tinkering to something more formal and systematic.

Hannan *et al.* (1998) in their study comparing medical and teaching practitioners, quote a teacher who states:

> There is an excellent body of research being produced across a wide variety of education-related topics but like many teachers, often we aren't aware of it/how to access it. It's not until you become involved in further study that you realise exactly where to obtain material for your field of study.
>
> (p.19)

Everton *et al.* (2000), reporting on studies of teachers' attitudes to and use of research evidence, suggested that interest in, and use of, research tended to correlate with higher level study in education, noting that:

> The results suggest a trend whereby interest in research appears a function of 'extended' professional development since those with further quali-fications exhibit the greatest interest.
>
> (p.171)

Hargreaves (1999a) writes that:

> Knowledge validation is capable of greater sophistication in schools where teachers have themselves undertaken research for a higher degree and are able to apply investigative skills to their practices in a climate of identifying and sharing what works.
>
> (p.129)

While study for a higher qualification such as a Master's degree may be one way to develop these skills, it is not the only route. Increasingly, teacher training institutions are including elements of research training in both undergraduate and postgraduate teacher training programmes, so that teachers coming into the profession are equipped with some research training. (For an examination of how this affects the students' perception of their practice, see Smith and Coldron (2000).) Indeed, the Standards for the Award of Qualified Teacher Status listed by the DfEE (DfEE, 1998) state that trainees should be able to demonstrate that they:

> are aware of, and know how to access, recent inspection evidence and classroom-relevant research evidence and know how to use this to inform and improve their teaching.
> (p.4)

For teachers in post, research consortia such as those being supported by TTA funding provide a valuable route for the development of research skills through participation alongside university researchers. This kind of teacher-researcher partnership may be especially valuable if:

> involvement of teachers with research and researchers is a crucial element in promoting effective practice.
> (Everton et al., 2000, p.180)

The EPPI Centre intends to offer 'training programmes for potential users of research such as teachers, students, parents, school governors and education authorities' (EPPI, 2000). Further, it may reasonably be argued that if a culture of using research evidence becomes established in schools, then this will facilitate the development of teacher research skills within the school itself.

In terms of professional development and the use of research by teachers, it is interesting to note the suggestion in the paper by Everton et al. (2000) that, because of the way in which evidence-based practice requires teachers to examine their own practice,

> it may require considerable emotional adjustment on the part of the teacher before research findings based on other colleagues' practice in other schools can be applied to one's own situation.
> (p.179)

On this basis, it would be reasonable to suggest that those new to the profession would need time to develop their own confidence before taking the messages of research on board. An alternative view is that the use of educational research in the development of teachers' practice is important for teachers throughout their careers, but especially so at the early stages, when their learning is necessarily at its fastest and most fundamental.

(Counsell *et al.*, 2000, p.468)

We might all agree with Cameron's (1998) aspiration that

in a research-based profession, individuals would cultivate 'A researching mind' throughout their careers.

(p.3)

However, we should be clear that the implications of this may be neither simple, nor without their emotional cost. Dobby (1999), however, writing about the evidence-based healthcare movement, strikes an optimistic note:

Practitioners found the movement extraordinarily empowering. It enabled them, for the first time, to take real charge of their own professional development in a truly competent way and this improved professional pride and morale to a very significant degree.

(p.4)

If adopting evidence-based practice contributes to increasing teachers' eroded sense of autonomy, it may be valuable indeed.

The 'secret garden' or 'ivory tower' of the teacher working in his or her isolated classroom has, in many ways, long gone. All educational practitioners are increasingly required to scrutinise data, to compare their performance (at least in terms of examination results and pupil attendance) with that of others, and to set targets. Teachers are, more and more, held accountable, and required to justify their practice. Increasingly the use of wider sources of evidence is being considered as a route to improvement within our schools. The use of evidence, and especially of research evidence, however that is conceived, is seen as highly desirable.

In this context, personal professional development will require taking on board the ideas of evidence-based practice, and of developing the skills needed to make critical use of evidence to inform practice.

The essence of professional development, and especially of its education component, is that it involves the learning of an independent, evidence-informed and constructively critical approach to practice within a public framework of professional values and accountability.

(Bolam, 1999, p.3)

The government and the TTA are promoting 'teaching as a research and evidence-based profession *as a means of improving teaching and learning and raising standards*' (TTA, 2000b, p.1, my emphasis). There is, arguably, little evidence on which to base this policy. Whether it is successful will depend, in no small part, on what practitioners come to see as their role in an evidence-based profession.

References

Bassey, M. (2001) 'A solution to the problem of generalisation in educational research: fuzzy prediction', *Oxford Review of Education* **27**(1), 5–22.

Bird, E. (2000) 'Accessing the evidence: towards the research-informed age', in Moon. B., Butcher, J. and Bird, E. *Leading Professional Development in Education*. London: Routledge-Falmer.

Blunkett, D. (2000) 'Influence or irrelevance: can social science improve government?', *Research Intelligence* **71**, 12–21.

Bolam, R. (1999) 'The emerging conceptualisation of INSET: does this constitute professional development?' Paper presented at SCETT annual conference, 26–28 November, Dunchurch, Rugby.

Cameron, L. 'Research and EAL: ways forward for the profession'. Education-line, http://brs.leeds.ac.uk/~beiwww/beid.html accessed 28.3.01.

Centre for Evaluation and Measurement (2000) *What is 'Evidence-based' Education?*
http://www.cem.dur.ac.uk/ebeuk accessed 7.3.01.

Coe, R., Fitz-Gibbon, C. and Tymms, P. (2000) 'Promoting evidence-based education: the role of practitioners', round table presented at the British Educational Research Association Conference, Cardiff University, 7–10 September.

Cordingley, P. (2000) 'Networking Partnership Seminar: Introduction'. Teacher Training Agency Seminar, London, 16 March.

Cordingley, P. and the National Teacher Research Panel (2000) 'Teacher perspectives on the accessibility and usability of research outputs'. Paper presented at the British Educational Research Association Conference, Cardiff University, 7–10 September.

Counsell, C. *et al.* (2000) 'The usefulness of educational research for trainee teachers' learning', *Oxford Review of Education* **24**(3 and 4), 467–82.

Critical Appraisal Skills Programme (CASP) and Health Care Libraries Unit (HCLU) (1999) *Evidence-based Health Care. An Open Learning Resource for Health Care Practitioners, Unit 2*. Luton: Chiltern Press.

Davies, P. (1999) 'What is evidence-based education?', *British Journal of Educational Studies* **47**(2), 108–21.

Davies, P. (2000) 'The relevance of systematic reviews to educational policy and practice', *Oxford Review of Education* **26**(3 and 4), 365–78.

Department for Education and Employment (DfEE) (1998) *Requirements for Courses of Initial Teacher Training, Annex A: Standards for the Award of Qualified Teacher Status*. Circular 4/98. London: DfEE.

Department for Education and Employment (DfEE) (2000a) *Research into Teacher Effectiveness: A model of teacher effectiveness*. Report by Hay McBer to the DfEE, June 2000.

Department for Education and Employment (DfEE) (2000b) *Threshold Application: Guidance Notes (England)*
http://www.dfee.gov.uk/circulars/dfeepub/mar00/120300/page7.htm accessed 22.3.01.

Department for Education and Employment (DfEE) (2000c) *Advanced Skills Teachers: Promoting Excellence*
http://www.dfee.gov.uk/ast/brochure/p_14.shtml accessed 22.3.01.

Dobby, J. (1999) 'Issues of quality in research reviews: lessons to be drawn from the experience of the evidence-based health care movement'. Paper presented at the Annual General Meeting of the National Foundation for Educational Research, London, 13 October
http://www.nfer.ac.uk/conferences/health99.htm accessed 20.3.01.

EPPI (Evidence for Policy and Practice Information and Coordinating Centre) (2000) What the centre can offer:
http://eppi.ioe.ac.uk/about_offer.htm accessed 2.3.01.

Everton, T., Galton, M. and Pell, T. (2000) 'Teachers' perspectives on educational research: knowledge and content', *Journal of Education for Teaching* **26**(2), 168–82.

Fitz-Gibbon, C. T. (1996) *Monitoring Education: Indicators, Quality and Effectiveness*. London: Cassell.

Hammersley, M. (1997) 'Educational research and teaching: a response to David Hargreaves' TTA lecture', *British Educational Research Journal* **23**(2), 141–61.

Hannan, A., Enright, H. and Ballard, P. (1998) *Using research: the results of a pilot study comparing teachers, general practitioners and surgeons*
Education-line, http://www.leeds.ac.uk/educol p.21 accessed 20.3.01.

Hargreaves, D. (1996) 'Teaching as a research-based profession: prospects and possibilities', TTA Lecture.

Hargreaves, D. (1999a) 'The knowledge-creating school', *British Journal of Educational Studies* **47**(2), 122–44.

Hargreaves, D. (1999b) 'Revitalising educational research: lessons from the past and proposals for the future', *Cambridge Journal of Education* **29**(2), 239–50.

Hill, A. (2000) 'The experience of evidence-based healthcare', in Moon, B., Butcher, J. and Bird, E. (eds) *Leading Professional Development in Education*. London: Routledge-Falmer.

Hillage, J. *et al.* (1998) *Excellence in Research on Schools*. London: DfEE.

Leach, J. and Shelton Mayes, A. (1998) *School-Based Research and School Improvement: A Staff Development Pack for Senior Staff and Teachers in Secondary Schools*. Dunstable: Folens Publishers.

Office for Standards in Education (OFSTED) (2000) *PANDA Report*. London: OFSTED.

Pendry, A. and Husbands, C. (2000) 'Research and practice in History teacher education', *Cambridge Journal of Education* **30**(3), 321–34.

Sebba, J. (1999) 'Developing evidence-informed policy and practice in education'. Paper presented at the British Educational Research Association Conference, University of Sussex at Brighton, 2–5 September.

Smith, R. and Coldron, J. (2000) 'How does research affect pre-service students' perceptions of their practice?' Paper presented at the British Educational Research Association Conference, Cardiff University, 7–10 September.

Teacher Training Agency (TTA) (1996) *Teaching as a Research-based Profession*. London: TTA and Central Office of Information.

Teacher Training Agency (TTA) (2000a) *Improving Standards: Research and Evidence-Based Practice*
http://www.canteach.gov.uk/info/library/tta00_03.pdf accessed 7.3.01.

Teacher Training Agency (TTA) (2000b) *Promoting Research and Evidence Based Practice (REBP)*
http://www.canteach.gov/uk/info/research/index.htm accessed 2.2.01.

Tooley, J. and Darby, D. (1998) *Educational Research: a Critique. A Study of Published Research*. London: OFSTED.

Chapter 23

Action research as a professional ideal

Richard Winter

Editors' Note: Practitioner action research has been a significant feature of two decades of educational literature. In this brief extract, Richard Winter argues that practitioner action research is part of the general ideal of professionalism and affirms it as a form of learning which is an intrinsic outcome of professional experience.

For a long time now, professional educators have been claiming the value and the possibility of research as an activity which could and should be an integral part of professional work, as opposed to a separate activity carried out by specialist academics upon professional workers.

> The general organisation of research is that one set of people (researchers) carry out research on another set of people (for example, teachers). . . . There are a number of reasons why the chances of such research having practical outcomes are small.
> (Bartholomew, 1972)

> A specialist research profession will always be a poor substitute for a self-monitoring educational community.
> (MacDonald and Walker, 1975)

The specific form of research which is adapted to this purpose is summed up in the phrase 'action research':

> Action research might be defined as: the study of a social situation with a view to improving the quality of action within it . . . (The) total process – review, diagnosis, planning, implementation, monitoring effects – provides the necessary link between self-evaluation and professional development.
> (Elliott, 1982, p.ii, p.1)

The overall claim for the value of action research by practitioners has a number of aspects. Firstly, professional workers are in a position to avoid the split between theoretical and practical understanding which bedevils the

297

institutional role of the academic social scientist; hence the use of the term 'action research', indicating the basic unity of theoretical and practical knowledge. Professional workers are not, therefore, to be thought of as the 'objects' of research into professional practice but always (at least) as collaborating research workers and (ideally) as well placed to initiate and carry out the investigation and development of the practices and understandings in which they are involved. (This is not to deny the possibility that outsiders of different kinds may make valuable contributions as facilitators, expert consultants, etc.) Hence the complete phrase which describes the activity is 'practitioner action research'.

This phrase ('practitioner action research') describes both a viable mode of organising educational 'research', and also an ideal which is already inherent within the role of 'professional' worker. Practitioner action research is thus part of the general ideal of professionalism, an *extension* of professional work, not an *addition* to it. It thus points to a form of learning which is an intrinsic outcome of professional *experience,* and to a form of involvement with practical experience which is intrinsically *educational.*

This is a way of asserting the real value of small-scale research and development projects carried out by practitioners on a part-time basis, concurrently with their professional work. The development of understanding and the initiation of innovative practice are therefore not to be thought of as the prerogative of an elite of academics or managers, but a possibility and even a responsibility for professional workers in general. Hence the assertion of the viability of practitioner action research is the assertion of a democratic social and political ideal, the ideal of a creative and involved citizenry, in opposition to the image of a passive populace awaiting instruction from above. The significance of this argument is strengthened by the ever-increasing number of workers of different categories who claim that they too are 'professional' workers, and are thus entitled to the consideration appropriate to their expertise and their responsibilities.

A substantial body of writing elaborates these claims and describes methods and examples of work; see for example: Elliott and Adelman, 1974; Nixon, 1981; Kemmis *et al.*, 1982; Elliott, 1982; Walker, 1985; Carr and Kemmis, 1986; Winter, 1987. The practitioner action research tradition thus has available principles, methods and examples of work. The range of procedures is varied and powerful enough to enable practitioners to respond constructively to the rapidly changing series of issues which structure professional work, as a result of historical changes and government policies. Indeed, the speed of these changes, and the speed with which new policy directives are produced 'on high' are going to require precisely the form of creative, innovative professionalism evoked by the practitioner action research ideal. This is especially important if we as teachers are to retain any sort of significant control over our working lives, and if managerial directives are to generate anything other than a combination of massive organisational confusion, plummeting morale, and a sequence of vacuous policy documents gathering dust on various shelves and notice-boards.

References

Bartholomew, J. (1972) 'The teacher as researcher', *Hard Cheese*, No. 1. London: Goldsmiths College, University of London.

Carr, W. and Kemmis, S. (1986) *Becoming Critical*. Lewes: Falmer Press.

Elliot, J. (1982) 'Action-research: A framework for self-evaluation in schools', Working Paper No. 1, *Teacher–Pupil Interaction and the Quality of Learning*. London: Schools Council (mimeo).

Elliott, J. and Adelman, C. (1974) 'Classroom action research', *Ford Teaching Project*. Norwich: University of East Anglia.

Kemmis, S. *et al.* (1982) *The Action-Research Planner*, 2nd edn. Victoria: Deakin University Press.

MacDonald, B. and Walker, R. (1975) 'Case study and the social philosophy of educational research', *Cambridge Journal of Education* 5(1).

Nixon, J. (ed.) (1981) *A Teacher's Guide to Action Research*. London: Grant McIntyre.

Walker, R. (1985) *Doing Research*. London: Methuen.

Winter, R. (1987) *Action Research and the Nature of Social Inquiry*. Aldershot: Gower Publishing.

Chapter 24

Why are class teachers reluctant to become researchers?

Roger Hancock

Editors' Note: This chapter takes a close look at the realities and practicalities of practitioner action research. It considers carefully the relationship between the work of 'researchers' and the work of 'teachers'.

Introduction

> To date, the United Kingdom's new Teacher Training Agency has been able to identify only a small, if significant, body of research findings directly focused on classroom practice and enhancing it: more is needed.
> (TTA, 1996, p. 1)

There have been important developments in the past 20 years with regard to Lawrence Stenhouse's (1975) vision of teachers integrating research into their classroom practice. Teachers have contributed as practitioners, researchers and writers to some classic collaborative action research projects like, for instance, the Humanities Curriculum Project (e.g. Stenhouse, 1968, 1971; MacDonald, 1973), the Girls into Science and Technology (GIST) Project (Smail *et al.*, 1982; Kelly *et al.*, 1984), and the Pupil Autonomy and Learning with Microcomputers (PALM) Project (Somekh, 1991). Teacher research has been generated by award-bearing courses and higher degrees (e.g. Lewis, 1988, Falkner *et al.*, 1992) and some of this work has been published in journals, bulletins, local collections and edited books gathered together by experienced researchers (e.g. Vulliamy and Webb, 1992; Bell *et al.*, 1994). Teacher research has also been greatly supported by research networks like the pioneering CARN (Classroom Action Research Network) (e.g. Ryan and Somekh, 1991) and by institutions like, for instance, Kingston University (Lomax and Jones, 1993) and Canterbury Christ Church College (Frost, 1995).

These are all very significant and desirable developments and I have no wish to devalue the importance of what appears to be a gathering teacher research movement. However, as my title suggests, my impression is that the great majority of classroom teachers remain uninvolved. They shy away from seeing themselves as researchers and they are reluctant to write about their teaching practice. Writing in the mid-1970s, Stenhouse anticipated the difficulties:

> I concede that it will require a generation of work . . . if the majority of teachers – rather than only the enthusiastic few – are to possess this field of research.
> (Stenhouse, 1975, p.142)

If more teachers are to become involved then it seems crucial to have a good understanding of the basis of this teacher reluctance. This chapter offers four areas of explanation – teachers' status, teachers' working conditions, teachers' confidence and, lastly, the difficulties that teachers experience when they try to integrate outsider research methodologies into their day-to-day practice. I then conclude by highlighting some of the ways in which teacher research might be effectively supported.

Teacher status and public expectations

> wise parents and wise children know that growth, education and enrichment depends on a deep collaboration between the natural God-given knowledge of parents and the professional knowledge of teachers – there's a complementarity here. Alas, what we have is a teaching profession which feels itself to be not trusted by government and which feels that government is almost setting the parents against the teachers. This cannot be constructive.
> (Milroy, 1992)

The history of the teaching profession is a history of a struggle for status. Teacher professional association activity, although often focusing on front-line issues like pay and workloads, can be seen, at a deeper level, to be about 'building up public appreciation of the value of education and the worth of the teacher' (Tropp, 1957).

Traditionally, class teachers have never been expected to comment on the theory and practice of their work and very few have done so. Those who research classroom practice tend to be former classroom teachers working in higher education, educational psychologists and those in advisory or inspection posts. To a large extent, classroom teachers' skills and knowledge are, at best, underestimated, and at worst, disregarded – by parents and the general public, by politicians, by the children and, curiously, by many teachers themselves. A further downgrading of an already poorly regarded workforce has been particularly in evidence over the past ten years when there has been a sustained period of political and public criticism of teachers.

There never has been a public expectation that teachers would write about the theory underpinning the classroom craft. Indeed, it can be argued that there is a tradition of public and political questioning about the very existence of any significant educational theory at all – an anti-intellectual and anti-professional stance. For instance, in the early 1990s, Kenneth Clarke, as Education Secretary, frequently referred to teachers' concerns as 'silly' and applauded an uncomplicated approach to educational practice and decision making. It should, nevertheless, be recognised that even common sense has a theoretical base – 'useful is good theory' (Brook, 1992).

Professionals who are able to integrate research with practice – e.g. doctors, educational psychologists, architects, management consultants – do not find themselves on such shaky theoretical ground. They are seen as possessing a body of knowledge that is not easily acquired by others and, generally speaking, they are held in some regard by the public. In contrast, there is a lack of agreement about the knowledge needed for teaching and a 'yawning gap between theory and practice' (Hargreaves, 1996, p.2). Teaching children (particularly primary-aged children) is something that many people feel they can do without any professional training or experience.

In short, teachers' understanding of teaching and their insights into the way in which children learn has generally not been recognised as a valid form of professional knowledge which is worthy of very much respect. Teachers, therefore, have not been made to feel they do something that merits research and dissemination.

Teachers' working conditions

Teachers, as a class, work under less-than-professional conditions with increasingly complex demands for academic, social and psychological expertise in demographically diverse settings.
(Hollingsworth, 1994, p.51)

A class teacher's work is intensely social with a heavy investment of 'self' (Nias, 1993). This arises from the historically determined context in which teachers find themselves – one adult managing the behaviour and learning of a large group of children – but also from the interactive nature of teaching. Teachers teach classes of children but they are also expected to build relationships with individuals. Teaching is probably as much about teachers 'giving' their personalities as it is about teaching the curriculum – a substantial amount of 'what gets taught is the teacher' (Nias, 1989, p.14).

The great outnumbering of children to teachers results, understandably, in a professional preoccupation with control and the skills that maintain classroom order. Much teacher energy and creativity is directed towards managing and controlling the class. Many teachers, particularly those in the early stages of their careers, live daily with the thought that they might – at some point in the lesson, the week or their careers – lose control.

An orderly classroom learning environment is achieved through a delicately balanced cluster of skills which includes a preparedness to make ongoing adjustments to teaching plans and intentions. However, the relationship between teacher and taught is best understood as a refracting rather than a transmitting medium (Hamilton, 1973, cited in Stenhouse, 1975). This gives rise to curious educational paradoxes, like, for instance, the fact that different pupils can learn different things from the same event and well-planned lessons can fall flat while unplanned lessons can go well. This 'illogical' and unpredictable dimension to teaching is professionally very bewildering and testing. Certainly, it is not generally taken into account by those outside teaching, most of whom subscribe to the 'illusion of causality' (Crites, 1986) – i.e. teachers teach and pupils therefore learn what is taught.

Hofkins (1994) captures a core element of a teacher's role when she talks of a teacher being a 'ringmaster ensuring all performers are on task'. Successful 'crowd' management requires close monitoring of individuals, sub-groups and the collective mood of the class. Although, if only for sanity's sake, teaching has to have routines, it also needs to be spontaneous and sometimes prepared to 'go with the flow'. These are subtle skills demanding well-developed professional abilities and intuitions which are built up over many class teaching encounters. In any one day, a teacher handles multiple child interactions with their attendant voices, emotions and volume levels. Indeed, teaching is a highly emotional, if not passionate, enterprise and this has been a neglected dimension in recent years. William Lodge Paley, a National School teacher in 1824, captures the extent to which feelings are involved:

> (I am) so teased with teaching that my soul feels heaviness and my spirits dullness.
> (Mitchell, 1991, p. 32)

For the classroom teacher, teaching is overwhelmingly a 'doing' activity. It requires constant attention to the here and now of pupil life – a 'shifting, unpredictable, capricious world' (Nias, 1989, p.13). The teaching day has a very crowded skyline. Although many teachers find themselves working through their lunch breaks, they still come to the end of a day with outstanding items on the list of things to do. Teachers encounter difficulties finding time when they urgently need to telephone a doctor or the bank and those outside schools often find it difficult to make telephone contact with teachers.

Teachers have little timetabled time for preparing teaching resources, liaising with parents, writing up records, consulting with colleagues or simply thinking about their work. Such essential professional activities have to be squeezed into tightly marked daytime moments or confined to evenings, weekends and holidays. And yet, many teachers will say they wish they had more time with their pupils in order to meet their learning needs (see Lortie, 1975). There is increasing evidence to suggest that government reforms have resulted in further work overload for many classroom teachers (Hargreaves, 1993; Campbell and Neill, 1994).

Teachers' working conditions militate against any activity that is not contributing to the 'hands on' work with pupils. Two teachers involved in a collaborative research project on children's thinking make this clear:

> Anyone who has experienced the concentrated action a teacher faces daily will ask: Why would a teacher further complicate life by trying to collect information on a very complex area of educational theory?
>
> (Hull *et al.*, 1985, p.92)

Any slack in the system is quickly taken up by an ever-present surplus of pupil-related work. In short, the nature of class teachers' working conditions is excluding of all other activities, particularly an activity as demanding as research. It seems pertinent to ask why teachers were ever adopted as researchers (see Lawn, 1989). Research is another level of work requiring its own time, training, creative energy and commitment, and understandably, most teachers are too fatigued to contemplate it.

Confidence and having something to say

> What came through to the National Commission was the extent to which teachers' own self-confidence had been undermined by the way in which they had been undervalued by government and by the media.
>
> (Kennedy, 1996)

If teaching has always been short-changed in the public's ranking of worthwhile occupations, then a case can be made for thinking that things have become considerably worse for teachers in recent times. The way in which the Education Reform Act (1988) was conceptualised and imposed runs counter to some of the most basic principles regarding ownership of change, and as

Sikes (1992, p.48) reminds us – 'imposition generally implies criticism'. Teachers have been left feeling reproached, challenged, besieged and 'grieving' (Nias, 1993) for lost practices and professional identities. In their study of 400 infant teachers, Campbell and Neill (1994) concluded that recent educational reforms rode on the back of teachers' conscientiousness and almost 50 per cent of those studied felt their own sense of professionalism had been damaged. The National Commission on Education (NCE, 1993, p.195) commented, 'Morale is low in the teaching profession'.

The radical nature and restless speed of government reforms and their various revisions and adjustments have disorientated many in the profession, particularly the more experienced – those who had developed, over time, personalised ways of doing the job, those with 'experientially-based confidence' (Sikes, 1992, p.49). The National Curriculum and its assessment structure has required that teachers learn a new pedagogic language in order to 'deliver' a politician's curriculum. The government has challenged teachers' professional experience, judgement and expertise and the net effect is that teachers are left with an overwhelming impression that they must try a lot harder in order to be better. Such was the level of professional confidence and dignity that most have done as they were told, often, as Campbell and Neill (1994) suggest, at the expense of their self-image as competent and effective professionals.

Meanwhile, government tinkering continues unabated with a string of reforms. In 1996, speaking of proposals for a new national curriculum for teacher training, Doug McAvoy, General Secretary of the National Union of Teachers, commented:

It's change upon change without any consultation. The government is about to reform its own reforms.
    (McAvoy, 1996)

The effect on a beleaguered profession is to reaffirm the message that politicians are the professional educators and teachers are 'marginalised victims' of reform (Hargreaves and Goodson, 1995). Innovation no longer resides within a professional domain; it is now delivered to schools by a political bureaucracy. Teachers have little part in drawing up an agenda for change (Nixon, 1989).

Interestingly, government reforms have probably led to a considerable increase in the amount of planning and writing done by teachers. However, this has not been writing of a spontaneous or creative kind – writing by one who wants to write because there is something burning to say. It is the equivalent of the dubious classroom practice which requires children to write to a title that has suddenly appeared 'out of the blue' on the blackboard.

To a very considerable extent, teachers have been usurped as creative and thinking professionals. It is now possible that they believe less in themselves than they ever did – less in themselves as professionals with something worthwhile to say about children's learning and development. Truly teachers have had their wings clipped and the idea that they should research their practice in a grass roots way has lost much ground.

Research and the class teacher

I became a writer partly because I was slightly detached from my family.
(Mason, 1992)

For a number of years, doubt has been cast on the extent to which the more traditional (academic) forms of educational research are relevant to classroom teachers who work in the diverse and variable settings of classrooms (e.g. Nixon, 1981; Carr and Kemmis, 1986; Pollard and Tann, 1987; McNiff, 1988; Elliott, 1988). Nevertheless, teachers have been encouraged to take a research stance on their practice through the use of alternative approaches. For instance, Carr and Kemmis (1986) write, 'teachers must be researchers'. McNiff (1988, p. xiii) comments, 'Action research presents an opportunity for teachers to become uniquely involved in their own practice' and Pollard and Tann (1987, p.23) believe that 'critical reflection and systematic investigation' of teaching practice should be an integral part of classroom life. Such writers have recommended 'teacher friendly' forms of research like self-evaluation, reflection, action research, action enquiry, and case study. And, as indicated at the beginning of this chapter, many teachers have successfully researched educational issues using these approaches.

A noteworthy feature of the teacher research movement is the role of outsiders. Elliott (1991, p.47) has drawn attention to this:

One of the interesting things about the school-based action research movement is that it has been led and sustained by academic teacher educators operating from the higher education sector.

If most teacher research depends upon outsiders in order to get off the ground, then there is reason to question whether even the alternative methodologies are feasible in the classroom situation.

Jackson (1968) and Taylor (1970) provide examples of early insights into teachers' professional behaviour in classrooms. Jackson studied a group of American elementary teachers and was struck by the immediacy of life in the classroom and the way in which this made teachers look for quick solutions to complex classroom issues. Jackson (p.159) commented:

> Were she [the teacher] seriously to try untangling the web of forces that combine to produce reality as she knows it, there would be no time for anything else.

In his study of the way teachers plan their teaching, Taylor (1970, p.71) provided similarly interesting insights when he wrote:

> It may well be that the planning is undertaken instinctively, governed by rule-of-thumb, drawing on successful experience, by feel and intuition rather than by reference to explicit criteria employed in a systematic manner.

Hull *et al.* (1985), in a collaborative research project between teachers and a small team of university staff, found the school staff were at first very tentative about getting involved and surprisingly unfamiliar with the 'culture' of research. They write, 'the professional teacher community does not embrace a research tradition' (p.99).

Brown (1989) is concerned that outsiders' models have dominated the thinking on teaching in classrooms and asks the question: what does classroom teaching look like from a teacher's perspective? She found that teachers work spontaneously from their own situations and that this does not tally well with a more systematic 'define objectives – plan activities – evaluate achievement of objectives' approach. Hammersley (1993) suggests that the rigour inherent in most teacher research approaches could militate against the actual practice of teaching and the way in which teachers need to 'operate under great pressures of immediacy and complexity' (p.438). He believes that we should be concerned to raise the status of teaching as an activity *per se* and not necessarily through associating it with research.

Some writers, like, for instance, Armstrong (1980) and Rowland (1984) have advocated 'observational' approaches to researching classroom life. These are inspiring studies and, on the face of it, they contain replicable methodologies for teachers. However, it needs to be noted that they were possible because the authors had time to observe. They were not carrying a full teaching load as well as observing, researching and writing.

Action research has received a high profile as a friendly methodology for teachers wishing to study and improve their practice. Reporting on their experience of action research in a community college, Cooper and Ebbutt (1974, p.70) found it 'possible' to participate in action research although the 'constraints of the day-to-day secondary school situation' reduced its effectiveness.

Elliott (1991), who has long been a leading protagonist of the method, draws into question the logic of established action research ways of approaching issues in schools:

> When one is faced with a practical problem, it is better to take the calculated risk of getting it wrong, and adjusting one's action strategy retrospectively, than that of not doing anything about the problem until one has fully understood it.
>
> (p.24)

Elliott argues that the above approach to classroom problems is more reflective of the 'natural logic' of teachers' practical thinking.

Johnston (1994) questions if action research is a 'natural' process for teachers. She identifies the barriers which prevent teachers from carrying it through on their own. She mentions teachers' strong orientation to practice, their continued belief that research is done by professional researchers, the isolation of individual class teachers which makes collaborative research difficult, and their lack of time and training in the necessary research skills. Echoing Hammersley (1993), she is concerned that teachers might be seen as lacking because they appear to need outside help in order to engage with action research. She concludes that there is a dissonance between action research and teaching:

> Teachers' reluctance to take on action research may arise because action research, although appearing on the surface to be a natural part of what is considered to be good teaching, actually does not fit with the processes that reflective, inquiring teachers use.
>
> (Johnston, 1994, p.43)

Dadds (1995) observes that teachers experience action research very differently from the way in which it is represented theoretically in the literature. She offers a penetrating account of the potential value of action research to a committed teacher-researcher; however, she is also honest about the difficulties and sees success to be dependent upon the 'fortitude of teachers working . . . within severe time constraints' (p.169).

So, although many teachers have been able to integrate research into their classroom teaching, there is reason to think that recommended outsider methodologies, like action research, are by no means straightforward.

Perhaps this dissonance is part of a larger difficulty related to the research role itself. Smetherham (1978, p. 98) suggests that the very act of doing research separates one 'from the thoughts and interests of those cohabiting the observed social world'. The maintenance of a research identity necessarily results in a degree of detachment from the here and now being studied. Participants who carry out 'insider' research have to grapple with this. Good professional practice requires that teachers give full attention to children's ongoing needs – the 'ethic of care'. However, observing the situation and collecting data must, to some extent, take them away from this interpersonal engagement. So, there is a sense in which research may actually conflict with good teaching practice.

Summary and conclusions

> Nothing exists until we write about it.
> (Ross, 1995)

This chapter has addressed class teachers' lack of enthusiasm for classroom-based research. (A more 'playful' approach might have involved asking why researchers are reluctant to become class teachers!)

I have identified four areas of difficulty:

- the lack of expectation that teachers should research and write about their professional practice;
- the demanding nature of teaching which leaves little time and energy for research;
- the current lack of professional confidence and marginalisation of teachers from government change agendas;
- the mismatch between many available research methodologies and teachers' professional ways of working in classrooms.

My purpose in revealing these difficulties is not to be discouraging of teacher research. As I said at the beginning of this chapter, I am committed to making teachers' understandings more widely available than they are at present. However, I think there is a need to develop clearer insights into teachers' reluctance in order to offer more effective support. And I do feel strongly that teachers need (and should expect) support if they are to take on research in addition to teaching.

By way of concluding, I want to look briefly at the idea of support. From the very beginning of the teacher-as-researcher movement there have been enterprising approaches to teacher involvement; however, there is now a particular need for imaginative and effective help.

I have argued that recent educational reforms have not been encouraging of grass roots practitioner research. Much has happened to make teachers feel powerless and disinclined to take the initiative. There is now a need for creativity with regard to establishing promising 'points of entry' for teacher research in a climate of imposition.

Three examples serve to show the sorts of measures that are needed. At Kingston University, lecturers have supported teacher research in the somewhat unpromising area of National Curriculum assessment and testing (Lomax and Jones, 1993). The authors state, 'teachers can work within the apparently strangling framework of national assessment to create something that is educationally worthwhile' (p.2). At the University of Greenwich there has been recognition of the potential for research that is offered by the Government's 'Special Educational Needs Parent Partnership Programme'. A lecturer provided school-based support to teachers in Tower Hamlets to assist them in developing and writing up projects in the area of home–school relations (Harland and Gale, 1997). Thirdly, the Teacher Training Agency (TTA) has announced a wish to bring teaching and research closer together and has made available small research grants for classroom-focused projects with a particular emphasis on effective dissemination of findings.

In addition to their creativity, these three initiatives illustrate an important principle with regard to establishing appropriate foci for teacher research. This is the need to achieve a high degree of overlap between the researched themes and classroom concerns. Given the difficulties of finding time for research, it makes a considerable difference if teachers feel that time spent on research is also directly benefiting their classroom work.

Given that research is an extra layer of work for teachers, it is important to provide the kind of practical support that will enable lift-off. Clearly this will vary from teacher to teacher but it seems that hands-on help is particularly welcomed. For instance, in the above example, the University of Greenwich offer teachers the choice of writing up their projects independently, writing them jointly with the tutor or delegating the writing-up to the tutor. Although most teachers are involved in teaching children to develop as writers, it seems that many teachers lack confidence as writers themselves.

As already noted, staff from higher education have traditionally carried the main support load so it seems important to look for other people who can increase the size of the 'support service'.

Head teachers are very well placed to encourage teacher research. However, head teachers (possibly even more so than class teachers) have experienced huge changes and increased work pressures in recent years (NAHT, 1993; Judd, 1996). It is difficult, therefore, to imagine that many could take on this facilitating role at this point in time; nevertheless, it is important to recognise that they could play a key enabling role in the development of a teacher research culture.

Most local education authorities (LEAs) still have a number of support, advisory and inspection staff (albeit much reduced) who can do much for the cause of teacher research. Such staff can provide an important service to class teachers by drawing attention to any exciting and innovative practice that they see from the 'privileged' position of a peripatetic observer. (It is actually very hard to be aware of successful practice when you are a class teacher who is very close to it and particularly when you are working in a climate in which many of those outside schools are suggesting that you are ineffective.) Teachers continue to hold to the view that research is an activity which is done by professional researchers based outside schools. Teachers therefore need support in order to see themselves as researchers and to see their practice as 'worthy' of research.

Many teachers feel the gap between their practice and research lift-off is very wide and video can be a very effective way of breaching this imagined divide. Videos create 'curiosity and reaction' (Anning, 1990, p.16) and help initiate the process of reflection. Video can be used to help teachers look objectively at their practice and can generate discussion and writing (see Hancock, 1995; Ferris and Hancock, 1997). A further benefit is the increased possibility of a research/practice overlap. Children are very motivated by video – to become both video makers and evaluators of classroom events. Parents can also be drawn in as videos can make the life and learning of schools more visible to the wider community (Hancock *et al.*, 1996).

With regard to choice of methodology, it seems desirable that no research approach is ruled out providing teachers feel motivated and involved. Golby (1989) believes that methodology relates to the research situation and its aims and is a matter of what is appropriate and possible. However, it seems important that there is acceptance of teachers' subjective and intuitive ways of understanding classroom processes – what Hart (1995) has termed 'interpretive modes' of enquiry. Teachers should be helped to cultivate personalised styles of writing which are likely to be more consistent with their professional ways of operating in classrooms and the nature of teachers' schoolwork (see Lawn, 1989). Case study has long been popular. Walker (1980) suggests that teachers make educational judgements on the basis of particular instances rather than referring to research findings and this makes them 'natural case study workers'. In recent years, a number of other teacher-centred approaches to inquiry, writing and research have become available. These include: 'narrative inquiry' (Connelly and Clandinin, 1990); the study of 'critical events' (Woods, 1993) and 'biography' (Thomas, 1995). All seem to offer teachers potentially meaningful ways of examining their implicit craft understandings.

Finally, Eisner (1988, p.19) has written:

> Researchers are beginning to go back to schools, not to conduct commando raids, but to work with teachers.

Although one hopes there have been less 'commando raids' in recent years, I feel these words continue to offer sound advice to all who are in a position to promote teaching as a research-based profession. It seems crucial that teachers' insights into children's learning are valued, captured in writing and made more widely available than they are at the present time.

Acknowledgements

I would like to express my thanks to Edward Korel, Titus Alexander, Harry Torrance, David Brook, Linda Harland and Margaret Meek Spencer for their interest in many of the ideas contained in this chapter.

References

Anning, A. (1990) *Using Video Recording for Teacher Professional Development*. Leeds: University of Leeds, School of Education.

Armstrong, M. (1980) *Closely Observed Children: the Diary of a Primary Classroom*. Oxford: Writers & Readers.

Bell, G. H., Stakes, R. and Taylor, G. (eds) (1994) *Action Research, Special Needs and School Development*. London: David Fulton Publishers.

Brook, D. (1992) Personal communication.

Brown, S. (1989) 'How do teachers talk about and evaluate their own teaching?', *Spotlight 12*. Edinburgh: Scottish Council for Educational Research.

Campbell, J. and Neill, S. (1994) *Curriculum Reform at Key Stage 1: Teacher Commitment and Policy Failure*. London: Longman.

Carr, W. and Kemmis, S. (1986) *Becoming Critical: Education, Knowledge and Action Research*. Lewes: Falmer Press.

Connelly, F. M. and Clandinin, D. J. (1990) 'Stones of experience and narrative enquiry', *Educational Researcher* **19**(5), 2–14.

Cooper, D. and Ebbutt, D. (1974) 'Participation in action research as an in-service experience', *Cambridge Journal of Education* **4**, 65–71.

Crites, S. (1986) 'Storytime: recollecting the past and projecting the future', in Sarbin, T. R. (ed.) *The Storied Nature of Human Conduct*. New York: Praeger.

Dadds, M. (1995) *Passionate Enquiry and School Development: a Story about Teacher Action Research*. London: Falmer Press.

Eisner, E. W. (1988) 'The primacy of experience and the politics of method', *Educational Researcher* **20**, 15–20.

Elliott, J. (1988) 'Educational research and insider-outsider relations', *Qualitative Studies in Education* **1**, 155–66.

Elliott, J. (1991) *Action Research for Educational Change*. Milton Keynes: Open University Press.

Falkner, D., Swann, J. and Stredder, K. (1992) Professional Development in Action Module E621, Certificate of Professional Development in Education. Milton Keynes: Open University Press.

Ferris, A. and Hancock. R., with Nicholson, A. and Maples, C. (1997) Nursery Education. A Video. Bilingual Primary Pupils Project/Hackney PACT. Queensbadge Buildings, Albion Drive, London E8 4ET.

Frost, D. (1995) 'Networking', *Educational Action Research* **3**, 249–51.

Golby, M. (1989) 'Teachers and their research', in Carr, W. (ed.) *Quality in Teaching: Arguments for a Reflective Profession*. London: Falmer Press.

Hamilton, D. (1977) 'At classroom level'. Unpublished PhD thesis, University of Edinburgh.

Hammersley, M. (1993) 'On the teacher as a researcher', *Educational Action Research* **1**, 425–45.

Hancock, R. (1995) The Chinese Independent School of Tower Hamlets. A video about the life and learning of a Chinese Saturday School. PICC Project, Tower Hamlets Learning Design Centre, English Street, London E3 4TA.

Hancock, R., with others (1996) 'Making school more visible to parents: an evaluation of the Harbinger video project', in Bastiani, J. and Wolfendale, S. (eds) *Home–School Work in Britain: Review, Reflection and Development*. London: David Fulton Publishers.

Hargreaves, A. (1993) 'Time and teachers' work: an analysis of the intensification thesis', in Gomm, R. and Woods, P. (eds) *Educational Research in Action*. London: Paul Chapman/Open University.

Hargreaves, A. and Goodson, I. (1995) 'Let us take the lead', *Times Educational Supplement*, 24 February, 15.

Hargreaves, D. H. (1996) 'Teaching as a research-based profession: possibilities and prospects'. Teacher Training Agency Annual Lecture.

Harland, L. and Gale, S. (1997) *Developing Home–School Links*. London: Learning by Design.

Hart, S. (1995) 'Action-in-reflection', *Educational Action Research* **3**, 211–32.

Hofkins, D. (1994) 'Mentors "ignored" trainees', *Times Educational Supplement*, 23 November, 13.

Hollingsworth, S. (1994) 'Feminist pedagogy in the research class: an example of teacher research', *Educational Action Research* **2**, 49–70.

Hull, C. *et al.* (eds) (1985) *A Room Full of Children Thinking: Accounts of Classroom Research by Teachers.* York: SCDC Publications-Longman.

Jackson, P. (1968) *Life in Classrooms.* New York: Holt, Rinehart & Winston.

Johnston, S. (1994) 'Is action research a natural process for teachers?', *Educational Action Research* **2**, 39–48.

Judd, J. (1996) 'Heads quitting profession in record numbers', *The Independent*, 23 May, 7.

Kelly, A., Whyte, J. and Smail, B. (1984) *Girls into Science and Technology Final Report.* University of Manchester, Department of Sociology.

Kennedy, H. (Member of the National Commission on Education) (1996) Keynote Address at the Helping Children to Succeed Conference at Swanlee School, Tower Hamlets, London, 27 April.

Lawn, M. (1989) 'Being caught in school work: the possibilities of research in teachers' work', in Carr, W. (ed.) *Quality in Teaching: Arguments for a Reflective Profession.* London: Falmer Press.

Lewis, I. (1988) 'Learning together: issues arising from outstation MA course experience', in Nias, J. and Groundwater-Smith, S. (eds) *The Enquiring Teacher: Supporting and Sustaining Teacher Research.* London: Falmer Press.

Lomax, P. and Jones, C. (eds) (1993) *Developing Primary Schools through Action Research.* Bournemouth: Hyde Publications.

Lortie, D. (1975) *School Teacher: a Sociological Study.* Chicago: University of Chicago Press.

MacDonald, B. (1973) 'Humanities Curriculum Project', in *Schools Council Research Studies Evaluation in Curriculum Development: Twelve Case Studies.* Basingstoke: Macmillan Education.

McAvoy, D. (1996) Speaking on the Six o'clock News, BBC 1, 12 June.

Mason, G. (1992) *In the Psychiatrist's Chair.* BBC Radio 4.

McNiff, J. (1988) *Action Research: Principles and Practice.* London: Macmillan.

Milroy, Father Dominic (1992) Head teacher of Ampleforth School and Chair of the Headmasters (*sic*) Conference. Interviewed for *Hard Words in the Classroom*, BBC Radio 4.

Mitchell, W. R. (1991) *Mr Elgar and Dr Buck: a Musical Friendship.* Settle: Castleberg Publications.

National Association of Head Teachers (NAHT) (1993) Press Release on resignations due to ill-health, 14 July.

National Commission on Education (NCE) (1993) *Learning to Succeed: a Radical Look at Education Today and a Strategy for the Future.* London: Heinemann.

Nias, J. (1989) *Primary Teachers Talking: a Study of Teaching as Work*. London: Routledge.

Nias, J. (1993) 'Changing times, changing identities: grieving for a lost self', in Burgess, R. (ed.) *Educational Research and Evaluation: for Policy and Practice?* London: Falmer Press.

Nixon, J. (ed.) (1981) *A Teacher's Guide to Action Research*. London: Grant McIntyre.

Nixon, J. (1989) 'The teacher as researcher: contradictions and continuities', *Peabody Journal of Education* **64**, 116–27.

Pollard, A. and Tann, S. (1987) *Reflective Teaching in the Primary School*. London: Cassell.

Ross, B. (1995) Said by Dr Zeigler, a prison psychiatrist, in the film *The Young Poisoner's Handbook*, directed by Benjamin Ross. An Electric Pictures/Polygram Filmed Entertainments.

Rowland, S. (1984) *The Enquiring Classroom*. Lewes: Falmer Press.

Ryan, C. and Somekh, B. (eds) (1991) *Processes of Reflection and Action*, CARN Publication 10B. Norwich: University of East Anglia.

Sikes, P. J. (1992) 'Imposed change and the experienced teacher', in Fullan, M. and Hargreaves, A. (eds) *Teacher Development and Educational Change*. London: Falmer Press.

Smail, B., Whyte, J. and Kelly, A. (1982) 'Girls into science and technology: the first two years', *School Science Review* **63**, 620–30.

Smetherham, D. (1978) 'Insider research', *British Educational Research Journal* **4**, 97–102.

Somekh, B. (1991) 'Pupil autonomy in learning with microcomputers: rhetoric or reality? An action research study', *Cambridge Journal of Education* **21**, 47–64.

Stenhouse, L. (1968) 'The Humanities Curriculum Project', *Journal of Curriculum Studies* **1**, 26–33.

Stenhouse, L. (1971) 'The Humanities Curriculum Project: the rationale', *Theory into Practice* **10**, 154–62.

Stenhouse, L. (1975) *An Introduction to Curriculum Research and Development*. London: Heinemann.

Taylor, P. H. (1970) *How Teachers Plan their Courses*. Slough: NFER.

Thomas, D. (1995) *Teachers' Stories*. Buckingham: Open University Press.

Tropp, A. (1957) *The School Teachers*. London: Heinemann.

Teacher Training Agency (1996) *Teaching as a research-based profession: promoting excellence in teaching*. London: TTA Information Section.

Vulliamy, G. and Webb, R. (eds) (1992) *Teacher Research and Special Educational Needs*. London: David Fulton Publishers.

Walker, R. (1980) 'The conduct of educational case studies: ethics, theory and procedures', in Dockrell, W. B. and Hamilton, D. (eds) *Rethinking Educational Research*. London: Hodder and Stoughton.

Woods, P. (1993) *Critical Events in Teaching and Learning*. London: Falmer Press.

Chapter 25

Classroom-based teacher development

Dennis Thiessen

Editors' Note: This heavily edited article gives a number of suggestions as to how teachers can use their own classrooms as the site for their personal development in order to improve their practice.

[. . .]

Three modes of Classroom-based Teacher Development (CBTD) are possible: teachers on their own, teachers with teachers, and teachers and students. For each mode, I outline approaches which emphasise building from, studying or changing existing classroom practices. Numerous references already exist which describe how teachers work alone or with others in teacher development[1] and I briefly review some of these through the lens of CBTD. There are comparatively fewer examples of teacher–student approaches, however. Yet directly engaging teachers and students together in teacher development realises the conditions of CBTD most thoroughly and extensively. I therefore devote greater space to these. Ultimately, though, all three modes of CBTD are necessary and mutually supportive.

Teachers on their own

Probably the most enduring mode of teacher development occurs on the job as teachers diligently work alone in their classrooms searching for, trying out and modifying strategies that best respond to the needs of their students. In early career, teacher development centres on the basic goal of survival in a lonely and often professionally isolated occupation. Teachers learn their trade in the 'school of hard knocks' through repeated trial-and-error cycles. Classroom experimentation with new practices by experienced teachers is a self-directed

---

1. Connelly, F. M. and Clandinin, D. J. *Teachers as Curriculum Planners: Narratives of Experience.* Toronto and New York: OISE Press and Teachers' College Press, 1988; Chapters 4 and 5 offer numerous 'tools for reflection' that teachers can use on their own or with others to better understand themselves as practitioners.

programme that teachers initiate to improve their learning environment.

Self-improvement projects should be more than instructional adjustments, however. When CBTD is undertaken by teachers without direct influence from colleagues or students, they should also learn about themselves and the implications of their practices for their classrooms.[2] Self-understanding is not, or need not be, egocentric or narcissistic. It can also inform teachers about the experiences of their students. As Connelly and Clandinin state,

> if you understand what makes up the curriculum of the person most important to you, namely, yourself, you will better understand the difficulties, whys, and wherefores of the curriculum of your students. There is no better way to study curriculum than to study ourselves.[3]

. . . Approaches where teachers write their own journals do not directly address how students and teachers share control (power), are not situated in the classroom (environment) and are not interactive or normally transformative (action). Yet these conditions can be incorporated indirectly into journal writing if teachers frame their written reflection in terms of decisions, relationships and norms in their own classrooms. (See Jennifer Moon's Chapter 28.) For example, teachers may write about incidents which describe their struggle to work effectively with reluctant or disruptive students. In these journal entries, teachers may think about tests of control (power) in the classroom (environment) and possible solutions (action) to the problem. Figure 25.1 introduces classroom-based teacher development approaches which teachers can carry out alone.

I. Constructing classroom routines. These involve teachers developing a more critical awareness of everyday classroom operations. In CBTD teachers do not only clarify the consistencies and inconsistencies of their taken-for-granted classroom norms, the roles they insist on, or the way they do things. They also act to remove obstacles to or gaps in their preferred curriculum. Teacher development is part of this constant attention to the mundane.

---

2. Many resources are available for teachers who want to guide their own development: Connelly and Clandinin, op. cit., note 1; Handal, G. and Lauvas, P. *Promoting Effective Teaching: Supervision in Action.* Milton Keynes, Society for Research into Higher Education and the Open University, 1987; Haysom, J. *Inquiring into the Teaching Process. Towards Self-Evaluation and Professional Development.* Toronto: OISE Press, 1985; Hunt, D. *Beginning with Ourselves: In Practice, Theory, and Human Affairs.* Toronto: OISE Press, 1987; and Pollard, A. and Tann, S. *Reflective Teaching in the Primary School: A Handbook for the Classroom.* London: Cassell, 1987, provide teachers with strategies and frameworks to enquire into, reflect about, and reform their practices.
3. Connelly and Clandinin, op. cit., note 1.

I. Constructing classroom routines

1. *Organising curriculum 'artefacts':* Each teacher determines her lesson plans, units of study, resources, desk arrangements, and displayed materials. She coordinates and analyses the use of these 'artefacts' in ways which support her curriculum priorities.[4]

2. *Managing the environment:* Each teacher compares what she does and anticipates doing to maintain the efficiency and order of classroom activities. In particular, she focuses on how the implicit and explicit rules regulate her actions and those of her students.[5]

II. Documenting one's actions

3. *Maintaining journals:* Each teacher describes and comments on the significant people, situations, forces, or events that permeate past and present classroom experiences. The translation of experience into written or audiotaped journal entries generates insights about everyday occurrences.[6]

4. *Engaging in self-evaluation:* Each teacher becomes a self-monitor, systematically describing a teaching episode, analysing it from different points of view, evaluating the underlying assumptions and values, and acting on any perceived contradictions, problems or dilemmas. It is a cyclic process of constructive and critical review.[7]

III. Adapting teaching and learning strategies

5. *Self-directed development:* Each teacher initiates changes in how teaching and learning occur in the classroom. She considers and experiments with different strategies, examines the intended and unintended consequences of available alternatives, and adopts those which improve the quality of teacher and student interaction.[8]

Figure 25.1 Independent teacher development experiences

---

4. Burgess, R. *In the Field: An Introduction to Field Research.* London: George Allen & Unwin, 1984; Connelly and Clandinin, op. cit., note 1.

5. Pollard and Tann, op. cit., note 2.

6. Holly, M. *Keeping a Personal-Professional Journal.* Seelong: Deakin University Press, 1984: Tripp, D. 'Teachers' journals: an illustrated rationale for teacher/ researcher partnership in curriculum research', a paper presented at the annual meeting of the American Educational Research Association, San Francisco, Calif., 1986; Tripp, D. 'Teachers, journals and collaborative research', in Smyth, J. (ed.) *Educating Teachers: Changing the Nature of Pedagogical Knowledge.* London: Falmer Press, pp.179–92, 1987.

7. Oberg, A. 'Professional development through self-evaluation', in Holborn, P., Wideen, M. and Andrews, T. (eds) *Becoming a Teacher.* Toronto: Kajan & Woo, 1988.

8. Loucks-Horsley, S., Harding, C., Arbuckle, M., Murray, L., Dubea, C. and Williams, M., *Continuing to Learn: A Guidebook for Teacher Development.* Andover and Oxford: Regional Laboratory for Educational Improvement of the Northeast and Islands, and National Staff Development Council, 1987; Iwanicki, E. and McEachern, L. 'Teacher self-improvement: a promising approach to professional development and school improvement', *Journal of Staff Development* **4**(1), 62–77, 1983.

II. Documenting one's actions. Here, teachers are educational critics of their own practices. They transform their spontaneous sense of instrumental effectiveness or practicality into a thoughtful and rigorous review of some fundamental theme in classroom learning. Various forms of recording, journal keeping and self-evaluation provide teachers with ways to track, judge and reconsider their experiences. In this approach, teachers develop from the informed interrogation of themselves.

III. Adapting teaching and learning strategies In these adjustments, teachers alter their pedagogical actions in the classroom. They are independent, one-teacher versions of action research. With these approaches, teachers use their initiatives as change agents to facilitate their own development.

Teachers with teachers

Teachers learn much from each other. They cite fellow teachers as the most valuable source of professional development.[9] In recent years, teacher development approaches which build on collegial and collaborative work among teachers have become prominent in the discourse on school improvement and educational change.[10] Peer coaching,[11] advising teachers,[12] cooperative professional development[13] and mentoring[14] are all examples of this mode of teacher development.

Not all teacher-to-teacher development approaches meet the conditions of CBTD, however. For example, some coaching approaches are part of a more

---

9. Flanders, T. 'Teachers' realities, needs and professional development', in Butt, R., Olson, J. and Daignault, J. (eds) *Insiders' Realities. Outsiders' Dreams. Prospects for Curriculum Change.* Curriculum Canada IV, Vancouver: Centre for the Study of Curriculum and Instruction, University of British Columbia, 1983.
10. See Fullan, M. 'Change processes and strategies at the local level', *Elementary School Journal* **85**(3), pp.391–421, 1985; and Wideen, M. and Andrews, I. (eds) *Staff Development for School Improvement: A Focus on the Teacher.* London: Falmer Press, 1987.
11. See Seller, W. 'A coaching model for professional development'. Paper presented at a meeting of the American Educational Research Association, San Francisco, Calif., 1986; and Showers, B. 'Teachers coaching teachers', *Educational Leadership* **42**, pp.43–8, 1985.
12. Mai, R. 'The advisory approach as a form of professional growth', in Honey, K., Bents, R. and Corrigan, D. (eds) *School-Focussed Inservice: Descriptions and Discussions.* Reston, VA: Association for Teacher Educators, 1981.
13. See Glatthorn, A. *Differentiated Supervision.* Alexandria, VA: Association for Supervision and Curriculum Development, 1984; and Glatthorn, A. 'Cooperative professional development: peer-centred options for teacher growth', *Educational Leadership* **45**, pp.31–5, 1987.
14. Galvaz-Hjornevik, C. 'Mentoring among teachers: a review of the literature', *Journal of Teacher Education* **37**, pp.6–11, 1986.

comprehensive training model[15] which use teaching models or results from previous studies to direct what teachers should learn and how they should work together. Cadres of expert and peer coaches often guide and support the process. Coaching systems become vehicles for transfer training, driving paired teachers to the efficient, effective and congruent uses of desired teaching models. These coaching approaches generally focus on learning and, at times, occur in the classroom, but they do not address the CBTD conditions of power, action and reference points.[16] Though they are interactive, the limited enquiry of much peer coaching is neither reflective nor transformative.

. . . When teachers work together in planning or support groups, they discuss the implications of changes for their classrooms but do not necessarily extend their joint efforts to classroom applications. Figure 25.2 on p.322 outlines six teacher-to-teacher development approaches.

I. Building joint endeavours. In CBTD partnerships, teachers extend how they presently work together in schools. This entails more than redistributing labour or capitalising on the knowledge of others. Rather, teachers consciously attend to the relationship between their planning and their teaching. They deliberate about preferred practices. They search for possibilities and alternatives. And in all this, they learn from their ongoing interactions.

II. Probing for meaning. In this set of approaches, teachers apply strategies which require them to research into each other's practices. Such 'research' or enquiry emphasises portrayals, interactions and interpretations more than measurements, detached observations or statistical analyses. These CBTD approaches range from reflective reviews about classroom experiences to participant observations in the classroom. In them, teachers get beneath the surface meanings of classroom events to make sense of their efforts to facilitate and share responsibility for learning. In each case, teachers develop from the informed insight of and exchange with colleagues.

III. Promoting collaborative development. Here, teachers cooperate to change their classroom practices. Approaches such as peer coaching or clinical supervision become genuinely reciprocal in CBTD. Teachers generate and sustain the energy for change within their evolving relationship.

---

15. Joyce, B. and Showers, B. *Student Achievement Through Staff Development*. New York: Longman, 1988.
16. See Hargreaves, A. and Dawe, R. 'Paths of professional development: contrived collegiality and the case of peer coaching', *Teaching and Teacher Education* **3**(3), 1990.

I. Building joint endeavours

1. *Exchanging expertise:* Two teachers combine their classes in a unit of study. One teacher is the 'expert' organising the unit activities while the other teacher is the 'assistant' learning from the 'expert' how the unit should be implemented. In a subsequent unit, the team teaching roles are reversed.[17]

2. *Planning cooperatively:* Two or more teachers work together to plan for classroom instruction. They pool strategies and resources, compare ideas, determine the structure and emphasis in topics and approaches, and evaluate the success, merit and worth of their products.[18]

II. Probing for meaning

3. *Comparing vignettes:* Teachers create stories, describe situations, or develop memos and cases of important classroom experiences. Through conversation or written communication, they react to each other's accounts.[19]

4. *Learning through participation:* Teachers become 'insiders' in each other's classrooms. They are active observers participating as team teachers, support people or students to discover the unique and complex realities of what happens.[20]

III. Promoting collaborative development

5. *Elaborating practical theories:* Teachers counsel each other in ways which make explicit the basis of decisions and actions in the classroom. They examine the relationship (and tension) between their espoused theories and their theories-in-use to define and direct their separate and shared improvement.[21]

6. *Enhancing professional dialogue:* Teachers form partnerships to generate critical insights into and improvements of classroom practices. The 'supervised' teacher determines the focus of observation but negotiates with the partner how the observations are gathered, interpreted and used.[22]

Figure 25.2 Teacher-to-teacher development experiences

---

17. Taylor, M. (ed.) *Team Teaching Experiments.* London: NFER Publishing Company, 1974.
18. Little, J. 'Teachers as colleagues', in Richardson-Koehler, V. (ed.) *Educators' Handbook: A Research Perspective.* New York: Longman, pp.491–518, 1987; Little, J. and Long, C. *Portraits of School-Based Collegial Teams.* San Francisco: Far West Laboratory, 1985.
19. Connelly and Clandinin, op. cit., note 1; Lieberman, A. 'Documenting professional practice: the vignette as a qualitative tool'. Paper presented at the annual meeting of the American Educational Research Association, Washington DC, 1987; Miles, M. 'Innovative methods for collecting and analyzing qualitative data: vignettes and pre-structured cases'. Paper presented at the annual meeting of the American Educational Research Association, Washington DC, 1987.
20. Day, C. 'Classroom based in-service teacher education: the development and evaluation of a client-centred model'. Occasional Paper 9. Falmer: Education Area, University of Sussex, 1981; Woods, P. *Inside Schools: Ethnography in Educational Research.* London: Routledge and Kegan Paul, 1986.
21. Handal and Lauvas, op. cit., note 2.
22. Ruddock, J. 'Partnership supervision as a basis for the professional development of new and experienced teachers', in Wideen, M. and Andrews, I. (eds) *Staff Development for School Improvement: A Focus on the Teacher.* London: Falmer Press, 1987, pp.129–41.

They learn from monitoring each other's implementation of an innovation and reviewing the changing patterns of their partnership.

Teachers and students

Of the three modes of CBTD, approaches which involve teachers and students are the least discussed and practised, yet the ones that have the greatest potential. . . . In CBTD, the nature of the partnership in any teacher–student development experience should incorporate the following three principles:

1. Teachers and students are active participants in all aspects of classroom life.
2. The different positions of teachers and students in the classroom limit the extent to which they work as equal partners.
3. The symmetrical dimensions of teacher–student relationships sustain and extend the partnership.

Teachers and students are the main characters on the classroom stage. Traditionally, students are less involved in 'behind-the-scene' actions that frame what happens in the classroom. In CBTD, however, students participate with teachers in the determination, planning, adaptation, and evaluation of teacher development initiatives.

In terms of qualifications and formal responsibilities, the position of teachers is quite different from that of students. Teachers are older, have more formal education, know more about the content and process of teaching, and probably rely on a broader and more diversified range of experiences. Teachers have more status, with more official responsibility for the curriculum as intended and practised. In most cases, they are expected to stimulate student learning, create an efficient and effective learning environment, and establish and manage the direction, appropriateness and standards of what students do. They are neither colleagues nor peers with students. The roles of teachers and students in these areas are not reciprocal. When teacher development approaches need the expertise of qualification or the voice of authority, teachers dominate the relationship with students.

Yet there are areas of symmetry in teacher–student relationships that should not be overlooked. Teachers and students live in the classroom and in relation to each other with similar *definition*, *agency* and *rights*. Both are learners, developing from their common situation and evolving relationships. Within the context of the classroom, teachers and students mutually *define* what and how CBTD happens.

I. Sharing teaching and learning

1. *Negotiating the curriculum:* Teachers involve their students in decisions about the purposes, organisation, content, approaches and evaluation of learning.[23]
2. *Forming teaching teams:* Students not only become cross-age or peer tutors for other students but also join with teachers to develop and extend their collective understanding of approaches to teaching.[24]
3. *Problem posing:* Students in concert with teachers investigate, discuss and act on issues relevant to their lives in the school and the community. Teachers and students combine reflection and action to take charge of their own learning.[25]

II. Examining classroom phenomena

4. *Creating investigative clubs:* Students work as a research unit which initially advises teachers about the focus and direction of a classroom research project. As the study evolves, students and teachers together collect, interpret and triangulate data.[26]
5. *Inquiring into student learning:* Teachers combine enquiry and teaching in ways that probe the nature of learning in the classroom. In-depth accounts emerge from intensive and varied interactions with students.[27]
6. *Evaluating teaching:* Teachers engage students in a critique of teaching, exploring what constitutes effective teaching and how various teaching strategies influence what happens in the classroom.[28]

III. Improving what happens

7. *Transforming teacher–student interaction:* With the aid of videotapes, students and teachers analyse their mutual efforts to implement innovative practices. In particular, they focus on ways to change the form, substance and orientation of their working relationship.[29]
8. *Altering the curriculum in use:* Teachers, consultants, and students form action-research groups to enhance their capacity to bring about meaningful changes. A critical comparison of the curriculum intended by teachers and the curriculum construed by students reveals what and how classroom and school realities should change.[30]
9. *Culture making:* In innovations, students and teachers develop alternative strategies to establish new norms and conditions in the culture of the classroom. They come to a mutual understanding of what matters in their new 'world'.[31]

Figure 25.3 Teacher–student development experiences

23. Boomer, G. (ed.) *Negotiating the Curriculum: A Teacher–Student Partnership.* Sydney: Ashton Scholastic, 1982; Boomer, G. 'Students and the means of production: negotiating the curriculum', in Schostak, J. and Logan, T. (eds) *Pupil Experience.* London: Croom Helm, pp.231–51, 1984.
24. Hedin, D. 'Students as teachers: a tool for improving school', *Social Policy* **17**(3), pp.42–7, 1987.
25. Wallerstein, N. 'Problem-posing education: Freire's method for transformation', in Shor, T. (ed.) *Freire for the Classroom: A Sourcebook for Liberatory Teaching.* Portsmouth, NH: Heinemann, 1987.
26. Pollard, A. 'Studying children's perspectives – a collaborative approach', in Walford, G. (ed.) *Doing Sociology of Education.* London: Falmer Press, pp.95–118, 1987.

In terms of *agency*, teachers and students construct their own meaning and actions in the classroom. Each teacher or student is the expert on his or her own past, present or future experiences. Previous classroom situations, reactions to present circumstances and anticipations of future realities influence how each teacher or student views and shapes his or her opportunities as a learner. Teachers and students have to respect, understand and work with each other's agency in any CBTD activity.

Another area of symmetry is the human *rights* which underpin teacher–student relationships. Both teachers and students have rights to fair treatment and participation. Such rights compel one party to inform, consult, and deliberate with the other party about judgements and actions which affect the relationship. The rights shared by teachers and students in the classroom are the foundation upon which CBTD builds.

The symmetrical dimensions of definition, agency and rights give a form of equality to teacher–student relationships. Students have the same expectation and obligation as teachers to influence classroom experiences. Though the symmetry cannot alter the inequalities of qualification and experience, it can modify the ways in which teachers use their formal responsibilities. Some inequalities persist: students remain as significant but junior partners. Nevertheless, when the symmetry of the partnership dominates, the active engagement of both partners becomes the dynamic force in CBTD.

Figure 25.3 on p.324 lists nine examples of teacher–student development approaches organised into three groups: sharing teaching and learning, examining classroom phenomena and improving what happens. For the three approaches in each group, I elaborate one approach and discuss the adaptations of the other two within the CBTD framework.

I. Sharing teaching and learning. Experiences in this approach are constructed to enhance the ways in which teachers and students already work together. This might include, but will also go beyond, matters of determining

27. Rowland, S. *The Inquiring Classroom: An Introduction to Children's Learning.* London: Falmer Press, 1984.
28. McKelvey, J. and Kyriacou, C. 'Research on pupils: a teacher evaluation', *Educational Studies* **11**(1), pp.25–31, 1985.
29. Hull, C. 'Pupils as teacher educators', *Cambridge Journal of Education* **15**(1), pp.1–8, 1985.
30. Oldroyd, D. and Tiller, T. 'Change from within: an account of school-based collaborative action research in an English secondary school', *Journal of Education for Teaching* **12**(3), pp.13–27, 1987; Kemmis, E. and McTaggart, R. (eds) *The Action Research Planner*, 3rd edn. Geelong: Deakin University Press, 1988.
31. Rudduck, J. 'Introducing innovation to pupils', in Hopkins, D. and Wideen, M. (eds) *Alternative Perspectives on School Improvement*. London: Falmer Press, pp.53–66, 1984; Ruddock, J. 'Curriculum change: management or meaning?', *School Organization*, **6**(1), pp.107–14, 1986.

student interests and encouraging active learning. Students are also part of those decisions which determine classroom structures and activities.[32] Both teachers and students 'seek to question each other's ideas, to reinterpret them, to adapt them and even to reject them, but not to discount them'.[33] In CBTD, as I have defined it, the distinction between teachers and students blurs and melds into a partnership. Teacher development in this view should involve joint efforts which extend the scope and mutuality of teacher–student interactions.

In Australia, Boomer established a network of teachers committed to negotiating the curriculum with students.[34] Students in elementary and secondary schools were empowered to construct, in collaboration with their teacher, the unfolding conditions and priorities of their own learning. The students and the teacher discussed proposed units of study, examining their feasibility, appropriateness, relevance and surrounding constraints. Cooperatively, the intentions of, approaches to and structures for the unit were planned. The negotiated frameworks of such units are open to constant scrutiny and revision as students and their teachers live through the practical implications of their negotiations. The curriculum here remains problematic, with students and their teachers in a process of 'constructive struggling'[35] to build meaningful and valued curriculum experiences. The work of Boomer illuminates the increase in experimentation, deliberation and institutional literacy that develops as students participate within the classroom decision-making process. The power of students is acknowledged and integrated into the organisation and improvement of classroom learning. Some of the teachers in Boomer's network reduced student involvement to input on decisions about content or methods. In CBTD, however, students should negotiate as many decisions as possible with their teachers.

Two other forms of sharing teaching and learning – forming teaching teams and problem posing – involve modified versions of cross-age or peer tutoring[36] along with the dialogical pedagogy of Freire[37] to emphasise the partnership of teachers and students. Cross-age or peer tutoring becomes CBTD when teachers teach all students about teaching and then work with them in small groups as rotating teaching teams for the rest of the class. Problem posing requires a critical examination of 'generative themes', personally and socially relevant issues which have the potential to enhance

32. Skilbeck, M. *School-Based Curriculum Development*. London: Harper & Row, 1984.
33. Rowland, op. cit., note 27, p.1.
34. Boomer, G. (ed.) *Negotiating the Curriculum: A Teacher–Student Partnership*. Sydney: Ashton Scholastic, 1982; and Boomer, op. cit., note 23.
35. Boomer, 'Students and the means of production', op. cit., note 23.
36. Hedin, op. cit., note 24.
37. Wallerstein, op. cit., note 25.

learning. In this endeavour, repeated cycles of reflection and action enable teachers and students to develop within and beyond their initial partnership.

II. Examining classroom phenomena. Here, CBTD occurs through joint efforts by teachers and students to conceptualise, implement and interpret the study and evaluation of classroom practices. Such investigations lead to more than mere appreciation of the insights of students[38] or improvements in teachers' abilities to enquire into the world of their students.[39] In CBTD, rather, students should be not simply research subjects but research associates, perhaps even co-investigators and co-evaluators. Teacher development results from the discoveries made during collaborative classroom research.

Pollard[40] enlisted a group of 11- or 12-year-old students to help him study the social world of the elementary school. The group, formally known as the Moorside Investigations Department, interviewed each other and peers in their school, advised Pollard about the content and tactics in his study, and reviewed his interpretations of their world. If Pollard was to understand the culture of students from their vantage point, he needed their help. He commented:

They helped me to decide who was likely to be available for interview next, operated recorders, initiated discussions, labelled and catalogued the cassettes and helped me considerably by discussing my analysis as it unfolded, I offered them the role of 'experts' – which in many senses they were. What was familiar to them was relatively strange to me. I played the role of the naive adult so that whilst I was there to 'learn', they, perhaps a little flattered and entertained by my interest, agreed to 'teach'.[41]

---

38. See Allen, J. 'Classroom management: students' perspectives, goals, and strategies', *American Educational Research Journal* **23**, pp.437–59, 1987; and Hammersley, M. and Woods, P. (eds) *Life in School: The Sociology of Pupil Culture*. Milton Keynes: Open University Press, 1984.

39. See Ball, S. 'Participant observation with pupils', in Burgess, R. (ed.) *Strategies of Educational Research: Qualitative Methods*. London: Falmer Press, 1985; Fine, G. and Sandstrom, K. *Knowing Children: Participant Observation with Minors*. Newburg Park, Calif.: Sage Publications, 1988; Hook, S. *Studying Classrooms*. Geelong: Deakin University Press, 1981; Simmons, H. 'Conversation piece: the practice of interviewing in case study research', in Adelman, C. (ed.) *Uttering, Muttering, Collecting, Using and Reporting Talk for Social and Educational Research*. London: Grant McIntyre, 1981; and Walker, R. *Doing Research: A Handbook for Teachers*. Cambridge: Cambridge University Press, 1985.

40. Pollard, op. cit., note 26.

Creating investigative clubs legitimises the knowledge which students possess about their classroom experiences. For CBTD, teachers should recognise that understanding the experiences of students is a metaphor for understanding and consequently developing the experiences of teachers.

Enquiring into student learning involves an ongoing case study of how the interaction of teachers with each of their students facilitates learning.[42] In a third approach – evaluating teaching – students are included in an interactive review of what teachers do.[43] In this CBTD experience, students should formatively evaluate teaching acts to improve classroom learning.

III. Improving what happens. This approach commits teachers and students to justified changes in their classroom world. Students are not just beneficiaries of change or objects of training.[44] They are not only strategic agents in innovations planned by others.[45] They are also the authors of change, partners with teachers in the improvement of classroom life. Teacher development in this approach should occur within deliberate and sustained attempts to change the interdependent curriculum experience of teachers and students.

A variation of this approach involves transforming the very nature of the interaction between teachers and their students. In this respect, Hull[46] has conducted interesting work with students as teacher educators. In his work with secondary school teachers in England, Hull made videotapes of lessons. From the tapes, Hull's teachers selected those sections which they felt would promote reflection and discussion with students. During the next meeting of the class, the students observed and reviewed what the tape revealed. Initial tendencies to react to the novelty of viewing their peers and themselves, combined with hesitancy about commenting on the practices of their teacher, gave way to a form of 'constructive critical discourse' between students and teacher. Through extended dialogue and evaluation, students and teachers worked as 'fellow conspirators or collaborative colleagues' to define and improve their interaction. Hull concluded:

Teacher educators should take urgent steps to promote the view of teacher education as an ongoing enterprise in which teachers and pupils work

---

41. Ibid., p.108.
42. Rowland, op. cit., note 27.
43. McKelvey and Kyriacou, op. cit., note 28.
44. Joyce and Showers, op. cit., note 15.
45. Furtwengler, W. 'Reading success through involvement – implementation strategy for creating and maintaining effective schools'. Paper presented at a meeting of the American Educational Research Association, San Francisco, Calif., 1986.
46. Hull, op. cit., note 29.

together through the principles of research to refine classroom practice. Teacher education is not separate from the education of pupils, any more than understanding the processes of education is separate from 'getting educated'.[47]

In CBTD, students should increase their participation in this teacher–student partnership by being involved in recording, editing and production decisions about video or audiotapes of practice.

Another approach – altering the curriculum in use – continuously compares teachers' and students' images of their present and anticipated learning opportunities.[48] Enquiry, in this form of CBTD, should uncover the differences between teacher and student perspectives and use these discrepancies to assess and stimulate curriculum change. Culture making should approach innovations as occasions for teachers and students to reconsider and, where necessary, reconstruct life in the classroom. The imaginative energy of teacher–student partnerships should guide this community-building enterprise.[49]

Conclusion

The improvement of teacher development is not fundamentally about increased input from teachers, consistent time for consultation and follow-up, greater availability for human and financial resources, more sophisticated training strategies, or adaptive organisational structures. These changes are only important if they are part of a reconceptualisation of teacher development, which begins with teachers as the primary agents of their own development and builds from the relationships they form with students in the classroom. CBTD works within a set of conditions that makes this reconceptualisation possible.

Ultimately, the bottom-line justification for CBTD is that it should generate informed and justified improvements in classroom practices. CBTD focuses on student and teacher learning: gives control to teachers in concert with key stakeholders (especially colleagues and students); is situated within the cultural realities of the classroom: consciously combines personal, educational and social reference points, and pursues significant changes in classroom practices through considered and collaborative actions. In CBTD teachers can work alone or in concert with their colleagues and students.

47. Ibid., p.8.
48. Oldroyd and Tiller, op. cit., note 30.
49. See Rudduck, 'Introducing innovation to pupils', op. cit., note 31: Rudduck, 'Curriculum change', op. cit., note 31.

Development is stimulated by more deliberate considerations of daily experiences, intensive examinations of fundamental classroom processes, or committed efforts to changing how the classroom works.

Figure 25.4 portrays how the major modes and emphases of CBTD interact. The categories of Figures 25.1, 25.2. and 25.3 are distributed within the cells. The dotted lines indicate that the categories can overlap. For example, attending to ongoing experiences may reveal either areas for further study or directions and strategies for change. Or an action-research project introduced by an individual teacher may expand to include other teachers and students.

Figure 25.4 itself is offered as an organiser for teachers in planning, implementing and evaluating their CBTD activities. Each cell presents a conceptual strategy for the creation of activities based on who is to be involved in CBTD (the mode) and what kinds of activity are going to be involved (the emphasis). Taken together, the nine cells act as an *aide-mémoire* to the range of CBTD possibilities.

. . . Careful consideration and inclusion of each condition is necessary for CBTD, as I have defined it.

EMPHASIS

		Attending to ongoing experiences	Studying areas of importance	Implementing new practices
MODE	Teacher–Student	Sharing teaching and learning	Examining classroom phenomena	Improving what happens
	Teacher–Teacher	Building joint endeavours	Probing for meaning	Promoting collaborative development
	Teacher Alone	Constructing classroom routines	Documenting one's actions	Adapting teaching and learning strategies

Figure 25.4 Interaction of modes and emphases

In most emphases and modes, CBTD directly:

1. Centres on improving the quality of learning for students and teachers (focus).
2. Combines personally meaningful, educationally defensible and socially justifiable practices (reference points).
3. Engages in reflective, interactive and transformative experiences (action).

The intent of these three conditions, however, is not always realised. For example, the focus can easily concentrate on developing teachers and assume an impact on student learning as a consequence of changes in teaching practices, or it can concentrate on developing students while ignoring the complex connections with teacher learning. Reference points can also respond to the most immediate and visible demands and avoid the social implications of teacher development strategies. Similarly, actions can easily shift to instrumental modifications and consequently limit considerably the nature of interaction, scope of reflection and depth of transformation.[50] Rigorous efforts are necessary to resist compromises in these three conditions.

For the most part, CBTD only indirectly:

4. Occurs in the complex and changing situation of classroom life (environment).
5. Supports those who have the most influence on and stake in what happens (power).

Under their present circumstances, teachers frequently situate their development outside the classroom. For example, they plan and train for later classroom applications or think back to earlier experiences to re-examine their practices. Such prospective or retrospective strategies attend to, but do not occur within, the classroom. When the environment condition is only indirectly applied, CBTD loses the opportunity to embed improvement within the dynamic cultural realities which teachers and students share and create.

The least prevalent condition, power, is only actively present in the least prevalent mode – that of teachers and students. It is not common for teachers to share control of classroom activities and decisions with their students. Until teachers infuse their development experiences with a genuine search for partnership with students, CBTD will remain hollow and incomplete.

CBTD is not simply a change in venue from more traditional workshop or conference settings. It is not simply a shift in time, method or person. It is an alternative orientation, one which uses the five conditions I have specified to create a dynamic, contextually rich and meaningful learning environment for everyone. In particular, CBTD proposes to re-establish the importance of the classroom as the key cultural and contextual force for teacher development and teachers, in collaboration with their students, as the primary agents in that process.

---

50. Miller, J. 'Atomism, pragmatism, and holism', *Journal of Curriculum and Supervision* **1**(3), pp.175–96, 1986.

Chapter 26

Sustaining improvement through practitioner action research

Hilary Burgess

Editors' Note: This chapter picks up some of the points raised in the previous chapter. It suggests ways in which a practical, structured and realistic approach to investigating classrooms can lead to important professional insights. 'Young' teachers in this chapter means teachers of all ages who are in the early stages of their teaching career.

Can practitioner action research be used to sustain improvement in practice? Many teachers who employ action-research strategies only do so because it is part of a course leading to a qualification that will help them in their careers. Another reason may be that for a period of time they become involved in a large action-research project led by researchers who are external to the school. Action research in schools, therefore, often reflects circumstances in which teachers are under an obligation to some organisation, group or individual outside their own school (Feldman and Atkin, 1995). Few teachers, it would appear, use action research on a regular basis as a tool to help them to improve the quality of their teaching and understanding of classroom processes. However, if practitioner action research is to be of real value to teachers in terms of improving practice it needs to be embedded in what is happening inside schools. This chapter will examine how practitioner action research can be used to support teachers on a regular basis as they seek to improve the quality of teaching in their classrooms. It will begin by examining definitions of action research and the conditions required if it is to be used successfully for improving practice. Frameworks and methods of action research will be explored through examples of teachers who have conducted action-research projects. Finally, how practitioner action research can be sustained as a regular part of teachers' work will be considered.

What is action research?

There are many different forms of research and action research is only one of the ways in which educational settings can be studied and explored. The main feature of action research is that many of the activities that take place in school such as planning, teaching, evaluation and curriculum development are integral to the process of carrying out the research. Action research makes it possible to study both the processes and product of teaching, an essential characteristic for improving classroom practice. The quality of the learning outcomes will depend upon the quality of the learning processes. Action research, therefore, can add to the usual cycle of curriculum evaluation practice (plan, act, and review) to include monitoring of the process in action. The review process becomes systematically based on information gathered while the actions being evaluated were undertaken. Action research, therefore, can be seen as a spiral of self-reflection that is a continuous process.

Action research allows teachers to reflect upon their own practice in a structured and systematic way and has very close links with the notion of the reflective practitioner (Schon, 1983). A central feature of action research, therefore, is the self-evaluating practitioner in the research process. However, action research is more than self-reflection on practice as it involves drawing on relevant theory and the work of other practitioners, examining relevance for teaching, and modifying widely held ideas to fit practice in a particular context. Such a process, it can be argued, results in the emergence of the informed expert practitioner.

There have been many definitions of action research. For example, Elliott (1991) has defined it as: 'The study of a social situation with a view to improving the quality of action within it' (p.69), while Avison (1997) describes action research as an attempt to 'link theory and practice, thinking and doing, achieving both practical and research objectives' so that in fact it is 'a pragmatic approach which desires to "come to terms" with the world' (p.197). Winter (see Chapter 23 in this volume) sees action research as a professional ideal where research is an integral part of professional work. He uses the phrase 'practitioner action research' as he considers it encompasses a viable way for teachers to organise research, and an ideal that is inherent in the role of the professional worker. Practitioner action research, therefore, is an extension of the role of the teacher and not an addition to it. It is this notion of action research that I will be using in this chapter as it allows the possibility for sustaining research as part of teachers' repertoire of skills for improving their practice.

Why should action research be part of teachers' repertoire of skills? It can be argued that action research allows teachers to make use of the knowledge and many experiences they already possess so that they can build on what they know rather than having to rely upon outsiders before further professional development can take place. Many teachers may be convinced that what they have to offer from their own experiences is not worthwhile and too personalised to further their professional development. However, teachers who have even only a few years' experience in the classroom will have already gained many insights into the complex nature of teaching. Recognising the value of past experiences and making use of these in terms of career development has often been linked to ages and stages in adult development (Oja, 1989) and many factors, including cultural, societal and personal values and aspirations, will have an influence. Oja identifies two broad perspectives that can be used to examine developmental growth in adults. She describes these as life age/cycle theorists and cognitive-developmental stage theorists. The life age/cycle perspective argues that growth occurs through predictable life events and maintaining social and interpersonal roles and relationships. The cognitive-development stage theorists describe events as making transformations in the way adults construct and make meaning of experience. However, both these ways of thinking about adult development may have something to offer young teachers planning professional development. Each perspective recognises the early to late twenties as a period of getting out into the world and finding one's place in the teaching profession. It is a period of time when commitments may shift, and others in the form of mentors, can play a very significant role (see Chapter 10 in this volume). Oja's own research from the action-research project that she undertook on change in schools (ARCS – Action Research on Change in Schools) indicated the willingness of beginning teachers to be involved in the project but that their concerns were more focused upon their own classroom practice. She concludes that where teachers can feel supported in new learning they are willing to take risks and respond to challenges to improve their teaching thus enabling continued professional development. How young teachers can come to terms with their professional uncertainty is illustrated through an example from Dadds (1995) who quotes an excerpt from a teacher who had to take on the responsibility of teaching two handicapped children in her mainstream class. The teacher had many doubts about teaching children with special needs and used this as an opportunity to carry out an action-research project to explore the experiences of handicapped pupils in a mainstream school. The teacher commented:

One evening last year, when I got home, I wrote this. It's Monday the 12th, 11.40, and I had to deal with my first fit with Darren. Maria was not around, and it was an event which I knew I would eventually have to cope with. It was not a bad one and Darren did not flail. The first indication was that one of the children called out 'Please miss, Darren's having a fit'. His arm had become oddly shaped and he began to work his mouth, and his eyes stared. I knew the object was to get him into the recovery position.

But he's heavy and I can feel my heart racing. I feel flushed. The children are watching to see how I am going to cope. Actually getting him down is a great physical effort. I eventually do it with the help of the children who help me with his legs. I know I must remember to keep his air passage clear and his head to one side. I talk to him all the time. I'm half kneeling on one side of him with his weight on my other leg. He is out, gurgling rhythmically to himself for about three-quarters of a minute. It seems much longer. He begins to come round, and immediately wants to get up. This is a struggle because he is still very unsteady. After a fit I knew that Darren generally likes to sleep. Another member of staff relieves me and takes him away. I immediately feel exhausted. I feel a weakness in one of my legs after the weight of Darren on it. But I am a little elated. I've got through the first one and it felt like a hurdle I knew I would have to take. He had come out of it okay. I felt a bit pleased with myself and relieved. I knew that if it happened again, I could do it again.

(Dadds, 1995, pp.55–6)

As Dadds comments: 'Here is professional development in the making; alive, emotive, knowledgeable, dangerous, committed, human' (Dadds, 1995, pp.55–6). This kind of professional development cannot come from attending courses outside school. The professional learning experience this teacher gains, comes from dealing with the situation in practice and thinking through afterwards what happened and how she felt. It demonstrates the researcher role and the teacher role fusing into one as the committed teacher investigates not only what occurred but also how she and the other pupils responded to the event.

The value of school-based professional development is clearly recognised in the DfEE document *Learning and Teaching* (DfEE, 2001) where the Secretary of State for Education reports that the intention is to 'build the capacity of all schools to become professional learning communities and manage time for professional development effectively. We will identify and share the excellent practice that already exists, and work to understand better the conditions that lead to this excellent practice' (p.7). Such a statement suggests the possibility of moving away from what many educationalists have seen as a delivery model of teaching where the teacher is viewed as a technician who is there to implement curriculum reform introduced by outside policies. If teachers are to seize this opportunity to have an input into curriculum development and pupil learning in their own classrooms then they will need the right kind of conditions in school to support such work as well as the skills required to undertake practitioner action research.

Supportive contexts for practitioner research

What conditions will support teachers' involvement in practitioner action research? The first condition would appear to be the disposition of the action researcher who needs to have a commitment to improving his own practice, a willingness to question and consider alternatives, a willingness to be responsible for his actions and intentions and sufficient confidence in his own ability as a source of improvement (Stevenson, 1995). However, many factors may affect commitment and motivation, such as, personal life experiences, career and the prevailing culture of the school.

Institutional contexts can influence attitudes of teachers and determine whether the time and space is available for the professional development of young teachers. Stevenson has argued that there needs to be both a 'framework and a language for expressing assumptions, beliefs, ideas and value commitments, and an analytical framework for guiding reflection, critique, and the search for alternative possibilities for practice. Without a language of critique for examining educational claims and an ability to articulate alternatives, the result can be a willingness to accept the status quo' (p.202).

He goes on to conclude that action research attempts to integrate self-reflection on individual intentions and practices and the consequences of those practices. The process of continuous reflection and subsequent revised planning and action occurs through conversations with both the self and others. Individuals, therefore, become responsive to situations and think reflexively about their teaching. What does being reflexive mean?

Reflexivity can be defined as 'a particular dialectic between the research project as a constructed entity, and how people participate in constructing it, especially the researchers' (Tripp, 1998, p.39). In practitioner action research the results of reflection are continuously transformed into practice and the practice continuously provides reasons for reflection and development of these practical theories. This characteristic aspect of action research is called reflexivity. Weaknesses in practical theories are slowly detected and useful action strategies emerge from the constant movement between action and reflection (Altrichter *et al.*, 1993).

The kinds of conditions that will enable both individuals and groups to be reflexive in their teaching require a language and framework for analysis at both the individual and institutional level and a community that encourages practitioner enquiry alongside personal and collaborative support (see Burgess, Chapter 10, in this volume). Practitioners will also need to understand the methods of action research and develop their skills in this area if it is to become an effective tool for professional development.

Developing skills in practitioner action research

Practitioners regularly reflect on and work to improve their practice. Action research has the same purpose and yet it is not a replacement but rather a means of enhancing the skills teachers already have, by enabling them to work through everyday problems. It provides methods for studying and improving practice in a systematic, rigorous and a collaborative way (Stevenson, 1995). The methods that can be used in action research can be both objective and subjective. In this chapter I am going to focus upon three methods that I believe are central to effective practitioner action research. These are, keeping a reflective journal, observation, and using conversational interview strategies. In discussing these methods of action research I will also be considering the ethical issues involved in their use. Discussion of a wide range of other methods can be found in several sources (MacIntyre, 2000; McNiff *et al.*, 1996; McKernan, 1991; McNiff, 1988).

The research journal

Many approaches to research advocate keeping a record of the research process in the form of a log, research diary, journal, field notes, or audiotapes. Does it matter what kind of record is kept? Holly and McLoughlin (1989) distinguish between keeping a log, diary or a journal in the following way. A log, they suggest, is a record of what happened that is unencumbered by interpretation. It is not purely for personal use and facts are recorded systematically to provide objective data about the event being studied. A diary records personal experiences and observations over a period of time. It contains spontaneous forms of writing and although many have been published it is usually a very personal document about the writer's feelings and daily life. Journals are similar to both in that they can include facts and personal and spontaneous thoughts. Holly and McLoughlin argue that the journal is written with the intention of returning to it, to learn from interpretation of what it contains, and in this way it is distinctively different from either a log or a diary.

Journals used in practitioner action research can be one of the most important research methods that teachers can employ. Viewed as a companion to the whole process and not just as a way of collecting and recording data, it can help to build on everyday skills and is often easier to organise than any other research method. It can be carried around and picked up and used without having to pre-plan and make the sort of special arrangements that interviewing or other methods require. Unstructured observation notes can be immediately jotted down in the journal alongside ideas about research issues, thus providing continuity in the research process. Keeping a journal in this way will ensure that data collection is not artificially separated from analysis and reflection.

In particular, the use of journals has been noted by some teachers as central to their professional growth when kept over a period of time. As one teacher commented of her journal keeping:

> When I first began writing, I cited mainly those things about teaching that were not to my satisfaction. When I look back I was very disenchanted about where I was as a teacher and my enthusiasm as a teacher. I had thought many times about leaving this profession . . . just to get a break from the many demands that teachers receive from students, administrators, parents and the community.
> (Holly and McLoughlin, 1989, pp.272–3)

A journal, therefore, is a personal document, a record of events, feelings and thoughts that have relevance for the writer. It can record a mass of data and alert teachers to developing thought as well as progression or lack of progression in pupil learning. A journal captures the feelings and beliefs about individual lessons and events as they occur without the distortion of past recollections (McKernan, 1991).

There are, however, both advantages and disadvantages to keeping journals as one primary teacher found:

> Once the decision had been made, everything was data. It had its advantages and disadvantages. The main advantage is that I have been able to form a far wider perception of the gender issues in general, both inside and outside school. The main disadvantage is that it becomes a way of life. I found I couldn't stop collecting data. Every event or happening has been viewed as data collection, even the recent Funday!
> (Dadds, 1995, p.64)

The data gathering became all consuming for this teacher as she recognised that her journal could 'seep into parts of life that other methods fail to reach' (Dadds, p.64).

Journals, therefore, can be powerful action-research tools. Where they are returned to and shared with colleagues they can be valuable in stimulating further reflection, analysis and discussion. Journals can also help the action researcher to identify topics for close scrutiny through observation and informal interview.

Conversational interviews

In social research many forms of interviewing can be used, from formal, tightly structured interviews, semi-structured interviews to informal conversational interviews. I have chosen to focus upon the latter as within the process of action research the conversational interview appears to offer the most flexible way of working for teachers and is sympathetic to the way collaboration informs and is part of action research.

Conversational interviews can develop from notes made in a journal, or an everyday conversation begun in the staffroom. They can access the thoughts, attitudes and opinions that lie behind behaviour and the perceptions of individuals (Altrichter *et al.*, 1993). For example, a pupil may perceive behaviour viewed as disruptive by the teacher, entirely differently. The conversational interview can provide access to the perceptions of both pupils and teachers in a way that observational methods are not able to do. It is, however, important to be aware of the limitations of conversational interviews as they will only reveal what the interviewee wishes to be known. They are also dependent on the interpretations individuals place upon events and situations at the time they occur. Some respondents may withhold information for reasons known only to themselves. Setting up the right conditions for conversational interviews is particularly important and not easy to achieve in a school as one action researcher, reported by Dadds (1995, p.45), discovered.

> She explained that the two teacher interviews 'took place before school' and she felt it worth commenting that there was 'hence the lack of background noise'. Here was improved sensitivity to the contextual constraints of interviewing. The noisy lesson which had gone on alongside the interviews in the first research project had been borne in mind. On the other hand, Vicki also mentioned the relative brevity of these interviews in the second study. This may have been the price paid for peace and quiet gained before lessons as colleagues gave precious, but limited, time. Here, Vicki may have been continuing to discover the roundabouts and swings of small-scale, insider research.

Background noise and brevity of time are not the only issues that may affect the right conditions for an interview. Other factors such as the level of content and relationship between interviewee and interviewer may affect the outcome of the data collected. For example, teacher interviews with pupils will be affected by the previous relationship that has been built up and issues of trust, affection or animosity will play a part in the conversation.

In terms of analysing both journal and conversational interviews, the role of the critical friend is central to the analysis of action research and can also be mutually supportive. The critical friend may be another teacher or group of teachers in the school, the tutor, or another teacher outside the school. The conversation needs to be a two-way process so that a dialogue between action researcher and critical friend emerges. Conversations which focus on data, or extracts from a journal, or observations, can make the interchanges powerful and be a useful political tool in a department in a secondary school or small primary school. Brenda Spencer (1993) described her methods and how she used a critical friend in her action-research project on formulating a school policy on assessment for young children.

> The methods of fact finding, data gathering and evaluation that I used in my research have depended largely on descriptive accounts by individuals working in a small school. The data gathering for the purposes of monitoring took several forms: staff responses to an initial questionnaire about their assessment practices; minutes and tape recordings of meetings; recorded discussions with a critical friend; draft and final documentation about policy; and a reflective diary. Where possible I used the method of triangulation: getting a picture of the same event from different sources of evidence.
>
> The personal reflective diary and the opportunity to discuss issues with my critical friend were key factors in my evaluation of the work. The diary contained the plans, agenda and record of staff's contributions. The evolution of my ideas of how the project should progress is delineated. Finally my own personal reflections on the conduct of each meeting gives an additional perspective on the situation.
>
> (Spencer, 1993, p.83)

This statement encapsulates the range of methods used by the teacher in her action-research project with young children. In particular, it identifies the value of keeping a reflective diary, or journal and the crucial role that a critical friend can play. Opening the data to others can enable all the participants to engage in the story revealed by the information.

Observational strategies

Observation is part of the normal process of teaching as teachers observe individual pupils and groups of pupils working in many learning contexts. However, most action resulting from the daily observations of teachers in lessons is based on intuition and often unfocused. More systematic observation can overcome the diffuseness of completely unstructured observation and also helps to prevent bias in the collection of data.

Teachers engaged in action research are likely to be at the centre of action so it is useful to invite other teachers to become engaged in the process and work collaboratively on the project. Such collaboration can be valuable in developing strategies for teachers to use on a regular basis, as Janet Mulholland's account of an action-research project on pupil assessment in a primary school shows:

> we began to pilot a method of whole child observation which we considered would be very helpful in informing the assessment procedure that was due to be installed. There were several problems associated with this. We all agreed that in the first few instances observations were difficult to complete. Diversions in particular were difficult to ignore. We agreed that stopping at the designated time was often hard. Frequently we became too interested to see what would happen next. We found that the children were usually aware that they were being watched. We were not able to make notes without arousing curiosity, either of the subject child, or others in the area, or both. . . .
>
> It was important to observe children in a variety of situations and on different days. This was highlighted for me in a series of observations that I undertook on one boy who was bright, intelligent and co-operative in most situations but when crossed exhibited quite different characteristics. Had I relied on the evidence of two of the observations alone this would not have been picked up. We discussed the need to sustain evidence of the success or failure of any intervention procedures. This was important to highlight changes or progress in the passage of time. I believe that knowing the children well is not achieved by a one off investigation but by a constantly reviewed and renewed process.
>
> (Mulholland, 1993, p.65)

Teachers working together to design their own observation schedule, or make notes over set periods of time, have the advantage that it is designed to suit the type of action-research project being pursued. However, it is important to be clear about the purpose of the observation and what it is being used to reveal. Decisions about what kind of action is important to observe and what are less relevant data are important to decide before the observations begin. An essential ethical decision, of course, is how the data from the observations will be used.

Ethical issues permeate every aspect of an action-research project and the use of journals, conversational interviews and observations will all bring ethical dilemmas that teachers will need to resolve. Teachers conducting action research will need to consider many of the following questions. What are the effects of the method of data collection? Are conclusions supported by proper evidence? Can confidentiality be assured? Is the practitioner researcher taking advantage of a position of power within the school? Is the action research authentic to the concerns of participants? None of these are easy questions to address and all need careful consideration by practitioners conducting action research. Further in-depth discussion and analysis of ethical issues can be found in several texts on action research (McNiff *et al.*, 1996; Altrichter *et al.*, 1993; Burgess, R. G., 1989).

Journals, conversational interviews and observation all hold possibilities as methods of research that can be sustained by teachers over a period of time. They are all adaptable to the daily life of busy practitioners and all provide rich sources of data that can lead to action in terms of curriculum development and pupil learning in the classroom. For teachers in the early stages of their career in school they can be dynamic tools for finding out more about classroom processes and furthering individual and collaborative professional development.

Sustaining practitioner action research

At the beginning of this chapter I suggested that few teachers voluntarily engaged in action research without the stimulus of an external researcher or a course of study leading to a qualification. I have tried to show the value of teachers undertaking action research on a regular basis through the discussion of methods and examples of other teachers involved in action-research projects. Action research as an effective tool for professional development needs to be seen as intrinsically desirable and not extrinsically inspired (Feldman and Atkin, 1995) to work successfully for teachers in schools. The action-research agenda needs to be that of the teachers if it is to be a self-sustaining enterprise. As Goodson (1992) argues, it is important to know about teachers' priorities and careers if professional development in schools is to be understood. He uses the analogy of a folklorist who realised that it was the people who sang the songs who were more important than the songs themselves. This seems an important concept to bear in mind when focusing upon the developing practice of young teachers. The vulnerability that teachers can feel when analysing aspects of their classroom practice needs to be handled sensitively by those who collaborate with them in action-research projects. In addition, a sense of developing professionalism needs to be recognised by those involved if practitioner action research is to be self-sustaining.

Inner motivation, however, does not necessarily bring with it clarity about the processes of practitioner action research which has been described by Cook (1998) as a very 'messy' procedure. In particular, writing up can be problematic as teachers struggle with the sanitised accounts of published research, trying to match their own misshapen and untidy data to these systematic and organised texts. If there are mechanisms within schools to facilitate studying the results of other teachers' work, young teachers will be able to share and articulate their developing needs in their own professional development.

Professional learning is not simply a matter of applying the theories of others to practice in schools. It is about the complex relationship of knowing and doing. It is about asking questions, analysing and interpreting feedback, and changing established practice. It is about retaining a professional curiosity in the learning of pupils. Sustaining improvement through practitioner action research is an emotional as well as an intellectual journey and a challenge to all those who wish to have a stake in the future of teaching in primary and secondary schools.

References

Altrichter, H., Posch, P. and Somekh, B. (1993) *Teachers Investigate their own Work: An introduction to the methods of action research*. London: Routledge.

Avison, D. E. (1997) 'Action research in information systems', in McKenzie, G., Powell, J. and Usher, R. *Understanding Social Research: Perspectives on Methodology and Practice*. London: Falmer Press.

Burgess, R. G. (ed.) (1989) *The Ethics of Educational Research*. Lewes: Falmer Press.

Cook, T. (1998) 'The importance of mess in action research', *Educational Action Research* **6**(1), 93–109.

Dadds, M. (1995) *Passionate Enquiry and School Development: A Story about Teacher Action Research*. London: Falmer Press.

Department for Education and Employment (DfEE) (2001) *Learning and Teaching: A Strategy for professional development*. London: DfEE.

Elliott, J. (1991) *Action Research for Educational Change*. Buckingham: Open University Press.

Feldman, A. and Atkin, M. (1995) 'Embedding action research in professional practice', in Noffke, S. E. and Stevenson, R. B. (eds) *Educational Action Research: Becoming Practically Critical*. New York: Teachers' College Press.

Goodson, I. F. (1992) 'Sponsoring the teacher's voice: teachers' lives and teacher development', in Hargreaves, A. and Fullan, M. G. (eds) *Understanding Teacher Development*. London: Cassell.

Holly, M. L. H. and McLoughlin, C. S. (1989) 'Professional development and journal writing', in Holly, M. L. and McLoughlin, C. S. (eds) *Perspectives on Teacher Professional Development*. Lewes: Falmer Press.

MacIntyre, C. (2000) *The Art of Action Research in the Classroom*. London: David Fulton Publishers.

McKernan, J. (1991) *Curriculum Action Research: A Handbook of Methods and Resources for the Reflective Practitioner*. London: Kogan Page.

McNiff, J. (1988) *Action Research: Principles and Practice*. London: Macmillan.

McNiff, J., Lomax, P. and Whitehead, J. (1996) *You and Your Action Research Project*. London: Routledge/Falmer.

Mulholland, J. (1993) 'Observing pupils and listening to parents: aspects of a primary school policy on pupil assessment', in Lomax, P. and Jones, C. (eds) *Developing Primary Schools through Action Research*. Bournemouth: Hyde Publications.

Oja, S. N. (1989) 'Teachers: ages and stages of adult development', in Holly, M. L. and McLoughlin, C. S. (eds) *Perspectives on Teacher Professional Development*. Lewes: Falmer Press.

Schon, D. (1983) *The Reflective Practitioner: How Professionals Think in Action*. New York: Basic Books.

Spencer, B. (1993) 'Formulating a whole school policy on assessment for 3–8 year old children', in Lomax, P. and Jones, C. (eds) *Developing Primary Schools through Action Research*. Bournemouth: Hyde Publications.

Stevenson, R. B. (1995) 'Action research and supportive school contexts: exploring the possibilities for transformation', in Noffke, S. E. and Stevenson, R. B. (eds) *Educational Action Research: Becoming Practically Critical*. New York: Teachers' College Press.

Tripp, D. (1998) 'Critical incidents in action enquiry', in Shacklock, G. and Smith, J. (eds) *Being Reflexive in Critical Educational and Social Research*. London: Falmer Press.

Chapter 27

Exploring the value of action-research methodologies: three case studies

Jane Devereux, Ian Eyres and Mike Price

Editors' Note: Practitioner action research can take a number of forms and is appropriate to teachers throughout their career. This is illustrated by examples in this chapter.

The three case studies described in this chapter provide real accounts of practitioner research work undertaken by teachers at different stages of their professional career. Each is an account of teachers engaging in action research in their own school. All of the studies enable one to experience the excitement, dilemmas and challenges that are encountered when working in this way. Winter (1988) makes a useful point about how research, written up as case studies, can have a general applicability to those working in different contexts. He argues that they have the form of a plurality of 'voices' and writers can organise the data to bring out the discrepancies and contradictions. The material can be presented as a story that does not require the reader to accept it, but anticipates a continuing analytical response from the reader who is therefore, in one sense, a collaborator in the research process. Such a process is true to practitioner action research as a procedure for encouraging professional development.

Each case study presents a brief outline of the research question, the methodology(ies) used, and the outcomes, interspersed with reflections on the process. Across all the case studies a wide range of issues are raised, some critical and difficult to address. These honest accounts are presented very differently but this reflects the different settings, the level and size of the particular research.

Case studies, as Cohen and Manion (1994) suggest, have several advantages that make them attractive to educational researchers. Their strength is that they:

- are based in reality;
- allow some generalisations within the context;
- recognise the complexity of social situations;

- provide rich descriptive material that can be revisited often for reinterpreting;
- are a 'step into action';
- present research or evaluation data in a more publicly accessible form. (Adapted from Cohen and Manion, 1994, p.123)

These accounts, though modest in scale, each incorporate a discussion of the above dimensions. In particular, they will allow those about to undertake some kind of action research to anticipate events and difficulties at the planning stage of their own small-scale research or investigation.

Two of the case studies are based in primary and early years settings and examine literacy and questioning skills respectively. The third concerns the teaching of mathematics and is based in the secondary sector. The teachers involved in the case studies range from a recently qualified teacher to an experienced deputy head, and the context of the case studies ranges from one teacher working with two nursery nurses to a two-school, collaboratively organised project.

Case Study 1 describes an experienced teacher, working with her colleagues to reduce the discrepancy between the numbers of children attaining National Curriculum level 4 in reading and writing at the end of Key Stage 2 (KS2). Critical to this study is the use of a range of data collected at various points to enable her to evaluate, reflect on and modify practice.

Case Study 2 is one teacher's attempt to explore her own questioning skills and those of her nursery nurses. They were particularly concerned about their use of 'open' and 'closed' questions as part of their interactions and how productive these were in terms of extending and challenging children's ideas and learning. As they set about their work they became aware of many other facets that impinged on this seemingly straightforward research question. Aspects of practitioner action research that are particularly significant in this study include the importance of shared understandings when working with colleagues, using common instruments for gathering evidence and validating such evidence and its interpretation.

Case Study 3 is a collaborative mathematics project across two contrasting secondary schools. It explores the development of effective use of two-line scientific calculators at KS3. Issues raised relate to the nature of 'proper' evidence to support conclusions, the authenticity of action research to the concerns of participants and the limitations of involvement in small-scale curriculum development projects as contexts for practitioner research.

Case Study 1

By Ian Eyres

Improving writing standards at Key Stage 2

Introduction

At the time of the study, the teacher, a deputy, was unit leader for Years 5 and 6, coordinating the work of three vertically grouped classes in a primary school in Cambridge. She had been at the school for two years when she undertook this work. The school was a large (370 on roll plus 50 nursery children) primary school with an intake very diverse in terms of both ethnic and socio-economic factors. An OFSTED inspection in 1998 found the school to have serious weaknesses, particularly in the areas of planning and monitoring and evaluation and all the school's staff had been working hard since that time to ensure a more favourable judgement at the next inspection. In undertaking this study the teacher had the twin purposes of developing an aspect of the curriculum, together with the way it is managed within school and of developing her own role and expertise.

The study

The area chosen to work within was literacy. The project period was within the National Literacy Strategy's (NLS) implementation phase. In particular, one of the targets within the school's 1999–2001 development plan was to reduce the discrepancy between the numbers of children attaining National Curriculum level 4 in reading and writing at the end of KS2. In the 1999 end of Key Stage tests, 98 per cent of Year 6 (Y6) children attained level 4 for reading, while the comparable figure for writing was only 57 per cent.

The decision as to how to make progress in this area was the result of ongoing discussions in a number of forums. The raising of standards was (in part thanks to OFSTED) high on the school's agenda, and therefore a frequent theme within staff meetings, meetings of the Senior Management Team, and the weekly unit planning meetings. The teacher took part in all of these, often in a leading role. The school also had regular support from one of the county's literacy consultants. However, most detailed discussions took place within the Y5/6 unit, as this is where the particular teaching strategies were to be implemented.

In working on this project there was an unusual amount of 'hard' data to deal with, principally the children's texts (including past test answers) and records of assessments, and this gave a starting point. An initial analysis of the 1999 writing tests (in part guided by the QCA's analysis (QCA, 1999a)) enabled her, together with her two colleagues, to identify seven strategies:

- teaching of handwriting outside the literacy hour;
- implementation of the NLS Key Stage 2 spelling programme;
- more teaching time spent on narrative rather than non-narrative writing;
- increased emphasis on learning outcomes in every aspect of lesson planning and teaching;
- use of guided group times to evaluate children's writing against learning objectives;
- setting of individual writing targets for children;
- regular spelling and handwriting homework.

Since the stated aim of the project was to achieve a quantitative improvement in outcomes at the end of Key Stage assessment, in a narrow sense the only indicator of success would be the May 2000 results. However, any view of educational innovation as 'implementation' at the start of the year and seeing the results at the end would be, to say the very least, naive! Throughout the year the three colleagues were able to make ongoing observations and evaluations, modifying their approach where appropriate. Often these observations were the subject of informal discussions as well as the subject of formal unit meetings. During the year, certain features became apparent.

- Strategy elements closely linked to the assessment process were having an effect. For example, it had been noted that, in 1998, several children had fallen below the threshold for level 4 by only a few marks, and that attention to spelling and handwriting might make the necessary difference. The strategy of giving separate and specific attention to these two areas of learning showed positive results early in the year.
- Children were seeing their own progress. Perhaps the most obvious example of this is in the area of spelling, where a focus on commonly made errors meant that in some children's writing the overall proportion of errors within a given text fell significantly in a relatively short space of time. Making learning objectives specific helped many children towards assessing their own progress within a lesson. The teacher's observation that more able children were beginning to make reference to these, led to a strategy of pairing children for the revision stage of writing. Children pursued their individual targets with some enthusiasm, and although there had been a concern that this strategy might reduce children's sense of ownership in their writing, this did not appear to be the case.

Unfortunately, demands on teacher time both during and outside the literacy hour meant that it was impossible to give children adequate personal feedback and the strategy was modified to a more manageable one based on group targets.

- Teachers felt that they were gaining greater control over what the children were learning. The more explicit use of learning objectives, shared with the children, and the separate foci on spelling, handwriting and writing made assessment and self-assessment much easier, to the point where with some children it became automatic. Feedback on writing within the guided writing sessions allowed further reinforcement of objectives.

It would be easy to describe the development of these strategies as unproblematic. With hindsight, all appear (eventually at least) to have led smoothly to practice supporting higher attainment. However, there lies beneath all these initiatives the scope for a tension between an emphasis (in the name of public accountability) on achieving higher numerical scores for the school, and a need to meet the learning needs of individual children. This tension, which emerged fairly often in unit meetings, may have been intensified by colleagues' perception of the teacher's role in a senior management team responsible for target setting. Although the effect of all this could easily have been negative, the ever present challenge to justify strategies on the grounds that they genuinely supported children's learning led all three teachers to observe children closely in lessons and to assess their writing carefully. At the same time the teachers sought to refine and optimise their own practice in the process.

Strategies for gathering evidence during the project involved the collection of all relevant documents – mainly assessment data (including samples of children's writing) and minutes and notes taken at meetings where work in progress was discussed. The teacher was then able to draw on these when writing her final report. With hindsight, she regrets not keeping a journal during the project period. Due to this omission, some detail in her account has inevitably been lost, in particular data on the kinds of reflective and critical discussions held with colleagues and of the observations made of children's learning. What is beyond doubt, however, is that these critical discussions and observations did indeed influence the progress of the work at every step. It is also clear that it was far from the case that the teacher was working alone. As well as interrogating her proposed innovations, colleagues both within the Y5/6 unit and across the school were able to share examples of their own practice with her too.

Conclusion

At a time when primary teachers across England were getting to grips with a new, or at least newly formulated, framework for teaching literacy, learning for this teacher, in this area, was reinforced both through examination of her own practice and through regular discussion with expert colleagues. These experts were the school's literacy coordinator (herself involved in ongoing NLS training) and the county's literacy consultant.

As an exercise in professional development the teacher's view was that her research was very effective. Unlike the case of out of school courses, everything she learnt was of direct relevance to the context of her own classroom. Much was of relevance to the wider school too, so that 'cascading' her new knowledge was at once less necessary and more easy to achieve – no one could say that it wouldn't work! Evidence for its success as a school improvement strategy is supported both by OFSTED's judgement that 'very good progress has been made in raising standards in reading and writing' (OFSTED, 2000) and by the numerical data. In 2000 the end of Key Stage 2 tests showed that the gap between reading and writing scores had reduced from 41 per cent to 21 per cent.

Like much of the agenda for primary schools in the opening years of the twenty-first century, this research was driven by quantitative considerations. Statistical targets, however, can only be achieved by qualitative developments in the classroom and its reflection on these which is at the heart of this study.

Case Study 2

By Jane Devereux

Investigating the types of interaction between early years practitioners and children in particular areas of the nursery

Introduction

This case study is an account of some work undertaken by a teacher in her third year of teaching while on a Certificate of Professional Practice course at her local Higher Education Institute (HEI).

Her reasons for undertaking this research (apart from providing data for her end of course assignment), arose out of concern that some days she seemed to spend a lot of time organising and controlling the children rather than spending that time for teaching and learning. As a newly qualified teacher, she had tried to use open-ended questions and thought her questioning technique was satisfactory. However, the arrival of an eager newly qualified nursery nurse, who appeared to be skilled at asking children a range of questions, made her think about her own interactions. At one of their weekly planning sessions, the new nursery nurse asked about approaches to supporting children as they worked on their own interests and projects. The teacher was interested in what prompted her to ask such a question. The response that the nursery nurse had not really heard much questioning of children about what they were doing, had at first shocked the teacher. But on reflection, she felt she could not say categorically whether open-ended questioning (or any form of questioning) was, or was not, a frequent teaching strategy in the nursery.

The action-research process

Defining the question and planning the approach

After some discussion with her line manager, and her tutor on the HEI course, the teacher decided to explore exactly what kind of interactions were taking place. Having recently attended a one-day, in-service course on questioning and science in the nursery, she saw an opportunity to investigate, through exploring science, whether or not her personal anxieties were founded. Her first step was to revisit some of the materials she had received on her INSET day and notes from her PGCE course. Second, she spoke briefly with her team to ascertain their interest and willingness to participate in collecting evidence. Third, she consulted her head teacher to negotiate time for planning. The head suggested that the teacher and her team of three adults should conduct an initial study with the children in a range of settings, including outside in the garden and in the playground. Their aim was to see if interactions were predominantly organisational and instructional rather than open and challenging, and time would be built in on the next training day for them to plan the initial investigation.

As a team, they decided to observe and record all questions asked by staff but limit their data collection to four areas of the nursery in the first instance and to use three ways of doing this. The areas chosen were the writing area, water tray, the role-play area inside, and outside they focused on the digging area. Every Tuesday and Thursday afternoon there were two extra adults in the nursery, which made it an ideal time to release one adult to gather data.

Before they began to work on all four areas a draft observation schedule was designed and tried out by each member of staff observing children working with an adult while using the sand tray. Each of the staff had one attempt at observation over a ten-day period. A meeting at the end of this time allowed all to share the experience of being watched and watching each other.

Some interpersonal tensions were felt at this meeting. All participants felt threatened by being watched so closely by colleagues as well as being concerned about their ability to record data using the schedule.

Differences in the way each recorded the information were raised and a second simpler schedule was designed to overcome these problems (see Figure 27.1) The new schedule required the observer to record the type of question, and to do it in units of time.

A timetable for observation was drawn up and agreed with the head.

Gathering data

The next few weeks were busy and two out of the ten observation sessions had to be forfeited because of visitors to the school and staff illness. Notes were made about the context and nature of the activities in which the children were involved.

This phase of observation provided a mass of information that needed analysis. Each person was observed at least twice and had the same number of attempts at observing. The observation sheets were stored until the Easter break.

Analysing the data

Over the Easter break the teacher spent some time collating and analysing the data. From the information she was able draw a graph to show the frequency of questions in relation to the variety of questions/interactions. The results showed that, to their surprise, there was considerable questioning taking

Type of Question	Date: Context: Observer:			
	1st 5 minutes	2nd 5 minutes	3rd 5 minutes	4th 5 minutes
Open	✓✓✓	✓	✓	✓✓
Closed	✓✓✓ ✓✓✓	✓✓✓✓✓	✓✓✓	✓✓✓✓✓ ✓✓

Figure 27.1 Observation schedule

place. It was most frequent at the beginning of the afternoon sessions and was particularly strong in the 'water' and 'writing' areas. The analysis of their questions showed that, in fact, they asked a range of different types of questions but the majority were short, focused questions that did not allow children to express their own ideas, but rather expected them to guess the answer in the teacher's head. Open-ended questions were less frequent, but tended to be used more in the role-play area and outside. Within the 'writing area' and the 'water area' the questions were more mixed, with a higher proportion of tighter organisational questions. The graphs were shared with the team and several informal discussions took place exploring the implications for their practice.

At this stage the deputy head provided some useful comments on the investigation. She contacted one of her friends who had a particular interest in questioning in science, who worked at a local HEI. This led to the group, particularly the teacher, reading some of the literature in this area (Harlen and Jelly, 1997; de Boo, 1999; Harlen, 2000). This unexpected diversion meant that the original timetable slipped but the value of their reading helped to refine and inform their evaluation of the data gathered.

Evaluation

With hindsight it was felt that researching the literature and talking with more experienced colleagues at the beginning of the investigation would have perhaps helped them shorten the overall timescale. If they had read some of the literature on action research (for example, MacIntyre, 2000), they may have had less difficulty designing their observation schedule. Another benefit may have been an increased and shared understanding of different question types that would have helped when observing. As it was, much of the learning about different types of question, and the ability to identify them in action, was developed 'on the hoof' as they undertook the observations. Several questions worthy of further investigation arose from this very small-scale study, some of which were taken up over the following few weeks by her team. For example:

- Why were more open-ended questions asked in certain areas of the nursery?
- Did people work differently with the children in these areas?
- Did they have different expectations of the children in the different areas that limited their approach to the children?
- Was their own knowledge of the kind of things children might need to know or be able to do, sufficient for these different areas?
- Were all the staff equally able to ask open and closed questions? If not, what can be done to help develop these skills?

- Does the kind of provision and the way it is presented to the children limit the need or opportunity for open-ended questioning?

Subsequently the group spent some time on developing their ability to form open-ended questions and, after a term of working on their skills, observed each other again. The results showed that there was more consistency between the team in the number of open-ended questions they asked and where they asked them.

During the next stage of their research they chose to explore the factors that affected the kind of interaction they wanted to encourage in the different teaching spaces in the nursery. This time they were more cautious and spent some time trying to define the problem with the help of a literature search, and through discussion with more experienced colleagues to help inform their discussions.

Conclusion

A successful project was completed by the teacher. She obtained her certificate and the nursery team developed a culture of sharing and questioning their day-to-day teaching that built upon their individual strengths, and their growing confidence to be constructively critical about their practice.

Case Study 3

By Mike Price

Making effective use of two-line scientific calculators in mathematics at Key Stage 3

Introduction

This case study will address two principal themes:

1. The potential of external 'steering' and collaboration between schools to support classroom-focused enquiries.
2. The possible limitations of involvement in a collaborative curriculum development project as a setting for individual practitioner action research.

The study is written from the perspective of the principal 'steerer' and the evaluation is informed by interview data from the heads of the two mathematics departments involved.

Background and motivation for the project

A wide-ranging review of research in mathematics education (Askew and Wiliam, 1995, p.30) has concluded: 'Calculators can improve both performance and attitude.' This research principally concerned younger pupils' use of basic four-function calculators. However, a subsequent review of research into calculator use at Key Stages 1–3 highlighted 'a lack of relevant evidence on the secondary phase' (SCAA, 1997). This review also concluded:

> There are indications that, while schools acknowledge the need to train pupils to make effective and considered use of calculators, they may not be according this sufficiently high priority.
> (p.35)

In the 1990s there have been *two* major technological advances in calculator development: graphic calculators with visual display screens and two-line scientific calculators with editing facilities. For graphic calculators, research and development has focused on their educational potential, initially for post-16 mathematics but also, more recently, for Key Stages 3–4 (Ruthven, 1996). However, the potential of two-line scientific calculators has been relatively neglected.

Two-Line Calculator Project plan

The initial conception of this project was the author's, a university teacher and education consultant, and a project action plan was negotiated with the education manager of a leading calculator manufacturer. The commercial imperative for involvement in such a project was the production of a substantial professional development resource for national dissemination (see Price, 2001). But, in the process of developing such a resource, systematic enquiry involving practising teachers, both in the classroom and in team discussions, formed an integral part of the project plan.

The project team comprised the two steerers and four volunteer mathematics teachers from two contrasting secondary schools: the head of department and an assistant teacher from an 11–16 city school and an 11–14 suburban high school. Both the departments were well known to the author through their involvement in school-based initial teacher training, and the two assistant teachers were both keen to explore and develop their classroom practice using this new technology. The team's work extended over a six month period and funding by the calculator manufacturer included the costs of three half day and evening meetings involving the two steerers and one teacher representative from each school. Other evaluation meetings were also held separately with the two departments, which were each provided with a class set of two-line calculators and a matching model for overhead project use. The agenda for developing effective use of these calculators was defined to focus throughout on three principal questions:

1. To what extent can the use of these calculators enrich the mathematical treatment of Key Stage 3 topics?
2. What is involved in developing pupils' keyboard skills with these calculators and how do pupils respond?
3. What is the potential of a class set of these calculators, with a matching projection model, to motivate and support whole-class interactive teaching methods?

Both the project's timetable and agenda were challenging, but the discipline of involvement served to motivate classroom experimentation and concentrate the minds of all the participants.

Progress, evidence and achievements

The first key question was investigated by reviewing existing calculator resources and National Curriculum documents for Key Stage 3, and team brainstorming of the possible range of topics and treatments. Ten different topics were identified for development in three phases:

Phase 1: Prime Factors and Formulas with Pi
Phase 2: Fractions, Percentages, Operation Priority and Metric/Imperial Conversions
Phase 3: Random Number Simulations, Sequences, Indices and Word Problem Solving.

In each phase the author took responsibility for drafting detailed lesson specifications on agreed lines, to include the main learning objectives, essential calculator facilities, suggestions for whole-class introductory and plenary work, pupil task sheets for individual or collaborative work, and possible extensions. The teachers undertook to trial each lesson with an appropriate class, to keep notes and records of pupils' responses and their own lesson evaluations, and to provide focused oral feedback in team meetings. The wide coverage of topics did not permit an iterative approach to the trial and refinement of the lesson specifications.

Over the six months all members of the team developed a strong conviction about the potential of these calculators to shape the teaching of a surprising range of Key Stage 3 topics in number, measures and algebra, as listed above. All the teacher members had previously taught these topics and made some use of calculators but the adoption of the two-line model as a *leading* tool in lessons was a major advance. The key phrase here, from one departmental head, is 'using the calculator *to teach* [her stress] these mathematics topics'. In the particular case of fractions, she added: 'This is a topic which I did not teach effectively nor with interest before adopting these calculators'. The team's conclusions are based on trials in only two schools over a relatively short period. But national dissemination through the published resource pack will provide an opportunity for feedback and testing of these conclusions on a much larger scale.

The second key question is focused on pupils' responses to the use of these calculators. The teachers kept notes on their observations of, and feedback from, their pupils, and also collected some samples of pupils' written work for assessment. In evaluation meetings the teachers reported and compared their findings, including the impact on pupils with reference to their own previous experiences and expectations for the topics and classes involved. The first striking feature of the impact of these calculators on pupils was the top line of the two-line display, where what you press is what you see, including a scrolling facility to manage overspill. The second striking feature was the capacity to monitor entries key by key, and edit entries, before seeing an answer, which appears instantly in the second line on pressing the equals key. The third striking feature was the facility to replay and edit complete key sequences after seeing an answer, and get instant feedback on the effect of any changes, without any need to retype the key sequence involved (see Figure 27.2). These facilities were generally highly motivating for pupils and they rapidly gained confidence and competence in using this potential. Teachers also reported that the use of these calculators helped to develop more independent learning, including more use of methods based on trial and improvement, and investigation of alternative possibilities, e.g. by asking 'What if . . .?'

The lesson specifications for particular topics were also judged to have helped to boost pupils' motivation for some commonly regarded as 'boring' or difficult topics, including fractions, operation priority and indices. Based on some assessment of pupils' written work and test results, teachers also pointed to some improvements in pupils' understanding of particular topics, but quantitative evidence was not submitted. Nor was any attempt made to collect quantitative evidence about pupils' responses to and attitudes towards the use of these calculators. But one strong positive indicator of impact was reported by both schools. For each class involved in the trials there were requests from a number of pupils to purchase the two-line calculator through the mathematics department.

The third key question is focused on the teacher's use of the two-line projector model as a visual aid to develop whole-class interactive teaching. The project team's thinking here was influenced by the National Numeracy Strategy's advocacy of stronger components of whole-class interactive teaching, and the potential of transparent calculators in particular (QCA, 1999b, p.59):

> Transparent calculators used with an overhead projector are invaluable in promoting whole class discussion, as everyone can see the display and the effect of entering or changing any number or operation.

The reference here was to basic calculators but the potential applies *a fortiori* to two-line scientific models. Furthermore, the potential of whole-class interactive teaching is currently being developed as part of the Strategy's extension to Key Stage 3. The project team was keen to address these priorities as part of its agenda.

First encounters with the classroom use of the projector calculator by teachers served to identify a number of simple practicalities, including the need for a separate board or flipchart to allow recording alongside the projector screen. The first striking feature of the projector calculator for the teachers was its power as an attention-grabbing and attention-keeping tool for whole-class teaching. Switching on the display generated widespread feelings of eager anticipation in the trial lessons. Such feelings tended to persist beyond the initial novelty of first encounters. The second striking feature was the potential of the projector display to play a leading role in teacher demonstration, explanation and questioning. The two-line display, editing and replay facilities provided a strong focus for interactive teaching and negotiation of the development of a topic with pupils. The transparent calculator allows all the pupils to see every key press and the immediate displayed consequences. In the case of *graphic* calculators, transparent keyboards have not yet been developed for projector use.

In some topics, particularly fractions, percentages and sequences, the calculator was used alongside tasks requiring pupils to use and develop their *mental* calculation skills. Here the teachers were particularly struck by the programming facility using the ANS key, to generate sequences and stimulate short and lively sessions of oral and mental practice. Further outcomes of the work for the participants deserve mention. In one trial school, which the head of department has since left, it has become departmental policy to promote the use of whole class sets of calculators for direct teaching of a range of topics and to restrict the incidental use of calculators by pupils for basic calculations. Finally, all members of the project team, including the two steerers, have

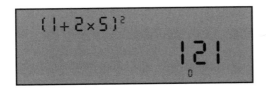

Figure 27.2

significantly advanced their personal calculator skills and use of the full range of two-line facilities through involvement in the project.

Curriculum development or action research?

In a recent survey of small-case action research projects the Teacher Training Agency (TTA, 2000, p.2) concluded 'teachers are more likely to interest themselves in research which contains real, accessible, classroom-based illustrations and examples'. The calculator project was certainly strongly oriented towards practical outcomes, and was driven throughout by a wide-ranging agenda, strict timetable, and commercial product orientation. But the process of working also involved elements of systematic enquiry by practitioners, both inside and outside classrooms, and the use of largely qualitative evidence from classroom trials, to support formative evaluation leading to a publication with potential for national dissemination by a leading calculator manufacturer. Admittedly, the evidence base is limited in its quality and quantity, and an iterative approach to trialling each lesson topic was not attempted. However, such a project has the potential to provide a strong framework within which individual teachers can research and develop aspects of their own classroom practice, as part of their continuing professional development. The Teacher Training Agency (2000, p.12) has concluded: 'Collaboration within and across schools is an effective and supportive way of conducting research.' A number of concomitant challenges are also identified and the responses of the project to these will serve to highlight the benefits of collaboration with external steering:

1. *Making time:* The project was externally funded to cover the costs of two teachers' attendance at meetings throughout the six-month period. One departmental head attended all the meetings but this strictly limited her colleague's involvement in the full team.
2. *Steering:* The project was jointly led by the author and the education manager for the calculator manufacturer.
3. *Writing and dissemination:* The author was contracted to undertake all the written drafting up to publication.

4. *Unanticipated events:* One departmental head moved school before the end of the project but her individual involvement continued. One assistant teacher volunteered to attend all the meetings but sickness and maternity leave led to a sharing of roles.

Conclusion

The limited evidence for generalisation from the work of this project has been admitted, and a number of conclusions might well be investigated more closely. A recent small-scale study of *graphic* calculator use concluded that this tool helped to overcome common pupil misconceptions about graphs and improved pupils' understanding, and teachers' confidence in using new technology was enhanced (Gammon and Smart, 1997). Similar findings were suggested in relation to the many other mathematics topics investigated in the two-line calculator project.

As part of the National Numeracy Strategy, the Department for Education and Employment (2001) has published an unprecedented detailed *Framework for Teaching Mathematics: Years 7 to 9*. Included herein are many examples of the use of ICT – including scientific calculators (but with no mention of two-line models!), graphic calculators and spreadsheets – to enrich the Key Stage 3 mathematics curriculum. These national prescriptions leave much potential room for further focused research and development by teachers, to make effective use of these technological tools within mathematics classrooms.

In conclusion: the three Case Studies

An essential purpose for these case studies was to illustrate the wide range of contexts in which action research is possible and valid. Second, they were used to present a selection of approaches for exploring real situations, and answering the burning questions that teachers pose about what is happening in their classroom. Each study provides a commentary on the benefits of pursuing different approaches, and it is significant that each investigation raised further questions and pointed clearly to the need for more than one kind of evidence to ratify initial findings.

In the current climate of accountability and testing, it is not surprising that the studies look particularly at teaching and learning issues. Ian Eyres comments in his case study, that the initial quantitative aim of such projects often have to include a more qualitative approach. The cyclic nature of action research as drawn by Kemmis and McTaggart (1981) and illustrated in Figure

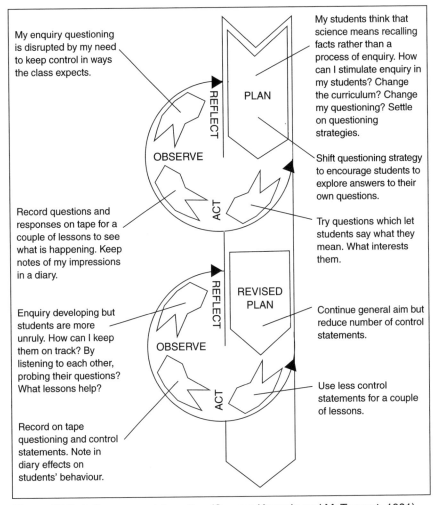

Figure 27.3 Action research in action (Source: Kemmis and McTaggart, 1981)

27.3, gives strength and form to what at times may seem a messy way of working. The fact is that some investigations seem to raise as many new questions as they answer. Data may, sometimes, provide contradictory evidence to that which was anticipated. Nevertheless, informed, focused insights into what was going on in their classrooms, and into what they themselves were doing, have provided evidence to confirm the need for change of current practices.

Whether the results of such a study can be shared and used to inform practice beyond the institutional setting of the particular research study is dependent on the nature of the research and whether or not this accords with other research in the same field. For example, the questioning case study links directly to growing evidence that supports the need for teachers and early years practitioners to use a variety of questioning skills, especially open-ended questions to support learning. The early years study is a much smaller study and describes in detail the process, while the other two studies have wider implications and relate to external factors. What is very clear, however, are the significant benefits of classroom research for all those involved in the case studies described.

Acknowledgements

Case Study 1: The authors would like to acknowledge the help of Celia Greenaway in the development of this case study.

Case Study 3: The authors would like to acknowledge the help of Casio Electronics Co. Ltd, Martin High School, Anstey, Leicester (teachers Jan Richardson and Will Read) and Rushey Mead School, Leicester (teachers Pearl King and Parul Patel) in the development of this case study.

References

Askew, M. and Wiliam, D. (1995) *Recent Research in Mathematics Education 5–16*. London: HMSO.

Cohen, L. and Manion, L. (1994) *Research Methods in Education*. London: Routledge.

de Boo, M. (1999) *Science 3–6: Laying the Foundations in the Early Years*. Hatfield: Association for Science Education.

Department for Education and Employment (DfEE) (2001) *Framework for Teaching Mathematics: Years 7 to 9*. Sudbury: DfEE Publications.

Gammon, A. and Smart, T. (1997) 'Girls, calculators and graphic concepts', 4-page summary in *Teacher Training Agency Teacher Research Grant Scheme, Summaries of Findings 1997*. London: TTA.

Harlen, W. (2000) *Teaching, Learning and Assessing Science 5–12*. London: Paul Chapman Publishing.

Harlen, W. and Jelly, S. (1997) *Developing Science in the Primary Classroom*. London: Longman.

Kemmis, S. and McTaggart, R. (1981) *The Action Research Planner*. Melbourne: Deakin University Press.

Macintyre, C. (2000) *The Art of Action Research in the Classroom*. London: David Fulton Publishers.

Office for Standards in Education (OFSTED) (2000) *Inspection report: St Matthew's Primary School*, Cambridge (Inspection No. 209519). London: OFSTED.

Price, M. (2001) *Developing Effective Use of Two-Line Scientific Calculators at Key Stage 3*, Casio Electronics Co. Ltd, Fiona Crooks (Education Manager, Unit 6, 1000 North Circular Road, London NW2 7JD).

Qualifications and Curriculum Authority (QCA) (1999a) *Analysis of the 1999 Key Stage 2 English tests*. London: QCA.

Qualifications and Curriculum Authority (QCA) (1999b) *Teaching Mental Calculation Strategies*. Sudbury: QCA Publications.

Ruthven, K. (1996) 'Calculators in the mathematics curriculum: the scope of personal computational technology', in Bishop, A. *et al.* (eds) *International Handbook of Mathematics Education*, Pt 1, 435–68. Dordrecht: Kluwer.

School Curriculum and Assessment Authority (SCAA) (1997) *The Use of Calculators at Key Stages 1–3*. Hayes: SCAA Publications.

Teacher Training Agency (TTA) (2000) *Patterns and Issues Emerging from the Third Year of the TTA Funded Teacher Research Grant Scheme 1999*. London: TTA.

Winter, R.(1988) 'Fictional-critical writing: an approach to case study research by practitioners and for in-service and pre-service work with teachers', in Nias, J. and Groundwater-Smith, S. (eds) *The Enquiring Teacher: Supporting and Sustaining Teacher Research*. Lewis: Falmer Press.

Chapter 28

Learning through reflection

Jennifer Moon

Editors' Note: Jennifer Moon offers practical advice on the use of personal journals to aid reflection in this selection of extracts from her book.

Developing reflective practice in experienced practitioners

The desirability of reflective practice in teaching is assumed in the literature – that it is good to be a reflective teacher. However, much of the literature is about reflection in student teachers. Sometimes it is difficult to dissociate the literature that concerns the development of reflective student teachers from that of reflective practising teachers, and as these two groups are substantially different in their likely uses of reflection, this might be a little surprising.

Wildman and Niles (1987) describe a scheme for developing reflective practice in experienced teachers. This was justified by the view that reflective practice could help teachers to feel more intellectually involved in their role and work in teaching, and enable them to cope with the paucity of scientific fact and the uncertainty of knowledge in the discipline of teaching.

Wildman and Niles were particularly interested in investigating the conditions under which reflection might flourish – a subject on which there was little guidance in the literature. They designed an experimental strategy for a group of teachers in Virginia and worked with 40 practising teachers over several years. They were concerned that many would 'be drawn to these new, refreshing conceptions of teaching only to find that the void between the abstractions and the realities of teacher reflection is too great to bridge. Reflection on a complex task such as teaching is not easy'. The teachers were taken through a programme of talking about teaching events, moving on to reflecting on specific issues in a supported, and later an independent, manner.

Wildman and Niles observed that systematic reflection on teaching required a sound ability to understand classroom events in an objective manner. They describe the understanding in the teachers with whom they were working, initially as being 'utilitarian ... and not rich or detailed enough to drive systematic reflection'. They suggest that teachers rarely have the time or opportunities to view their own or the teaching of others in an objective manner. Further observation revealed the tendency of teachers to evaluate events rather than review the contributory factors in a considered manner – in effect, standing outside the situation or progressing to the higher levels of reflection in terms of Van Manen's model (1991).

Helping this group of teachers to revise their thinking about classroom events became central in the work with them. This process took time and patience and effective trainers. The researchers estimate that the initial training of the teachers to view events objectively took between 20 and 30 hours, with the same numbers of hours again being required to practise the skills of reflection.

Wildman and Niles identify three principles that facilitate reflective practice in a teaching situation. The first is support from the administrators in an education system, enabling them to understand the requirements of reflective practice and how it relates to teaching students. The second is the availability of sufficient time and space. The teachers on the programme described how they found it difficult to put aside the immediate demands of students in order to give themselves the time they needed to develop their reflective skills. The third is the development of a collaborative environment with support from other teachers. Support and understanding were also required to help teachers on the programme to cope with the products of their reflection. Becoming reflective meant, for example, that they became aware of aspects of their professional life with which they were not comfortable, and they required support to cope with the situations or change them. Wildman and Niles make a summary comment: 'Perhaps the most important thing we learned is that the idea of teacher-as-reflective practitioner will not happen simply because it is a good or even compelling idea.'

The work of Wildman and Niles suggests the importance of recognising some of the difficulties of instituting reflective practice. Others have noted this, making a similar point about the cultural inhibitions in the teaching profession about reflective practice. Zeichner and Liston (1987) point out the inconsistency between the role of the teacher as a (reflective) professional decision maker and the more usual role of teacher as technician, putting into practice the ideas of others. More basic than the cultural issues is the matter of motivation. Becoming a reflective practitioner requires extra work (Jaworski, 1993) and has only vaguely defined goals with, perhaps, little initially perceivable reward and the threat of vulnerability. Few have directly questioned what might lead a teacher to want to become reflective. Apparently, the most obvious reason for teachers to undergo work towards reflective practice is because teacher educators think it is a good thing.

There appear to be many unexplored matters about the motivation to reflect – for example, the value of externally motivated reflection as opposed to that of teachers who might reflect by habit. LaBoskey (1993) talks about the process of changing 'common-sense thinkers', who are externally motivated to reflect, into 'pedagogical thinkers', who reflect habitually.

[. . .]

Learning through reflection – the use of learning journals

Probably all of us reflect. For those who do, being reflective can be an orientation to their everyday lives. For others, reflection comes about when the conditions in the learning environment are appropriate – when there is an incentive or some guidance. The remainder of this chapter focuses on the practical activities that will provide a context in which reflection can be encouraged. The activities are mostly no more than situations in which various conditions that favour reflection are accentuated or harnessed in a formalised manner, as they are, for example, in a learning journal. The activities are grouped for convenience according to these 'accentuated conditions' – though there will be much overlap.

Because the use of journals as a vehicle for reflection in educational situations is becoming common, and because the literature on writing journals is relatively abundant, the use of journals to enhance learning and practice warrants this subject being covered in a chapter on its own. . . .

There are various words used in the literature in a synonymous manner to 'journal', such as log, diary, dialectical notebook, workbook and autobiographical and reflective writing. Sometimes it is called a profile and a 'progress file' (NCIHE, 1997). Precisely defining words seems to be fairly unhelpful here so by 'journal' is meant predominately written material that is based on reflection and is relatively free writing, though it may be written within a given structure. A journal is written regularly over a period of time rather than in a single session. Within this generalised form there are many variations, and this chapter is an attempt to capture the essence of the activity in its relation to reflection in order that it can be applied elsewhere. It 'imposes form on experience' (Grumet, 1989).

Journal writing in education and professional development is not restricted to the disciplines for which writing is the main representation of learning (Young and Fulwiler, 1986; Fulwiler, 1987). Some of the more unusual descriptions of how journals are used come from the quantitative disciplines, such as engineering (Gibbs, 1988), maths (Selfe et al., 1986; Korthagen, 1988), physics (Grumbacher, 1987; Jensen, 1987). Journals are used in

English and the humanities (Belanoff, 1987), philosophy (Kent, 1987), professional education and development – for example, Wolf (1980), James (1992, 1993), Knowles (1993), Johns (1994), Hoover (1994), Hatton and Smith (1995), HEBS (1997) and Handley (1998). Walker (1985) describes the use of journals in religious contexts, and Christensen (1981) and Redwine (1989) describe journal use in general adult education.

In terms of the manner in which reflection functions in relation to learning in journal writing, the reflection is primarily in a represented form on paper, though it may be electronic or spoken into an audio-recorder, and the learning comes from the process of representing and reading back. Journal writing also provides a means by which learning can be upgraded – where unconnected areas of meaning cohere and a deeper meaning emerges. These processes can be directed towards a wide range of outcomes or purposes in improvement of the learning practice itself.

Like so much of the literature on reflection in education, assessment of the value of the reflective process is difficult. Even more than in most literature on reflection, the accounts of journal writing tend to be written by enthusiasts, often journal writers themselves, and it is likely that few who do not feel at ease with reflective writing would encourage others to try it. There are a few evaluative studies, but while hard evidence is hard to quantify, many reports convey enthusiasm and expression of value in learners (Selfe *et al.*, 1986; Morrison, 1996, for example).

The nature of the outcome of journal writing will depend on the prior structuring of the whole exercise, but then the same structure may be used to fulfil a number of different aims, hence the notion of a unified outcome is problematical. For example, for Rainer (1978), one of the main writers on journal writing, a journal is a means of learning to be free with oneself. Cooper (1991) sees it as attending to one's immediate needs, providing a sense of nurturing. For Progoff (1975), it is finding one's voice. It can be therapeutic – Holly (1991) says 'Just writing makes me feel better', or it is seen as a method of fostering creativity (Christensen, 1981). For Berthoff (1987), it is the 'language of speculation' and a form of 'learning how to think', of keeping things 'tentative' and a means 'to forestall closure'.

Holly (1989) refers to the meta-cognitive effect of journal writing in the way that it 'facilitates consciousness of consciousness which enables critical self-enquiry'. Such reflection might require a particular form of guidance and structure to ensure that both of the stages of initial observation and later reflection on reflection can occur. Wolf (1988) stresses the initial stage of this as the 'snaring [of] moments of experience for later analysis'. It tends to be the potential for self-criticism of journal writing and the development of understanding of the personal construction of knowledge that are rationales for the use of journal writing in professional contexts (Bruner, 1990).

For example, Calderhead and James (1992) describe their use of 'recording and profiling' as a means of enabling student teachers to conceptualise the nature of their own professional development, understanding their prior educational experiences in relation to their current re-evaluation of these experiences.

[. . .]

The forms of journal writing

Journals come in a range of shapes and forms and many consist of several different types of writing, some being more personal and others more structured. The provision of structures in journal writing seems to have several purposes. Structure can help learners starting reflective writing. It can ensure that they reflect on the appropriate issues and help them 'move on' in their thinking and learn from the reflective processes. In this connection, it is worth noting the distinctions between those forms of writing that are 'one-off' recording and those to which the writer returns for further reflection.The differences between structured and unstructured forms of journals is somewhat arbitrary.

Unstructured forms
Free writing and reflecting. This form is usually chronological, though may not involve writing every day.

Recording relating to an ongoing event or issue. There is some element of record keeping here.

Double-entry journals. The initial recording of the experience is made on one part of the journal, for example on one side of a page and this may be factual. At a later time, the writer reflects further on the written account of the experience and writes thoughts on the other side. The writing in this second session may be designed to reach conclusions about action.

Structured forms
Autobiographical writing. There is an autobiographical element to journal writing. It may not be chronological and may be related in some way to the current time, such as relating a previous experience that is similar to one in the present (as in Progoff, 1975). Autobiographical writing may accompany a portfolio, making sense of the materials in terms of personal development.

Structure is given in the form of exercises. The exercises may be the same at each writing session or different (examples of exercises are given later in this chapter).

Structure is given in the form of questions to answer or guidance about issues to be covered. The questions might ensure that the appropriate areas of material are covered.

The journal is used to accompany other learning and the structure is determined by that learning. The intention is that the writer thinks again about the initial experience and draws conclusions from the second 'look'. A journal might accompany work on a dissertation or a research project. Recording the reflective processes that occur during the selection of a topic on which to work can be helpful.

Structure is provided within the journal itself and the writer chooses where to write. Progoff's 'intensive journal' is an example of this structure. The writer moves about within the sections of the journal according to the content of his or her writing or what he or she wants to work on. There are many sections with associated methods of working. Dream, fantasy and image, current and past experiences, and summaries of life periods are among the areas of functioning that are covered in this way (Progoff, 1975; Hallberg, 1987).

Profiles or portfolios. There is another group of 'life accounts' that are not usually called 'journals', but can have the same effect. Portfolios tend to include other documents alongside reflective writing that summarise and interrelate the content. The content may be other than written accounts, such as graphic material, stories or poetry.

Practical issues in journal writing – some considerations

Again, the practical issues covered here tend to be viewed in the context of the classroom or formal education setting. There are a number of decisions to make that are likely to influence the quality of the learning that results from the process, and the motivation with which learners engage in writing. . . . Writing in a journal is alien for many learners, and it will help to 'sell' the idea if the purpose behind it and the anticipated learning that should result is clearly articulated.

The purpose for which a journal is to be written is likely to determine its design and structure. There may be writing tasks that are given regularly or periodically, such as reflection on teaching practice each week or on events or books read, and there may be the encouragement for free personal reflection as well. A loose-leaf arrangement will encompass all possibilities and can enable a learner to sequence the material in an order that is appropriate for them. Personalising a journal provides a sense of ownership of it and dissociates it from more formal learning materials. It will help learners to identify this task as one that requires a different orientation to that more usually adopted in learning situations (Francis, 1995).

A statement of the purpose will also suggest criteria on which any assessment will be based. Several different methods for grading or marking this sort of material are illustrated in the literature. The journal itself may be assessed or a question set where the response requires learners to use the material of their journals (Morrison, 1996). Where the journal itself is assessed, a competence-based assessment – 'competent', on the basis of known criteria, or 'not yet competent' – may be more appropriate than grading. A variation on this is to guarantee a basic mark for an adequate journal and to give additional marks for evidence of particular qualities of reflection or learning (Kent, 1987).

Most journal designs allow the possibility of some free or personal writing. If the journal is to be assessed, there is the issue of the privacy of the free writing to be considered. Material will be written differently if it is to be seen – and the learning from it will be different – than if it is purely private. Loose-leaf arrangements mean that private reflections can be removed before a journal is assessed or, alternatively, private pages can be stapled.

Privacy in the form of confidentiality of material is an issue if learners are encouraged to work with peers on reflecting or to share the products of it. It is widely accepted in the literature that there is much to be gained by learners if they work with others or in groups. 'Critical friends' (Hoover, 1994; Francis, 1995) or co-counselling arrangements can maintain the learning process from a journal, and can prevent the learner from avoiding material or 'going around in circles'. The availability of emotional support can help those who find themselves in areas of emotional discomfort. Systems of peer support may suffice. Francis suggests that structured writing is less likely to generate such discomfort, but, equally, does not necessarily provide the psychological space in which emotional matters can be worked through.

Another consideration that may emerge from the nature of the journal is how often or how much writing should be done and this may be guided by assessment criteria. Extensive 'rambling' may be both a problem for marking and an excuse for avoiding meaning and learning. On the other hand, very brief writing may not go beyond a description of events. Allied to the matter of how much to write is the location for the writing. Reflective writing takes time and adding it to normal study time after class may be unfair on learners (Thorpe, 1993), but then class situations may not be conducive to reflection.

One approach to this is to ask learners to jot down notes and ideas in class to be pursued later.

In terms of the learning to be achieved from journal writing, it is important to build into the process some situations in which learners are required to re-read their material. Discussions or assignments on matters that have been recorded can encourage this process, though Walker (1985) suggests that a re-reading of the whole out of the context of assessment enables the learner to get a sense of the development that has taken place.

Getting started

The fact that not everyone finds reflection or reflective writing easy has been pointed out a number of times and the implication of this is that journal writing needs to be introduced carefully. Knowles (1993) describes the ways in which he gently encourages teaching students to write their personal history accounts. He talks of the development of 'open, safe and respectful learning environments' and the acceptance of personal experience as having value for learning to teach. He shares his own experiences and talks about the task with the learners, allowing them to 'complete the assignment in almost any way that promotes the growth of individuals' professional knowledge and skills and their satisfaction with the completed account and process'. Francis (1995) and Walker (1985) describe how they use a series of exercises in reflective writing to introduce the idea before they talk about the journal itself.

A particularly helpful idea for the introduction of journal use that is reported by Gibbs (1988) from Garry and Cowan (1986) is that students who have participated in the experience of journal writing one year should write guidance notes for the students who will be doing so in the following year. The notes produced by a group of engineering students include the following suggestions for starting to write:

- start with 'what is on top' at that time or by writing down an anecdote;
- or start by thinking about the quality of ideas and experiences – for example, the strengths or weaknesses of them;
- or start with the previous entry or, where appropriate, previous comments of the tutor.

The students say that it is helpful to consider who the writing is intended for and keep exploring and probing to get at the deep meanings with efforts being made to work towards truths uncovered in experience.The writing is a process of seeking advice from the self for imminent action and of seeking the next questions that require responses.

Working in the context of the professional training of trainers with an educationally mixed group of adults, Handley (1998) initiates the use of a learning journal by discussing learning styles. Participants pair off and each describes to the other a significant learning experience and, from the manner of the description, they decide their preferred manner of learning. They use a learning styles questionnaire (Honey and Mumford, 1986) to determine learning style, then discuss their styles and the implications of them for their teaching and learning. In their role of trainers (and this would apply to any educators), they need to recognise that their manner of teaching is likely to be derived from the manner of their own learning. The writing of a journal is initiated in a detailed recording of a significant learning event of the day that is described as it happened.The learners then read it over, reflecting on it and its implications for learning and action.The writing is discussed in a short, small group session the next morning. This exercise is completed on the first day of a course that lasts several weeks. Also, on each of the subsequent four residential days, an incident in the day is written up in the same way. On the last evening, they summarise their reflections of the whole week, looking at the implications of this for their workplace practice. There are assignments to be completed over the whole of the six-month course (with two other residential components) and the learning journal is used as a reflective tool to accompany other elements of the assignment. While the material of the first week of the journal is not assessed, the other journal sections accompany the assignments as part of the assessed work. Judgement is on a competency basis.

Exercises for use in journals

The exercises and activities described below are particularly suited to forming part of the structure of journal writing, though they can be used independently. They may be used as 'one-off' exercises in the process of journal writing or as a regular element of its structure. The purpose of the exercises can usefully be seen as means by which the process of reflecting is facilitated, sometimes deepened or directed, rather like loosening the soil (Progoff, 1975). . . .

Writing from different angles
Writing in the present tense can increase the intensity of a described event, which may mean that more understanding is derived from the experience. An altered point of view of the self may be gained by writing about the self in the third person or as if it was at a different stage of life (older and younger).

Metaphor

Finding a metaphor for a person or an experience can enable the subject matter to be explored in a new way. Metaphor has, for example, been used as a means of exploring the concepts of teaching and learning by students in teacher education (Francis, 1995).

Unsent letters

Cooper (1991) suggests writing 'unsent letters' as a journal exercise. The writer chooses a person they keep in mind on the occasion of writing and writes them a letter 'honestly and deeply', but keeps the letter in the journal, using it to communicate with themselves rather than the other. The content of the letter may be emotional or could be directed to a prominent theoretician in the learner's discipline, with the content being academic reflection.

Reflection on a book or reading assignment

Learners may reflect on a book or media presentation that has some relevance to the writer's life or studies. Kent (1987) describes her use of this exercise with philosophy students and D'Arcy (1987) describes the use of journal writing 'as a kind of running commentary' on the reading and writing tasks of her students. She comments that the freedom of the journal writing 'enabled the students' own voices to be heard in their writing'. An example is given of the thoughts of a 14-year-old student on the opening of Shakespeare's *Romeo and Juliet*.

A critical friend

A critical friend might read the journal entry and make comments deliberately to promote deepening of the reflection.

Responding to questions

The questions might be set in advance by a teacher or could be posed in a peer support situation. A group might take turns in setting questions for themselves. Morrison (1996) suggests a useful framework of questions for the personal, professional, academic and evaluative areas of development.

Describing the process of solving of problems

Korthagen (1988) and Selfe *et al.* (1986) ask their mathematics students to describe the processes of solving a mathematical problem.

Focusing on a past experience that has relevance for current learning

The experience might be a period of learning, schooling, being nursed and so on. Writing this material in the present tense will make it easier to examine attitudes prevailing at the time and to relate them to understandings in the present.

Lists

Rainer (1978) suggests that a list can generate an unexpected topic for reflection or enable learners to focus on a particular topic prior to writing. A list might be written on 'things I am good at' or 'things I would like to change in the way I . . .' (think, act and so on), for example.

Stepping stones

Stepping stones is an exercise modified from Progoff (1975) and is a very effective way of loosening memory. Doing the exercise usually has the effect of generating surprise in the writer as to the range of memories she has on a particular topic or person or issue in her life.

The writer starts with a topic in mind – education, learning experiences, a person, a religious belief – anything. In chronological order, she lists her first memory of that topic in terms of a word or short phrase, then a second, a third and so on coming towards the present time, maintaining the order and not reaching more than eight to ten items. By the time the most recent event has been written, other examples that occur chronologically earlier in the sequence will have arisen in the mind and a new sequence from earliest to the present (eight to ten) can be written to include them and so on. Some of the memories may be obvious candidates for more detailed reflection.

If this exercise is run in a group situation where everyone is working on lists of the same topic, a round of sharing one or two memories each is likely to spark off more memories and therefore more sequences to be written.

The stepping stones exercise is a valuable means of finding significant but maybe unexpected material on which to reflect further. It is interesting, too, that the stepping stones listed for a particular topic on one day will differ considerably from the list generated on another day and that in itself is worth exploring.

Period reflections

This is also an exercise modified from Progoff (1975). Looking back over a year or two, most people can discern that their lives can be divided into periods of time, with each period of time having a theme. The theme may be expressed as an idea, a title or even an image. Once the identity of the theme has been made, the period of time may be the subject of review and Progoff suggests that the 'feeling' about the period is collected in an image for the period.

Dialogues with people

Both Rainer and Progoff describe the use of imaginary dialogues with other people. The 'other' is likely to be a significant person in the writer's life in the present or past, but not necessarily someone known personally. The person may, for example, be a mentor, 'wisdom figure', spiritual leader or a dead or absent parent.

Progoff suggests that the writer 'gets in touch' with the other by means of several techniques, such as a stepping stones exercise (see above) in which the stepping stones of the writer's knowledge or acquaintance with the other are written before the dialogue is begun.

Dialogues with events and projects

A very useful series of sections in Progoff's book (1975) deal with dialogues with different elements of a person's life. One that is particularly significant in an educational situation is a dialogue with work, where the imaginary dialogue with work with which the writer is engaged is written out. In the formal learning situation, this might be a project or essay or, on a larger scale, a career and so on. The dialogue addresses the 'work' as if it is a person, and there is likely to be a specific topic that is the subject of the dialogue. The writing of an essay, for example, might seem to be 'blocked' or a career not progressing and so on.

Progoff suggests that all of the dialogues are set up in a similar manner to the dialogues with people, using the stepping stones technique to engage with the subject. Other areas for dialogue work are society, the body, events, situations and circumstances.

Working with dreams and imagery

Working in a journal with dreams and imagery is as legitimate as working with conscious thoughts and feelings. They are just as much products of the brain and can bring interesting and useful new areas of content to a journal. Working in this way may usefully circumvent emotional blocks. There are many different ways of working with dreams and images (see Shohet, 1985; Reed, 1985).

Past, present and future

This technique can bring unexpected considerations to bear on an area of life. Around ten minutes is spent reflecting and writing on a past occurrence. In the professional context, it might be a period of practice or learning or an event. There is no interpretation, just a description. The next 10 to 15 minutes are spent writing down future associations and anticipations that arise in free association from the description of the past material. This is then brought into the current time in an integrated account that includes consideration of the meanings and its implications for the present.

SWOT analysis

A SWOT analysis is a commonly used tool that facilitates thinking about some issue or event. It may be used in an evaluative manner or as a prelude to change. In either case, such an analysis can provide useful material for further reflection and can 'move thinking on'. A SWOT analysis can be performed on an event, an ongoing situation or organisation. It involves the separate noting of issues under the four words that make up the acronym – strengths, weaknesses, opportunities and threats.

References

Belanoff, P. (1987) 'The role of journals in the interpretive community', in Fulwiler, T. (ed.) *The Journal Book*. Portsmouth, NH: Heinemann.

Berthoff, A. (1987) 'Dialectical notebooks and the audit of meaning', in Fulwiler, T. (ed.) *The Journal Book*. Portsmouth, NH: Heinemann.

Bruner, J. (1990) *Acts of Meaning*. Cambridge, Mass.: Harvard University Press.

Calderhead, J. and James, C. (1992) 'Recording student teachers' learning experiences', *Journal of Further and Higher Education* **16**(1), 3–12.

Christensen, R. (1981) '"Dear diary": a learning tool for adults', *Lifelong Learning: the adult years*, October.

Cooper, J. (1991) 'Telling our own stories', in Whitehead, C. and Noddings, N. *Stories Lives Tell: Narrative and dialogue in education*, New York: Teachers' College Press.

D'Arcy, P. (1987) 'Writing to learn', in Fulwiler, T. (ed.) *The Journal Book*. Portsmouth, NH: Heinemann.

Francis, D. (1995) 'Reflective journal: a window to preservice teachers' practical knowledge', *Teaching and Teacher Education* **11**(3), 229–41.

Fulwiler, T. (1987) *The Journal Book*. Portsmouth, NH: Heineman.

Garry, A. and Cowan, J. (1986) 'To each according to his need', *Aspects of Educational Technology*, Vol. XXI. London: Kogan Page.

Gibbs, G. (1988) *Learning by Doing: A guide to teaching and learning methods*. Birmingham: SCED.

Grumbacher, J. (1987) 'How writing helps physics students become better problem solvers', in Fulwiler, T. (ed.) *The Journal Book*, Portsmouth, NH: Heinemann.

Grumet, M. (1989) 'Generations: reconceptualist curriculum theory and teacher education', *Journal of Teacher Education* **40**, 13–17.

Hallberg, F. (1987) 'Journal writing as person making', in Fulwiler, T. (ed.) *The Journal Book*. Portsmouth, NH: Heinemann.

Handley, P. (1998) Personal communication.

Hatton, N. and Smith, D. (1995) 'Reflection in teacher education – towards definition and implementation', *Teaching and Teacher Education* **11**(1), 33–49.

Health Education Board for Scotland (HEBS) (1997) *Promoting Health: A short course in developing effective practice*. Edinburgh: HEBS.

Holly, M. (1989) 'Reflective working and the spirit of enquiry', *Cambridge Journal of Education* **19**, 71–80.

Holly, M. (1991) *Keeping a Personal–Professional Journal*. Victoria: Deakin University Press.

Honey, P. and Mumford, A. (1986) *Using Our Learning Styles*. London: Honey Publications.

Hoover, L. (1994) 'Reflective writing as a window on preservice teachers' thought processes', *Teaching and Teacher Education* **10**, 83–93.

James, C. (1992) *The Personal Professional Profile: A rationale for practice*. School of Education, University of Bath.

James, C. (1993) 'Developing reflective practice skills – 'the potential'. Paper presented to 'The Power of the Portfolio' national conference, 12 November.

Jaworski, B. (1993) 'Professional development of teachers – the potential of critical reflection', *British Journal of Inservice Education* **19**, 37–42.

Jensen, V. (1987) 'Writing in college physics', in Fulwiler, T. (ed.) *The Journal Book*. Portsmouth, NH: Heinemann.

Johns, C. (1994) 'Nuances of reflection', *Journal of Clinical Nursing* **3**, 71–5.

Kent, O. (1987) 'Student journals and the goals of philosophy', in Fulwiler, T. (ed.) *The Journal Book*. Portsmouth, NH: Heinemann.

Knowles, J. (1993) 'Life history accounts as mirrors: a practical avenue for the conceptualization of reflection in teacher education', in Calderhead, J. and Gates, P. (eds) *Conceptualizing Reflection in Teacher Development*. London: Falmer Press.

Korthagan, F. (1988) 'The influence of learning orientations on the development of reflective teaching', in Calderhead, J. (ed.) *Teachers' Professional Learning*. London: Falmer Press.

LaBoskey, V. (1993) 'A conceptual framework for reflection in preservice teacher education', in Calderhead, J. and Gates, P. (eds) *Conceptualizing Reflection in Teacher Development*. Falmer Press, London.

Morrison, K. (1996) 'Developing reflective practice in higher degree students through a learning journal', *Studies in HE* **21**(3), 317–32.

National Committee of Inquiry into Higher Education (NCIHE) (1997) *Report of the National Committee of Inquiry into Higher Education* (The Dearing Report).London: NCIHE.

Progoff, I. (1975) *At a Journal Workshop*. New York: Dialogue House Library.

Rainer, T. (1978) *The New Diary*. Los Angeles: J. P. Tarcher Inc.

Redwine, M. (1989) 'The autobiography as a motivational factor for students', in Warner Weil, S. and McGill, I. (eds) *Making Sense of Experiential Learning.* Buckingham: SRHE/Open University Press.

Reed, H. (1985) *Getting Help from your Dreams*. Virginia Beach, Va: Inner Vision.

Selfe, C., Petersen, B. and Nahrgang, C. (1986) 'Journal writing in mathematics', in Young, A. and Fulwiler, T. (eds) *Writing Across the Disciplines*. Upper Montclair, NJ: Boynton/Cook.

Shohet, R. (1985) *Dream Sharing*. Wellingborough: Turnstone Press.

Thorpe, M. (1993) 'Experiential learning at a distance', in Boud, D., Cohen, R. and Waler, D. (eds) *Using Experience for Learning*. Buckingham: SRHE/Open University Press.

Van Manen, M. (1991) *The Tact of Teaching*. New York: The State of New York Press.

Walker, D. (1985) 'Writing and reflection', in Keogh, R. and Walker, D. (eds) *Reflection: turning experience into learning*, London: Kogan Page.

Wildman, R. and Niles, J. (1987) 'Reflective teachers: tensions between abstractions and realities', *Journal of Teacher Education* **3**, 25–31.

Wolf, J. (1988) 'Experiential learning in professional education: concepts and tools', *New Directions for Experiential Learning* **8**, 17.

Young, A. and Fulwiler, T. (1986) *Writing Across the Disciplines*. Upper Montclair, NJ: Boynton/Cook.

Zeichner, K. and Liston, D. (1987) 'Teaching student teachers to reflect', *Harvard Educational Review* 23–48.

Chapter 29

Teaching's long revolution: from ivory towers to networked communities of practice[1]

Jenny Leach

Editors' Note: This chapter is about the use of information and communications technology (ICT) by teachers. It links with Chapters 10 and 11 in suggesting that learning takes place collaboratively in communities of practice, and that such communities express and define their practice through the tools that they use.

Introduction

Information and communications technology (ICT), together with a variety of other technological tools and artefacts, have throughout history been fundamental to the development of professional practice. We are unlikely, for example, to visit a doctor's surgery that has no thermometer or blood pressure gauge. Until recently, an architect's office would have been unthinkable without drawing boards, maquettes, and a myriad of drawing implements, while most lawyers routinely use fax machines for contacting solicitors at a moment's notice. Be it doctor's surgery, science laboratory, library, law court or place of worship, it is the unique combination of technology, books and resources, choice and arrangement of furniture, that enables a specific practice to be instantly identifiable more or less anywhere in the world, and at any period in time.

Most professionals in the UK have been engaged in quite significant changes to their daily work routines, as the rapid developments in information and communications technology of the last decade begin to be capitalised on and integrated within different 'communities of practice' (Lave and Wenger, 1991; Rogoff, 1994; Wenger, 1999). The pace of adoption of the World Wide Web in particular has revolutionised Internet use, eclipsing all technologies before it. Created as recently as 1994, by the end of 1995 it had 9 million users and 179 million by June 1999. Projected figures suggest 700 million by 2001

---

1. This is an edited version of a longer paper written for the Centre For Research and Development in Teacher Education (CReTE). The complete version, including links to cited websites can be found at http://www.crete-ou.org

and 2 billion by 2007 – one-third of the population of the planet. Between January and April 2000 the Internet population in the UK grew by 1.8 million users, from 7,821,000 to 9,631,000. These rapid developments in the use of web technologies, including electronic mail and multiple user domains have enabled new and established communities to develop in hitherto unimagined ways. Some of these changes have enabled greater efficiency of working practices, facilitated perhaps by sophisticated record-keeping databases, or more powerful work tools. Medical practices and dental surgeries for example, have substituted cumbersome filing cabinets with computerised patient records, in order to ease the record-keeping process. Lawyers now use computers to check the progress of a client's case or point of law, or use e-mail to contact solicitors. The drawing boards, so resonant of architectural practices, have been largely replaced by computer screens and customised design software.

In many professions, at least in the developed world, new computer and telecommunication networks have not only made day-to-day routines of the workplace more *efficient* or *extended*; they have *transformed* the nature of work itself, as completely new knowledge and skills are created. (Streibel (1993) and McCormick and Scrimshaw (2001) discuss this three-level analysis of ICT use.) Occupations such as accountancy, stockbroking and marketing, for example, are significantly changed by the introduction of databases that identify patterns and problems in current practice, as well as in the quantitative aspects of future development. Large chemical engineering companies now expect researchers to employ computers to carry out sophisticated simulations of chemical processes impossible by other means. Surgeons achieve ground breaking surgery with digital scanners, while forward-looking architects use computer software to facilitate innovative design processes. Bennett (2001) argues that leading-edge computer technology needs to be an essential component of university level architecture and design programmes, if such courses are to prepare students to participate in the real world where use of such technologies is already the norm.

Learning: the enterprise of teaching

But in what ways can ICT enhance the practice of teachers? To answer this question we need first to look at teaching's unique enterprise: the advancement of learning. Alison Gopnik (2000) has pointed out that our developing understandings over the last decade of how human minds work and how people learn (Gardner, 1999; Greenfield, 2000; Bransford *et al.*, 1999; Moon, Chapter 11 in this volume;) might well be the equivalent of the scientific physiology that so transformed medical practice over a hundred years ago. For this reason, she argues, the history of education in the twenty-first century, quite aside from the use of new technologies, may well turn out to be as significant as the history of medicine in the nineteenth century. We now know, for example, that our brains grow and develop in quite phenomenal ways during our lifetimes, but they also develop in response to the specific contexts, experiences and purposes in which, and for which, we use them (Greenfield, 2000). We also know that learning is not a discrete, abstract process of cognition taking place exclusively in the mind, but is essentially social in nature, stretched over, not divided among mind, body, activity, other people and tools in particular settings (Lave, 1988). Rather than being an accumulation of discrete skills and information, learning is also a process of developing *identity* – of becoming. It transforms who we are, what we can do – and what we believe we are capable of doing in the future. From this perspective learning entails both *processes of* knowledge building and *places* where the interaction between experience and competence can lead to new ways of knowing (Wenger, 1999). 'Communities of practice' (Lave and Wenger, 1991; Rogoff, 1994; Wenger, 1999) such as families, workplaces, leisure time groups are these places.

The concept of a 'community of practice' is not just a matter of social category, nor simply a synonym for a group, team or network; it does not depend on working in the same building, nor on having the same professional title; though it may include some or all of these factors. A community of practice is defined as 'participation in activity about which participants share understandings concerning what they are doing and what that means for their lives and their communities' (Lave and Wenger, 1991, p.98). Such practice arises from what Wenger has described as the sustaining of 'dense relations of mutual engagement', organised round a shared history of learning (Wenger, 1999, p.74). Three essential dimensions define such a practice:

- joint enterprise – an agreed, negotiated *purpose* or *goal* with mutual *accountability*;
- mutual engagement – a common *activity*; participants play distinctive *roles* in this joint work;
- shared repertoire – a distinctive *discourse* framing a shared *understanding* of *concepts*, *tools* and *resources* of practice.

We rarely think of our day-to-day teaching job as learning, since what we learn *is* our practice. Yet it is through the shared repertoires and the particular discourse of the schools of our choice that we navigate together with colleagues the complex environments of classrooms, staff meetings, parents' evenings and OFSTED visits, imperceptibly becoming familiar with, and creating, a wide range of activities, knowledge and artefacts.

Professional identity is redefined over time as we develop fresh knowledge, take on different roles, and new ways of participating in the overlapping educational practices we inhabit, leave and join. In the first week of our first term we *are* a probationary teacher; by the year-end we have *become* Year 3's class teacher, Year 9's Form Tutor, or a *member* of the History Department. Just as in families daughters become sisters, mothers, aunts, grandmothers, or as in football clubs trainee footballers become football stars, coaches, managers, so in educational communities we become science coordinators, expert teachers, heads of year, mentors, senior managers, advisory teachers, educational researchers.

This 'crucial', yet 'subtle' concept of a 'community of practice' has explanatory power for teacher learning in particular, because as a theory of how people learn it is based on research within authentic adult working practices. It offers a way of analysing teacher development that is strikingly different from that which has traditionally been employed in teacher research (Putnam and Borko, 2000).

The role of ICT in creating more effective educational communities of practice

ICT has the potential to provide educators with access to a vast array of information, including data for analysis, digital libraries and websites. It also enables access to people that provide information, feedback, and motivation; as Hargreaves writes:

> ICT provides opportunities for networking for professional knowledge creation, shared tinkering and concurrent dissemination on a scale and at a rate that has hitherto been unimaginable.
> (Hargreaves 1999, p.139)

A school or educational institution is a 'constellation' of diverse practices (see Figure 29.1) which may have members in common, share artefacts and technologies, have geographical relations; share overlapping styles and discourse; compete for the same resources (Wenger, 1999, p.74). At this level of practice senior managers, classes (i.e. pupils together with their teacher(s)), office staff, and various cross-functional teams such as year teams and subject faculties can be said to be their own communities, with specific purposes and goals. Each of these groups will use ICT to enact and support core values, practices and identities, in ways that are relevant to their unique interpretation of the educational enterprise. From this perspective the view of ICT as a set of discrete, generic skills to be acquired by individual teachers is fairly

Figure 29.1 An example of a constellation of practices of a secondary school

meaningless. ICT within educational communities is not one thing, but a range of practices, software and hardware technologies, modes of representation and interactions assembled by individuals, communities and groups in myriad ways to add up to *their* (not *the*) use of ICT.

The following sections consider some of the ways in which ICT can enhance and extend teacher practice and give examples of its use in specific communities. They also indicate new communities of practice that are emerging. The following headings will be used to provide a framework for considering the different applications of ICT within practices:

Informational
Communicative
Disciplinary
Productive
Pedagogic
Research.

Informational tools: knowledge building within teacher communities

The World Wide Web (WWW or 'the web') is a massive assortment of information connected together in such a way that makes it possible for members of specific communities to search for and access information of mutual interest. Many educators now use the Internet as an information source as a matter of routine, either to extend their own subject knowledge or to widen access to subject-related classroom resources. Of the 300 teacher respondents to a web questionnaire posted on the Open University Learning Schools Programme's (LSP) teacher website, 52 per cent ranked access to *subject and phase resources* as one of their top three purposes for using the web environment.

Lesson plans published on the Internet are a growing resource for teachers. Sites like Schoolzone include web links to lesson resources, as well as offering hundreds of their own resources. Teachers can submit their own lesson plans too. This site, in common with most other teacher-focused sites categorises its resources into 34 subject areas. The National Grid for Learning's (NGFL) Virtual Teachers' Centre classifies its resources according to the major National Curriculum subjects of England and Wales, while Nine, the national educational website in Northern Ireland and the Learning and Teaching Scotland site make similar subject-specific provision.

Some websites offer templates for lesson plans, or feedback on plans, while the BBC Education site offers Teacher Notes to accompany educational TV programmes together with recommendations for activities. The LSP web questionnaire also revealed that when repondents were asked to specify 'one url/web site you regularly access', they chose a website that had a direct relation to their subject specialism. Maths teachers, for example, use sites like Mathsnet for maths resources, puzzles and conundrums. English teachers make regular use of sites about authors to support their subject knowledge or students' study of texts, the BBC On-Line Arts section, for example. Geographers frequently access an Internet site that collates the readings of the last 20 earthquakes in the world. Some use this information with pupils in order to get them to develop a hypothesis from the data, which can be tested by subsequent classes studying results from different earthquakes.

Increasingly creators of information sites for teachers are beginning to see the advantage of incorporating a communicative dimension; the rationale is explored in the next section.

Communicative tools: supporting networked communities of practice

Because many new technologies are interactive (Greenfield and Cocking, 1996), they can create and sustain the kind of coherence and ongoing collaboration that transforms mutual engagement into a community of practice. ICT can enable new environments to develop in which members can collaboratively learn by doing, consistently receive feedback, refine their understanding, and jointly build new knowledge (Bereiter and Scardamalia, 1993). In this way groups can build up a shared history of learning.

The development of the Internet has allowed many geographically dispersed communities to emerge based on shared interests such as hobbies, mutual support, or even criminality with diasporic cultural and linguistic groups sharing concerns, ideas and decision making as never before (Graddol, 1997). In addition to facilitating highly focused communities, web communication tools also position people within networks that place them in wider flows of global cultural, political, economic and educational resources,

> the boundaries of markets, nations, cultures and technologies become increasingly permeable, and require people to think of themselves as actors on ever more global stages.
> (Miller and Slater, 2000, p.19)

Despite the extensive research that indicates successful learning (including teacher learning) extends over time and develops in communities, structured opportunities for teachers to work alongside each other in the workplace to exchange or develop new resources remain the exception rather than the rule. Planned visits to colleagues' classrooms and schools are rarely resourced. Opportunities for new practitioners to attend INSET, particularly that which focuses on innovations in pedagogic practice, are infrequent. ICT can support teaching communities in overcoming professional isolation – and hence learning. Connectivity between schools and their local communities, including homes, enables a medium for creating local and global communities that include teachers, administrators, students, parents, practising scientists, artists, writers and other specialists. It can help teachers benefit from being able to share their experiences with others, wherever they may be. Such activities have been accomplished through websites that not only provide information but also create:

- opportunities for collaborative tasks;
- discourse around common text/resources;
- discussion of data about student learning;
- a focus on shared decision making.

Of respondents to the LSP survey, 75.4 per cent ranked 'Exchange of teaching and learning ideas' in their top three purposes for using the web, one-third ranked it as their top priority; 63.2 per cent ranked 'Contact with fellow subject specialists' among their top three purposes and 29 per cent ranked it their first priority. Some examples of teacher-related communicative practices include: Questions to experts; On-line Mentoring, Learning Circles and Tele-field trips (teachers who take pupils to historical sites, zoos, museums, field trips, etc., can work with students to share experiences and observations with others locally or globally).

385

Web technologies also have the potential to support teachers in longer-term collaborations and the assembling of shared resources that are vital to community building. Many communicative sites for teachers, however, are often little more than 'forums for exchanging titbits and opinions' (Roschelle and Pea, 1999). Research shows that high quality on-line teaching and moderation of conferences are of critical importance if teachers are to use them as an integral and valuable part of practice (Salmon, 2000). The OU's LSP e-environment uses the communicative software *FirstClass* and has developed as one of the world's largest teacher e-communities. Since its inception between April 2000 and February 2001 some 24,068 teachers have accessed its various subject and phase-related conferences. Participants in this and associated programmes report the value of close contact with other practitioners, subject-related electronic resources, as well as the opportunity to exchange teaching and learning ideas (Leach, 2000). Findings indicate these new e-environments provide secure settings within which trainees, or more experienced teachers can learn to develop, extend and even change their practice.

Tools of the disciplines: supporting the development of authentic practices

All too frequently what pupils learn in formal schooling are a range of 'school' or institutional practices unrelated to the world outside. This includes 'school ICT'[2] which is often quite divorced from ICT use beyond the classroom walls. For example ICT is often primarily used in secondary schools in subjects such as Business Studies, IT or Maths; for a limited range of activities such as spreadsheets or databases; as a purely individual activity; and seen as marginal to drama, RE, or English Literature. Such perceptions are often reinforced by statutory curriculum requirements (see Leach and Moon, 2000).

In reality, research has shown that ICT can enable teachers of whatever subject or age group to provide:

- more effective teaching of core disciplinary concepts;
- an extension of the range of tools currently available to pupils within the subject;
- exciting curriculum possibilities;
- new opportunities and contexts for learning grounded in authentic practices outside of school.

---

2. See Banks, Leach and Moon (1999) for a discussion of the distinction between 'school' and 'subject' knowledge.

English specialists on the Open University's Learning Schools Programme, for example, are invited to look at the way ICT can be used to support learning in a range of literacy practices, such as interpreting and composing literary texts for a variety of audiences (see Table 29.1). One English department in the Programme uses desktop publishing programmes to enable pupils to compose real texts for external audiences, such as brochures about the school for prospective pupils and parents. Students also have the opportunity to work with local publishers, and to use the powerful computers that are part of their daily practice. Mathematics teachers by contrast, will use entirely different combinations of ICT for mathematical purposes, exploring data, observing mathematical pattern, visualising geometry.

Computer software can thus support subject-related habits of mind, significantly extend learner competence, and motivation. In addition, ICT enables teachers to provide pupils with direct experience in a variety of

Literacy Specialists' Activity	How will ICT help?
Composing texts	Word processing, e-mail, computer conferencing; digital cameras; voice recording software; multimedia
Focusing on audience/purpose; presenting texts	E-mail; computer and video conferencing, desk top publishing; web authoring; databases and spreadsheets; multimedia software; presentation software
Transforming texts	Word processing; desk top publishing; hypermedia
Exploring information	CD-ROM; Internet; video conferencing; electronic mail
Reading texts	Internet; CD-ROM; talking books
Asking 'What if?' questions	Simulation; databases; internet text debates; video and computer conferencing
Identifying features of text	Word processors; Text Disclosure Programme
Developing knowledge about language	Text Disclosure Programme; Internet; CD-ROM

Table 29.1 Opportunities for exploiting ICT within literacy practices (from Leach and Scrimshaw, 2000)

authentic communities – to try them on for size. Beverly Caswell's (Leach and Moon, 2000, Caswell, 2001) classroom community of nine- and ten-year-olds, for example, uses the Computer Supported Intentional Learning Environment (CSILE) Knowledge Forum technology as an integral tool for working and learning. The software helps Caswell create an authentic scientific community across a ten week period when pupils study Madagascan Hissing Roaches belonging to the adult research community at the University of Toronto's Zoological Department, local to the school. Questions entered by pupils into the Knowledge Forum database ware used to identify research questions, as well as support and scaffold scientific thinking. Daily e-mail communication between pupils and the Zoo Department supplement weekly face-to-face meetings.

It is important for post-holders such as subject coordinators in primary schools, Key Stage 3 subject leaders, and heads of department to develop their knowledge of these kinds of learning opportunities as they lead colleagues in curriculum development issues.

Productivity tools: supporting communities in the work of alignment[3]

Productivity tools based on new technologies are software applications that enable professionals to carry out routine, everyday tasks more effectively. Many generic software tools (word processors, desk top publishing, spreadsheets, etc.) can be used to develop the kind of artefacts essential to teachers' practice – 'points of focus' around which any community of practice organises and negotiates meaning between its members. In schools these typically include pupil worksheets, lesson plan templates, registers, calendars or assessment databases. Table 29.2 gives some examples of such productivity tools that teachers might make use of.

Productivity tools can also be useful in the work of alignment. Alignment helps to define a community's broad vision and aspirations to other communities. It is the process by which groups communicate their core purposes, needs and methods to closely related groups in the hope that they will share in their common enterprise. All teachers are often engaged in liaison with related communities – families of pupils, inspectors, future parents, to name but a few. ICT can help in this work of alignment in a variety of ways; many software tools enable schools to present themselves vividly and publicly to a range of interest groups. Tools such as *Powerpoint* can be

---

3. For a definition of the concepts 'points of focus' and the 'work of alignment' see Wenger, 1999.

Year/subject department team activity	How will ICT help?
Contacting students, parents, future parents, governors.	Word-processing templates; web site; e-mail.
Presenting information to pupils, parents, governors, inspectors.	E-mail; desk top publishing; web authoring; multimedia software; presentation software such as Powerpoint; databases and spreadsheets.
Accessing information from international sources about good practice in schools.	CD-ROM; Internet; computer and video conferencing; electronic mail.
Accessing networks for exchange of information and ideas on effective leadership and school improvement.	Internet; computer and video conferencing; electronic mail.
Exploring pupil outcome data.	Computers enable class teachers and senior managers to work with school PANDA and PICSI data, which can be presented in a variety of ways. This supports interpretation and analysis.
Developing knowledge about how ICT can be used as a tool for pupil learning and school improvement across the curriculum.	Computer conferences; Listserves. Websites such as DfES site on school-based research and Hay/McBer site on teacher effectiveness.
Planning and target setting for individual pupils and whole school improvement.	Electronic access via web to OFSTED inspection and school performance data; YELLIS and local authority data. Use of statistical packages to explore school data.

Table 29.2 Opportunities for exploiting the power of ICT within and between year and subject department practices

used to make presentational slides and stored electronically. These can be modified with ease, or updated year on year to suit different purposes and audiences (e.g. pupils in lessons, governors' meetings or parents' evening). School journeys, drama productions or classroom events can be captured on digital cameras and the resulting (still or moving) images incorporated into such presentations via the computer.

School websites enable different groups within a school (students, subject departments, year teams, etc.) to present information to the audience of their choice. Office staff can ensure the school calendar is available for parents, senior managers can focus on the aims of the school with prospective parents in mind, while pupils can show grandparents poems, stories or art work they have written and published on the site.

Pedagogic tools: supporting communities in new practices

Marx *et al.* (1998) have developed a threefold categorisation of applications of ICT (multimedia, productivity tools, information and communication systems) as a conceptual framework for teacher professional development. They have designed, and developed a variety of web-based tools for teachers based on this categorisation that combine the applications discussed in previous sections of this chapter. This software is intended to 'scaffold complex cognition such as organising, synthesising, problem solving, and applying new understanding'. The Project Integration Visualisation Tool (PIViT), for example, supports innovations in the planning process, providing a design window that allows teachers to collaborate on concept maps, incorporate curriculum objectives, teacher activities and artefacts. A network enables teachers to exchange annotated PIViT plans electronically and discuss them on-line.

Databases have also been established on the web to assist teachers in a number of subject areas. One consists of a video archive of lessons taught by mathematics specialists, Lampert and Ball (1998). These lessons model inquiry-oriented teaching, in which students work to solve problems and reason and engage in discussions about the mathematics underlying their solutions. The videotapes allow users to stop at any point in the action and discuss nuances of teacher performance with colleagues. Teachers' annotations and an archive of pupils' work associated with the lessons enrich the resource. The CD-ROM and associated network *Iliad* (Swarbrick, 2001) provides a similar facility for Modern Languages teachers across six European countries. Many such sites are based in the US. *Moving Words* (Leach and O'Hear, 2000) is a prototype site for the professional development of UK-based teachers, aiming to provide new approaches to literacy around the theme of the *Literature of Other Cultures and Traditions*. As well as suggesting new possibilities for pedagogy it trials innovative uses of ICT. Three guiding questions provide a central focus for discussion around hypertexts; text mapping and audio and video presentations. Hyperlinks to related texts (e.g. National Curriculum requirements, skeletal lesson plans, key themes and concepts) and a discussion forum are integral to the site.

Such innovations provide *pedagogic tools* (Salamon *et al.*, 1991) for teacher development in the sense that web technology is used to:

- focus explicitly on supporting, developing or changing a teacher's understanding of a concept;
- aid collaboration between teachers;
- situate a teacher's own practice in a specific context.

Such *'pedagogic sites'* (Leach and O'Hear, 2000) presume a high level of teacher involvement, including interactivity and production. They have the potential to extend practices by developing understanding of the subject, encouraging the creation of new products and enabling those products to be shared publicly.

Research tools: supporting communities in the work of accountability, imagination and change

Defining a joint enterprise is a process, not a static agreement. It produces relations of accountability that are not fixed constraints or norms. These relations are manifested not as conformity but as the ability to negotiate actions as accountable to an enterprise. The whole process is as generative as it is constraining. It pushes the practice forward as much as it keeps it in check. An enterprise both engenders and directs social energy. It spurs action as much as it gives it focus. It invites ideas as much as it sorts them out.
(Wenger, 1999, p.84)

One element of a community's joint enterprise is mutual accountability, the working out of what matters and what does not, what actions are good enough and when they need improvement or refreshment. Such regimes of accountability (Wenger, 1999) within communities help to define the circumstances under which members feel concerned or at ease with what they are doing, some aspects may be expressed in policies, rules, standards or reports. While ICT has been used to support such tasks in schools for many years, it has often only been used in the school office, or by individuals. Now systems are available which allow data to be shared with ease on school Intranets between senior management teams, year teams, subject departments, special needs departments – even parents and pupils. Such systems help with record keeping, target setting, report writing, while also supporting the associated calculations and manipulations of information required to make practice accountable to externally imposed regimes of accountability (see Table 29.3 and also Bird, Chapter 22 in this volume). ICT can also reduce the time spent on such tasks, as well as enabling more sophisticated analyses to be carried out.

Other forms of accountability within communities are highly informal and unsystematic. A study reported by Leach and Shelton Mayes (1998) found that teachers regularly undertook informal evaluations after lessons or in the staffroom, although the majority did not consciously think of such activity as evaluation (see also Bird, Chapter 22). Despite a long-standing tradition of school-based research, formal research practices are often seen as remote from the day-to-day concerns of teachers and classroom. There is, however, a strong argument for educational communities of practice to be involved in research into their own practice. Teachers are best placed to identify issues and questions for their schools, carry out investigations and, most importantly, act on those findings to bring about school improvement and change. When many staff within a school are involved, this can create a genuine climate of inquiry that can have an important effect across different groups, serving as a model for learning as a whole. Such work allows school communities to decide for themselves what counts, to identify questions that are significant and pertinent to their concerns.

ICT can support this process in many ways (see Table 29.3), providing access to electronic data and research journals as well as to systematic research reviews (Bird, Chapter 22). ICT also allows hitherto separately bounded research and school-based communities to connect. Teachers experienced in the key concerns of schools and classroom can work alongside colleagues experienced in the processes, tools and discourse of research practices. In new, joint networks such as mentor conferences, university-based professional development programme conferences, or specially focused research projects, this distributed knowledge can be far more powerful than the hitherto solitary ivory towers – be they of classroom or university.

Imagination is a fundamental element of our experience of the world and our place in it. Through imagination we recognise our practices as learning histories reaching back into the past. We also conceive of new developments, explore alternatives and envision future possibilities. The work of imagination, through questions and research, is a critical aspect of effective educational communities. It allows novice teachers to imagine their future identities as members, indeed leaders of existing and newly developing communities of practice. It opens up broader choices and new competencies. ICT supports this work of imagination, enabling teaching communities to:

- make thinking explicit and reflective;
- participate in creative thinking – making inspired hypotheses, articulating probing questions;
- engage in collaborative thinking;
- envision future possibilites for teaching and learning.

As we have seen, selection and use of ICT defines professional communities. For technology is not simply a tool, or a resource, or a context for working, it is an expression of our practice. We choose the tools. We define the direction of that practice.

Research practices	How will ICT help?
Accessing research data, research reports, pupil outcome data.	Web access to electronic journals and databases such as EPPI and Campbell systematic reviews of educational research; PANDA and PICSI data interpretation and analysis.
Carrying out literature searches.	CD-ROMs; web access to electronic journals.
Sharing and discussing research questions, methods.	Computer conferences; Listerves. Websites such as Hay McBer site on teacher effectiveness and DfEE school-based research site.
Disseminating research to peers, parents, governors, inspectors, potential partners.	Desk top publishing; web pages; multimedia software; presentation software such as Powerpoint; databases and spreadsheet.
Participating in aligned research communities.	On-line professional development study; mentors conferencing with ITT providers; conferences supporting university–school linked research projects.

Table 29.3 Opportunities for exploiting the power of ICT within and between research practices

References

Banks, F., Leach, J. and Moon, B. (1999) 'New understandings of teachers' pedagogic knowledge', in Leach, J. and Moon, B. (eds) *Learners and Pedagogy*. London: Paul Chapman.

Bennett, R. (2001) 'Om'nium: a research iniative proposing strategies for quality; collaborative on-line teaching and learning', *Education, Communication and Information* **1**(1).
http://www.open.ac.uk/eci accessed 31.5.01.

Bereiter, C. and Scardamalia, M. (1993) 'Technologies for knowledge-building discourse', *Communications of the ACM* **36**(5), 37–41.

Bransford, J. D., Brown, A. L. and Cocking, R. C.(eds) (1999) *How People Learn: Brain, Mind, Experience, and School*. Committee on Developments in the Science of Learning, National Research Council, National Academic Press.

Caswell, B. and Lamon, M. (1999) 'Development of scientific literacy: the evolution of ideas in a knowledge building classroom', in Leach, J. and Moon, B. (eds) *Learners and Pedagogy*. London: Paul Chapman.

CSILE: Computer Supported Intentional Learning Environment http://csile.oise.utoronto.ca/ accessed 31.7.01.

Gardner, H. (1994) *The Disciplined Mind*. New York: Basic Books.

Gopnik, A. (1999) 'Review of Howard Gardner's *The Disciplined Mind*: what all students should understand', *New York Review of Books*, 6 May, 33–5.

Graddol (1997) *The Future of English*. London: The British Council.

Greenfield, S. (2000) *Brain Story*. London: BBC Publications

Greenfield, P. M. and Cocking, R. R. (1996) *Interacting with Video*. Norwood, NJ: Ablex.

Hargreaves, D. (1999) 'Teaching as a research based profession', in Moon, B., Bird, E. and Butcher, J. (eds) *Leading Professional Development*. Paul Chapman: London.

Lampert, M. and Ball, D. L. (1998) *Teaching, Multimedia, and Mathematics: Investigations of Real Practice*. New York: Teachers. College Press.

Lave, J. (1988) *Cognition in Practice: mind, mathematics and culture in everyday life*. New York: Cambridge University Press.

Lave, J. and Wenger, E. (1991) *Situated Learning*. Cambridge: Cambridge University Press.

Leach, J. and Shelton Mayes, A. (1998) *School-Based Research and School Improvement*. Dunstable: Folens.

Leach, J. and Scrimshaw, P. (1999) 'Teaching in English', in *English: Learning Schools Programme* (to accompany CD-ROM *English*). Open University Publications.

Leach, J. (2000) 'Breaking the silence: the role of technology and community in leading professional development', in Moon, B., Bird, E. and Butcher, J. (eds) *Leading Professional Development*. London: Paul Chapman.

Leach, J. and O'Hear, S. (2000) 'Voices on the Web'. Paper presented to the British Education Research Association, Cardiff, September.

Leach, J. and Moon, R. E. (2000) 'Pedagogy, information and communication technologies and teacher professional knowledge', *Curriculum Journal* **11**(3), 385–404.

Marx, R. W. *et al.* (1998) 'New technologies for teachers' professional development', *Teaching and Teacher Education* **14**(1), 33–52.

McCormick, R. and Scrimshaw, P. (2001) 'ICT, knowledge and pedagogy', *Education, Communication and Information* **1**(1). http://www.open.ac.uk/eci accessed 31.7.01.

Miller, D. and Slater, D. (2000) *The Internet: an ethnographic approach*. New York: Berg.

OISE (2000) *Computer Supported Intentional Learning Environment* http://csile.oise.utoronto.ca/ accessed 31.7.01.

Putnam, R. T. and Borko, H. (2000) 'What do new views of knowledge and thinking have to say about research on teacher learning?', *Educational Researcher* **29**(1), 4–15.

Rogoff, B. (1994) 'Developing understanding of the idea of communities of learners', *Mind, Culture and Activity* **1**(4), 209–29.

Roschelle, J. and Pea, R. (1999) 'Trajectories from today's WWW to a powerful educational infrastructure', *Educational Researcher* **28**(5).

Salamon, G., Perkins, D. N and Globerson, T. (1991) 'Partners in cognition: extending human intelligence with intelligence theories', *Educational Researcher* **20**(3), 2–9.

Streibel, M. J. (1993) 'Instructional design and human practice, what can we learn from Grundy's interpretation of Habermas' Theory of Technical and Practical Human Interests?', in Muffoletto, R. and Knupfer, N. N. (eds) *Computers in Education: social, political and historical perspectives*. Creskill, NJ: Hampshire Press.

Swarbrick, A. (2001) 'Iliad'. Paper presented to the British Educational Research Association, Cardiff, September 2000.

Wenger, E. (1999) *Communities of Practice*. Cambridge: Cambridge University Press.

Index

Author Index

Subject Index